'A' Level English Law

Sixth Edition

R. S. Sim, LLB(Hons) (Liverpool), CertEd,
of Gray's Inn, Barrister
Regional Chairman of the Social Security Appeal Tribunals
and Medical Appeal Tribunals
Chairman of the Vaccine Damage Tribunal
Formerly Principal Lecturer in Law
at Manchester Polytechnic
Formerly Chief Examiner in Law
with the Associated Examining Board
and the Joint Matriculation Board

P. J. Pace, LLB(London), LLM(Manchester)
of Gray's Inn, Barrister
Principal Lecturer in Law
at Manchester Polytechnic

London
Butterworths
1984

England	Butterworth & Co (Publishers) Ltd, 88 Kingsway, LONDON WC2B 6AB
Australia	Butterworths Pty Ltd, SYDNEY, MELBOURNE, BRISBANE, ADELAIDE, PERTH, CANBERRA and HOBART
Canada	Butterworth & Co (Canada) Ltd, TORONTO and VANCOUVER
New Zealand	Butterworths of New Zealand Ltd, WELLINGTON and AUCKLAND
Singapore	Butterworth & Co (Asia) Pte Ltd, SINGAPORE
South Africa	Butterworth Publishers (Pty) Ltd, DURBAN and PRETORIA
USA	Butterworth Legal Publishers, ST PAUL, Minnesota, SEATTLE, Washington; BOSTON, Massachusetts, AUSTIN, Texas and D & S Publishers, CLEARWATER, Florida

First edition	1964
Reprinted	1965, 1966
Second edition	1967
Reprinted	1968, 1969
Third edition	1970
Reprinted	1972
Fourth edition	1974
Reprinted	1976
Fifth edition	1978

© Butterworth & Co (Publishers) Ltd 1964, 1967, 1970, 1974, 1978, 1984

British Library Cataloguing in Publication Data

Sim, R. S.
    'A' level English law.—6th ed.
    1. Law—England
    I. Title   II. Pace, Peter J.
    344.2   KD661

ISBN Hardcover 0 406 65707 6
ISBN Softcover 0 406 65708 4

Typeset by Cotswold Typesetting Ltd, Gloucester, and
Printed by Billings Bookplan, Worcester

This Edition is respectfully dedicated
to the memory of
Dennis Michael Millie Scott

Preface to the sixth edition

It is with a deep feeling of sadness that I write the Preface to the sixth edition of this textbook. In August 1983 my co-author, Mike Scott, died suddenly and unexpectedly while working on this edition. It is to his memory that this edition is respectfully dedicated.

In the preparation of the new edition I have been joined by my colleague at Manchester Polytechnic, Peter Pace. We have each been responsible for the preparation of different sections of the work but are jointly responsible for the whole.

The passage of time has meant that updating has become necessary. The radical change in the A.E.B.'s syllabus and the advent of the J.M.B.'s syllabus have meant that a new edition has been delayed while these new syllabi could be digested, bearing in mind the needs of the student and the particular problems of the textbook writer. New material has been added throughout each of the existing chapters (apart from two chapters deleted) and new sections and chapters have been added. The whole work has undergone rearrangement.

No *one* book ever does, or indeed should, cover all the subject-matter of an 'A' Level syllabus. As examiners at different levels for the G.C.E. and others for over 20 years it is our belief that this edition forms a most suitable basic text which covers the groundwork and which will hold the subject together.

For further reading a short selection of other works has been added in an Appendix. Other appendices give guidance on how to approach the study of law and develop a good examination technique, with sample papers as examples.

Our gratitude is expressed to both the Joint Matriculation Board and the Associated Examining Board for kind permission to reproduce the questions from their papers appearing in Appendix 2.

At the last moment the opportunity has been taken to include the Occupiers' Liability Act 1984. Generally, the law stated is as it was available to us at the beginning of April 1984.

R. S. Sim
P. J. Pace

Preface to the first edition

The justification for this book lies in the fact that at present there is no text book on the market specifically designed for the needs of students preparing for the General Certificate of Education law paper at 'A' level of the Associated Examining Board. 'A' level students for any subject require a basic textbook which provides an adequate treatment of the whole syllabus. This type of book we have attempted to write. For this reason the book has been divided into two parts corresponding to the two papers of the 'A' level examination. This means that a much more detailed treatment than is usual in a textbook on the general principles of English law has been given to the law of contract which forms the subject matter of Paper II. We have also emphasised the historical growth of the law and its institutions.

As this book is written for students in colleges and schools which are unlikely to have the facilities of a law library where reference to law reports and other legal literature can be followed up, we have tried to avoid the usual array of citations which are commonly found in legal textbooks. It has thus been our standard policy to confine our citations in the text to the name and year of a case only, but for the benefit of teachers and others who may wish to have appropriate references our publishers have kindly compiled a list of cases and statutes where these may be found.

Our gratitude is due to all who have influenced our own learning – our tutors, our colleagues and our students. In particular we would like to thank Mr Barber, a student of Holborn College, who prepared the table on pages 94–97, Mr David Kobrin, LLB, our much respected colleague and Lecturer in the Commerce Department of Holborn College who did us the great service of critically and constructively reading a large part of the first draft, Mrs Lorna M. Sim who typed part of the manuscript and Mrs Anne-Marie Scott, L-ès-L, for constructive literary criticism of part of the work. Finally, our thanks are due to Mr Kay Jones, Mr Partridge, and Mr Harrison of Butterworths for their guidance and tolerance at all times.

Errors and omissions are our sole responsibility, and it has been our aim to state the law as it existed on 1 September 1964.

It is our hope that in addition to providing students with a suitable textbook we have awakened a feeling for the law and an interest in its study which will inspire them to greater things.

October, 1964

R.S.S.
D.M.M.S.

Contents

Table of Statutes

References in this Table to *Statutes* are to Halsbury's Statutes of England (Third Edition) showing the volume and page at which the annotated text of the Act is set out in part or in full.

PAGE

PAGE

Table of Cases

PAGE

Part one

General

Summary

Chapter 1
The origin of law and the state

The United Kingdom, which consists of England, Wales, Scotland and Northern Ireland, is one political unit but each of the constituent countries is not governed by the same set of laws. The English legal system operates only within England and Wales. Northern Ireland has a legal system similar to that in England, whereas Scotland has a very different system which has been influenced to a considerable extent by the laws of ancient Rome. There are, however, two important links between the three countries. The British Parliament at Westminster can and does legislate for all three territories and the British House of Lords exercises certain powers as a final appeal court from all three territories in certain cases. Our study in this book is of the origin of English law, its courts and in particular the English law of contract, but before proceeding to a detailed consideration of our task it is necessary to clarify in our minds the meaning to be attributed to certain fundamental concepts.

Law as a facet of philosophy

Philosophy is defined in the *Oxford English Dictionary* as

> 'the study of ultimate realities and general principles; a system of theories on the nature of things or of rules for the conduct of life'.

The philosopher asks such questions as, 'What is God?' and directs himself to the purpose behind life and human actions. The aim of law is to regulate the conduct of human beings in society. A philosopher will be interested in law as one minor part of his field of inquiry because he will want to know why laws are necessary, what their purpose is and how far they are just. The philosophy of law is called 'jurisprudence' or 'legal theory'. Its aim is to consider the nature, origin and classification of law. One of the most important ideas of the legal theorists is the idea of 'natural law'. The theory of natural law is based on the belief that there is a set of perfect rules for human conduct and the laws devised by men must be judged by these rules. Particular rules of natural justice are that the judge must be impartial and both parties must be heard. However, different views are held as to the rules of natural law and although its basic principles may influence a court of law today its rules are not binding on English courts.

3

There are said to be three approaches to jurisprudence, each supported by a school of thought. 'Historical jurisprudence' involves the study of the growth of law and in particular its relationship to the development of the state. Well-known members of the 'historical school' were Savigny (1779–1861), a German jurist and Sir Henry Maine (1822–88), Regius Professor of Civil law at Cambridge, whose ideas are discussed later in this book. The 'analytical school' of jurisprudence makes a study of the law as it is and analyses basic legal concepts. John Austin (1790–1859), first Professor of Jurisprudence at University College, London, was a leading member of this school. His idea of law is considered below. The third school of jurisprudence is termed 'sociological' and concerns itself with the working of the law in practice and its effect on society. Most of the work in this field has been done in the United States of America.

What do we mean by 'law'?

'Law' is a term which is used in many different senses all of which contain the common element of the law being a general rule of conduct. Thus there are the laws of science, the laws of morality and the law of God, among others. To a lawyer, 'law' has a far narrower meaning which has been defined by Sir John Salmond in his book, *Jurisprudence*, as 'the body of principles recognised and applied by the state in the administration of justice'. He goes on to say, 'In other words the law consists of the rules recognised and acted on by courts of justice.' The main element of law in this narrow sense is that it consists of rules which are enforced by the state. A well-known exponent of the law in this sense is John Austin who analysed the law, as he saw it, in his work, *The Province of Jurisprudence Determined*. To Austin, law is a command set by a superior being to an inferior being and enforced by sanctions (punishments). The superior being is the state and the inferior being is the individual. The sanctions are wide and include imprisonment, fines, damages, injunctions and decrees of specific performance.

Although Austin's theories have been doubted on many sides no one view of law has triumphed the world over and Austin's ideas have remained predominant in England at least.

Law and its relation to justice

The law as a body has as its aim the attainment of justice in society. The law is phrased as a series of principles each called *a* law. Justice is an abstract idea of right and wrong, fairness and equality. The aim of a given law is, therefore, to encourage the doing of what is right (just) in a particular set of circumstances. In order that the law may be known it must be specific. However, in its application to a particular set of circumstances a law may not always achieve the degree of justice hoped for. For example, it is a rule of law that taking the property of another person is a crime (theft) punishable by a fine or imprisonment or both. This rule of law would also appear to many people to accord with their idea of justice. But where a destitute man steals bread to give to his starving child the law may punish him for his crime and the same people who think that the law is just when it says that stealing is a crime may say that the law is unjust in this particular case. In general it may be said that a law which coincides with the people's idea of justice is more likely to be respected and as a consequence more easily enforced than a law which does not coincide with the people's idea of justice.

However, there are a vast number of regulatory crimes, concerned with such matters as the selling of food and liquor and the use of motor vehicles, which may be regarded as 'unjust' because liability may be imposed even though an accused was not at fault. Thus, for example, a person who consigned pure milk for sale was found guilty of selling impure milk when an unknown person adulterated the milk with water. As conviction does not involve the moral stigma that ensues on conviction for offences such as theft, society is prepared to accept strict liability, or liability without fault, as the price to be paid for a system of control which is administratively expedient. If the prosecution were required to prove that the accused was at fault in each and every case, the criminal courts would soon cease to function.

As well as the attainment of justice the law also seeks to impose some sort of social control. Although this is particularly important in the sphere of criminal law, the civil law is also concerned with this aspect in such areas as industrial relations, the formation and dissolution of marriage and town and country planning.

What is a state?

At several points in the above discussion we have used the word 'state', but what does this word mean? It is important that we should know because legal systems are administered almost entirely on the basis of the political unit known as the state. For international purposes the British state is the United Kingdom of Great Britain and Northern Ireland, though *English law* applies only to part of this state, i e to England and Wales. We may take as our definition of a state in the modern world the words of Sir John Salmond,

> 'a society of men established for the maintenance of peace and justice within a determined territory by way of force'.

As to the origin of states in this sense there are several theories, some of which are examined below.

Thomas Hobbes (1588–1679), the English political thinker, believed that before states came into existence men lived in an unhappy natural condition where their lives were 'solitary, poore, nasty, brutish and short'. In order to escape from this situation they surrendered their rights to do as they pleased (their sovereignty) to a powerful ruler (thenceforth known as a sovereign) who ensured their safety. Hobbes's theories were used to justify the actions of the monarchy. The king as sovereign could do as he pleased; his powers had been given to him voluntarily and he was accountable not to his subjects but to God alone. This is known as the social contract theory and whatever may be its particular merits not all its supporters held the same view. John Locke (1632–1704), also an English political thinker, thought that the lot of early man was a happy one and that he surrendered only some of his rights to the sovereign in return for the latter's promise to keep him safe. Locke thought that where the sovereign failed in his obligation he could be removed and replaced by one willing and able to protect his subjects. This view of the social contract theory was used to attack the divine right of kings (an idea, prevailing particularly in the seventeenth century and earlier, that the king was appointed by God to rule over his subjects and was irremoveable by man). Jean-Jacques Rousseau (1712–78), the well-known '*philosophe*', favoured an interpretation more akin to that of Locke than Hobbes and his book *Du Contrat Social*, which suggested that when a ruler by bad government broke his contract his subjects were free to chose another ruler, was one of the seeds which germinated to produce the French Revolution.

There are many weaknesses in the social contract theory, but, above all else, it seems historically most unlikely that men banded together and voluntarily surrendered all or some of their rights to another being to be master of them. To suggest that this is true is to attribute to early man a refined political thinking of which he hardly seems to have been capable.

Another theory as to the origin of the state, known as the 'patriarchal theory' was advanced by Sir Henry Maine (1822–88) in his famous work, *Ancient Law*. He argued that the primeval unit of organisation among Indo-European peoples was the agnatic family, ie a family linked by blood relationship through the male line to a common relative who was the eldest male parent of the group. The head of the family was supreme. He had the power of life and death over all the members of the group and owned all the property in the possession of any member. Each family lived in isolation. The next stage towards the development of the state took place when several families banded together into a larger group. When a group of families felt itself sufficiently strong it refused to accept strangers or other families to increase its numbers. However, outsiders were not necessarily persecuted and when others came to live in the same area as the large family group, though not members of it by blood, they were gradually accepted as belonging to that area. So developed the new idea, not of blood relationship, but of local contiguity—living in the same territory. Here lies the beginnings of the state as we know it. The idea that a state must have connections with a defined territory is generally accepted today and is one of the assumptions on which international law is based.

As with the social contract theory, Maine's patriarchal theory has many detractors. Maine's theory by comparison is at least based on historical research and although certain aspects can be exploded it is still recognised as containing a large amount of truth.

Law, the state and the constitution

Every state has a government, and has some rules which lay down who shall govern and how. There may be a despot who makes his own rules as he goes along, there may be a booklet of rules decided upon by a referendum of all the people concerned, or there may, as in the United Kingdom, be an unwritten constitution derived mainly from the common law, statutes and 'conventions of the constitution' (which are rules relating to government and which are followed for practical reasons, although they are not enforceable as law). For example, in strict law the Queen could appoint as Prime Minister the leader of the smallest party to be returned after a General Election. This would be ridiculous and would not work. It is therefore a convention of the constitution that she appoints the leader of the largest party represented in the House of Commons, as he can secure the necessary votes to enable him to govern.

The constitution has grown up over the centuries and has been influenced by Acts of Parliament, decisions of judges, the Civil War of the seventeenth century and other historical factors. One may say that the constitution is greatly influenced by the law, and that the law is made and applied within a constitutional context.

At present there is a United Kingdom Parliament at Westminster with unlimited powers, but dissatisfaction has stirred in various parts of the Kingdom, and in the long run the situation is likely to change. The basis of change may well be the report to Parliament of the Royal Commission on the Constitution, a body set up to take evidence and make recommendations, and headed by Lord Kilbrandon. The Kilbrandon Report, which was published and debated in Parliament on 30 October 1973, recommended that there should be a Scottish and a Welsh legislative assembly with limited powers, in addition to the United Kingdom Parliament, with a Prime Minister of Scotland and a Prime Minister of Wales. If these recommendations should come into effect in the years ahead, there would be changes affecting the sources of law.

With a view to the possible implementation of change a referendum was held in Wales and one in Scotland. Both countries rejected the proposals for devolved powers to their own legislative assemblies. England, a part of the United Kingdom, was not consulted by referendum.

The sovereign power within the state

Each state has some person or body who exercises the ultimate authority or power. In a dictatorship the sovereign power would be exercised by a single person. In a democratic society power is shared and there are rules of the constitution attempting to prevent the abuse of power. An attempt is made to balance the powers of the legislature, the executive and the judiciary. However, in the United Kingdom we can say that Parliament (strictly the Queen in Parliament) is the sovereign legislative power. Parliament has unlimited legislative competence, known as the Sovereignty of Parliament. It can legislate on any matter and can delegate to others some of its power to legislate but it can always withdraw such power.

In enacting the European Communities Act 1972, which makes provision for the entry of the United Kingdom to the European Economic Community, it can be argued that Parliament surrendered its sovereignty and is now limited. A counter-argument says that the European Communities Act, like all other Acts, can be repealed, leaving Parliament still sovereign. In the final analysis such arguments of law fall to be decided by practical reality.

The constitution and Europe

It is against the background of the United Kingdom Constitution which governs who shall make the law, how it shall be made, and who shall apply it, that it is necessary to consider a notable change that has taken place with the entry of the United Kingdom into the European Communities under the provisions of the European Communities Act 1972.

The European Communities are based on three Treaties made by France, Germany, Italy, Luxembourg, Belgium and Holland. The first was the Treaty of Paris of 1951, which set up the European Coal and Steel Community (ECSC), the second and third were the two treaties of Rome of 1957 which set up, respectively, the European Atomic Energy Community (EURATOM) and the European Economic Community (EEC or, as it is popularly known, 'the Common Market').

Of the three Communities only the EEC is of practical importance for the purpose of this study, as the other two have little bearing on the general law. The three Communities were merged as respects their operation in 1967—but they remain separate organisations in theory. On 1 January 1973 the United Kingdom, Ireland and Denmark all joined the three Communities and became parties to, amongst others, the Paris and Rome Treaties, and the Brussels Treaty of Accession of 1972 (by which they agreed to join). These are known collectively as the 'European Treaties'.

The objects of the European Communities

The Communities, which owe their inspiration to M. Robert Schuman, French Foreign Minister in 1950, have a number of objects. The ECSC places the production of steel and coal produced in all ten member states under the authority of a single supra-national organisation and makes war between them impossible as armaments are thus indirectly controlled. EURATOM encourages atomic research, but it is the EEC that is of the greatest significance. It is an organisation which aims to weld Europe into a single prosperous area by abolishing all restrictions affecting movement of people, of goods and capital. When all customs duties have gone, there will be a single market in excess of 250,000,000 people available to all producers in the member states, and European manufacturers will be able to produce goods more cheaply, on the scale that is practised in, for example, the United States. Any person who wishes to go and work in any other member state will be able without formality to set off there and enjoy job equality with the local inhabitants.

The running of the European Communities

Every independent state is set up on the basis of national sovereignty, which means that it can, in theory, do anything it wishes. For example, it could in case of war shoot the prisoners of war that it takes, but such behaviour would soon bring retribution, and so states are generally wise enough to sign the Geneva Convention on prisoners of war and to behave in a humane manner. What they are doing, of course, is voluntarily giving up a part of their national sovereignty, but the advantages outweigh the disadvantages.

Similarly, the ten member states of the European Communities have voluntarily limited their sovereignty and have handed over some of their powers to supra-national institutions. The four main institutions of the European Communities are:

(i)   The Council of Ministers ('The Council')
(ii)   The Parliament
(iii) The European Commission
(iv)   The Court of Justice ('The European Court').

The Council meets periodically usually in Brussels and normally the ten Foreign Ministers of the member states will attend. Decisions are usually unanimous. The Council takes decisions on matters of major importance.

The Parliament is a consultative body of national MPs.

Direct elections

By resolution of the European Parliament a very important development intended to give ordinary people a real voice in running the European

Communities was introduced. They decided to increase the size of the Parliament to 410 members, proportionately divided among the nine member states to that there would be the following allocation: 81 each from the United Kingdom, Germany, France and Italy, 25 from Holland, 24 from Belgium, 16 from Denmark, 15 from Ireland and 6 from Luxembourg. Greece has since joined the Community.

Instead of being chosen, as at first from among existing MP's of each country, the new European members of parliament are elected in each country.

Each country has promised to hold these elections. If any one country failed to hold direct elections, there could be none in any of the ten countries, and democratic control of the Community would suffer.

The European Commission of 14 Commissioners, two each from the United Kingdom, Germany, France and Italy, and one each from each of the other states, is a unique institution. It makes proposals for policy which must either be accepted *in total* by the Council or rejected. The Commissioners can be dismissed only by the Parliament.

The Court of Justice has the duty of ensuring respect for the European Treaties, and judges cases between the Commission, the Council, the member states, and even in some cases private persons.

The European Communities and English law

Under the European Communities Act 1972, which gives the European Treaties the force of law in the United Kingdom, the Council of Ministers and the Commission may both make laws for ECSC, EURATOM and the EEC, which apply in England and Wales, while the Court of Justice of the European Communities may give judgment directly binding in English law on the UK government or on private persons. We have, in fact, had new sources of law since 1 January 1973.

European law

The Council and the Commission can make:

(i)   Regulations
(ii)   Directives
(iii)   Decisions.

These are the names of legislative documents issued in respect of the EEC and EURATOM. There are certain other forms of nomenclature in respect of ECSC, but these are of less importance. Prior to British entry into the Communities 41 volumes of these laws were passed, and are gradually being absorbed into English law. These laws are confined to small areas of the legal system and mainly affect such matters as agriculture, companies, competition and free movement of workers. A *Regulation* is of general application having the direct force of law in all ten states as soon as it comes into force and is binding in England without reference to Parliament at Westminster. It is said to be 'self-executing'. A *Directive* is binding on all member states, but the states must themselves bring the Directive into force by issuing their own statutory instruments within the time limit in the Directive. This is subordinate legislation.

A *Decision* may be addressed to a state, a person or a company and is binding only on the recipient. The Council and the Commission may also issue *Recommendations* and *Opinions* which, although not to be disregarded, are not binding in law.

The European Communities Act 1972 provides that judicial notice shall be taken of the European Treaties, The Official Journal of the Communities and 'any decision of, or expression of opinion by, the European Court'. Usually assertions made in court must be backed by proof, but there are certain facts that are so well known that it would be a waste of time to prove them, e g that Tuesday follows Monday or that water is wet. Courts accept the existence of such facts without demanding proof and this process is called 'taking judicial notice of' the fact in question. The judgments of the Court of Justice are a part of English law. The Court has ten judges.

Under Art 177 of the EEC Treaty of Rome any court in a member state from which there is no appeal (e g the House of Lords, the Judicial Committee of the Privy Council, and in certain matters the Court of Session in Scotland) and which has a case which turns on the meaning of one of the European Treaties, *must* suspend the case and send it to the European Court, which is situated in Luxembourg for a *preliminary ruling* on the meaning of the Treaty, unless the matter has already been decided by the European Court. Lower courts may, but need not, send such cases to Luxembourg.

There is a strict separation of function between the European Court and the national court. The European Court will, under Art 177, only declare the meaning of the Treaty, and nothing more. The national court must then decide the case before it by applying the Treaty as clarified to the facts of the case. A number of English courts have already used the Art 177 procedure. The Chancery Division of the High Court, for example, in the case *Van Duyn v Home Office* (1975) (European Court case No 41/74) consulted the European Court as to whether or not the United Kingdom could prevent a Dutch woman from entering the country. She maintained that the EEC Treaty, which gives freedom of movement to workers from other countries of the EEC, entitled her to entry, but the Home Office maintained that the UK was entitled to exclude her if she was associating with an organisation regarded as socially harmful to the UK. The European Court in its judgment of 4 December 1974 stated just that the Treaty must be interpreted as meaning that a member state in imposing entry restrictions is entitled to take into account the type of matter relied upon by the Home Office, and left to the Chancery Division the duty of making the final decision as between the two parties to the case in London.

A National Insurance Commissioner dealing with a claim for social security benefits from a person who had worked abroad for a time, and a Metropolitan magistrate wishing to know whether he could report a Frenchman who had committed drug offences are two further examples of English courts and tribunals using the procedure of Art 177 of the EEC Treaty to make a reference for a preliminary ruling on European law. Very interesting accounts of the relationship between English and European Law are to be found in the judgments of Lord Denning in the cases of *Application des Gaz v Falks Veritas* and *H. P. Bulmer Ltd v J. Bollinger SA*, both heard in the Court of Appeal in 1974.

The two functions of the European Court, that of hearing applications for a preliminary ruling under Art 177, and that of deciding cases between opposing parties, are quite separate.

Decisions of the European Court cannot be questioned in English courts. This is in contrast with foreign judgments which are not binding in England. The jurisdiction of the House of Lords as a final appellate court is now limited.

Each member state enforces the judgments of the European Court through its own enforcement system, and the European Court has no machinery for the enforcement of its judgments in or against member states. In practice the states always comply.

World legal systems

In the modern world, among the legal systems which exist to do justice between man and man, and man and the state, two types predominate; those based on the laws of ancient Rome, and those based on the common law of England. The Romans, who were methodical and resourceful, built up a system of law over a period of a thousand years. The greatest names in Roman law were those of Gaius, a famous jurist who lived in Rome about 150 AD, and Justinian who ruled the Eastern Empire from Constantinople between 537 and 565 AD. Justinian's claim to fame lies in the fact that he got his Chancellor, Tribonian, and 16 assistants to set out the whole law in a code called the *Digest*. They also prepared a students' book called the *Institutes* which is still in use today. The Romans had occupied most of western Europe and after the collapse of the western empire in the fifth century following the barbarian invasions the 'dark ages' descended and only the most primitive legal systems existed. Towards the end of the eleventh century interest in Roman law began to revive, but nothing was known of the *Digest*. However, by great fortune, there was discovered in Pisa and brought to Florence what is known as the *Florentina* – the only complete manuscript of the *Digest* to survive the dark ages. Following this the science of Roman law was recreated and the rediscovered law was adapted to meet the needs of almost every country in Europe except England and Ireland. With the colonisation of America and Africa and the desire of some oriental countries to adopt new legal systems, Roman ideas of law have spread around the world. Today, systems of law influenced in a greater or lesser degree by Roman law exist in most countries of western Europe, in almost all the states of South America, in Japan, Thailand and Turkey, and in Quebec and Louisiana. Many African countries including South Africa have Roman-influenced systems and, as mentioned previously, Scotland has benefited.

The common law of England which, like Roman law, has taken a thousand years to build has also spread around the world. British arms and settlers took it with them, and it has remained as a high-tide mark even where the tide of empire has ebbed. No country ever adopted the common law voluntarily, but once having enjoyed the benefit of it, no country has willingly given it up. Besides Australia, New Zealand and India common law countries include Canada (except Quebec), most of the United States and many countries of Africa.

Characteristics of English law

Although English law has developed a character of its own, this would be difficult to define exactly. It is, nevertheless, possible to identify the main characteristics that give individuality to our law. These are as follows:

(i) *The continuous growth of the law since Saxon times.* In the course of recent history most other countries have made a break with one system of law and changed to another. This has happened in a number of ways. In some cases, for example, there has been a sudden change to a code of laws based on Roman law. In other cases a system based on English law has been developed gradually. In England the law has been evolved and recorded continuously without any fundamental change in the system. This explains in part English respect for law and legal institutions. Neither rules of law nor institutions cease to exist through want of use. Examples of this are the revival in 1954 of the Court of Chivalry which had not sat for over 200 years and the current validity of the Treason Act 1351.

(ii) *The absence of a code of laws.* Codification in other countries has often been associated with the unification of law in the state and the introduction of Roman law. In England a unified system of law was achieved relatively early and there was no reception of Roman law. To produce a complete code of laws would be a difficult task.

(iii) *The system of precedent.* This is discussed below (see p 41).

(iv) *The influence of procedure.* Although at the present day the substantive law is much less influenced by the requirements of procedure than once was the case, it is still shaped to a considerable extent by the requirements imposed on it by procedure in times past.

(v) *The judicial character of the law.*　The case law of England was made by the judges, and it is this body of law that remains the basis of our system. Acts of Parliament assume the existence of case law, and it is the judges who declare the meaning of Acts of Parliament. The character and outlook of the judges has always, therefore, been a significant factor in the development of our law.

(vi) *The independence of the judiciary.*　The judges of superior courts hold office during good behaviour and can be removed only on an address from both Houses of Parliament. This has been so since the Act of Settlement of 1700 and no judge of a superior court has ever been removed from office since then. Owing partly to the Act and partly to tradition, the judges in fact arrive at their decisions without fear of government or other influence. They retire at the age of 75.

The judges' independence is preserved in this way as part of the separation of the judiciary from the control of the legislature and as a defence against arbitrary power exercised by the executive organ of government. The independence of the judiciary is one aspect of the separation of powers (see p 71, below).

(vii) *The independence of barristers and solicitors.*　The legal profession is divided into two main branches: barristers, and solicitors of the Supreme Court. Each branch is responsible for maintaining high standards of conduct among its members. Lawyers (which expression includes both barristers and solicitors) are not state officials and are not allowed to let themselves be swayed by political considerations in their legal work, or their choice of clients.

(viii) *The accusatorial procedure.*　In some foreign systems it is the function of the court to produce the evidence; this is called the 'inquisitorial' method of procedure. In English law under the accusatorial method of procedure the court (in the form of the judge) remains neutral and hears argument by both sides. This is generally so in both civil and criminal cases.

(ix) *Legal work in private hands.*　The reports of cases in court, explanatory editions of Acts of Parliament, and many books on court procedure are produced by private organisations, instead of by the state.

(x) *The small influence of Roman Law.*　This is mentioned below (see p 61, below).

Chapter 2

Classification of law and legal terminology

Classification of law

If somebody were told to classify human beings, without knowing for what purpose he had to do this, he would have an impossible task because there are innumerable ways of doing it; they may be classified by weight, age, religion or whatever comes to mind. The same sort of problem besets anyone wishing to classify law.

Usual classifications

Some of the more usual classifications are as follows:

(i) For the purposes of analytical jurisprudence we may adopt Austin's division of law into: the laws of God, positive law, and positive morality.

(ii) Another classification which may be adopted is to distinguish between law that applies within a state and law that prevails between states. The former is called 'municipal law', and the latter is termed 'public international law'. 'National law' is also the phrase applied to the law of a member state of the European Economic Community and here is contrasted with 'Community law'.

Public international law should be distinguished from 'private international law', or 'conflict of laws' as it is often called. Private international law is a part of municipal law so that in every country there will be a different version of it. It consists of the rules that guide a judge when the laws of more than one country affect a case.

(iii) A further classification is that which distinguishes between substantive law and adjectival law. The former consists of the rules that govern the people, while the latter consists of the rules that lay down the procedure for applying the law.

(iv) For the purposes of this book the most important classifications are those set out in the diagrams on the next page. These are the divisions into public law and private law, and into civil law and criminal law.

The distinction between public and private law is that the former is concerned with matters that affect the state as a community, while the latter is concerned with matters that affect the rights and duties of individuals among themselves. Constitutional law deals with such questions as the supremacy of Parliament, the position of the Crown and rights to personal freedom. Criminal law generally aims at punishing

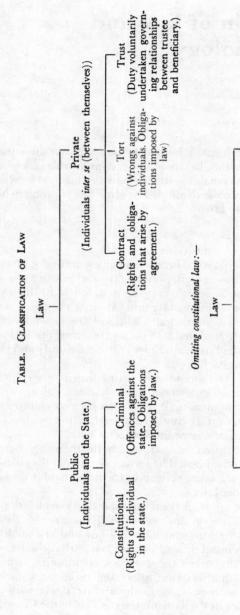

TABLE. CLASSIFICATION OF LAW

Law
- Public (Individuals and the State.)
  - Constitutional (Rights of individual in the state.)
  - Criminal (Offences against the state. Obligations imposed by law.)
- Private *inter se* (between themselves))
  - Contract (Rights and obligations that arise by agreement.)
  - Tort (Wrongs against individuals. Obligations imposed by law)
  - Trust (Duty voluntarily undertaken governing relationships between trustee and beneficiary.)

Omitting constitutional law :—

Law
- Criminal
- Civil
  - Contract
  - Tort
  - Trust

Note.—The first of the above diagrams illustrates a classification of the law that takes into account constitutional law. It contrasts public and private law. The second diagram illustrates a classification that ignores constitutional law. It contrasts criminal and civil law, the classification on which the organisation of the courts is based.

criminals and suppressing crime. Civil law is intended to give compensation to persons injured, to enable property to be recovered from wrongdoers and to enforce obligations (contracts and trusts).

Double liability for wrongdoing

Certain types of wrongdoing involve both criminal and civil liability. For example, if A obtains B's watch by deception, A may be prosecuted in a criminal court and sent to prison; B may also sue A in a civil court to recover the value of the watch.

There are cases where the same court will both punish the wrongdoer and award compensation to the person wronged. Thus a criminal court may both convict a man of criminal damage and order him to pay compensation.

In some cases it is not possible to pursue both civil and criminal remedies; for instance, if a person has been dealt with in a criminal court for a common assault or battery, he cannot be sued in a civil court for the same wrongful act. If the person attacked wishes to take civil proceedings, he must not institute criminal proceedings.

Legal terminology

Contract

Contracts are based on agreement. The law of contract is the branch of the law which determines when a promise or a set of promises is legally enforceable. The promises which are to be enforced form the contract.

Generally the essential elements in a contract are:

> an offer
> which is accepted
> both parties having capacity to contract,
> there being no
> > mistake,
> > misrepresentation, or
> > undue influence,
> the object being lawful, and
> both parties *intending* to enter legal relations.

For such an agreement to be *enforced* in the courts there must be consideration for the offeror's promise or the promise must be in the form of a deed.

For example:

> A offers to take B to the cinema:
> There are no intended legal relations.
> There is no promise by B.
> There is no contract.

A and B become business partners:

> Legal relations are intended.
> There is a promise for a promise (consideration).
> There is a contract.

Tort

Tort is based on an obligation imposed by law.
For example:

> A walks on the land of B.
> A has no agreement with B to keep off the land.
> A commits the tort of trespass.

A tort is a civil wrong. It is the breach of a general duty which is imposed by the law (and not agreed between the parties). It is remediable by a civil action for unliquidated damages (damages whose amount is left to the discretion of the court). Any person whose legal right is infringed may sue.
There must be:

> an act or omission
> done intentionally or negligently (or in cases of strict liability done independently of any particular state of mind);
> frequently there must be damage, although in some cases this is not a prerequisite of a right of action.

Trust

A trust is generally the relationship which exists between a person who holds property for another and that other. It is the relationship between the parties who are called the trustee and the beneficiary.
For example:

> A hands property to B telling him to hold it for C.
> A is the donor (or settlor if he makes a formal settlement or gives property by will).
> B is the trustee.
> C is the beneficiary.

Crime

A crime is a wrong to the state for which punishment is inflicted by the state, the proceedings usually being brought by the Crown.

The elements of a crime

The elements of a crime are: actus reus (a wrongful act) and mens rea (a guilty mind). For example, A stabs B (actus reus) with intent to kill (mens rea). Mens rea is not necessary for certain offences created by statute.

Indictable and summary offences

Indictable offences are generally more serious than summary offences. They are tried by jury. This means that after the judge and jury have heard the evidence of both sides, the jury will decide whether the accused is guilty or not. If the jury find the accused guilty the judge will decide on the sentence.

Summary offences are tried by magistrates without a jury. In this event the magistrates will decide both the question of innocence or guilt and the question of sentence is necessary.

By statute certain offences may be tried summarily or on indictment. If the trial is on indictment, this will mean jury procedure but the possibility of a heavier sentence if the accused is found guilty, since courts in which jury trials are heard have greater powers than magistrates' courts.

Arrestable offences and other offences

Under the Criminal Law Act 1967 a distinction is drawn between arrestable offences and other offences. An arrestable offence is one for which the sentence is fixed by law or for which the statutory penalty is at least five years' imprisonment and attempts to commit these offences. An arrestable offence is so called because in general a policeman or any member of the public may arrest *without warrant* anyone who commits such an offence. The power to arrest without warrant for non-arrestable offences is confined mainly to policemen.

Terminology of civil and criminal proceedings

Civil	*Criminal*
Plaintiff	The Crown
sues	prosecutes
defendant;	accused;
defendent liable	accused guilty
damages may be awarded;	a fine or imprisonment may be imposed:
damages go to Plaintiff.	the fine goes to the Crown.

Appeals

If there is an appeal the party appealing is known as the 'appellant' and the other as the 'respondent'.

Jurisdiction of a court

This expression has two meanings. It may be used in a geographical sense, e g the jurisdiction of the Court of Appeal is confined to England

and Wales. On the other hand it may be used in a sense that refers to the subject matter with which a court deals, e g the jurisdiction of county courts is confined to civil cases.

Law and fact

The distinction between law and fact is of considerable importance. An appeal may be allowed against a finding of fact or only on a point of law. Important as the distinction is, it is not always an easy one to make in practice. The judge will deal with questions of law i e rules of law and rules of evidence. The jury will decide questions of fact i e all questions which are not questions of law. To this simple approach there are exceptions as, for instance, where the judge decides whether words are capable of being malicious *in law* or whether goods are capable of being necessaries *in law* before leaving the question of whether the words are *in fact* malicious, or the goods necessaries, to the jury (see pp 198 and 243, below).

Primary fact and secondary fact

Secondary fact is fact which is deduced from or flows from primary facts. Lord Denning explained the relationship with these words:

> 'Primary facts are facts which are observed by witnesses and proved by oral testimony, or facts proved by the production of a thing itself, such as original documents. Their determination is essentially a question of fact for the tribunal of fact, and the only question of law that can arise on them is whether there was any evidence to support the finding. The conclusions from primary facts are, however, inferences deduced by a process of reasoning from them. If, and in so far as, those conclusions can as well be drawn by a layman . . . as by a lawyer, they are conclusions of fact for the tribunal of fact, and the only questions of law which can arise on them are whether there was a proper direction in point of law and whether the conclusion is one which could reasonably be drawn from the primary facts. . . . If, and in so far, however, as the correct conclusion to be drawn from primary facts requires for its correctness, determination by a trained lawyer . . . because it involves the interpretation of documents . . . the conclusion is a conclusion of law on which an appellate tribunal is as competent to form an opinion as the tribunal of first instance.' (*British Launderers' Research Association v Hendon Borough Rating Authority* (1949)). (See proof of custom p 39, below.)

Where a court takes notice of a fact without proof it is said to take 'judicial notice' of it. The court does this on rare occasions where the fact is widely accepted as such in society generally, e g water is wet. (See p 11, above.)

Chapter 3

The development of the law and the courts from Saxon times until 1875

Before the coming of William the Conqueror in 1066 there already existed a primitive legal system. The law consisted mainly of customary rules and dooms which were codes of law compiled by Anglo-Saxon kings. The dooms dealt mainly with such things as fines and methods of proof. The country was divided into shires, which were called counties after the Conquest, and the shires were sub-divided into hundreds and vills; the vills were of importance mainly in connection with police purposes. There was a court for each shire and each hundred. These were known as communal courts. In addition there were seignorial courts held by landowners for their free tenants, but there is some doubt about their functioning prior to the Conquest.

The shire court assembled periodically in the county town and was presided over by the sheriff who was a representative of the king.

The hundred courts had jurisdiction only over the local area and dealt with humbler matters than those that took the attention of the shire courts.

The effects of the Norman Conquest

William I established a strong monarchy with a centralised executive. Claiming to be the lawful successor of Edward the Confessor he began to rule the country through existing institutions. At first the county courts and hundred courts maintained their importance but eventually they dwindled into decay.

The Normans found themselves in the position of a minority ruling another race and were forced to devise a method of protecting themselves. Everybody had to be enrolled into a 'tithing' which was a group of ten families. The members of the tithing were jointly responsible for bringing to trial any member who had committed a crime. If they did not carry out this duty they had to pay a fine. A special fine had to be paid if a Norman was murdered, and unless the contrary was proved it was assumed that a murdered person was a Norman. The proof that the deceased was not a Norman was called 'Presentment of Englishry'. This system of law enforcement was called the Frankpledge system. In the course of time it died out as the two races gradually merged into one.

The courts that benefited most from the Conquest were the seignorial courts. Under the feudal system large landowners had authority over the tenants who lived on their estates, and the tenants were called together to act as judges. A distinction was drawn between the court baron which was used by freeholders, and the court customary which was used by villeins. Some of the hundred courts were taken over by feudal lords also. The important thing to realise is that these were, to use a modern expression, 'private enterprise' courts running at a profit taken from court fees, and offering justice that was backed by the landowner's military force. The courts were a form of private property but this did not seem shocking to people who lived in the feudal period when ideas of private property were very different from those of today and when there was no clear distinction between public and private law.

The Norman kings had a body to help them rule known as the *Curia Regis* (king's court). Although called a court it was in fact a body that had a number of functions, legislative, administrative and judicial. The kings were in the habit of travelling round the country and the *Curia Regis* used to meet wherever the king was. The great men who made up the *Curia Regis* were those to whom William had granted large tracts of land to be held in return for doing some necessary service, such as providing soldiers and arms. These men were know as 'tenants in chief' and the *Curia Regis* settled disputes between them. In addition to this the *Curia Regis* exercised a residuary right to give justice that had been inherited from the general principle of kingship as it existed in Anglo-Saxon times. By degrees there came to be two types of meeting of the *Curia Regis*, the great assemblies attended on important occasions by the tenants in chief and smaller, more frequent, assemblies at which royal officials were in the majority. Eventually the officials began to do specialised work with the assistance of staffs and from this beginning the courts of common law ultimately developed.

In 1086 William sent officials throughout the country to gather information for the compilation of a survey of the kingdom known as the Domesday book, and the dispatch of royal officials to various parts of the kingdom for administrative or judicial purposes was not an unusual event in the centuries that followed. William sent justices out as early as 1072. Henry II (1154–89), regularised this practice, and by the time of Henry III (1216–72) justices were sent round the country twice a year. One form that this type of activity took was the General Eyre. From the time of Henry II until 1340 in the reign of Edward III, justices were appointed to travel round the country every few years to enquire into the sources of royal revenue, to try prisoners in gaol, and to question local officials as to their behaviour since the previous General Eyre. All this was of course very unpopular.

King Henry II divided England into circuits and began regularly to send justices round the country to the towns on the circuits. One of his objects was to strengthen royal power by taking away work from the seignorial courts and this he did in various ways, one of which was by offering to prospective litigants a more satisfactory mode of trial than that used in the other courts. The great innovation of Henry II was a procedure which gave rise to the Grand Jury.

The modes of trial available in older times were of various types, but the most important were trial by ordeal, trial by compurgation and trial by battle. Trial by ordeal was a direct appeal to God and priests took part in the trials until the Lateran Council forbade this in 1215. In one type of trial by ordeal the accused had to eat a cursed morsel of bread and if he choked he was guilty; in another he had to carry a hot iron and if the wound healed after seven days he was innocent; he was similarly 'clean' if he sank in cold water. Trial by compurgation (also called 'wager of law') consisted of the defendant going to court with 11 oath-helpers so that all 12 could attempt to pronounce a word-perfect oath to the effect that the defendant was telling the truth. If any one of them made a slip of the tongue the defendant lost. Trial by battle was introduced by the Normans. It consisted of a judicially supervised fight. The late Professor Potter in his work on legal history gives Dyer's account of a trial in 1571. The contestants themselves could fight or could employ hired champions. The contestants who were bare-headed and clad in leather armour fought in a 60 foot square until one of them was forced to shout 'craven'. If the defendant could fight on until the stars came out he won. It is doubtful whether deadly weapons were used. By the nineteenth century trial by battle had long been obsolete and, following an attempt to make use of the procedure, it was finally abolished by an Act of Parliament in 1819.

Trial by jury was used for both civil and criminal cases in the royal courts; the original idea in jury trials was to summon to court a number of local men to give a verdict to the judge on some matter that they already knew all about from local knowledge. By the fifteenth century the system had changed to the present one whereby the jury gives a verdict only on the basis of what is related to them by others giving evidence as witnesses in court.

A legislative enactment called the Assize of Clarendon (1166), which was re-enacted and extended by the Assize of Northampton (1176), provided that 12 men of every hundred district must report to the king's justices every person who had committed a grave crime. This procedure was developed and from it emerged the Grand Jury which had the task of sifting the likely accusations from the improbably ones; in performing this function it was regarded as guarding the liberty of the subjects against the king. In this century it has been regarded as unnecessary and was abolished in 1933 by the Administration of Justice (Miscellaneous Provisions) Act of that year. A similar function to that of the Grand Jury is now carried out by the examining magistrates who hold a preliminary investigation into allegations of serious crime (see p 96, below).

When trial by ordeal went out of use as a result of the Lateran Council of 1215 the only procedure available that was regarded as suitable for the trial of allegations of serious crime was trial by jury; this was a new procedure, however, and the accused was not bound to accept such trial. The courts found themselves in a difficulty because if the accused did not consent to be tried by jury, he could not be tried at all. A statute of 1275 directed that persons refusing jury trial should be kept in hard prisons. The courts escaped from their difficulty by misinterpreting the statute to mean that the accused should be submitted to cruel torture; thereafter those who would not plead were put on the floor and loaded with heavy weights until they changed their minds or were crushed to death. This practice was called *Peine Forte et Dure*. In those days and even until 1870 when the Forfeiture Act was passed those found guilty of some serious crimes had all their goods and chattels forfeited to the Crown. If an accused who had considerable wealth knew that if he stood trial he would be found guilty and sentenced to death, he might choose to die under *Peine Forte et Dure* so that his relatives would get his goods on his death. Nowadays if somebody refuses to plead guilty or not guilty in court this is taken as a plea or not guilty and the trial proceeds. The jury which actually tried the case was called the Petty Jury and it survives today.

In civil matters Henry II introduced juries for the trial of questions of possession of land. Various actions were available; for example, if somebody had recently lost the seisin (possession) of his land he would follow the appropriate type of lawsuit called the *Assize of Novel Disseisin* to get it back from the intruder. If the wrongdoer had taken the land that the plaintiff should have occupied on the death of his ancestor he used the *Assize of Mort d'Ancestor*. These innovations were very popular and drew increased business to the royal courts, for the seignorial courts were prevented from summoning juries. By the thirteenth century, when the royal courts were well established, the seignorial courts were already in decline.

The development of common law

At the time of the Norman Conquest there was no central government and no legal system as we now understand it. William the Conqueror began the policy of centralisation that led to one government for the whole of the country, one legal system and one body of law. In order to gain the confidence of his subjects he needed to develop in them a sense of security. He did this by not imposing laws upon them, but by settling disputes by reference to local customs which were fairly administered by the itinerant justices. These justices held their authority under certain commissions, and from the time of Henry II were sent out at regular intervals.

The main purpose of the itinerant justices was to supervise local administration and tax collection but gradually the minor judicial powers they originally had increased in importance. There were three types of commission:

Gaol Delivery. The commission of gaol delivery empowered the itinerant justices to try all persons found in the gaols (it should be noted that at this time imprisonment was not a punishment).
Oyer and Terminer. Under the commission of Oyer and Terminer the justices were to try all cases of crime since the last visit.
Assize. The commission of assize gave power to try civil cases.

'Nisi Prius'. As a general rule trials of civil cases were held at Westminster but as a matter of convenience to the parties trial was allowed in local courts. A case would be formally set down for trial at Westminister 'unless before' (nisi prius) it came up for trial at Westminster it had been heard locally. The modern nisi prius, i e the Assizes, were presided over by High Court judges and other commissioners (e g in divorce cases), all of whom derived their authority from one commission that gave the powers of the three listed above. This system continued until 1974.

Early commissioners were clerics as this was the only class of persons who could read and write. Later, as a legal profession developed, the commissions were issued to lawyers. At first the itinerant justices administered local customs. They discovered the custom with the help of a jury and then applied it. Judges refused to apply bad customs and would discuss the merits of the various customs that had been 'discovered' at Westminster, agreeing on certain customs and rejecting others. In this way local custom gained the force of general law for local custom formed the basis on which the judges developed the common law.

As time went on the *Curia Regis* began to take on a more professional air and the various specialists began to separate into their own departments. It was this trend that led to the emergence at different times of the courts of common law. The first court to appear was the Court of Exchequer which had come into existence by 1200. At first it dealt only with revenue disputes, but as the fees earned by the judges depended on the amount of litigation conducted in the court, various devices were resorted to in order to increase the court's jurisdiction. The judges of the Court of Exchequer were known as Barons, and were headed by a Chief Baron. The Court of Common Pleas (also called the Common Bench) emerged from the *Curia Regis* next. In 1272 the first Chief Justice, as the head of the court was called, was appointed. He was assisted by other judges called puisne (younger or lesser) judges. The Court of Common Pleas was established because Magna Carta 1215 laid down that there should be a court in a 'fixed place' to carry out the same functions as the itinerant justices (see p 22, above). The place chosen was Westminster, and the court sat in Westminster Hall from the thirteenth to the nineteenth century. It was used mainly for actions by one subject against another particularly in trespass and debt. The third common law court to emerge was the Court of King's Bench. The first Chief Justice was appointed in 1268; the other judges were called puisne judges. Originally the Court of King's Bench followed the king round the country and, by reason of its close connection with the sovereign, became the most important of the three common law courts. Its civil jurisdiction was concurrent with that of the Court of Common Pleas in many matters; it was the only one of the three which had criminal jurisdiction, and in addition it controlled the activities of inferior courts by means of the prerogative writs (see p 90, below) which it developed. The three common law courts remained in existence until abolished by the Judicature Acts in 1875 (see p 33, below).

Forms of action

An action at common law was begun by the issue of a document known as a writ. This was purchased from the Chancery office, which was controlled by an important royal official, the Chancellor. The writ was a formal document containing the allegation of a wrong and directing the Sheriff to summon a jury to hear the dispute. As the writ contained the allegation it was essential that the correct writ should be chosen or the demandant (plaintiff) would be non-suited (i e told that he had chosen the wrong writ and would not be allowed to proceed thereon). A simple illustration of the difficulty caused by this highly technical system can be seen from the following example of writs available for wrongs against chattels:

(i)   A tears B's book but leaves him with the pieces—*Writ of trespass to goods.*

(ii)   A borrows B's book for fourteen days but then informs B that he will not return the book until after the examination six months hence—*Writ of detinue.*

(iii)   A borrows B's book and then sells it to X—*Writ of trover.*

In each of the above cases a wrong has been done to the property of B. In (i) B's possession of his book is unjustifiably *interfered with*. In (ii) B is *deprived of* possession of his book. In (iii) B's right of *ownership* is denied.

The choice of the writ was also important from the point of view of procedure as it determined which mode of trial (or form of action) was to follow. The writ of right, which was used to determine the question of ownership of land, enjoyed trial by the grand assize, a jury consisting of 16 men (four knights chosen by the sheriff who in turn chose 12 lawful men to assist them). However, at the option of the defendant, trial by battle could be employed. The writ of debt, which was used to recover a liquidated (ascertained) sum of money gave rise to trial by a petty jury of

12 lawful men but again there was an option – the defendant could choose trial by wager of law.

The forms of action were reformed in part in the nineteenth century and finally abolished by the Judicature Acts 1873–1875 (see p 33, below). Although they are no longer used their influence is still felt. (Maitland said 'they rule us from their graves'.)

Appeals from the Common Law courts

Although today a party to an action usually has a right to appeal from the decision of the trial court to a higher court on a point of law or, possibly, a question of fact, this type of right of appeal did not exist before the Judicature Acts. Instead there was a procedure by writ of error. It was possible to use this procedure only if it could be shown that there was an error disclosed by the record of the case, so that there were some types of error that could not be remedied. If the party who resorted to the writ of error was successful the result would be that the original judgment would be quashed (set aside), but no new judgment would be substituted for it. Courts entitled to hear a writ of error were said to have 'jurisdiction in error'. The Court of King's Bench had jurisdiction in error over the Court of Common Pleas. The other common law courts with jurisdiction in error were the Court of Exchequer Chamber and the House of Lords. There were at various times four courts bearing the name of Court of Exchequer Chamber. The first was established by statute in 1358 to hear errors from the Court of Exchequer. The second Court of Exchequer Chamber lasted from medieval times until the seventeenth century and consisted latterly of a meeting of the judges of the three common law courts to discuss difficult point of law that had come up for decision before one of the courts. The judges passed an informal resolution and the court in which the particular case was being tried gave its judgment in accordance with the resolution. The third Court of Exchequer Chamber was set up by statute in 1584 to hear errors from the Court of King's Bench in some types of case. The court consisted of judges from the Courts of Exchequer and Common Pleas. The House of Lords heard proceedings brought by writ of error from the courts set up in 1258 and 1584. Both these courts were abolished in 1830, and so was the jurisdiction in error of the King's Bench over the Common Pleas. Instead a new Court of Exchequer Chamber, the fourth, was set up and empowered to hear appeals from the three common law courts. The court consisted of all the judges of the two courts other than the trial court. An appeal lay from it to the House of Lords, until the court was abolished in 1875.

The Court of Chancery

In many cases it was not possible to obtain redress for a wrong from the courts of common law. This might be so because the law was defective in that no remedy existed or because the remedy the common law provided (damages) was unsuitable or, in some cases, because one of the parties involved was so important as to be able to defy the court. Where there were circumstances of the kind mentioned, those who were unable to obtain justice in the usual manner petitioned the king, who was regarded as the fountain of justice, for assistance. In early times many petitions were considered by the Council, as the *Curia Regis* came to be called by the fourteenth century. One of the most important members of the Council was the Chancellor. He was the king's chief minister and was generally an ecclesiastic. One of his duties was to supervise the Chancery offices from which writs were issued. In the course of time it became the custom to hand over petitions to the Chancellor to deal with, and eventually petitions were addressed direct to him. As a result of these developments the Chancellors began administering justice, and by the end of the fifteenth century they were doing this in their own court, the Court of Chancery, alongside the common law courts. The Chancellor, who was called the 'keeper of the king's conscience' because he was the king's confessor, approached his task in quite a different way from the common law judges. Proceedings in the Chancery Court were commenced not by a writ, but by a bill, as petitions were later called. When the Chancellor received a bill he would send a copy of it to the defendant together with a writ of *subpoena*, which was a command to the defendant to come before the Chancellor to answer the allegations made. As an ecclesiastic the Chancellor was determined to see that, as far as those who were summoned before him were concerned, none should have evil-doing weighing on his conscience. Therefore the Chancery Court's procedure differed considerably from that of the common law courts. The defendant found himself not before a judge and jury but before a clergyman who by skilled and persistent questioning probed to find the truth. If the Chancellor was satisfied that the defendant had done wrong, and that his conscience was burdened with guilt, he would order the defendant to make good the wrong and thus to clear his conscience. It was because of this approach to litigation that the Chancery Court was called a court of conscience. If a defendant refused to do the Chancellor's bidding he was sent to prison until he saw the error of his ways and decided to relieve his conscience. The fact that the Chancery Court acted not against the defendant's property but against his person was expressed by saying that it acted 'in personam'. The type of justice dispensed by the Chancery Court came to be known as 'equity'. During the early history of the Court of Chancery equity had no binding rules and each Chancellor gave judgment in a way that satisfied his own conscience. This led to considerable criticism of the uncertainty concerning the outcome of cases and by the end of the seventeenth century the criticism was made that equity varied with the length of the Chancellor's foot. Gradually equity built up a system of rules based on precedent in much the same way as the common law courts had done and the decision of cases no longer turned on the views of a particular Chancellor. As the Chancery Court became busier Vice-Chancellors were appointed to assist the Chancellor and additional Chancery Courts were established in various parts of the country. In this way there grew up in England a system under which two sets of courts existed side by side, one set administering the common law and the other administering equity. The achievements of the Chancellors were considerable. Equity built up the whole law of trusts (see p 17, above) and it developed the remedies of specific performance and injunction (see p 350, below).

As examples of the way in which equity developed we can consider the growth of the rules relating to trusts and mortgages. A trust was not recognised at common law, which took the view that the trustee was not bound to administer the trust property for the beneficiaries' benefit. Equity however would compel a trustee to administer the trust in accordance with his conscience and if he defaulted would imprison him until he made good the loss he had caused to the trust property. The idea was that the trustee should make good the loss for the good of his conscience. Equity thus acted as a court of conscience and against the person.

The common law position under a mortgage, where a person mortgaged his land to another in exchange for a loan of money that was to be repaid by a certain day, was that if the money was not repaid by that day, the land thenceforth belonged absolutely to the lender and the borrower remained liable to repay the loan. Even if the borrower obtained enough money later to pay off the debt he could not recover his land. Equity developed the maxim 'once a mortgage, always a mortgage' and allowed a borrower to insist on his land being returned to him when he was able to repay the debt, even though the agreed date for repayment had passed. Of course he would have to pay in addition some extra interest to cover the period during which he could not raise the money. This right, which still exists, is called the 'equity of redemption'. The real intention of the parties in such a case is that the right to the land shall be handed over only temporarily by way of security and the enforcement of the equity of redemption is an illustration of the equitable maxim, 'Equity looks to the intention and not to the form'.

When the Chancery Court first came into being the common law courts showed no resentment of the jurisdiction that it exercised. As time went on, however, a conflict began to develop. This conflict arose from the view held by the Chancellors that they ought to prevent a man from acting against his conscience, even though he was acting within his legal rights. If, for example, a man issued a writ in a common law court to enforce some right recognised by the common law and the Chancellor regarded it as being against the plaintiff's conscience to enforce his right, the Chancellor would issue an injuction forbidding the plaintiff to go on with his action. If he disregarded the injunction he would be imprisoned. The common law courts felt that they were suffering from unreasonable interference and in the reign of King James I (1603-25) a sharp personal conflict developed between the Chief Justice of the Common Pleas, Sir Edward Coke, and the Chancellor, Lord Ellesmere. The King acted on the advice of Sir Francis Bacon, an enemy of Coke, and decided that in matters of conflict between common law and equity, equity was to prevail. This was a great turning point in the history of equity and it was in the years following this decision that equity made its greatest contributions to the development of law. Its successes were to some extent offset by the fact that proceedings in the chancery courts were exceedingly slow and expensive. The situation was at its worst in the eighteenth century. Various reforms were made in the nineteenth century but these were inadequate. The Court of Chancery was abolished in the general reorganisation that took place in 1873-75 (see p 33, below).

Chancery appeals.   An appeal lay from a vice-chancellor to the Chancellor and, until 1851, from the Chancellor to the House of Lords. In 1851 the Court of Appeal in Chancery was established to hear appeals from the Court of Chancery. The court was staffed by two lords justice, the Chancellor and any vice-chancellor or the Master of the Rolls (a judge of the Chancery Court). This court was abolished in 1875.

Common law and equity

The relationship between common law and equity.   The common law was built up as a complete system and was independent of any other system. Equity, on the other hand, was developed to remedy the defects in the common law and would be meaningless if considered in isolation because it presupposed the existence of the common law. Because of the way equity developed it is difficult to define and indeed it may be said to have two meanings. In its earlier days it merely consisted of principles of fairness, equality and good conscience, but by the nineteenth century it had become a rigid set of rules standing side by side with the rules of common law, but administered in different courts. In its developed form equity could be defined as that body of law which was administered in the Court of Chancery before it was abolished in 1875. However, in common speech 'equity' may still be used to mean simply fairness.

Similarities and differences between common law and equity.   The two systems are similar in that both were developed from the beginning in an English context, both rely on the doctrine of precedent and both have been partly embodied in statutes. This last point is illustrated by the Sale of Goods Act 1893, which codified many common law rules relating to the sale of goods, and the Trustee Act 1925 in which are embodied many rules developed in the Chancery Court.

There are several important differences between common law and equity:

(i) In theory the rules of the common law have existed since time immemorial, while the rules of equity are admitted to have been created from time to time as the necessity arose.

(ii) The common law is a complete system while equity consists of certain rules devised to meet particular difficulties.

(iii) The common law was administered in the courts of common law before 1875 while at the time equity was administered in the Chancery Court.

(iv) If a person can prove that he has a right at common law, the court must grant him a remedy, whereas a plaintiff seeking an equitable remedy cannot be sure that it will be granted even if he makes out what appears to him to be a good case. This is so because equitable remedies are discretionary, i e the court has a discretion as to whether or not it will award the remedy. This discretion is exercised in accordance with well-established rules. For example, the court will take into account such matters as the previous behaviour of the plaintiff applying the equitable maxim that 'He who comes into equity must come with clean hands'. The effect of this maxim is that a person who has acted against good conscience will not be granted the assistance he seeks.

Other courts

The greater part of the work of fashioning English law was done by the courts of common law and the courts of equity, but there were, at various stages of history, a number of other courts that contributed to the growth of our law, and a few of the more important are described below.

The House of Lords. In former times the House of Lords exercised first instance criminal jurisdiction. From the time of Magna Carta 1215 until 1948, members of the House were in some cases tried by the House, if accused of crime, instead of being tried by the ordinary courts. This situation was ended by the Criminal Justice Act 1948. Until the early nineteenth century the procedure of impeachment was used. This was a prosecution by the House of Commons of an accused person before the House of Lords. During the seventeenth century the House of Lords exercised first instance civil jurisdiction but abandoned it after a dispute with the House of Commons. As an appeal court the House of Lords had jurisdiction in error from the King's Bench, Exchequer and Chancery Courts.

The Courts Merchant. From medieval times there was an unwritten body of customary rules and practices observed by merchants who traded at fairs all over Europe. These rules were called the 'law merchant'. The law merchant which was internationally recognised was administered originally in England by the courts merchant which were of two types, Courts of the Staple established in certain towns, and Courts of Pie Powder which were held at each fair and market to settle disputes between traders. In the sixteenth and seventeenth centuries the courts merchant were declining in importance and the common law courts began to take over the law merchant and incorporate it into the common law, of which it now forms part.

One of the most important functions of the Courts of the Staple was to protect foreign merchants trading in England. Although in the sixteenth century the law merchant was not well administered by the common law courts, Lord Holt, in the seventeenth century, and Lord Mansfield, in the eighteenth, were instrumental in bringing about the absorption of the principles of the law merchant (commercial law) into the common law.

The High Court of Admiralty.   This court dates from the fourteenth century. It had jurisdiction over matters connected with the sea. Until the nineteenth century it had criminal jurisdiction in respect of crimes committed at sea. The court was often in conflict with the common law courts because all the courts wished to extend their civil jurisdiction at the expense of the others. The fortunes of the High Court of Admiralty fluctuated in this respect, the court being more prosperous in the sixteenth century. In 1875 the court was abolished.

The Ecclesiastical Courts.   These came into existence long before the Reformation. In each diocese the bishop held a court that had jurisdiction over both clergy and laity. The law that was originally administered was the canon law of the medieval church. With the Reformation Henry VIII (1509–47) became head of the Church of England and the ecclesiastical courts began to administer what became English ecclesiastical law. Besides dealing with offences committed by clergy and church matters, these courts exercised jurisdiction in connection with wills and the administration of deceased persons. In addition they had jurisdiction over matrimonial matters such as judicial separation and legitimacy. They lost both of the last types of jurisdiction in 1857 (see below). Ecclesiastical courts continue to function today (see p. oo, below).

The Court of Probate.   This court was set up by the Court of Probate Act 1857 and it took over from the ecclesiastical courts their jurisdiction in the matter of wills and the estates of deceased persons. It was abolished in 1875.

The Court for Divorce and Matrimonial Causes.   The Matrimonial Causes Act 1857 transferred to this court the matrimonial jurisdiction of the ecclesiastical courts. The Act, in addition, made it possible for the first time to secure a dissolution of marriage, or 'divorce' as it is usually called, through the court. Previously the only way to obtain a divorce was by promoting a private Act of Parliament at considerable expense. This court was abolished in 1875.

The Conciliar Courts. The *Curia Regis*, which became known in the course of time as the Council, retained jurisdiction in legal matters even after the common law courts had broken away from it. It was due to this that further courts were able to develop in later times. These courts, which are known as the conciliar courts, had more political than legal significance, although they did develop some important parts of the law. The most important of these courts was the Court of Star Chamber which came into existence some time in the fifteenth century and lasted until 1641. The Tudor kings used the court to enforce the power of the Crown in the troubled times following the Wars of the Roses. The most important Act that recognised the jurisdiction of the court was the Star Chamber Act of 1487. The court brought order to the country. In exercising its criminal jurisdiction it developed the law in relation to criminal libel, conspiracy, forgery and fraud. In addition it had a varied civil jurisdiction which overlapped with that of the common law courts. The court, which for a time had been popular, eventually became an instrument of royal oppression and was abolished when the monarchy fell. Another conciliar court was the Court of Requests which existed from 1493-1642. It was a court of equity and was originally concerned with administering justice to poor men. In spite of opposition from the common law courts it became popular for a time. When the court ceased to exist in 1642 it left a gap in the legal system, since no other courts were suitable for the trial of small cases. In the eighteenth century new local courts called courts of request were set up to try small cases and these continued to exist intil the new county courts were created in 1846 (see p 77, below).

The reforms of 1873–75

The Supreme Court of Judicature Act 1873, which came into operation in 1875, made a comprehensive reform of the system of superior courts in this country. The Act set up the Supreme Court of Judicature which was divided into the High Court and the Court of Appeal. It provided for the abolition of the following courts and the transfer of their functions to the High Court: the Court of Queen's Bench, the Court of Common Pleas, the Court of Exchequer, the High Court of Admiralty, the Court of Probate, the Court for Divorce and Matrimonial Causes, the London Court of Bankruptcy (which dated from 1869), and the courts created by commissions of assize. In addition it abolished the Court of Exchequer Chamber and the Court of Appeal in Chancery and vested their functions in the Court of Appeal. Under the Act the High Court was originally divided into five divisions, namely, the Chancery Division, the Queen's Bench Division, the Common Pleas Division, the Exchequer Division and the Probate, Divorce and Admiralty Division. In 1880 the number of divisions was reduced to three, by the merging of the Exchequer and Common Pleas Divisions into the Queen's Bench Division. The Administration of Justice Act 1970 replaced the Probate, Divorce and Admiralty Division by the Family Division| (see p 81).

The Judicature Acts finally abolished the forms of action and introduced new rules of procedure for the courts that were brought into being. The procedure relating to the issue of writs and to other stages of litigation was much simplified. Another important provision in the Supreme Court of Judicature Act 1873 was s 25 which dealt with conflicts that had existed between common law and equity before the coming into force of the Act. Many points of difference were dealt with specifically and a single rule to be followed in all courts was laid down for the future; sub-s (11) of s 25, which was the final sub-section, dealt with all cases not specifically mentioned by laying down a general principle in the following words:

> 'Generally in all matter not hereinbefore particularly mentioned, in which there is any conflict or variance between the Rules of Equity and the Rules of the Common Law with reference to the same matter, the Rules of Equity shall prevail.'

An example of a particular rule laid down by s 25 is well furnished by s 25 (7) which deals with time being the essence of a contract| (see p 311, below). Before 1875 at common law, if the parties fixed a time for the performance of the contract, time was always of the essence of the contract (i e the contract was held to be broken if not fulfilled in time), but in equity time was of the essence only if one of the following three conditions was present: (i) if the contract declared time to be of the essence; (ii) if, even though time was not originally of the essence, one party had defaulted or unreasonably delayed performance within a specified time, provided it was reasonable: or (iii) if the nature of the contract was such as to make time of the essence, for example a contract to sell perishable goods. The effect of s 25 (7) was to abolish the common law rule and to make the equitable rule applicable in all courts.

Reform of ancient local courts

A large number of ancient and local courts escaped the reforms of the last two centuries and still live on, albeit as shadows of their former selves. The Law Commission published a report in 1976 entitled '*Jurisdiction of Certain Ancient Courts*' which was presented to Parliament by the Lord Chancellor, and which became the basis of s 23 of and Sch 4 to the

Administration of Justice Act 1977. This report is an interesting document which refers to various surviving classes of courts as well as a number of courts mentioned by name. It pointed out that although certain ancient courts had not sat for many years, an apparently moribund inferior court might be revived as a result of an application for mandamus, and recommended that certain courts should cease to have any jurisdiction to hear and determine legal proceedings but should be allowed to carry on other customary business. These recommendations were incorporated into the Act of 1977 mentioned above.

It is not possible here to list all the classes of court and individual courts dealt with by the 1977 Act, but it is interesting to note that among the courts which still exist and carry out restricted functions are certain Hundred Courts, Courts of the Staple and Courts of Pie Powder.

The 1977 Act specifically preserves the jurisdiction of 32 ancient courts to carry on certain customary businesses. For example, File Bideford Manor Court may deal with the appointment of 'a people's warden, tything man and waywardens', the Court Leet and Court Baron of the Ancient Manor of Bowes in the County of Durham may concern itself with the presentation of the audited accounts of the manor and the City of London Court of Hasting may continue with the enrolment of wills and deeds.

The Supreme Court Act 1981

This is an Act to consolidate the constitution, jurisdiction and practice of the Supreme Court. At the same time certain changes have been made and the law has been restated in a more modern and coherent manner.

Changes in the structure of the superior courts since 1875

Courts existing in 1874
and merged in 1875

Courts created in 1875
High Court

Court of Queen's Bench

Queen's Bench Division

Court of Common Pleas

*Common Pleas Division

Court of Exchequer

*Exchequer Division

Court of Chancery

London Court of Bankruptcy }   Chancery Division

Court of Probate

*The Common Pleas and Exchequer Divisions were merged with the Queen's Bench Division in 1880.

Court of Divorce	}	Probate, Divorce and
Court of Admiralty		Admiralty Division
Court of Appeal in Chancery	}	Court of Appeal
Court of Exchequer Chamber		

Courts abolished and created after 1875

1907—Court for Crown Cases Reserved abolished

1908—Court of Criminal Appeal established

1951—Courts-Martial Appeal Court established

1956—Crown Courts at Liverpool and Manchester established

1957—Restrictive Practices Court established

1963—Court of Ecclesiastical Causes Reserved established

1966—Court of Criminal Appeal abolished. Court of Appeal divided into a Civil Division and a Criminal Division

1970—Administration of Justice Act: Family Division replaces Probate, Divorce and Admiralty Division; Admiralty Court and Commercial Court in Queen's Bench Division

1971—Courts Act: Assizes, Quarter Sessions and Crown Courts replaced by new Crown Court
    Industrial Relations Act: National Industrial Relations Court set up

1972—European Communities Act: as from 1973 European Court jurisdiction extended to United Kingdom

1974—Trade Union and Labour Relations Act: National Industrial Relations Court abolished

1975—Employment Protection Act: Employment Appeal Tribunal set up

1977—Patents Act: provision for Patents Court as part of Chancery Division

Chapter 4
Sources of law

Before we begin our study of this topic we must consider what we mean by the expression 'sources of law' because it can have several meanings. First of all, it can mean the records where the law is to be found. This head covers the law reports and statutes and is known as the 'literary source'. Second, it means the authority which gives force to the rules of law, i e the state. In this country the law derives its authority, expressly or impliedly, from Parliament. This is termed the 'formal source'. Third, the phrase refers to the causes which induce the creation of law but which do not themselves create it. The deliberations and recommendations of the Law Commission may result in Parliament considering a particular question and legislating to cover the point. The work of the Law Commission (see p 65, below) would be classified under this third head as a 'historical source' of law. Religious beliefs and moral standards are also historical sources of law. Fourth and lastly, there are the means by which law is brought into existence. In England and Wales today this covers the process of legislation, adjudication and possibly custom. This may be termed the 'legal source'. Thus the Wolfenden Report (historical source) brought about the process of legislation (legal source) whereby Parliament gave its authority (formal source) to the Street Offences Act 1959. What Parliament decided is to be found in the Act (literary source).

A. Principal sources

The following sources of law which have most influenced and created English law are dealt with in their historical order of appearance.

1 Custom

Nature and origin of custom

Custom has its origin in the usage or practice of people in doing a certain thing in a certain way and one of its characteristics is that it is not consciously formed.

> 'Usage is the spontaneous evolution by the people or part of them of rules of conduct the existence and general acceptance of which is proved by their regular observance' (Holland).

Usage developing into customary law is the oldest form of law-making and in its early stages depends for its validity on the willingness of those who generally follow the usage to submit to it. As a state develops, more conscious and deliberate methods of law-making are used: in England, particularly adjudication and legislation. Thus, as a state develops, the scope for the evolution of new customs over a period of time gets less and less and in modern England is *almost* non-existent, but not quite. Most of our law now has its authority in statute and case law but occasionally new customary rules may arise. However, where custom is recognised it must comply with several stringent requirements which are discussed below.

Custom is of two main types

Binding custom may be subdivided into (i) particular or local custom and (ii) general custom. Both types are limited in their application by the rules which must be satisfied before these are recognised by the courts.

(i) *Local custom.*   A local custom is a usage which has obtained the force of law and is binding within a particular area or place upon the persons and things which it concerns. In practice a plaintiff or defendant relying on a local custom must plead it and give particulars of it. At the trial the existence of the custom is proved like any other fact, e g by documentary evidence or the oral testimony of the old inhabitants of a village. Where it has already been the subject of litigation it must still be pleaded but the reported decision may be given in support. Some customs, such as gavelkind in Kent, are so well known that the courts take judicial notice of them. A modern example of a local custom is to be found in the case of *New Windsor Corpn v Mellor* (1975) where an 81-year-old lady successfully established the customary right of local inhabitants to indulge in lawful sports and pastimes on an area of land in the middle of New Windsor. It was alleged that the right went back at least to AD 900.

(ii) *General custom.*   A view once widely held was that the common law was simply a body of general customs and judges did not make new law by their decisions but merely declared pre-existing customs. Evidence of this is to be found in the earliest text books many of which were entitled *Lex et Consuetudinis Angliae* (Law and *Customs* of England). Many of the early Year Books state that the 'Common Law of the Realm is the common Custom of the Realm'. As late as the time of George III, Blackstone wrote that

> 'judicial decisions are the principal and most authoritative evidence that can be given of the existence of such custom as shall form part of the Common Law'.

But this identification of common law and custom is no longer accepted as correct. Common law is built up of case law which is in the main new law and not pre-existing customary law. In its early development the common law adopted a wealth of rules of customary origin. Many common law rules thus owe their origin to ancient custom but far more owe their origin to judicial decisions given over the centuries.

The question occasionally arises whether new customs of binding force can arise. In view of the wide scope of statute law and the numerous requisites of a valid custom this would seem unlikely – but it is possible. Most of the rules of the 'law merchant' grew up outside the common law and were absorbed into it in the seventeenth and eighteenth centuries. Negotiable instruments are, however, the only case in which a general custom arising after the year 1189 has been recognised as supplanting the common law.

Tests for custom

Before the law will recognise a *local* custom nine tests must be satisfied.

1 The custom must have existed since time out of mind – known as the test of immemoriality or antiquity. A custom was only recognised if it had been observed for a long time and eventually the method of calculating the time became fixed by reference to 1189, being the first year of the reign of Richard I. The party alleging the custom must prove it, but in practice the courts do not require positive proof right back to 1189. If he proves the custom as far back as living memory goes, and further by records, a presumption arises in his favour. Once the presumption of antiquity has arisen the burden of proof then falls on the other party to disprove the existence of the custom at some time since 1189.

2 The custom must have been continuously in operation without lawful interruption. This does not mean that a custom must have been *continuously exercised* but that at all times it must have been possible to exercise it lawfully. If it were legally unenforceable for even a short time it would not be recognised as a valid custom.

3 The custom must have been exercised peaceably, openly and as of right – *nec per vim, nec clam, nec precario*. The basis of custom is that it is exercised by consent and any secret or forcible exercise cannot be with consent. Furthermore, an exercise of a 'right' which depends on the granting of permission cannot be a valid custom for clearly, if there had been a right, permission would have been unnecessary.

4 The custom must not be unreasonable in the eyes of the law. This is a question of law for the judge and, in relation to general custom and mercantile custom, is the test which is concentrated on. In the case of *Day v Savadge* (1614), a custom, which allowed an officer of the City of London Corporation to certify what customs of the City were valid in matters in which the Corporation was interested, was held to be invalid because it was unreasonable. In another case the lord of the manor under an alleged manorial custom took minerals from under a tenant's copyhold land without paying compensation for subsidence and consequent damage. This too was held to be unreasonable (*Wolstanton Case* (1940)).

5 The custom must be certain. In *Lady Wilson v Willes* (1806), an alleged custom that the tenants of a manor might take from the manorial common as much turf as they required for their lawns was held to be unreasonable and uncertain.

6 The custom must be compulsory. Custom is

'legally effective only because, and only so far as, it is recognised by law as the expression of an underlying principle of right approved by those who use it' (Salmond).

7 The custom must be consistent with other customs – otherwise they cannot all be good.

8 It must not be contrary to any statute.

9 It must apply to a definite locality. Local customs apply only to the things or inhabitants of a particular area such as a shire, a borough, a parish or a manor.

When the courts are considering the validity of an alleged *general* custom (see p 38, above) they do not require that the custom should have existed since 1189, nor do they require it to be confined to a particular locality. The other tests, enumerated above must, however, be satisfied. (*Alfred F. Beckett Ltd v Lyons* (1967).)

Is custom law?

We now ask ourselves whether customary *law* exists in its own right or whether customary *rules* become law when recognised and enforced by the courts. There are several views on this jurisprudential problem and one is dealt with here.

To the English jurist, Austin, law is the will of the sovereign power within a state – in this country the Queen in Parliament. Therefore, only the formal commands of the sovereign power and methods recognised by the sovereign power as law-making can create law. In England this means legislation and case law, the latter being promulgated in courts created by statute. It follows from this that custom is not law till recognised as such by the legislature or by the courts, at which time it becomes enforceable, not as a custom but as an Act of Parliament or a precedent.

Conventional usage

To be distinguished from custom in the strict sense of binding rules of law is that body of rules sometimes known as custom which binds *only by agreement*, express or implied, of the parties concerned. For clarity this type of custom is called conventional usage. Because such usage is not binding of itself it can be excluded by agreement but as a general rule usages of a trade or particular area are impliedly included in contracts within the trade or area. It was said in *Hutton v Warren* (1836) that 'the parties did not mean to express in writing the whole of their agreement but to contract with reference to certain known usages'.

Before the usage will be implied it must have existed for so long and become so well established that it is reasonable to incorporate it by implication in an agreement where there is no express term to the contrary. In *Smith v Wilson* (1832) a usage of the fur trade that 'a thousand rabbits' meant one thousand two hundred rabbits was implied in a contract. In *Dashwood v Magniac* (1891) a custom of Buckinghamshire that 'timber' included beech as well as the usual oak, ash and elm, was recognised.

2 Judicial precedent

History of the doctrine of binding precedent

The doctrine of judicial precedent, whereby the decisions of certain courts are binding on other courts, is of comparatively recent origin and is certainly little more than a hundred years old. The early theory as to the nature of the common law was that the judges merely declared its existence, which lay in custom. If this is at all true (and of part of the common law it is true) there cannot be conflicting decisions declaring the same custom. As early as the time of Edward I (1272–1307) the idea of judicial consistency can be seen in contemporary writings but this is not the same thing as *binding* precedent. From the sixteenth century onwards, with the development of printing and the improvement in the standard of reporting, cases were cited more frequently. By the nineteenth century it was clearly stated in the opinion of Baron Parke given to the House of Lords in 1833 in the case of *Mirehouse v Rennell* that precedents must be regarded in subsequent cases and it was not for the courts 'to reject them and to abandon all analogy to them'. The reorganisation of the courts which took place in the nineteenth century, culminating in the major reconstruction brought about by the Judicature Acts 1873–1875 and the Appellate Jurisdiction Act 1876, made easier the task of recognising a hierarchy of the courts. Another considerable factor influencing the development of the doctrine was the creation of the Council of Law Reporting in 1865 which raised the standard of the reports (see p 63, below).

Equity had its origin in the jurisdiction of the Lord Chancellor to do justice where the common law failed. It was not based on any declaratory theory so it was not felt that there was any need for consistency in the decisions of the Chancellor until comparatively late in its development. Towards the end of the seventeenth century criticism of equity as being uncertain intensified and from that time onward equity also moved towards a system of binding precedent. The reorganisation of the courts and the formation of the Council of Law Reporting were also of considerable influence here.

Judicial precedent today

The process of adjudication, whereby after argument before a judge a decision in a dispute is given, forms one of the two most important means by which the law is created. In reaching his conclusion the judge will formulate and apply a legal principle. In accordance with certain rules this principle may form a guide (binding or persuasive) for the future. This regard for precedent has not always held sway in England and in many other parts of the world today is not a system which is followed.

Before embarking on an enquiry into the situations where precedents are binding or otherwise it is first necessary to draw certain distinctions.

The decision and the ratio decidendi

In most cases which come before the courts the judge has to decide in favour of one of two parties to a dispute. His words, 'I give judgment for the plaintiff' or, 'I find for the defendant' are his decision inter partes (as between the parties). This decision is of the utmost importance to the parties to the litigation. But a judge will give reasons for reaching this decision and in these reasons lies the ratio decidendi (the legal reason for deciding) or the legal principle behind the decision. This is important for the future. The decision binds only the parties whereas the ratio decidendi may bind others in similar disputes in the future. The distinction is well drawn in the case of *Re Waring* (1948). W left annuities to H and L 'free of income tax'. In 1942 in an appeal to which H was a party, the Court of Appeal held that in the circumstances of the case income tax must be deducted. In 1946 in a similar case between different parties the House of Lords overruled the Court of Appeal case of 1942. H and L in 1948 *both* applied to the Chancery Division to determine whether their annuities should be paid in full in view of the decision of the House of Lords in 1946. The Court held that H's annuity was to be paid less income tax. As his claim to the full amount had been litigated and the matter decided (res judicata), it could not, therefore, be reopened. But L was not a party to the 1942 case. If L had applied to the Chancery Division between 1942 and 1946, the court of first instance would have been bound by the Court of Appeal's decision. However, as it was, L made his application in 1948 and the court followed the ratio of the 1946 House of Lords' decision.

For illustration of the principle of res judicata see *Public Trustee v Kenward* (1967) and *Re Manly's Will Trusts (No 2), Tickle v Manly* (1976).

The ratio decidendi

The word 'decision' is often loosely used to cover all the words a judge says in the course of his judgment but strictly speaking a 'decision' is only part of the judgment.

A judgment consists of:

1 a statement of the facts and an indication as to which of these the judge considers material to a consideration of the law,
2 an account of the reasoning towards the actual decision (this involves a discussion of the precedents and is of most interest to a lawyer), and
3 the actual decision inter partes.

The ratio decidendi may be defined as the legal principle applied to the facts by the court (or judge) in reaching its decision. There are many views as to what the true meaning of the phrase 'ratio decidendi' is. Professor Goodhart takes the view that it is the legal principle in relation to the *material facts* as found by the jury or judge sitting alone. Other writers take the view that where full argument has been heard on facts as assumed to exist, *even though they are not in issue*, any resultant statement of the law by the judge is part of the ratio decidendi.

Briefly the ratio decidendi may be said to be the legal principle behind the decision. This is in contrast to other statements of legal principle put forward in the judgment but which are not directly relevant to the matters in issue. Such comments given in the course of a judgment are called obiter dicta (matters spoken by the way).

Binding and persuasive precedents

Precedents which fall within this category are decisions of the superior courts which have not been reversed or overruled or abrogated by statute. A decision is 'reversed' when an appellate court allows an appeal against that decision. A decision is 'overruled' when in another, later case a higher court reaches a decision which is based on a legal principle inconsistent with the earlier decision of the lower court. A *binding* precedent is one which the court *must* follow whether it is in sympathy with the decision or not. Each court must decide for itself whether in a given case there is a precedent binding on the court and covering the given case. If there is a binding precedent but the court decides that it does not cover the facts of the given case it is said to 'distinguish' the precedent. *Persuasive* precedents are those which are not binding but to which respect is paid.

Binding precedent. Whether a court is bound by a previous decision covering the point in question is dependent upon its position in the hierarchy of the courts. Until 1966 the position was that the House of Lords was bound by its own previous decisions (*London Street Tramways Co v LCC* (1898)) except where the previous decision had been reached per incuriam (without sufficient care) as where a relevant Act of Parliament or an earlier decision had not been noticed, or where subsequent legislation had altered the law. The present position is that the House of Lords is now prepared, where it appears right to do so, to disregard its own precedents. This was made clear in July 1966 when the Lord Chancellor made the following statement on behalf of himself and the Lords of Appeal in Ordinary:

> 'Their Lordships regard the use of precedent as an indispensable foundation upon which to decide what is the law and its application to individual cases. It provides at least some degree of certainty upon which individuals can rely in the conduct of their affairs, as well as a basis for orderly development of legal rules.
>
> Their Lordships nevertheless recognise that too rigid adherence to precedent may lead to injustice in a particular case and also unduly restrict the proper development of the law. They propose therefore to modify their present practice and, while treating formal decisions of this House as normally binding, to depart from a previous decision when it appears right to do so.
>
> In this connection they will bear in mind the danger of disturbing retrospectively the basis on which contracts, settlements of property and fiscal arrangements have been entered into and also the especial need for certainty as to the criminal law.
>
> This announcement is not intended to affect the use of precedent elsewhere than in this House.'

The Practice Statement itself raises the problem of its relationship to the doctrine of binding precedent. It has been argued that the Practice Statement is self-contradictory because, while it is operative, that is one decision of the House of Lords from which that court cannot depart. The other, and perhaps better, view is that the Practice Statement, like other statements by courts about their own *practice*, falls outside, and is not subject to, the rules relating to ratio decidendi and obiter dictum.

In *Jones v Secretary of State for Social Services* (1972) the House of Lords followed a previous decision of its own *(Dowling's Case)* even where it felt this case to have been wrongly decided. The House argued that the point of *Jones'* case involved the interpretation of a complicated statutory provision affecting only a small number of people and that if it were causing difficulty to the government department concerned the minister had appropriate access to Parliament to remedy the decision. However, in the case of *British Railways Board v Herrington* (1972) the House of Lords declined to follow its own previous decision in *R. Addie & Sons (Collieries) v Dunbreck* concerning child trespassers even though this decision had been passively approved of by Parliament in 1957 (the Occupiers' Liability Act, dealing with the duty of care owed by occupiers to persons on their premises, did nothing to alter the law relating to the duty owed to trespassers). In *Herrington's Case* the House held that an occupier owed a duty to take reasonable steps to enable trespassers to avoid a danger where the occupier knew of the danger to the trespassers. The British Railways Board was held liable to a boy aged six who crawled through a hole in a fence and then on to an electrified line. (The law on this point is now to be found in the Occupiers' Liability Act 1984, see p 172, below.)

The law was changed in *Herrington* because their Lordships saw a change in social attitudes since their earlier decision. In *Miliangos v George Frank (Textiles) Ltd* (1976) the House of Lords departed from a previous decision, which stated that awards of damages in English courts had to be expressed in sterling, because of changed circumstances, i e rapidly inflating rates of exchange. Damages were awarded in Swiss francs (see p 344, below).

In *Khawaja v Secretary of State for the Home Department* (1983) Lord Scarman, in the House of Lords, considered the meaning of the words, 'when it appears right to do so'. He said:

'This formula indicates that the House must be satisfied not only that adherence to the precedent would involve the risk of injustice and obstruct the proper development of the law, but also that a judicial departure by the House from precedent is the safe and appropriate way of remedying the injustice and developing the law. The possibility that legislation may be the better course is one which, though not mentioned in the statement, the House will not overlook .... Provided, however, due attention is paid to the dangers of uncertainty in certain branches of the law (especially criminal law) the House, as it has already in a number of cases made clear, will, if it thinks right, depart from a previous decision whether the decision be ancient or modern and whether the point of law arises on the construction of a statute or in the judge-made common law or equity'.

An explanatory note issued to the press along with the Practice Statement pointed out that the relaxation of the former position will enable the House to pay greater attention to judicial decisions reached in the superior courts of the Commonwealth.

Since the accession of the United Kingdom to the European Communities, the House of Lords is bound by certain decisions of the Court of Justice of the European Communities (see p 10, above). Although not bound to do so, the European Court generally follows its own previous decisions.

The position of the *Court of Appeal (Civil Division)* is clearly stated in the judgment of Lord Greene in *Young v Bristol Aeroplane Co* (1944). The Court is bound by decisions of the House of Lords, by its own decisions and decisions of former courts of co-ordinate jurisdiction, such as the Court of Exchequer Chamber and the Court of Appeal in Chancery. To this general rule there are three exceptions given by Lord Greene: (1) The Court of Appeal must decide which of two conflicting decisions it will follow. (2) The Court must not follow one of its own decisions which is inconsistent with a later decision of the House of Lords. (3) The Court will not follow decisions given per incuriam (through want of due care) as where the Court's attention was not drawn to relevant binding authorities – a House of Lords' decision or a statute. Over the years there has been a tendency, particularly under the guidance of Lord Denning as Master of the Rolls, for the Court of Appeal to develop additional exceptions where it was not bound to follow its own previous decisions. In *Davis v Johnson* (1978) Lord Denning said that the question of whether the Court of Appeal is bound by one of its own previous decisions is one of practice for the Court itself to decide. However, on appeal in the House of Lords, it was clearly stated that the rule laid down in the *Bristol Aeroplane* case as to precedent is still binding on the Court of Appeal. One of the reasons given by the House of Lords for re-asserting the rule was the increasing number of divisions in the Court of Appeal combined with the need for legal certainty. Another reason given was that the Court of Appeal is not the final court in the appellate system.

The *Court of Appeal (Criminal Division)* is bound by the decisions of the House of Lords, and in general by its own decisions and those of the former Court of Criminal Appeal and the former Court for Crown Cases Reserved. However, in view of the fact that in criminal cases life and liberty is often at stake, more latitude is allowed in deviating from its own previous decisions than is the case with the Civil Division of the Court of Appeal. Where a full court of the Criminal Division is assembled, it may overrule its own previous decision. (*R v Taylor* (1950)).

We shall see (p 100, below) that in certain cases where an accused has been acquitted on the basis of an arguably wrong direction on the law by the trial judge to the jury, the point of law in question may be referred by the Attorney General to the Court of Appeal (Criminal Division) for its opinion. The status of an opinion, which is contrary to the trial judge's view of the law, as a binding precedent is unclear. Furthermore, would a later Court of Appeal (Criminal Division) be bound by one of its earlier 'opinions' as opposed to an earlier 'decision'?

The jurisdictions of the Civil Division and of the Criminal Division are mutually exclusive. The decision of one court is not binding on the other even though they are of co-ordinate authority. It should be noted, however, that under the Civil Evidence Act 1968, s 11, in any civil proceedings, the fact that a person has been convicted of an offence is admissible evidence to prove that he committed that offence, thus displacing the old law which laid down that in civil courts convictions were not admissible in evidence, and required fresh proof of the offence.

In civil cases the *Divisional Courts* are bound by the decisions of the House of Lords, the Court of Appeal (Civil Division) and by their own previous decisions. In criminal cases it was thought that the Divisional Courts were bound by the Court of Criminal Appeal but in view of the fact that the Administration of Justice Act of 1960 has provided for an appeal in criminal matters from the Divisional Court of the Queen's

Bench Division direct to the House of Lords it is suggested that in future the Divisional Court will not be bound by the decisions of the Court of Criminal Appeal, nor by those of the new Criminal Division of the Court of Appeal.

The Divisional Court is not obliged to follow a Court of Appeal decision which is inconsistent with statute or a House of Lords decision. It may also decide between two or more of its own conflicting decisions and is not obliged to follow one of its own decisions reached per incuriam.

The *High Court* is bound by the House of Lords, Court of Appeal, and the Divisional Court of the same Division, though in the last case judges of the Chancery Division are given considerable latitude.

The *Crown Court* is part of the High Court and has first instance jurisdiction in criminal cases.

The *Employment Appeal Tribunal* was set up under the Employment Protection Act 1975, to hear appeals on points of law from Industrial Tribunals. Its decisions are in practice binding on Industrial Tribunals and it is bound by the House of Lords and the Court of Appeal. However, it is not bound by the decisions of the Queen's Bench Division or Chancery Division, nor by the former National Industrial Relations Court, although, in practice, it will give careful consideration to decisions of these courts.

The *County courts* are bound by the House of Lords, Court of Appeal and the High Court.

The *Judicial Committee of the Privy Council* is not strictly bound by its own decisions (advice) or those of the House of Lords. However, the Judicial Committee will rarely depart from previous decisions, especially in constitutional matters. As it is a final appellate tribunal for the territories appealed from it is not surprising that it is not bound by decisions within those territories.

Decisions of the Judicial Committee are of persuasive force only in English Courts but, as its members are in many instances also Lords of Appeal in Ordinary, they are of highly persuasive force.

Persuasive precedent. Persuasive authority is allowed to decisions of English Courts not binding on the court in question, obiter dicta of English judges, decisions of judges of other common law systems and, in the absence of such authority, to Roman law and the works of text book writers. In each case the weight attached to such authority is always a matter of degree. Where a case has been decided by a judge whose judgments have stood the test of time that case will be of highly persuasive authority. Where time has been taken by the court before delivering judgment it is of great force. Where a case has not been defended it may not have been fully argued before the court and so will carry little weight.

Where a Court of Appeal decision is by a two-one majority and the two reached their decision for different reasons it is not a very persuasive authority before the House of Lords.

Reversing, overruling, disapproving and distinguishing

Once a legal principle has been stated as the ratio decidendi of a case it will stand as a binding or persuasive authority according to the court in which it was formulated. As a result of later cases its authority may be diminished or completely lost and various words are used to describe the effect that a later case has on an earlier case.

A case is said to be *reversed* when on appeal the appellate court disagrees with the point of law which decided the matter in the court below and hence gives its decision in favour of a different party. A case is *overruled* when in a later and separate case a higher court decides a similar matter on the basis of a different and conflicting legal principle. Thus the ratio decidendi of the higher court is to be followed and the earlier decision of the lower court is no longer good law.

The word *disapproved* is used when in a later case, without overruling an earlier case, the court gives its opinion that the earlier case was wrongly decided. Where the ratio decidendi of a later case is not wide enough to cover the earlier case it cannot overrule it but if the court expresses an opinion (by way of obiter dictum) that the earlier case is wrong in law it is said to *disapprove* it.

A case is *distinguished* when in a later case the court draws some point of difference or distinction between the earlier case and the one before the court. *Distinguishing* is the device frequently used by a court which wishes to avoid following the decision of a higher court which would otherwise be binding on it. If the lower court can find some material distinction *on the facts* between the earlier case and the present one it is not bound by the earlier decision. The rule in *Rylands v Fletcher* was not applied in *Read v Lyons* because on the *facts* there was no escape (see p 200, below) and in *Wakeham v Mackenzie* (1968) the case of *Maddison v Alderson* was distinguished on the court's interpretation of the facts (see p 260, below).

Advantages and disadvantages of our system of judicial precedent

The following are the advantages of a system of judicial precedent:

1 Such a system leads to an element of certainty in the law. If a client seeks advice from a solicitor, he wants to know his legal position. As the courts follow previous decisions according to the scheme outlined above it will be possible to give the client advice in most cases (– but not all!). The position is admirably expressed by Scrutton LJ, in *Hill v Aldershot Corpn* (1933), Court of Appeal). When faced with a problem of statutory interpretation in relation to which there were existing precedents he said,

'If I had a free hand to construe the statutes without reference to the decisions I should probably have arrived at a different conclusion from that which I have with some difficulty reached. Such a decision would no doubt be welcomed by various non-judicial writers who have protested against too careful adherence to the principle known as *stare decisis*, following decisions of co-ordinate and superior courts, though you do not agree with them. But, in my view, liberty to decide each case as you think right without any regard to principles laid down in previous similar cases would only result in a completely uncertain law in which no citizen would know his rights or liabilities until he knew before what judge his case would come and could guess what view that judge would take on a consideration of the matter without any regard to previous decisions.'

It will be apparent that the statement by the House of Lords in 1966 allowing itself greater flexibility when considering its own decisions detracts from the element of certainty.

2 The law is able to grow as the needs of society alter. New rules arise out of concrete fact-situations. The law abounds in detail and is, as Professor Kiralfy puts it, 'forged slowly on the anvil of reality'.

3 Under such a system the law is flexible. A general ratio decidendi may be extended to various fact-situations. Thus the statement of what in law is a duty of care for the purposes of the tort of negligence in a case concerning the liability of a manufacturer of ginger beer to the eventual consumer has been considered in relation to the duty of a crane manufacturer to a site foreman who assembled the parts of a crane supplied, in relation to the liability of a motor cyclist, who was involved in a crash, to a pregnant fishwife not touched by the physical impact and in relation to a taxi-driver who by his negligence in reversing his vehicle caused illness to a mother in a bedroom.

The following are the disadvantages of the system:

1 Once a hierarchy of binding precedent has been established a certain amount of rigidity is introduced into the law. In the above case of *Hill v Aldershot Corpn*, Scrutton LJ, held himself bound by a previous House of Lords decision and said,

'I regret the result, because I think the consequences of the decision, though in accordance with an Act of Parliament as interpreted by the House of Lords, are ridiculous.'

As much as the learned Lord Justice regretted it he was bound to give a decision he himself declared to be ridiculous.

2 In order to avoid rigidly applying a principle the courts are sometimes keen to distinguish between a previous case and the one before them. This leads to endless hair-splitting. Moreover, the proliferation of fact-situations gives rise to much litigation and many reports. These two

factors combine to make the law, in many instances, most uncertain. In order to verify a case-law principle there are over a thousand law reports in which to search. Although the advent of computer-based retrieval systems will give ready access to authorities the position is not simplified because the cases will still have to be read through in an effort to assess their possible application to the particular facts under consideration.

3 It is sometimes said that the development of the law through new precedents is too slow and too irregular. Legislators can think over a whole field of law and provide in advance for new legal principles and further provide for exceptions and definitions. Case law cannot so readily do this and in many instances justifies Bentham's criticism that it is 'dog's law' – you do something wrong, you are hit, then you realise you have done something wrong. In order to introduce some uniformity into the law there are certain standing committees, the most important of which is the Law Commission, and special committees are continually being formed (see p 65, below).

3 Legislation

Opposite is shown an example of a statute. It is a short one, but others run to hundreds of pages. The words 'Chapter 4' mean that it is the 4th Act of Parliament of 1977. Each Act is a chapter of the statute book. The long name (which in other statutes may be several lines long) is printed *below* the words '1977 Chapter 4'. Next come the 'words of enactment' which begin 'Be it enacted . . . .' and which appear in every Act to show that it has gone through the proper Parliamentary process.

The *operative* part of this Act has only one section, Section 1. The short title is used to refer to the Act in any official papers or books.

Legislation is the formulation of law by the Queen in Parliament. After a Bill has been approved of by both Houses of Parliament and received the royal Assent it becomes an Act of Parliament, also known as a 'statute'. Acts may be passed both to alter the existing law, both statute and case law, and for the purpose of making new law. Historically, custom was the first creator of law and customs were altered by fictions, by equity and finally by legislation. Maine, in his *Ancient Law*, points out that this is the historical order in which these agencies for reform often appear.

Each Parliament is supreme in its power and can undo or alter the work of its predecessors. This position has been reached as a result of many hundreds of years of growth. The early acts of legislation were known by different names – ordinances, assizes, provisions, but are now known as Acts of Parliament, or statutes. The view that Parliament is supreme did not pass without dispute from the judges but was established by the end of the seventeenth century.

A *consolidating statute* is one which gathers together *several* Acts on one

ELIZABETH II

c. 4   1

Roe Deer (Close Seasons) Act 1977

1977 CHAPTER 4

An Act to Amend the Deer Act 1963 with respect to close seasons for roe deer.   [17th March 1977]

BE IT ENACTED by the Queen's most Excellent Majesty, by and with the advice and consent of the Lords Spiritual and Temporal, and Commons, in this present Parliament assembled, and by the authority of the same, as follows:—

1. Schedule 1 to the Deer Act 1963 (which prescribes close seasons for deer of the species and descriptions therein mentioned) shall be read and have effect as if under the heading " Roe Deer (Capreolus capreolus) " in the said Schedule there were inserted the words—

Close seasons for roe deer. 1963 c. 36.

" Buck.........1st November to 31st March inclusive.".

2.—(1) This Act may be cited as the Roe Deer (Close Seasons) Act 1977.

(2) This Act shall come into force on the 1st day of November 1977.

Short title, and commencement.

PRINTED IN ENGLAND BY BERNARD M. THIMONT
Controller of Her Majesty's Stationery Office and Queen's Printer of Acts of Parliament
(383686)

topic and re-enacts them so that all the statute law on that topic can be found in the same Act. *A codifying statute* involves the enactment of the *whole law* on a particular subject. Thus it always includes in part law that was formerly case law. The Sale of Goods Act 1893 is a well-known example of this. *Statute law revision* embraces the reprinting of old Acts of Parliament with a view to omitting obsolete sections.

Two original copies of an Act of Parliament are kept, one in the Public Record Office and the other in the House of Lords. Since the early eighteenth century unannotated Queen's Printers copies of Acts have been accepted in court as prima facie evidence of the original Act. Only on very rare occasions are they ever challenged. Members of the public may buy a Queen's Printers copy from one of Her Majesty's Stationery Offices (HMSO). The earliest statutes were referred to by the name of the place where they were passed, but when the *Curia Regis* (the early form of Parliament) became fixed at Westminster this was found to be inconvenient and reference to the first words were used. The practice today is to give an Act a short title, such as the 'Law of Property Act 1925'.

Opposite is an example of a statutory instrument. It is followed by an explanatory note to help understand it.

Mr Callaghan and Mr Healey were using the powers given to them by the Finance Act 1976 (Chapter 40 of 1976) to raise the duty on tobacco.

Common law and statute

1 *Origin.*   Statute law begins with the reissue of Magna Carta 1225 and has increased regularly year by year until it is now of enormous bulk. However, the most fundamental part of our law is common law. Common law grew out of existing custom and was already a system before many statutes had been passed. Statutes presuppose the existence of common law, adding to and altering it. Without the common law many statutes would have no meaning. On the other hand common law without statute would still be a system, albeit a very imperfect one.

2 *Conflict.*   Where statute law and common law conflict statute prevails. This is because the very existence of law, according to the English view of law expounded by Austin, depends upon its imposition and enforcement by superior being. In England this is, and has been for centuries, the Queen in Parliament. Thus the enactments of the superior being have the greatest force within the state. The common law is recognised by implication. Statute can override the common law but no development of the common law can destroy statute.

3 *Obsolescence.*   A precedent which is old and has not been before the courts for years may be regarded as obsolete. This is never true of an Act of Parliament. Thus the right of trial by battle was claimed as late as 1819 in *Ashford v Thornton*. The right was granted by a Statute of Henry II and its *exercise* had become obsolete though the *right* remained.

STATUTORY INSTRUMENTS

1976 No. 2134
CUSTOMS AND EXCISE
The Tobacco Products Duty (Increase) Order 1976

Made - - - - -	15*th December* 1976
Laid before the House of Commons	15*th December* 1976
Coming into Operation - -	1*st January* 1977

The Lords Commissioners of Her Majesty's Treasury by virtue of the powers conferred on them by section 6 of the Finance Act 1976(**a**), and of all other powers enabling them in that behalf, hereby make the following Order:—

1.—(1) This Order may be cited as the Tobacco Products Duty (Increase) Order 1976.

(2) The Interpretation Act 1889(**b**) shall apply for the interpretation of this Order as it applies for the interpretation of an Act of Parliament.

(3) This Order shall come into operation on 1st January 1977.

2. The rates of duty in force under the table in section 4(1) of the Finance Act 1976 shall be increased by ten per cent.

James Callaghan.
Denis Healey.
Two of the Lords Commissioners
of Her Majesty's Treasury.

15th December 1976.

CUSTOMS AND EXCISE

EXPLANATORY NOTE
(*This Note is not part of the Order.*)

This Order increases the rates of the duty of excise on tobacco products by ten per cent with effect from 1st January 1977. The old and new rates are thus:

		Old rates	*New rates*
1.	Cigarettes	20 per cent of the retail price	22 per cent of the retail price
2.	Cigars	£2.765 per lb	£3.0415 per lb
3.	Hand-rolling tobacco	£2.400 per lb	£2.640 per lb
4.	Other smoking tobacco and chewing tobacco	£1.550 per lb	£1.705 per lb

4 *Source.*   The common law presents great difficulties in determining what is law. In early times there were only poor and spasmodic reports. Improvement in the standard of law reporting and the establishment of the doctrine of judicial precedent have considerably lessened these difficulties. Statute law may be found in one of the official copies of an Act of Parliament kept in the House of Lords or the Public Record Office, but in practice the Queen's Printers' copies are accepted as authentic.

5 *The future.*   As the industrial, commercial and private life of the country become more complex and are changing with increasing rapidity, statute law will play an ever more important part in our legal system. Employment law may be cited as an example. The idea of a statutory redundancy payment was introduced to the statute book in 1965, unfair dismissal in 1971, and several individual employment rights in 1975, all of which were consolidated in 1978 in the Employment Protection (Consolidation) Act.

Statutory interpretation

An Act of Parliament may be regarded as the will of the legislature expressed in a document, and it is from that document that one must discover what the legislature intended. The object of interpretation is to discover this intention. When it is clear what is meant by the words used, the rules of interpretation are irrelevant. Where the meaning is not clear from the face of the statute, questions of interpretation arise. The legislature is to be taken as meaning what it has in fact said – not what the courts think it said. Therefore, as a general rule only the words used may be referred to. However, the rules relating to interpretation of statutes are so numerous, have so many exceptions, and several are so flatly contradictory, that some writers hold the view that there are in effect no rules at all. The brief discussion of a few of these rules which follows will demonstrate the general approach of the courts and some of the problems that arise.

There are several *presumptions* which guide a judge when he is called upon to interpret an Act. There are presumptions that the Act applies to the whole of the United Kingdom but no further, that the Crown is not bound, that the statute is not retrospective and that the common law is not altered. As the early common law was based on custom, it existed as a system long before the effect of statutes began to be felt. It is more fundamental than statute. Therefore any alteration of the common law must be perfectly clear. An example of the working of this last presumption is to be found in the Criminal Evidence Act 1898 which allowed a spouse to be called as a witness for the prosecution or the defence without the consent of the accused. In *Leach v R* (1912) the House of Lords said that this provision must be strictly construed as it altered the common law rule which did not allow a wife to testify against her husband. The House, therefore, interpreted the Act to mean that the wife was allowed to give evidence but that she could not be compelled by the prosecution to give evidence (i e she became a 'competent' but not a 'compellable' witness). In *Sweet v Parsley* (1969, House of Lords), a school teacher who had a farmhouse in the country was convicted of being concerned in the management of premises used for the purpose of smoking cannabis, contrary to s 5 of the Dangerous Drugs Act 1965. The teacher lived in Oxford and visited the house only to collect the rents due. At the time the police visited the farmhouse she was in Oxford. In the section no mens rea was referred to, but the House of Lords held that where Parliament creates an offence without reference to mens rea one will be presumed. The appeal to the House was allowed. In the words of Lord Reid:

> 'Our first duty is to consider the words of the Act; if they show a clear intention to create an absolute offence, that is the end of the matter. But such cases are very rare, Sometimes the words of a section which creates a particular offence make it clear that mens rea is required in one form or another. Such cases are quite frequent. But in a very large number of cases there is no clear indication either way. In such cases there has for centuries been a presumption that Parliament did not intend to make criminals of persons who were in no way blameworthy in what they did. That means that, whenever a section is silent as to mens rea, there is a presumption that, in order to give effect to the will of Parliament, we must read in words appropriate to require mens rea.'

In addition to the presumptions there are certain other *aids* to a judge. *Internal aids* such as the title of the Act, its preamble (setting out its purpose), headings to sections and Schedules may be looked at in appropriate circumstances, but not marginal notes as these are not inserted by Parliament. Acts usually contain their own definition sections. *External* guidance such as text books in general may not be used. The *Oxford English Dictionary* may be referred to as a guide to the ordinary meaning possessed by words used in the Act. Judicial decisions on the meaning of particular words are binding in accordance with the scheme of judicial precedent explained above but words may not have the same meaning in different Acts so that a case that decided the meaning of a word in one Act may be only of persuasive authority when deciding its meaning in a different Act. The Interpretation Act 1978 consolidates the Interpretation Act 1889 and various other Acts and gives effect to recommendations of the Law Commission. The Act gives a particular meaning to various words and expressions used in legislation unless a contrary intention appears. For example, the Act says that the masculine gender includes the feminine and the singular includes the plural (s 6), references to the time of day are to Greenwich mean time (s 9) and Sch I contains a five page list of 'words and expressions defined'.

Since 1980 the courts have been permitted to look at *Hansard* (the official report of the debates and proceedings in the House of Commons) as an *external* aid to the construction of a statute. The question of what weight is to be attached to *Hansard* and how it is to be used is for the courts to decide. Parliament used to forbid counsel to refer to *Hansard* in argument, so it would have been improper for judges to refer to it when counsel would have been unable to comment on the words and arguments of ministers and MPs expressed in the House. As a practical proposition it could be time consuming and expensive for both judges and counsel to be obliged to read *Hansard* in search of clarification, which might not even be there. Also, what has been said in the course of a heated or lethargic political debate might be of little guidance as to the intention of Parliament as a whole. (See *Davis v Johnson* (1978) HL.)

While discussing the advisability or otherwise of reference to *Hansard* as an external source of interpretation, reference is often made to the *travaux préparatoires* which are looked at by the judiciaries of several European states and even by our own judiciary when resolving doubts about the meaning of community legislation. However, the European Economic Treaty *requires* regulations and directives to state the reasons on which they are based. Hence it is the practice of the EEC Commission when making proposals to the EEC Council to accompany them with explanatory memoranda, which set out the reasons in expanded form. These are true *travaux préparatoires*. They are prepared dispassionately, yet even these are seldom referred to by the European Court of Justice when interpreting community legislation.

Where a United Kingdom Act of Parliament incorporates an international treaty, *travaux préparatoires* preceding it may be considered if they are publicly available and they unequivocally point to a particular legislative intention (see *Fothergill v Monarch Airlines Ltd* (1980) HL).

An analogy to continental *travaux préparatoires* is more closely found in the reports of such bodies as the Law Commission, which are prepared with reforming legislation in mind. Where legislation is passed as a result of such a report, the report may be referred to in order to identify the problem or mischief which the Act was intended to deal with but may *not* be referred to in order to interpret the enacted words in a way consistent with the report. (*Black-Clawson International Ltd v Papierwerke Waldhorf-Aschaffenburg AG* (1975) HL.) The construction of the words of an Act is for the court and no one else.

A particular rule of interest is the ejusdem generis (of the same kind) rule. Where two or more particular words are followed by general words the general words are to be read in relation to those particular words. For example, the Betting Act 1853 prohibited the keeping of a 'house, office or other place' for betting with persons resorting thereto. The question arose as to whether Tattersall's Ring (an open air enclosure reserved for certain bookmakers) fell within the statute. The court applied the ejusdem generis rule and said that 'or other place' referred to other covered accommodation and did not, therefore, include Tattersall's Ring.

Finally, a few words might be said about the so-called canons of construction. The 'Literal Rule' says that, where there is no ambiguity, the literal or usual meaning must be given to words even though hardship results. The remedy for the hardship lies in an amending Act of Parliament. The intention of Parliament is to be discovered in the expression of its will in the words of the Act and not in Parliament's state of mind as seen by its interpreters.

An extension to, or offshoot of this rule, is the 'Golden Rule' of interpretation which has been expressed thus:

'the grammatical and ordinary sense of the words is to be adhered to unless that would lead to an absurdity or repugnancy or inconsistency with the rest of the instrument, in which case the grammatical or ordinary sense of the words may be modified so as to avoid such absurdity, repugnancy or inconsistency and no further' (per Lord Wensleydale in *Grey v Pearson* (1857) HL).

An application of the rule may be seen in the interpretation put upon s 57 of the Offences against the Person Act 1861 which provides that any person who 'being married, shall marry' commits the offence of bigamy. The legal definition of marriage says that both parties to a marriage must be single. It would, therefore, seem impossible to commit bigamy because no person 'being married' can 'marry'. However the courts have interpreted the word 'marry' as meaning 'going through a ceremony of marriage'.

Another canon of construction is the 'Mischief Rule'. This provides that in cases of ambiguity the courts may look at the old law to discover the wrong (mischief) which the Act sought to remedy and then interpret the words of the Act in the light of this knowledge. This rule is also known as the rule in *Heydon's Case* (1584), the case in which the Barons of the Exchequer formulated the rule. An interesting illustration of this rule and of the conflict between principles of interpretation is *National Real Estate v Hassan* (1939). In the 1930s speculators were buying dilapidated houses cheaply with the aim of suing the tenants for failure to repair as they were obliged to do by the covenants in their leases. In this way they hoped to make a profit. In 1938 an Act of Parliament was passed to stop this practice and the question arose as to whether the Act applied only to landlords who bought property after the Act came into operation or whether it applied to all landlords seeking to enforce repairing covenants. Although there is a presumption that statutes do not have retrospective effect this was not applied. The court chose to apply the 'Mischief Rule'.

The court looked at the law before the Act of 1938, discovered the mischief and interpreted the Act so as to enable the court to relieve against the hardship caused by actions brought on repairing covenants, i e gave the Act a retrospective effect.

Lord Denning in the Court of Appeal gave impetus to the development of the 'purposive approach' to the interpretation of statutes. This approach was favoured by the Renton Committee (a Committee appointed by the Lord President of the Council to inquire into *The Preparation of Legislation* Cmnd 6053 (1975)). Under the purposive approach the courts adopt such a construction as will promote the general legislative purpose underlying the provision in the Act. See the Court of Appeal in *Nothman v London Borough of Barnet* (1978) but note the Court of Appeal was not followed on appeal to the House of Lords.)

Now that the United Kingdom is a member of the European Communities English courts are sometimes called upon to interpret the meaning of any Treaties of the Communities or a Community Instrument. The European Communities Act 1972 provides that such questions shall be treated as questions of law and, if they are not referred to the European Court, they shall be decided in accordance with the principles laid down by any relevant decision of the European Court. Thus it follows that in interpreting Community legislation the English courts are bound by the decisions of the European Court which is outside the area of jurisdiction of the English courts. The purposive approach is particularly appropriate when interpreting the more general words of European legislation, most notably the Treaty of Rome. The European Court of Justice has said that the courts of the member states must gather the meaning of Community rules from the wording *and the spirit* of the Treaty *(Bulmer (H.P.) Ltd v J. Bollinger SA* (1974)).

Delegated legislation

In modern times legislation has become the chief means by which the law is developed to meet the new situations of a rapidly developing society. But to keep pace with detailed development over many fields Parliament has had to resort more and more frequently to delegated legislation, i e laws passed by a body to whom Parliament has given limited power to make new laws. Acts of Parliament can never be ultra vires (beyond the powers of Parliament) because the Queen in Parliament is the supreme power within the state. Delegated legislation can, however, be challenged in the courts on the ground that it is ultra vires, i e that the party to whom the power to make laws has been given has acted beyond his powers. This is because the powers conferred by Parliament on other bodies are always limited to particular, defined purposes. Rules made beyond the powers given are void because they are not made under the direct or delegated power of Parliament.

Delegated legislation has increased in bulk considerably since the last war. All wars tend to produce a desire for social reform and the last one saw an enormous development of state enterprise – social legislation covering the Health Service, Education, Coal Mining and National Insurance. But while Parliamentary time is short, and the scope of activities within its control so vast, delegated legislation will tend to increase.

One unhappy feature of this trend is that matters of law-making are moving more and more out of the control of elected representatives of the people and more and more into the hands of a permanent civil service. Thus Parliament passes an Act creating a National Health Service but Parliament does not have the time to consider all the relevant details of administration when the Act is passed nor does it have the time to give consideration to the daily routine of running the Health Service. Therefore the main Act delegates certain powers to the Minister of Health who makes rules having the force of law within the scope of the authority delegated to him. But the minister himself is too busy to deal thoroughly with these matters and in many cases problems are investigated, and a new rule phrased, entirely by civil servants. The minister's function is to sign the document containing the rule and thereby give his, and Parliament's, authority to it. However, Parliament does, in theory at least, retain some control. Thus under the Statutory Instruments Act 1946 ministerial orders and regulations (known as 'statutory instruments') may be submitted to Parliament and will cease to be operative if either House so resolves within 40 days; in some important matters *approval* by both Houses is necessary. Whether or not a statutory instrument must be laid before Parliament depends upon whether such a procedure is required by the statute under which the relevant powers were delegated. There are many cases where statutory instruments are not laid before Parliament. However, in both Houses of Parliament there are committees whose job it is to scrutinise statutory instruments and to draw the attention of Parliament to cases where subordinate authorities appear to be abusing their powers.

Another example of delegated legislation is local authority bye-laws. Such bye-laws often require confirmation by a Minister of State (e g the Minister of Health where bye-laws under the Public Health Acts are made) and in all cases must not go beyond the powers originally given to the local authority.

4 European law

Regulations, Directives and Decisions are binding in England since the accession of the United Kingdom to the European Communities on 1 January 1973. The European Communities Act 1972 provides that all rights, powers, liabilities, obligations, restrictions, remedies and procedures under the European treaties are to be given immediate effect in English law and such rights are to be referred to as 'enforceable Community rights'. Judges in court must accept the authority of European Law. With the passing of time the volume of such laws will steadily increase (see further p 10, above).

European law is already introducing new concepts into England. For example, the European Communities have a common policy for agriculture which is to be carried out in all the member states in accordance with the same rules of law. The legal position is that in carrying out its duties the state authority is subject to European law and must follow the case-law of the European Court in Luxembourg.

The European Court has developed a number of principles of law which the authority (or any British civil servant) must obey in furthering Community policy.

One such principle to be observed is the 'Principle of Proportionality' which has accordingly become a part of the law of England, although so far very few English solicitors or barristers have come into contact with it. It is a rule which helps to protect the ordinary man against abuse of power by civil servants. If a state authority took a decision, for example, which involved farmers in unnecessary expenditure such a decision would be contrary to the Principle of Proportionality and the farmers concerned could start proceedings in the High Court to recover damages.

The Principle was raised before the European Court in the *Internationale Handelsgesellschaft* Case (No 11/70) where the Advocate-General said on 2 December, 1970 '. . . the Principle of Proportionality, . . . citizens may only have imposed on them, for the purposes of the public interest, obligations which are *strictly necessary* for those purposes to be attained'.

B. Subsidiary sources

Apart from means by which law is created there are other sources which have to a greater or lesser extent influenced the development of the law.

1 Law merchant

The customs of foreign merchants have played a part in influencing the development of English commercial law. The merchants of western Europe generally followed the law of the Italian commercial cities, hence the influence of Roman law was quite strong in this field. The more developed commercial law of the foreign traders found favour in the large ports and the fairs which they visited and special courts were set up to give speedy justice (see p 31, above). From the seventeenth century onwards the customs of merchants and many of the rules of the law merchant were incorporated into the common law. In this way many rules relating to bills of exchange and the sale of goods were judicially adopted and years later became part of our statute law in the Bills of Exchange Act 1882 and the Sale of Goods Act 1893 (see pp 273 and 381, below).

2 Roman law

Roman law has had little influence on the development of English law. There certainly has not been any large-scale reception of it, as has been the case with most other European countries. Several principles of our law are often expressed in Latin but this may be explained in two ways: Latin was widely spoken at the time the rule was formulated or the English rule was so similar to the Roman one that Roman terminology was used. It is not surprising that similar, developed civilisations should have similar problems and attempt to solve them in similar ways without the second necessarily being influenced by the first.

Roman law was taught in England as early as the thirteenth century but formed no part of the training given at the Inns of Court where most lawyers were trained. Graduates in Roman Law (known as civilians) practised in the Ecclesiastical and Admiralty courts and it is here that the influence of Roman law is most felt. The medieval church played a large part in the distribution of a deceased's property and the informal 'soldier's will' recognised originally by the ecclesiastical courts and now adopted by our law is of Roman origin.

3 Canon law

After the Conquest, ecclesiastical and secular jurisdiction became quite distinct, ecclesiastical courts having sole jurisdiction over matters spiritual and kindred matters, e g marriage, legitimacy and wills. In particular, the concept of the prohibited degrees of relationship is of Canon law origin and the general principle of 'good conscience' in equity is almost certainly considerably influenced by a study of Canon law which all the early Chancellors would have followed. However, over the whole field of English law the influence of Canon law has been but slight.

4 Textbooks

The works of jurists have had almost no effect on the development of English law. In Rome, the replies of the jurists to questions put to them had, in certain cases, the status of law. In England, text books and learned articles are of use as a source of ideas for practitioners, and in argument counsel may use the ideas and adopt the argument of a writer but he cannot cite his work as authority for a proposition stated by counsel. Again, there is a rule of rapidly diminishing importance, that the works of a living author cannot be referred to at all in court.

However, early in the development of our law, when there were but few reports and many of these were unreliable, text books of a rudimentary sort were written by leading practitioners, many of whom were judges. Some of these are regarded as authoritative statements of the law of their time. Examples of these are: *Tractatus de Legibus et Consuetudinis Angliae* (treatise on the laws and customs of England) by Glanvil who was Chief Justiciar to Henry II. This deals with the criminal law and land law of the twelfth century. Littleton, who was Chief Justice of the Common Pleas in the fifteenth century, wrote *Tenures*, a book dealing with the various estates in land and incidents attached to the holding thereof. Chief Justice Coke, writing in the early seventeenth century, is famous for his *Reports* and his *Institutes*, which in four parts covered a wide cross-section of English law and brought Littleton's *Tenures* up to date. This part of the *Institutes* is known as *Coke upon Littleton* and is one of our most famous legal text books.

In modern times we have reliable reports and much detailed legislation so the scope for text book writers is greatly diminished. However, a few well-known writers have had the distinction of court recognition of their work. For example, Pollock's definition of consideration was accepted by the House of Lords in *Dunlop v Selfridge* (1915) and Winfield's definition of nuisance was accepted in *Read v Lyons* (1947) and today there is an increasing tendency for judges to refer both to dead and living writers, notably during his lifetime Dr Cheshire's work on *Private International Law* and Cheshire and Fifoot on *Contract* were often cited. A noticeable trend in modern criminal law cases is that judges often find support for their legal opinions in such modern works as Glanville Williams' *Textbook of Criminal Law* and Smith and Hogan's *Criminal Law*.

5 Law reporting

In England and Wales law reporting is not carried out by the government but by private enterprise and over the centuries there has been considerable lack of system in our reports. This lack of system could lead, and on occasion has led, to considerable difficulty. The law is what it is because it has been so *decided*, not because it has been *reported*, but in the nature of things we are forced to rely on reports in order to discover the law. However, it must be remembered that unreported decisions are law and in the case of an appeal, the transcript of the case is available in the Bar Library on request by the legal profession and the parties to a case. Historically the year 1875 saw the most important event in law reporting so we shall divide our study into reports before and reports after that date.

The earliest reports are the Year Books which appeared in the Middle Ages and which were annual compilations dealing in the main with matters of procedure and practice rather than rules of substantive law. (This is not surprising when we realise that at this early time law was closely bound up with procedural writs: see p 00, above). They are mainly concerned with the pleadings and arguments of counsel and judges and were probably written from notes made in court. Their language is difficult and with the arrival of the more comprehensive Abridgments of the Year Books by Fitzherbert (1516) and Brooke (1568) they went out of use by the middle of the sixteenth century.

At about the same time the first of the private or 'named' reports began to appear. These were produced and published by individuals under the name of the reporter and vary tremendously in quality. Some are treated with great respect, others almost always viewed with suspicion. Coke's Reports (1572–1616) are treated as authoritative (the report of *Heydon's Case* (see p 57, above) and of *Pinnel's Case* (see p 231, below) are by Coke) whereas doubt attaches to the accuracy of those of Espinasse of whom it was once unkindly said that he only ever heard half of what went on in court and reported the other half. Many of the private reports have been republished in collected form together with an index, e g the collection known as the English Reports which covers the period 1220–1886.

There were many criticisms of the named reports. Many of them were inaccurate. They were very expensive, and there was considerable delay in publication, being published months or even years after judgment had been given. In 1865 the four Inns of Court co-operated to create the Council of Law Reporting which in 1870 became the Incorporated Council of Law Reporting. The aim was to satisfy the need of the profession for accurate reports of recent cases. The new system proved a great success and today the reports of this body, which enjoy the benefit of being revised by the judges and contain a summary of the arguments of counsel, are known simply as the *Law Reports*.

In addition to this series there still exist a number of reports published by other organisations. Of these, virtually the only remaining general reports are the *All England Law Reports*, published by Butterworths, which began publication in 1936 on a weekly basis in response to a demand for a service combining speed with accuracy, The judgments contained in this series are now also revised by the judges but, though they give a list of cases referred to during the arguments of counsel, the arguments themselves are hardly ever reported. Generally these reports appear a few weeks after the decision and a larger number of cases are included than in the *Law Reports*. In 1953 the Incorporated Council of Law Reporting also began a weekly series on a similar basis known as the *Weekly Law Reports*. Now the All England Reports have been extended backwards from 1936 in a series called the *All England Reports Reprint*.

Any report of a case that is vouched for by a member of the bar may be cited in court and all the series of reports mentioned above satisfy this condition. Should there be a divergence between the words of a judgment as reported in various reports the *Law Reports* version will be preferred.

The Times newspaper publishes reports of cases of legal and general interest usually within 24 hours of the decision but not all the judgment is given and part may be summarised.

Today, in addition to the general series of law reports, there are special series covering shipping cases, restrictive trade practices cases, tax cases, industrial cases, criminal appeals, and other specialised fields of law.

The European Court publishes the 'Reports of Cases before the Court' in English and the other languages of the European Communities. This series was not published in English until 1973, but the earlier volumes of reports, which began in 1952, have now all been translated into English, a task which took a team of translators four years to complete (a member of this team was D. M. M. Scott, one of the original authors of this work).

The 1980s has seen the beginning of a new development with the application of computer-based information retrieval systems to the transcripts of the official shorthand note of cases heard in court, particularly the Court of Appeal. The traditional view of the common law is that the law is what it is because it has been so *decided* – not because it has been so *reported*. Counsel in court have the right, a duty even, to cite all relevant authorities to the court in the course of argument. Ever since law reporting began there have been unreported cases. Over the years these worried no one. However, in 1973 the monthly *Current Law* began to contain a section with summaries of unreported Court of Appeal decisions. The weekly *New Law Journal* has begun a similar practice. The availability of information about unreported cases has led to them being researched more frequently by counsel and cited in court. The year 1980 saw the introduction of two computer-based systems, *Lexis* and *Eurolex*, which provide ready access to a wide range of reports, including American and European cases.

We now have an immediate practical problem. There exists the means of storing and retrieving all judgments in all courts. Far from saving time, this could involve a tremendous increase in the amount of research to be carried out by counsel for both sides and by the judge, who will probably be reading many of the unreported cases for the first time. This can only consume time and give rise to expense. In *Roberts Petroleum Ltd v Bernard Kenny Ltd* ((1983) HL) Lord Diplock, referring to transcripts of unreported Court of Appeal judgments, said that 'none of them laid down a relevant principle of law that was not to be found in reported cases: the only result of referring to the transcripts was that the length of the hearing was extended unnecessarily'.

The problem will not go away. With the increasing number of cases being heard and the several Divisions of the Court of Appeal all producing judgments which are *now* becoming more readily available, the problem intensifies. One solution would be to prohibit the citation of unreported cases. To do this would place even greater responsibility on the shoulders of editors who select cases for reporting and would probably lead to a big increase in the number of cases reported.

In *Roberts Petroleum Ltd v Bernard Kenny Ltd* Lord Diplock, considering the House of Lords' response to the problem of the citation of unreported cases, said:

'There are two classes of printed law reports: the two weekly series of general law reports, (a) the Weekly Law Reports of the Incorporated Council of Law Reporting, of which the more important, contained in volumes 2 and 3, are later reproduced in the Law Reports proper, together with a summary of the arguments of counsel, and (b) the All England Law Reports, which reports much the same cases as the former series; these do not err on the side of over-selectivity. Then there are the various series of specialised law reports which seem to have proliferated in the course of the last few decades; these may be useful in helping lawyers practising in specialised fields to predict the likely outcome of the particular case in which they are advising or instituting proceedings, by seeing how previous cases in which the facts were in various respects analogous were actually decided; but these specialised reports contain only a small minority of leading judgments in which some new principle of law of general application in the specialised field of law is authoritatively propounded, as distinct from some previously accepted principle being applied to the facts of a particular case. If a civil judgment of the Court of Appeal (which has a heavy case load and sits concurrently in several civil divisions) has not found its way into the generalised series of law reports or even into one of the specialised series, it is most unlikely to be of any assistance to your Lordships on an appeal which is sufficiently important to reach this House.

My Lords, in my opinion, the time has come when your Lordships should adopt the practice of declining to allow transcripts of unreported judgments of the Civil Division of the Court of Appeal to be cited on the hearing of appeals to this House unless leave is given to do so, and that such leave should only be granted on counsel's giving an assurance that the transcript contains a statement of some principle of law, relevant to an issue in the appeal to this House, that is binding on the Court of Appeal and of which the substance, as distinct from the mere choice, of phraseology, is not to be found in any judgment of that court that has appeared in one of the generalised or specialised series of reports.'

6 Law reform

An important influence on the development of the law today is the work of official bodies whose task it is to consider and make proposals for the reform of the law. The most important of these is the Law Commission, which was established by the Law Commissions Act 1965. The members of the Commission are appointed by the Lord Chancellor and must be suitably qualified by the holding of judicial office or by experience as a barrister or solicitor or as a teacher of law in a university. They are appointed on a full-time basis for periods of up to five years. The first Chairman of the Law Commission was Mr Justice Scarman who is now a Lord of Appeal in Ordinary. Their function is to keep the whole law under review with a view to its systematic development and reform and in particular its simplification, modernisation and codification. For this purpose the Commission may consider proposals for law reform referred to them; prepare programmes for the examination of different branches of the law, and undertake the examination of particular branches and formulate proposals for reform by means of draft Bills. It also studies relevant aspects of overseas legal systems. From time to time the Law Commission publishes a Working Paper with a view to stimulating discussion prior to the Commission formulating its proposals. The Working Paper is often commented on in professional journals, legal debates and in law schools. Discussions are often reported back to the Commission. As a result of its own researches and a consideration of the views of others, the Commission will later make its proposals for reform of the law. In 1982 the Law Commission published its *Working Paper No 81 on Minors' Contracts* (HMSO). In this discussion paper the Commission points to the unsatisfactory nature of the present law and offers alternative suggestions for reform. One is a simple reform lowering the age for contractual capacity to 16 years of age, below which age a minor could not be sued but he could sue the other contracting party, and the other is a far more complex series of alterations to the existing framework of the law. It is hoped the Law Commission will issue its proposals at a future date.

The Commission must also make an annual report on its proceedings to the Lord Chancellor. The first report, which was published in June 1966, included a report on the progress on the law reform programme, approved by the Lord Chancellor in September 1965. Among other items this programme covers the following branches of the law dealt with in this book: codification of the law of contract; consideration, third party rights and contracts under seal; civil liability for dangerous things and activities; interpretation of statutes, and matters involving anomalies, obsolescent principles or archaic procedures. As a result of the Law Commissions' proposals numerous statutes have been passed by Parliament including the Supply of Goods and Services Act 1982 (p 391, below).

In considering its programme the Commission consults with the chairmen of the Law Reform Committee and the Criminal Law Revision Committee, two bodies set up on a part-time basis by the Lord Chancellor and the Home Secretary respectively to consider specific questions of law reform which may be referred to them on civil law and criminal law respectively.

The Law Reform Committee consists of a small number of judges, barristers, solicitors and academics who meet to consider what changes in the law may be desirable, especially with reference to judicial decisions referred to it by the Lord Chancellor. The Limitation Act 1980 (p 352, below) embodies most of the recommendations made by this Committee in a Report to the Lord Chancellor. Other recommendations resulted in the Misrepresentation Act 1967. The Criminal Law Revision Committee also consists of judges and lawyers and advises the Home Secretary on reform of areas of the criminal law referred to it. In 1984 it produced its Report on *Sexual Offences* (Cmnd 9213), in which it recommended, among other reforms, the extension of the law of rape to married couples who are living apart. Earlier proposals led to the Criminal Law Act 1967 and the Theft Act 1968.

Where a question of wider importance arises the initiative for reform may come from a government department. The appropriate head of department may set up a committee to enquire and report. Alternatively, the Crown may order a Royal Commission. As a result legislation may be introduced by the government in Parliament. The Courts Act 1971 is the result of the work of the Royal Commission on Assizes and Quarter Sessions (Report 1969).

The Lord President of the Council appointed a Committee under the chairmanship of Sir David Renton, QC, MP, to inquire into and report on the all important subject of the *Preparation of Legislation* (1975).

7 Treaties

In an increasingly interdependent and uncertain world it makes good sense for states to seek to safeguard their vital interests, be they economic, social or security, by concluding international treaties. In the absence of any effective international sanction for the breach of a treaty, other than war, the effectiveness of treaties in protecting these interests largely depends upon what the jurist Austin termed a kind of 'international morality'.

Whatever term is used to describe a treaty, eg 'convention', 'protocol' or 'charter', there must be an *international agreement in writing between two or more sovereign states (or sovereign state and an international organisation, such as the United Nations) governed by international law*. English law holds that the power to conclude a treaty lies exclusively within the Royal prerogative and the exercise of this power cannot be challenged in the courts (*Blackburn v A-G* (1971)). The great constitutional lawyer Dicey defined 'Royal prerogative' as 'the name for the residue of discretionary power left at any moment in the hands of the Crown, whether such power be in fact exercised by the King himself or by his Ministers. Every act which the executive government can lawfully do without the authority of the Act of Parliament is done in virtue of this prerogative.' Thus, in effect, a treaty is concluded by the Government, though there is a long-standing practice of laying draft treaties before Parliament for 21 days.

A treaty may become part of our internal domestic law only where the United Kingdom Parliament has passed enabling legislation. An example of this situation is provided by the European Communities Act 1972 which gave internal effect to the Treaty of Paris (1951) and the two Treaties of Rome (1957) (see p 11, above). These treaties are of special significance in that, as exceptions to the general rule, they are a source of legal rights directly enforceable by the individual against the Crown in our courts.

Although treaties are usually concerned with economic matters, the protection of basic human rights has not been neglected. The European Convention for the Protection of Human Rights and Fundamental Freedoms (1950) seeks to protect the human rights set out in the Universal Declaration of Human Rights (1948), e g the right to life, the prohibition of inhuman treatment and forced labour, respect for private and family life and the protection of freedom of thought, conscience and expression.

The Convention is enforced by the European Commission of Human Rights, the European Court of Human Rights and the Committee of Ministers of the Council of Europe. Complaints of breaches of the Convention may be made to the Commission either by parties to the Convention or by individual citizens against a government which has recognised the right of individual petition, as has the United Kingdom government. If the Commission cannot reach a friendly settlement of the matter, it reports to the Committee of Ministers as to whether there has been a breach of the Convention. The matter may then be referred to the Court of Human Rights, provided the defendant state has accepted the Court's jurisdiction. It should be noted that only states have access to the Court; in the event of individual petition the citizen drops out of the case. An example of the Commission's work is provided by *Malone v United Kingdom* (1983). There it had come to light in Malone's criminal trial that the police had tapped his telephone. After he had exhausted all his remedies under his country's laws, as required by the Convention, by taking unsuccessful civil proceedings, he complained to the Commission. It upheld his complaint that there had been a breach of Art 8 of the Convention, which concerns the right to respect for private life and correspondence, and referred the case to the Court of Human Rights.

The United Kingdom government has often been the defendant in proceedings before the Court of Human Rights. In *Campbell and Cosans v United Kingdom* (1982) it was unsuccessfully alleged that corporal punishment administered in a Scottish school violated Art 3 of the Convention which forbids inhuman or degrading treatment or punishment. In *Hamer v United Kingdom* (1982) the refusal of the Home Secretary to allow a prisoner to marry was held to be contrary to Art 12, which upholds the right of men and women to marry and found a family.

The bill of rights provided by the Convention, with its important right of the individual to take action independent of, and even against his own government, has prompted unsuccessful moves in this country to make it enforceable before our courts. Equally unsuccessful have been other calls, notably from Lord Scarman, for an entrenched Bill of Rights to counter what is seen as an increasing tendency for the state to curtail civil liberties.

SOURCES OF LAW SINCE THE PASSING OF
THE EUROPEAN COMMUNITIES ACT 1972

English Law

Law from
English sources

Custom

Judicial
precedent

Legislation

Subsidiary
sources

Law from European
Community sources

European
treaties

Self-executing
legislation

Subordinate
legislation

Decisions of
the European
Court

Chapter 5

Governing Britain: legal aspects

The United Kingdom of Great Britain and Northern Ireland has no constitution in the sense used by most other countries, i e it has no one or main *written* constitutional document such as in Eire or the USA. Its rules are contained in a great many sources of the constitution such as statutes, decided cases and conventions and the practices of Parliament and books of authority. The government of a country is often said to fall into three main areas or organs of government (see Montesquieu's *L'Esprit des Lois*). These are the executive, the legislature and the judiciary. A modern constitution will provide for each of these areas to be governed by its rules and attempt to ensure that no one organ in the state has control over two, still less three, of these areas lest such excess of power should lead to tyranny. This is the concept of the Separation of Powers. In our constitution we seek to preserve a balance of power while at the same time preserving very considerable flexibility so that the constitution can work smoothly. The organs of government overlap each other. The constitution changes with time and public opinion to preserve the values, attitudes and ideas which are believed currently to be worthwhile.

The Executive consists of the Cabinet, Her Majesty's Ministers and the Civil Service. This huge organ of state, which carries out the will of the legislature expressed in enactments, is nominally headed by the Queen who chooses as her Prime Minister and head of the Executive the person who can command a majority in the House of Commons. Until the seventeenth century the monarch was the dominant power within the state. Now the monarch's role is largely titular without the real power of bygone days. Real power today is said to lie with the legislature. Certainly the legislature is supreme legally. It can make or unmake any law it wants to. However, in practice the Executive controls Parliament. Bills which are presented to Parliament are decided on by the Executive. The Prime Minister exercises enormous powers. The Prime Minister chooses her (or his) ministerial team all of whom are technically Her Majesty's Ministers. Ministers close to the Prime Minister become members of the Cabinet. The very existence and constitution of the Cabinet is largely a matter of constitutional convention (political practice) rather than Act of Parliament. The Prime Minister chooses who shall be the Lord Chancellor and who shall be the senior judges such as the Law Lords, the Lord Chief Justice and the Master of the Rolls. The

Lord Chancellor appoints magistrates, tribunal chairmen and other judges. It can easily be seen that the Executive, through the Prime Minister, quite legally is in the position of influencing the judiciary through the appointments system.

On the fall of a government the Lord Chancellor and other elected members of the Executive vacate their office.

The executive power of the sovereign has now passed to Her Majesty's Government which stands at the head of the administrative machine of the modern state.

The judiciary is headed by the Lord Chancellor, who presides as chairman in the House of Lords when it is sitting as a legislative chamber, the Lord Chief Justice, who is the senior criminal law judge, and the Master of the Rolls, who is the senior civil law judge. The last two judges sit in the Court of Appeal supported by many other Lord Justices of Appeal and High Court judges (for more on the judges generally see '*The Courts Today*', pp 77–105, below). The role of the judges in the constitution is to decide disputes between people within the state. In doing this the judges declare their subservience to the authority of Acts of Parliament (see *British Railways Board v Pickin* (1974)) but this has not always been their attitude. In the seventeenth century a great constitutional struggle took place. The divine right of kings to rule gave way to the controls exercised by Parliament over royal power. During this struggle the judges at times stood their ground against the Crown. Sir Edward Coke took a stand against government by royal proclamation in the *Proclamations' Case* (1611) with these famous words, 'The King hath no prerogative but that which the law of the land allows him'. At other times they argued that unreasonable Acts of Parliament were unlawful. This view was maintained with less and less enthusiasm into the eighteenth century. As they deal with the multitude of cases the judges push the boundaries of the law forward. They declare that they do not make law (that is for Parliament) but they continue to do so. Readers should consider the cases of *Rylands v Fletcher* (1868) and *Hedley Byrne and Co Ltd v Heller and Partners Ltd* (1964). (See pp 199 and 161, below.)

In addition to their role in resolving disputes and developing the law, the judges, in accordance with common law tradition, protect the weak against the powerful, the subject against the state. The judges protected a union member who had been expelled in breach of union rules (*Bonsor v Musicians' Union* (1955)) and they protected an airline against the state where the state, acting ultra vires (beyond its powers), had directed a licensing authority to withdraw the airline's licence to operate a transatlantic route (*Laker Airways Ltd v Department of Trade* (1977)). In the *Laker Airways* case the Court of Appeal pointed out that the Secretary of State at the Department of Trade could not alter a statute by guidance given to the Civil Aviation Authority but that an amending Act of Parliament could lawfully achieve the object desired by the Secretary of

State. The courts assert the right to examine the exercise of any discretionary power vested in the Executive.

The royal prerogative is now exercised in practice by the government of the day (the Executive). The prerogative is a discretionary power, exercisable by the executive government for the public good, in certain spheres of governmental activity for which the law has made no provision. Examples are the prerogative of war (requisitioning property for the defence of the realm), and the treaty prerogative (making treaties with foreign powers). (See p 67, above.) As this discretionary power is to be exercised by the executive for the public good it is subject to examination by the courts.

In order to preserve the impartiality of the judges they are protected from attack by those who are aggrieved by their decisions or who dislike their policies. The salaries of the judges are charged on the Consolidated Fund and as such do not come up for annual review by Parliament. The judges cannot be dismissed by due notice. They hold office until the age of 75, or in some cases 72 (Judicial Pensions Act 1959). Rarely can judges be sued for damages in a civil court for anything they do or say in the exercise of their authority. (A corrupt judge can be punished before the criminal courts e g for taking a bribe.) The procedure for the removal from office of a High Court judge is not free from doubt. In 1688 judges were given tenure of office during good behaviour. More modern legislation suggests that judges may be removed by the Crown for misbehaviour (e g an offence of moral turpitude or persistent neglect of duty) or on any ground in pursuance of an address from Parliament.

The legislature consists of the *Queen in Parliament*. The role of the Queen is largely a formal one. In law her assent is necessary to a Bill before it becomes law as an Act. The Houses of Parliament are two in number; the House of Commons and the House of Lords. Most Bills must receive the assent by both Houses before they pass to the Crown for the Royal Assent. In respect of Money Bills (Bills involving *only* provisions relating to money matters and certified as such by the Speaker) the House of Lords may exercise a delaying power only (Parliament Acts 1911 and 1949). The House of Lords is the second legislative Chamber composed of Lords Spiritual, hereditary peers, life peers and the Lords of Appeal in Ordinary (the Law Lords). As a non-elected body it is frequently subjected to criticism. Also its composition is criticised even by its supporters. The virtue of the House is that it is not so heavily committed to party politics as is the House of Commons and can look at problems in a different light.

The House of Commons is the main elected legislative body. A Bill begins life as an idea, probably outside Parliament within a government department or as a result of the work of a pressure group. The idea is put to a government minister, then to the Cabinet and if all goes well it will be drawn as a Bill. The Bill undergoes the following procedure in most cases.

First Reading. The title of the Bill is left on the table in the House of Commons so that members can see the subjects which will be arising in the future. No vote is taken.

Second Reading. The Bill is introduced by a minister who explains its general purpose. Discussion takes place, largely on party political lines, before a vote is taken. If the vote supports the Bill it moves to the Committee Stage. As the Executive which proposes the Bill has a majority in the House of Commons a Bill is rarely defeated at this stage.

Committee Stage. One of several standing committees, of 16 to 50 members reflecting the composition of the House (ie with an inbuilt government majority), considers the details of the Bill. It is usual for many amendments to be made but it is rare for an amendment to be successful unless it has government backing. Again the influence of the Executive in the legislative process can be seen to be very strong. The Executive controls what is introduced to Parliament, the time to be allocated to any matter and, by the vote, the Executive determines its success.

Report Stage. The Bill as amended is reported to the House. Amendments may be made at this stage or the Bill returned to committee for further consideration. Most frequently after the Report Stage a Bill proceeds immediately to the Third Reading.

Third Reading. The Bill, agreed on policy matters at the Second Reading and in detail in committee, is presented to the Commons in its final form for approval. If approval is given, and it almost invariably is, the Bill may proceed to the House of Lords where it undergoes a similar process before receiving the Royal Assent. The Bill then becomes an Act of Parliament.

Delegated legislation consists of rules of law which have been made by a person or body to whom a power to make laws has been given by Parliament. A local authority may be given power to make bye-laws. The Minister of Transport may be given power to make regulations in respect of safety standards of lorries etc. An Act may make provision for a new structure or set of rules and leave to the appropriate minister power to fix by Commencement Order the date on which the new provisions are to come into effect.

The volume of delegated legislation, which is very many times greater than legislation enacted by Parliament in a year, has increased dramatically with the development of the welfare state since the Second World War. More and more the major institutions of the state, such as the Department of Health and Social Security, are governing us by regulation made under the authority of an Act of Parliament. Such a process appears as if it will continue largely unabated for some time to come.

Control over delegated legislation is exercised in various ways but the sheer volume of delegated legislation plus the law arriving from Europe (since 1973) make impossible the task of knowing the law. A power might be delegated to a minister subject to his draft of the new rules he proposes being placed before the House of Commons and agreed to by a resolution of the House. This is said to be subject to an *affirmative resolution*. An alternative is for the new draft rule to be placed before the House of Commons to become law unless a vote is taken rejecting the proposed law within a certain number of days, say 40. This is called the *negative resolution* procedure. The courts also play a role here. Where the delegatee of a power, in purported exercise of his authority, exceeds that power he may be brought before the courts for the exercise of the power to be examined. Where the courts consider that the power has been exceeded they will declare the rules proposed or action taken to be ultra vires and void i e of no legal effect. (See *Laker Airways Ltd v Department of Trade* (1977).)

In order that rules passed under statutory authority should become more widely known the Statutory Instruments Act 1946 was passed. The Act provides that all statutory instruments as defined in the Act must be printed, numbered, published and sold. Delegated legislation is operative when made unless it states otherwise. Failure to comply with the need for publicity does not affect the validity of the instrument. Everyone is presumed to know the law. It is, therefore, possible to do an unlawful act in breach of a statutory instrument which has not been published. The wrongdoer may have no means of knowing what the law actually is. However, where a *criminal prosecution* is brought based on a failure to comply with an as yet unpublished statutory instrument, there is a defence based on the lack of publicity, unless the prosecution is able to prove that at the time the offence was committed reasonable steps to bring its purport to the notice of persons likely to be affected had been taken (s 3(2)). To make matters worse for the public, by s 8, the Treasury, with the concurrence of the Lord Chancellor and the Speaker, may make regulations exempting statutory instruments from the requirements of being printed and sold. Existing regulations cover a wide range of activities, such as regulations affecting a locality, which are part of a series or are bulky. An example of the working of the law is found in *Defiant Cycle Co v Newell* (1953). The company had been convicted of the offence of selling in contravention of the Iron and Steel Prices Order. On appeal to the Divisional Court the conviction was quashed because (i) the Schedules to the Order had not been printed, and (ii) no certificate of exemption from the requirement of printing had been made, and (iii) reasonable steps under s 3(2) had not been taken.

In any study of the constitution a phrase often read is 'the Rule of Law'. This is frequently an emotive phrase used by the person who utters it as a measure of the rightness or wrongness of an idea, a law or an action he is examining. It is often put forward as an abstract idea of what a constitution ought to attempt to maintain within a society or state. It means many things to many men.

Professor A. V. Dicey in his *Introduction to the Study of the Law of the Constitution* (1885) set out the rule of law in three parts, since when his ideas have been subject to examination and development by many other writers. Dicey wrote,

(i)   '. . . no man is punishable or can be lawfully made to suffer in body or goods except for a distinct breach of law established in the ordinary legal manner before the ordinary Courts of the land. . . .'

(ii) '. . . every man, whatever be his rank or condition, is subject to the ordinary law of the realm and amenable to the jurisdiction of the ordinary tribunals.'

(iii) '. . . the general principles of the constitution (as for example the right to personal liberty or the right of public meeting) are with us as a result of judicial decisions determining the rights of private persons in particular cases brought before the Courts; . . .'

It is an interesting exercise to see how far Dicey's concept of the rule of law is applicable in Britain today. His first principle relating to the ordinary courts is to a great extent true today. There are a few secret courts, or rather occasions where ordinary courts are held in camera (public excluded); for example on the grounds of national security (see the trial in April 1984 of Michael Bettaney the MI5 officer) or sexual capacity. Publicity may amount to contempt of court. In Northern Ireland trial by jury is avoided in the case of terrorist trials in the so-called Diplock Courts.

The large number of administrative tribunals which now exist are in derogation of the rule of law. However, such tribunals are usually subject to appeal with further appeal to the courts.

Dicey's second principle, that all men are subject to the ordinary law, has a great many exceptions. Diplomatic immunity places several hundred people, mainly in London, outside wide areas of legal control. Judges enjoy a special position (see p 73, above). Trade unions possess certain immunities from actions in tort based on acts done in contemplation of or furtherance of a trade dispute. Police powers of arrest without warrant can be an intrusion on civil liberty. The special immunity formerly enjoyed by the Crown has now been eliminated to a large extent by the Crown Proceedings Act 1947.

Dicey's third principle is largely true today. The constitution, such as it is, is part of the ordinary law of the land. The concept of parliamentary sovereignty has evolved over the years and is now enshrined in judicial decisions (see p 72, above).

Chapter 6
The courts today

The courts at present administering justice may be divided into civil courts and criminal courts.

Courts may be either courts of first instance (i e courts where cases are tried for the first time) or appeal courts. There are some courts which hear both civil and criminal cases or which hear cases both at first instance and on appeal.

First instance civil courts

The County Courts Act 1846 set up a new network of courts to administer civil law locally where small sums of money were involved. The present authority for the operation of these courts is the County Courts Act 1959, as amended, and the County Courts Rules. The Rules, which are a form of delegated legislation (see p 58, above), are set out in an annual volume known officially as the *County Court Practice*, but more generally as the *Green Book* from the colour of the binding. The Rules lay down the procedure to be followed in the courts, and they are amended from time to time. There are more than 400 county courts. The judges of county courts are selected from amongst the ranks of the circuit judges (see p 98, below) although the Courts Act 1971 provides that every judge of the Court of Appeal and of the High Court, as well as every recorder, shall be capable of sitting as a county court judge if he consents and is desired by the Lord Chancellor to do so. The judge is aided by a registrar who acts as assistant judge and is in charge of the office staff. Unlike the judge, the registrar is a civil servant and may be in charge of more than one court. He is a solicitor of at least seven years' standing.

County court jurisdiction

The most important matters with which county courts can deal are:

1   Actions in contract where the sum claimed does not exceed £5,000.
2   Actions in tort where the sum claimed does not exceed £5,000 with the exception of actions for defamation.
3   Matters of an equitable nature such as trusts, dissolution of

partnerships, and mortgages, where the amount involved does not exceed £30,000.

4   Actions concerning title to land and actions for recovery of possession of land where the net annual value for rating does not exceed £5,000.

5   Actions arising from disputes regarding the grant of probate or letters of administration where the estate of the deceased is *less than* £30,000.

6   Actions remitted to a county court from the High Court.

7   Like the High Court and magistrates' courts, county courts have jurisdiction over the adoption of children.

8   Some county courts outside London have bankruptcy jurisdiction; this is unlimited in amount. All bankruptcy cases in the metropolitan area are dealt with by the Bankruptcy Court of the High Court.

9   Those county courts with bankruptcy jurisdiction also have power to wind-up companies with a paid-up share capital not exceeding £120,000.

10   Some courts near the coast have Admiralty jurisdiction limited to £5,000 except in salvage cases where the limit is £15,000.

11   Undefended matrimonial causes. Under the Matrimonial Causes Act 1967 every matrimonial cause, such as actions for divorce, or nullity of marriage must be commenced in a divorce county court. If the action is not contested by the other spouse the action will be heard in the divorce county court, but if it is defended, it must be transferred to the High Court.

12   A great deal of miscellaneous work has been confided to county courts by various statutes, particularly those dealing with social matters like housing, and the welfare of children.

13   Although in many matters the High Court has a concurrent jurisdiction with the county courts, there are others over which the county courts have exclusive jurisdiction, which means that actions involving them cannot be commenced in the High Court. Examples are questions arising under the Rent Restriction Acts, the Hire-Purchase Acts and the Consumer Credit Act 1974.

In most cases an appeal lies from the county court to the Court of Appeal (Civil Division). An appeal based on a point of law can be raised in the Court of Appeal only where that point of law was raised in the county court (*Balchin v Buckle* (1982)). An appeal based on a point of fact lies subject to strict limits only. In this case the value of the subject matter of the case must exceed a certain figure which in the case of tort and contract is £200.

In some matters, particularly in contract and tort actions, the jurisdiction of the county courts is unlimited if both parties agree to the action being tried in a county court.

The judge may deal with any case. The registrar can deal with undefended cases and those where up to £500 is claimed unless a party objects to his doing so. By agreement between the parties the registrar can try any case. Usually the judge and the registrar sit alone but on rare occasions the judge sits with a jury of eight. This is possible where there is a charge of fraud against a party or where a defamation case is remitted to a county court by the High Court.

The jurisdiction of county courts is limited to their own locality, and actions must normally be commenced in the court for the district in which the defendant resides or carries on business, or in the court for the district in which the cause of action arose. In this connection it may be noted that the Welsh Language Act 1967 provides that in any legal proceedings in Wales or Monmouthshire the Welsh language may be used by any party, witness or other person.

The practical importance of the county courts lies in the fact that they, and not the High Court, are used for the conduct of the greater part of the civil litigation in this country. The Judicial Statistics, which are published annually by the Lord Chancellor's Office show that in 1982 the number of proceedings commenced in certain courts were as follows: High Court – Chancery Division 17,119, Queen's Bench Division 164,396, Family Division 280,762, county courts 2,301,364. Only 2,252 proceedings in the Queen's Bench Division were determined after a full trial, the remainder mainly being settled by the parties to the disputes. Only 168,682 of the county court cases actually went to trial before the judge or registrar, mainly because defendants paid what they owed soon after proceedings had been started against them.

The original aim of the county court system in 1846 was to provide a local court before which the ordinary man could take his differences. In practice it has not worked out as intended. The ordinary man is more likely to find himself in a county court as the losing defendant in an action brought by a large finance company, debt-collecting agency or mail order firm than as a successful plaintiff complaining about a consumer matter. As a result, a call for reform was made, pointing out the need for a small claims court free of the expense and complication of the county court. The needs of an unrepresented party under a simple system of procedure were stressed. Experimental small claims courts were established in London and Manchester in an attempt to show what could be done.

In the Manchester Arbitration Scheme for Small Claims the parties each submitted to the jurisdiction of the court by agreement. No jurisdiction existed *by statute*. Costs were £1 from each party. No enforcement machinery existed but in the event of a losing party not complying with the terms of a judgment an action could be brought in the county court to enforce the original contract to submit to the jurisdiction and comply with any award. Few such actions were needed and those brought were successful.

These experimental courts, funded both voluntarily and by the local authorities, paved the way for the introduction of an arbitration scheme in the county court in 1973. The small claims courts disappeared by 1980 through lack of funds. By 1981 a new county court arbitration scheme for claims not exceeding £500 was introduced. Now a small claim not exceeding £500 is *automatically* referred to arbitration by the registrar. In the interests of justice provision is also made for this referral to be rescinded in specific circumstances such as where a difficult point of law or a question of fact of exceptional complexity is involved or where the parties are agreed that the dispute should be tried in court. Arbitration is now covered by new rules of procedure under which the rules of evidence do not apply and the arbitrator may adopt any fair and convenient method of procedure. As it is rare that costs are awarded to the successful party, legal representation will also be rare.

Hopefully, the new arbitration scheme will come close to meeting the aims behind the creation of the original county courts.

The Supreme Court of Judicature

The Supreme Court which sits at the Royal Courts of Justice in the Strand, London, is divided into the Court of Appeal which does not hear cases at first instance, and the High Court of Justice which is the most important of the first instance civil courts together with the Crown Court. See the Supreme Court Act 1981.

The High Court is a superior court (see p 102, below), whose jurisdiction in civil matters is very wide although by statute there are various matters, such as those allocated to county and other courts, with which it cannot deal at first instance. As a matter of convenience the High Court is split into three divisions each handling cases of a different type. Legally any division is competent to try any type of case within the High Court's jurisdiction but in practice if a case were commenced in a division different from the one that usually handles the particular matter it would be transferred to the usual division at the expense of the party responsible. The High Court of Justice may sit anywhere in England and Wales.

Each division of the High Court has a head and a number of other judges known as puisne (literally 'younger') judges. The Maximum Number of Judges Order 1970 fixed the maximum number of puisne judges of the High Court at 75. They are allocated to divisions by the Lord Chancellor.

The head of the Queen's Bench Division is the Lord Chief Justice of England; some of his time is taken up by the task of presiding over the divisional court of the Queen's Bench Division (see below). There are about 43 puisne judges in the division. The head of the Chancery

Division is the Vice-Chancellor. There are ten puisne judges in the Chancery Division. The President of the Family Division is the head of the division and he is assisted by 16 puisne judges, including two women, Dame Elizabeth Lane and Dame Rose Heilbron. There is no limit to the amount in respect of which litigation may be commenced in any division. The work of the various divisions is allocated as follows:

1 *The Queen's Bench Division.* This is the division that deals with the greatest number of cases. Any action not allocated expressly to one of the other divisions will be tried in the Queen's Bench. In particular contract and tort actions are tried in this division. The division acts as a successor to the old courts of King's Bench, Exchequer, and Common Pleas. The Administration of Justice Act 1970 set up as part of the Queen's Bench Division an Admiralty Court and a Commercial Court.

2 *The Chancery Division.* The work of the old Court of Chancery forms the basis of the work done today by the Chancery Division. The matters mainly dealt with in the division are:

The administration of trusts (see p 29, above).
Mortgages.
Bankruptcy.
Company matters.
Partnership matters.
Specific performance of contracts (see p 350, below).
Contentious probate business, i e all cases concerning (i) the validity or
    otherwise of a will (which was part of the work of the old Probate,
    Divorce, and Admiralty Division) (ii) cases concerning the meaning
    of a will (which was always part of the work of the Chancery
    Division) (iii) cases concerning disputes arising as to estates where
    the deceased made no will.

3 *The Family Division.* This division, which was set up by the Administration of Justice Act 1970, replaces in part the old Probate, Divorce and Admiralty Division. The Admiralty work of the old division has been allocated to the new Admiralty Court of the Queen's Bench Division. Its contentious probate business has gone to the Chancery Division, while the non-contentious probate business of the old division has been allocated to the Family Division. Non-contentious probate business means, in practice, the office work done by the court officials in connection with the administration of the estates of deceased persons.

The Family Division has been assigned certain first instance and certain appellate business by Sch I to the 1970 Act. For example, it took over the wardship of infants from the Chancery Division, and the divorce business from the old Probate, Divorce and Admiralty Division. This includes hearing defended divorce cases, and where necessary dissolving validly celebrated marriages, making declarations that marriages for one reason or another are void altogether, and granting judicial separations to spouses (for appeals, see p 92, below).

Supreme Court Procedure

Procedure in the Court of Appeal and the High Court is governed by Rules of the Supreme Court which are drawn up and amended by the Rules Committee consisting of judges, barristers, and solicitors. The rules are laid before Parliament and published as delegated legislation. The Rules of the Supreme Court are available in looseleaf form from Her Majesty's Stationery Office. They are also set out with extensive notes in a publication known officially as the *Supreme Court Practice*, and more generally as the *White Book* from the colour of the binding. Procedure and terminology vary in the different courts, so that the outline of procedure in the Queen's Bench Division given below will not necessarily apply to the other divisions.

Queen's Bench Procedure. Proceedings commence with a writ which is issued by the plaintiff against the defendant calling on him to satisfy the claim or acknowledge service of the writ within fourteen days or risk having judgment given against him in his absence. The plaintiff fills in a form which is validated by being stamped and sealed after a fee has been paid. This is the writ, and a copy of it must be served on the defendant who enters an appearance by filling in another form and leaving it at the office from which the writ was issued. A writ may be obtained from the Central Office in London or from one of the local offices called district registries. The plaintiff then sends the defendant a statement of claim (which describes the harm he has suffered), and the latter sends the plaintiff a defence. These documents are called pleadings. After further exchanges of pleadings the parties' solicitors appear together before a Queen's Bench master who decides such preliminary questions as where the trial is to be held, and whether there is to be a jury. There is an appeal from the master to a judge in chambers (in private) and thence to the Court of Appeal.

The trial is usually before a judge sitting alone, but a jury may be demanded by either party in cases of defamation, malicious prosecution, false imprisonment, and at the request of the defendant only, fraud. Both sides may call witnesses to help establish their version of the facts and both may address the judge on their view of the law. Generally it is up to the plaintiff to prove his case, although there are exceptional cases. The decision of the judge is said to be based on the 'balance of probability' which means that the successful party need not prove his case 'up to the hilt'; if he can, it is so much the better, but all he need do is to persuade the judge that his case is more likely to be correct in fact and law than is the defendant's case.

If the plaintiff is successful he usually obtains a money judgment which the defendant must pay him. If the defendant does not pay there are various courses open to the plaintiff. He may get a writ of fieri facias (also called fi. fa.) issued. This authorises the sheriff to seize enough of the defendant's goods to satisfy the judgment debt. He may get at property which cannot be seized physically by having a receiver appointed to receive the defendant's interest. There are other possibilities as well.

Summary of the work of Queen's Bench Judges.

1 Taking civil cases at first instance in the Queen's Bench Division at the Royal Courts of Justice in London.
2 Taking civil cases at first instance on circuit in the provinces.
3 Taking criminal cases on appeal in the Court of Appeal (Criminal Division) together with judges of the Court of Appeal (Civil Division), if requested to do so (see p 100, below).
4 Taking criminal cases on appeal, and hearing applications for prerogative orders and habeas corpus in a divisional court of the Queen's Bench Division (see p 90, below).
5 Taking cases on appeal in the Courts-Martial Appeal Court (see p 101, below).

Prior to the coming into force of the Courts Act 1971, the High Court judges used to travel round the country, as they had done for 700 years, to take both civil and criminal cases at Assizes. In recent times the system has been unable to cope satisfactorily with the needs of the public, the Bench and Bar. Long delays developed, sittings were held in small towns, which, although they may have been important in medieval times had lost their position as centres of activity, and, furthermore the defects of the old system of rigidly defined assize circuits had repercussions on the system of Quarter Sessions. A Royal Commission under its Chairman, Lord Beeching, was appointed to look into the situation and the 'Beeching Report' was produced in 1969. This recommended that (i) both civil and criminal assizes should be abolished, (ii) quarter sessions (which were criminal courts – see p 98, below) should be abolished, (iii) High Court judges should be able to sit anywhere in England and Wales and not just at the old Assize towns, (iv) a single new court, the Crown Court, should be created to do all criminal work above the level of magistrates' courts (see p 95, below). These proposals have been implemented mainly by the Courts Act 1971. Although the old term Assizes is no longer used the judges continue to go on circuit and High Court trials are held in as many provincial centres as convenient. There are offices of the High Court called District Registries in many provincial towns, from which writs and other documents are issued; these are in the charge of district registrars who have practically the powers of Queen's Bench masters. Appeals lie from them to a judge in chambers in London.

Other Superior Civil Courts

In addition to the High Court proper there are a number of other courts associated with it; the most important of these are described below.

The Companies Court

This is a court of the Chancery Division where proceedings are tried before a single judge who is familiar with companies work. The work is divided into liquidation proceedings, which are concerned with the winding-up of companies, and chancery proceedings which include such matters as permitting companies, on proper grounds, to reduce their capital.

The Court of Protection

The Mental Health Act 1983 put the protection and management of the property of persons suffering from mental disorder under the jurisdiction of the Lord Chancellor, certain chancery judges and the Master of the Court of Protection. Although the judges make certain orders, in practice most of the work is done in an office building by civil servants. The court supervises dealings with the mental patient's property. Most of the dealings are carried out by a guardian called a 'receiver' who is usually a relative appointed by the court.

The Bankruptcy Court

This court comes under the jurisdiction of the Chancery Division and its judicial functions are usually discharged by a Registrar in Bankruptcy. It deals only with cases arising in the London area, other cases being heard at the appropriate County Court.

The Prize Court

The function of this court is to decide whether or not ships captured in wartime together with their cargoes should be treated as hostile, and be confiscated. By s 27 of the Supreme Court Act 1981 the court's jurisdiction has been transferred to the High Court.

The Restrictive Practices Court

This court, which was set up by the Restrictive Trade Practices Act 1956, consists of three High Court judges, one Scottish judge and one Northern Irish judge together with up to ten laymen qualified by their knowledge of or experience in industry, commerce or public affairs. The court may sit in divisions but there must be at least one judge and two other members to hear a case. The judges decide questions of law, but questions of fact are decided by a majority of the members of the court. In England there is an appeal, on questions of law only, to the Court of Appeal (Civil Division). The function of the court is to decide whether certain trading agreements fall within the Restrictive Trade Practices Act 1976 and if so, whether they can be justified on one of the grounds mentioned in the Act (see p 300, below). The court also has power to exempt contracts from the provisions of the Resale Prices Act 1976 (see pp 301, *et seq.* below).

The Employment Appeal Tribunal

This tribunal consists of judges nominated by the Lord Chancellor and lay members from both the employers' side and workers' side of industry. A quorum consists of a judge and two lay members. The tribunal hears appeals almost entirely on points of *law* from Industrial Tribunals hearing applications under the Redundancy Payments Act 1965, Equal Pay Act 1970, Trade Union and Labour Relations Act 1974, and the Sex Discrimination Act 1975, as well as under the parent Act, the Employment Protection Act 1975. Parties before the Employment Appeal tribunal may appear in person or by any person they wish, such as a trade union official or friend. Costs are not normally awarded.

Other Civil Courts

The Mayor's and City of London Court

This court is the successor of two older courts. It was abolished and re-established as a county court by the Courts Act 1971.

The Consistory Courts

The Bishop of every diocese of the Church of England has his own court called the Consistory Court, except in the diocese of Canterbury, where it is called the Commissary Court. It is presided over by the Chancellor of the diocese, except in the diocese of Canterbury, where the judge is called the Commissary General. Ecclesiastical law is administered in these courts. Appeals lie from these courts either to the appropriate Provincial Court, or in certain cases, to the Court of Ecclesiastical Causes Reserved.

Provincial Courts

The Province of Canterbury has at its head the Archbishop of Canterbury and is one of the two territorial divisions of the country for ecclesiastical purposes, the other being the Province of York, headed by the Archbishop of York. Each province has its own court, that of Canterbury being called the Court of Arches, and that of York being called the Chancery Court of York. Appeals from Provincial Courts are heard by the Judicial Committee of the Privy Council.

The Court of Ecclesiastical Causes Reserved

This court has first instance jurisdiction to try any Church of England Bishop or other clergyman accused of an offence involving a matter of doctrine, ritual or ceremonial. It also has certain appellate functions. An appeal lies to a body known as a Commission of Review which is appointed ad hoc.

The Court of Chivalry

This court, which tries such matters as allegations of the improper use of coats of arms, has an hereditary judge, the Earl Marshal of England, who is the Duke of Norfolk. It was revived in 1954 after being in abeyance for more than two hundred years.

Administrative tribunals

In modern times there has been a great deal of social legislation; it deals with many aspects of life and covers such matters as rent control, industrial disputes, and National Insurance. This legislation inevitably gives rise to disputes and provision must be made for settling them. The ordinary courts of law are accustomed to dealing with situations where very little discretion is needed; they find the relevant facts and apply the law to those facts. Once the facts and the law are ascertained the outcome is usually a foregone conclusion. Disputes that arise from social legislation are of such a type as to require administrative rather than legal decisions. In order to be able to make satisfactory administrative decisions the body charged with making them needs much wider discretionary powers than those possessed by the ordinary courts. Because of these considerations a considerable number of bodies known as administrative tribunals have been set up to settle disputes arising from social legislation in place of the ordinary courts. These tribunals have the discretionary powers they need. There are different tribunals for different types of dispute, and they have the advantage of including members who are expert in the subject with which the tribunal is concerned. Tribunal procedure is often speedier and less costly than court procedure. In many instances the statute that brings an administrative tribunal into existence gives little indication of the way in which the tribunal should approach its task. As a result tribunals often have to develop their own policies in this respect. Their decisions, therefore, are influenced by considerations of justice, expediency, and their own policy. Tribunals have been subjected to criticism on various grounds. It was said in particular that the rules of procedure in some tribunals were unsatisfactory, and that in many cases no reasons were given for decisions. Generally legal aid is not available for representation. Following the report of a committee that inquired into criticisms of tribunals, the Tribunals and Inquiries Act 1958 was passed. This Act authorised the setting up of the Council on Tribunals which is a body that reviews the working of tribunals; it also provided that in most cases reasons must be given for decisions on request by the parties, and that the Council on Tribunals is to be consulted when procedural rules for tribunals are being drawn up. Most of the law is now to be found in a consolidating statute, the Tribunals and Inquiries Act 1971. In some cases there is an appeal from a tribunal to a court of law, and even where there is no appeal, tribunals may to a certain extent be controlled by the prerogative orders (see p 90, below). There are exceptional cases in which social legislation is administered by the ordinary courts; for example the Rent Restriction Acts which govern the rents of unfurnished accommodation and the rights of tenants to remain in possession, are administered by the county courts. Examples of some tribunals are given below.

Social security appeal tribunals. Under the Health and Social Services and Social Security Adjudications Act 1983 appeals from decisions of adjudicating officers are heard by a Tribunal consisting of a legally qualified chairman and two lay side members. Decisions are by a majority. The President of the new Tribunal system is responsible to the Lord Chancellor for the administration of tribunals under him. There are seven regional chairmen, each of whom is assisted by a full-time chairman and several part-time chairmen who sit two or three times a month on average. In practice most appeals are heard by part-time chairmen. The function of the regional chairman is to organise the work of the tribunals in his region as well as sitting in the tribunal. This will involve work in connection with the appointment and training of clerks, members and part-time chairmen, a total of approximately 1,000 personnel in each region.

The tribunals hear appeals by claimants against the decisions of adjudicating officers under the social security legislation (mainly the Social Security Act 1975) e g claims for unemployment benefit, sickness benefit, single payments, supplementary benefit and family income supplement.

Claimants are seldom represented by a solicitor or barrister but in a number of cases, still a minority, they are represented by a friend, a trade union official, a person from a community rights group or a representative of the Citizen's Advice Bureau. The tribunal assumes a more inquisitorial role than is the case with the courts and industrial tribunals. A further appeal lies to the Social Security Commissioners.

Legal aid is not available to claimants before Social Security Appeal Tribunals.

Rent tribunals. These exercise powers granted by the Rent Act 1977. There are tribunals in most areas and the Minister concerned appoints the members. The tribunals fix the rent of accommodation in houses and flats when application is made to them. They have power to give tenants security of tenure (the right to stay in possession) for a limited period. An appeal lies on points of law to the divisional court of the Queen's Bench Division.

Special Commissioners of Income Tax.   The Special Commissioners are a body of civil servants who hear appeals against income tax assessments.

Lands Tribunal.   This hears appeals concerning the valuation of premises for rating purposes.

Judicial control of administrative tribunals

The Divisional Court of the Queen's Bench Division exercises control by means of the prerogative orders (see p 90, below) following a procedure introduced in 1977 and known as 'judicial review'.

Domestic tribunals

The term 'domestic tribunals' means disciplinary committees which exercise jurisdiction over groups of people, such as the members of a profession, a club or society or other association. There are many such tribunals, some having been established by statute and others simply by contract; the most important of them are described below.

The Benchers of the Inns of Court

The Masters of the Bench of each of the four Inns of Court have disciplinary powers over the barristers of their respective Inns. In 1966 the four Inns set up a Senate to take over from each Inn all disciplinary powers over barristers in respect of professional misconduct, other than the powers of pronouncement and carrying into effect of sentences for misconduct. The Masters of the Bench of each Inn agreed to carry into effect any sentence recommended by the Senate. An appeal by a barrister lies to the 'visitors' of his Inn (usually five High Court judges).

The Disciplinary Committee appointed under the Solicitors Acts

The Master of the Rolls, acting by authority of the Solicitors Act 1974, appoints from among the members of the Council of the Law Society a Committee to hear complaints against solicitors. It has power to strike solicitors off the roll, to suspend them temporarily from practice, or to impose a fine. The Committee is a separate body from the Council of the Law Society and the Society sometimes brings complaints itself. An appeal lies to a divisional court of the Queen's Bench Division.

Other professional committees

There are disciplinary committees for doctors, dentists and opticians. These were established by statute, and an appeal lies from them to the Judicial Committee of the Privy Council.

Judicial Control of Domestic Tribunals established by contract

In *Lee v Showmen's Guild of Great Britain* (1952), Denning LJ (as he then was) discussed the extent to which the courts would intervene in the decisions of domestic tribunals. He said that although the jurisdiction of a domestic tribunal is founded on contract, the parties are not free to make any contract they please. They cannot, for example, validly contract that the principles of natural justice shall be ignored, or that the tribunal shall be the final arbiter on questions of law. In connection with social clubs the courts will see that there is fair play, but will not otherwise interfere. In connection with domestic tribunals which sit in judgment on the members of a trade or profession, which can deprive a man of his livelihood, the courts will be much more ready to intervene, to see that the tribunal has observed its law and has interpreted its rules correctly. In particular the courts will decide the extent of the jurisdiction of a domestic tribunal.

Industrial tribunals

Consisting of a legally qualified Chairman assisted by two lay persons known as wingmen, these tribunals hear most disputes under recent statute law affecting employment; for example, redundancy, unfair dismissal, equal pay, sex and race discrimination. Appeal lies to the Employment Appeal Tribunal, in most instances, on a point of *law* only. Although called tribunals, the Industrial Tribunals appear to have all the characteristics of a court (see *A-G v BBC* 1979).

Civil courts of appeal

The High Court

The three divisions of the High Court all have appellate functions. Some of these are exercised by a single judge and some by two or more judges sitting together. A single judge deals with less important appeals; thus, for example, an appeal lies from the decision of a Queen's Bench Master to a Queen's Bench Judge in Chambers. The more important appeals are dealt with by *Divisional Courts*. It is important to use the correct nomenclature in this connection. The expression, for example, a Court of the Queen's Bench Division' means normally a hearing at first instance by a single judge, but the expression 'a Queen's Bench Divisional Court' means usually the hearing of an appeal by two or three judges of the Queen's Bench Division sitting together. Although in law two and sometimes even one judges will suffice, three usually sit in practice.

Appeals to the Queen's Bench Division

It is in this division that the most use is made of the Divisional Court. It has important functions in connection with criminal law which are mentioned below. The Tribunals and Inquiries Act 1971 provides for appeals to the Divisional Court from Rent Tribunals. Under the Solicitors Act 1974 there is an appeal to the Divisional Court from the Solicitors' Disciplinary Committee.

Prerogative orders and habeas corpus

It is convenient here to deal with the ability of the Queen's Bench Division to prevent the abuse of power by inferior courts, individuals, organisations, and even government departments. Although this is not strictly a question of appeal it is analogous to an appeal in some cases. This power of the Queen's Bench Division is one of the most important safeguards that Her Majesty's subjects can invoke to protect themselves against injustice. The remedies in question were originally called 'prerogative writs' because they used to be issued only on the application of the Crown. They were common law powers exercised by the old Court of King's Bench. The old procedure was simplified and various changes were made by the Administration of Justice (Miscellaneous Provisions) Act 1938 so that there now remains only one prerogative writ, which is habeas corpus and the other remedies are called prerogative orders. The current remedies are, therefore the prerogative orders of mandamus, prohibition and certiorari and the prerogative writ of habeas corpus. Application to the High Court for one of the forms of relief, an order of mandamus, prohibition or certiorari, is now made by the procedure known as *judicial review*, s 31 of the Supreme Court Act 1981. This new procedure introduced in 1977 is a result of the recommendations of the Law Commission in its *Report on Remedies in Administrative Law*.

Mandamus.   The name of the order means a command, and an order of mandamus is a peremptory command from the High Court. This order is used to compel the performance of a duty by some person or body of persons and it is for the individual asserting that there is a duty which the law requires to be done, to apply to the Queen's Bench Division. He must show that the person against whom he wants the order to be made is obliged by law to do something and is not just enabled to do something if he feels so inclined. Mandamus has been used against local authorities to make them produce their accounts for inspection and to make them hold an election of aldermen. Both of these things the local authority was legally bound to do. Mandamus may be used to compel inferior courts to deal with a case if they wrongfully refuse to do so. Although mandamus does not lie against the Crown it may be used to make a government department carry out a statutory duty to a citizen. The issue of the order is discretionary and the court will not grant it if there is a satisfactory alternative remedy.

Prohibition. This order is issued to prevent something from being done, unlike mandamus which orders something to be done. Although originally available only against courts, it can now be used against any public authority as well, although not against private persons or private bodies such as the committees of clubs. Prohibition is used to prevent inferior courts, tribunals, and other bodies in their exercise of judicial powers, from exceeding their jurisdiction. It is available also against bodies acting in a quasi-judicial capacity such as licensing justices, who are concerned with granting licences for the sale of alcohol. Prohibition is available against the Crown.

Certiorari. The use of certiorari is to bring before the Queen's Bench Division, from inferior courts, cases in progress or that have been adjudicated upon, so that the High Court may be 'certified' (informed) as to whether or not the inferior court has acted either in excess of its jurisdiction, or in disregard of the principles of natural justice. If the inferior court is found to have committed one of these transgressions its decision will be quashed. Certiorari is available also in cases where an inferior court has made an error which appears in the record of its judgment. The order is available against inferior courts and statutory bodies on which powers have been conferred by Parliament.

The principles of natural justice are the subject of some disagreement but almost certainly there will be a breach of the principles if any of the following rules are not observed:

1   No man may be a judge in his own cause. This means that if a person is likely to be personally interested in the outcome of a case, he must not take part in deciding it. Thus in *Dimes v Grand Junction Canal Proprietors* (1852) a decision of the Lord Chancellor was set aside because he was a shareholder in the canal company.

2   Both sides must be given the chance of being heard. This rule is rendered in Latin as *'audi alteram partem'*. If a judicial decision is reached without one or both sides being able to put their contentions forward the rule will have been infringed. If, however, a party has the opportunity to put his side of the case and does not bother to do so, there will be no breach of the rule. It does not matter if the manner in which the party is asked to put his views differs from the manner used by the courts; thus it was held in *Local Government Board v Arlidge* (1915) that where a party to an inquiry was asked to put certain of his contentions in writing this was an adequate way of complying with the rule.

3   The rules of natural justice will not have been observed if the decision has been arrived at in bad faith through the tribunal acting from some wrong motive.

Habeas corpus.   The purpose of this writ is to secure the release of a person unlawfully detained. The procedure is now largely governed by the Administration of Justice Act 1960. Application is made to a divisional court of the Queen's Bench Division if it is sitting, and otherwise to a single judge. If the application concerns a criminal matter or detention under the Mental Health Act 1983 a single judge is empowered to issue the writ or to refer the case to a divisional court which alone can refuse. In civil cases such as the detention of a wife or child at home a single judge may grant or refuse the application. Appeals in criminal cases lie from the divisional court to the House of Lords and in civil cases from the divisional court to the Court of Appeal (Civil Division) and thence to the House of Lords.

Appeals to the Chancery Division

The Divisional Court of the Chancery Division hears appeals on bankruptcy matters from county courts outside London; bankruptcies in London are dealt with by the Bankruptcy Court of the Chancery Division and an appeal lies to the Court of Appeal (Civil Division).

A single judge hears appeals from the Special Commissioners of Income Tax.

Appeals to the Family Division

Appeals lie to the Divisional Court from magistrates' courts on matrimonial matters such as orders for payment of maintenance.

The Court of Appeal (Civil Division)

The Court consists of the Master of the Rolls and 16 Lords Justices of Appeal. Usually three judges sit together, so that it is possible to have the court sitting simultaneously in four divisions. In certain types of case two judges may sit. In any case where there are an even number of judges who are evenly divided the case must be argued again by an uneven number of judges before appeal may be made to the House of Lords: s 54 of the Supreme Court Act 1981. Occasionally the Lord Chancellor appoints a judge of the High Court to sit in the Court of Appeal to make up a quorum. It is possible for a Lord Justice to sit alone at first instance. The court hears appeals on questions of law and fact and re-hears the whole of the case presented to the court below, relying on the notes made by the shorthand writer and the judge. On allowing an appeal the court may reverse the decision of the court below, amend that decision, or order a new trial. The courts from which an appeal lies to the Court of Appeal are mentioned on p 104, below. Since October 1966 the Court of Appeal, sitting in the criminal division, also has jurisdiction to hear criminal appeals. See p 104, below.

The House of Lords

In addition to its functions as a legislative body the House sits as a court of law. For this purpose it consists of the Lord Chancellor, nine Lords of Appeal in Ordinary, who are life Barons, and any other members of the House who hold or have held high judicial office. The qualification for a Lord of Appeal in Ordinary is 15 years at the Bar, or two years as a Supreme Court judge. The short name given to Lords of Appeal in Ordinary is Law Lords. Some of the Lords of Appeal in Ordinary are appointed from Scotland and Northern Ireland. The House is the highest civil court of appeal for England and Wales, Scotland, and Northern Ireland, and the highest criminal court of appeal for England and Wales and Northern Ireland only. Its criminal jurisdiction is discussed below. As far as England and Wales are concerned the House hears appeals from the Court of Appeal (Civil Division), provided that the appellant can obtain leave to appeal from either the Court of Appeal (Civil Division) or the House itself. The quorum for the court is three, but usually five members sit. Judgments delivered in the House are known as 'opinions', and are normally delivered to the parties in a printed form without being read aloud. This procedure dates from November 1963, prior to which oral judgments known as speeches were delivered. Speeches may still be made by any law lord who wishes to express himself orally.

The Administration of Justice Act 1969 makes provision for appeal from a single judge of the High Court, or from a Divisional Court on a point of law of general public importance, direct to the House of Lords in certain circumstances (popularly known as the 'leap-frog' procedure). A High Court judge may certify that a sufficient case for direct appeal to the House of Lords has been made out, justifying the application for leave to appeal. The point of law must relate to the construction of an Act or statutory instrument, or, alternatively, the point of law must be one where the judge is bound by a previous decision of the Court of Appeal or House of Lords.

The Judicial Committee of the Privy Council

The members of this body are the Lord Chancellor, the Lords of Appeal in Ordinary, and all Privy Councillors who have held high judicial office in the United Kingdom, besides certain other persons such as Commonwealth judges who have been appointed Privy Councillors. Two unusual features of the Judicial Committee of the Privy Council should be borne in mind. First, it is not strictly a court at all, but a committee of the Privy Council, and it delivers its judgments as 'humble advice' to Her Majesty. This advice used to be unanimous but since March 1966 dissenting members of the Privy Council present at the hearing of the appeal may express their dissent and state their reasons therefor. This is different from the position in the House of Lords where the judges may deliver five judgments all expressing various shades of opinion. Second, the Judicial Committee is not a part of the ordinary English judicial system, although it hears certain appeals that originate in England. The jurisdiction of the court is very wide. As far as England is concerned it hears appeals from Prize Courts of the Queen's Bench Division of the High Court, from the Provincial Courts of Canterbury and York (on questions of ecclesiastical law) and from such disciplinary bodies as the General Medical Council. In respect of territories overseas the court exercises both civil and criminal jurisdiction. It hears appeals from courts of the Channel Islands, the Isle of Man, and certain Commonwealth countries.

The European Court

The Court of Justice of the European Communities, the European Court for short, is the highest court within the European Economic Community. It should not be confused with the European Court of Human Rights which has a narrow jurisdiction in the human rights field among states who are parties to the Convention establishing the court. Nor should it be confused with the International Court at the Hague which deals with disputes between nations and is part of the United Nations organisation.

By the European Communities Act 1972 European law has become part of English law. Lord Denning has described it as 'an incoming tide' (*H. P. Bulmer Ltd v J. Bollinger SA*). The treaties, regulations, directives and decisions from the European Community are becoming more and more numerous and are altering our native law. However, the new law is not all-pervading. It applies only in respect of those matters contained in the treaties, notably the Treaty of Rome, such as employment law and economic areas. Generally it does not affect areas such as family, land law and criminal law. Rights arising under European law are known as enforceable community rights.

Article 177 of the Treaty of Rome is now, by virtue of s 2 of our own European Communities Act 1972, part of English law; indeed, it is applicable to the whole of the United Kingdom and Northern Ireland. Under this article, where in a case in the House of Lords a point of European law arises the House *must* refer the matter to the European Court for a preliminary ruling on the interpretation of the point of law involved. Lower courts faced with a point of interpretation of European law before being able to apply the law to the facts of the case and to reach a decision *may* refer the case to the European Court for a preliminary ruling.

The Court does not enforce its rulings but refers the case back to the court of the member state with its judgment set out as if an appeal had been made leaving the member state to apply the ruling so given through the enforcement machinery of its own courts.

The judges of the court are drawn from the member states. Advocates-general are appointed to assist the Court by presenting reasoned submissions on cases before the Court of Justice. The judges and advocates-general are chosen from persons of independence and experience of high judicial office or who are 'jurisconsults of recognised competence'. The appointment is by agreement of the governments of the member states for a period of six years, with part of the total number retiring every three years. The judges elect their own President for three years.

It is clear that from time to time, by inadvertence or otherwise, a conflict will arise between English law and Community law. Section 2 of the European Communities Act 1972 provides that existing and future Community law is part of English law. The European Court itself is very clear in its judgments that Community law is to prevail in the event of conflict even to the extent of overriding subsequent national enactments (*SA Simmenthal* (1978)).

The Court also has specific jurisdiction in cases involving individuals who have suffered damage caused by the Institutions of the Communities or their servants in performance of their duties, and in disputes between the Community and its servants under the Staff Regulations and Conditions of Employment.

First instance criminal courts

Magistrates' courts

The office of justice of the peace, or magistrate as it is also called, has existed for more than six hundred years. Justices, who need have no legal qualifications, are appointed by a document known as a Commission of the Peace. There is a separate commission appointing county justices for each county, and borough justices for a large number of boroughs. A justice has jurisdiction only in the county or borough to which he is appointed. Most justices are unpaid and receive only their expenses. Some boroughs have full-time paid magistrates who are lawyers and who are known as stipendiary magistrates. In London they are known as metropolitan stipendiary magistrates. Magistrates' courts sit as often as required. Procedure is regulated by the Magistrates' Courts Act 1952, as amended, supplemented by the Magistrates' Courts Rules, the Welsh Courts (Oaths and Interpreters) Rules and others, which are a form of delegated legislation. In order to try a case there must be at least two lay (non-lawyer) magistrates, or a stipendiary magistrate. Every magistrates' court has a clerk of the court. The Clerk to the Justices is a lawyer and he advises the justices on the law. There is no jury. Both the prosecution and the defence may call witnesses. Each side has the right to address the court both as to their version of the facts of the case, and as to the law involved. The parties may appear in person or may be represented by a barrister or a solicitor. The justices decide whether the defendant is innocent or guilty, and fix the sentence if he is found guilty.

Jurisdiction of magistrates' courts

Magistrates' courts have jurisdiction in both criminal and civil cases although their civil jurisdiction is very limited. Criminal offences are divided, according to their seriousness, into indictable offences (which may be tried before a jury) and summary offences (see p 18, above). From the point of view of the cases that can be tried in magistrates' courts, offences may be divided into three classes: (a) The more serious indictable offences which must be tried before a jury and cannot be tried by magistrates; (b) the least serious of the summary offences, which must be tried in a magistrates' court, and (c) all other indictable and summary offences which may, according to the circumstances, be tried in either a magistrates' court or before a jury. Magistrates may impose a fine of up to £2,000 and or up to a maximum of six months' imprisonment in most cases. Where a person who could have been tried before a jury has been found guilty by magistrates, he may be sent to the Crown Court (see below) for sentence if the magistrates consider that he deserves a greater punishment than they have power to inflict. The Crown Court can impose any sentence that could have been passed if the offender had been convicted after being tried on indictment before a jury. In such a case an appeal against sentence lies to the Court of Appeal (Criminal Division).

Examining magistrates (committal proceedings)

A person cannot be tried on indictment before a jury unless he is first brought before one or more magistrates so that they can hold a preliminary examination. When holding a preliminary examination, magistrates are not acting as a court. Their function is simply to decide whether or not a prima facie (reasonable) case can be made out against the accused. At the preliminary examination the prosecution must call their witnesses and address the magistrates to show the evidence that they wish to put before a jury. The accused may tell the examining magistrates what his defence would be or not as he wishes. The evidence of each witness is taken down in writing and signed by the witness and one of the justices. The records of what was said by the witnesses are called the depositions. After having heard the evidence the examining magistrate must decide either that there is no prima facie case against the accused, and release him, or commit (send) him for trial. If it is decided to commit the accused for trial, he must be sent to the Crown Court.

The Magistrates' Court Act 1980 lays down that where an accused is legally represented, a magistrate may commit for trial on evidence consisting of written statements, without considering the evidence, provided that the defendant's advocate does not wish to submit that the written statements disclose insufficient grounds for committal.

Juvenile courts

For the purposes of criminal law 'children' are defined as persons between the ages of ten and fourteen years, and 'young persons' are defined as those who are aged 14 or over but under 17 years of age. Any child or young person who is accused of a crime must generally be tried by a juvenile court. Under the Children and Young Persons Act 1963 a juvenile court must usually consist of three magistrates drawn from a panel of justices specially qualified to deal with juvenile cases. The court must include a man and a woman among its members. (For the sanctions that can be applied where a child or young person is found to have committed an offence see p 123, below).

Under provisions in the Children and Young Persons Act 1969, a child or young person is liable to be brought before a court only in the following circumstances: (a) if his health or development are being neglected or impaired; (b) if he is exposed to moral danger; (c) if beyond parental control; (d) if not being educated properly; (e) if guilty of an offence, excluding homicide, and is in need of care and control. In the case of those under 14, no criminal proceedings are possible, and they are subject only to civil proceedings in a magistrates court, which may make various orders for the care of such children.

Civil jurisdiction of justices

Certain administrative functions (mentioned on p 113, below) are performed by justices. In addition they have jurisdiction in affiliation and matrimonial matters. A woman with an illegitimate child may apply for a summons against the man she alleges to be the father and, if the court finds her allegation to be proved, it may make an 'affiliation' order against him. This means that he must pay a sum towards the maintenance of the child. It may also make an order that the husband must pay his wife a sum for the maintenance of herself and their children, and may award the custody of the children to one of the parents or to a third party.

Appeals from magistrates' courts

There are two possible ways of appealing from a decision of a magistrates' court. Firstly, the defence, but generally not the prosecution, may appeal to the Crown Court. This involves a complete re-trial with all witnesses giving evidence again. Questions of both law and fact will be judged afresh. A further appeal from the Crown Court then lies at the instance of either the prosecution or the defence to a divisional court of the Queen's Bench Division. This appeal can be on a point of law only. It is called an appeal by way of 'case stated'. This means that upon request by either party the magistrates must 'state a case', that is they must set out in writing their findings of fact and must identify the point of law on which the opinion of the High Court is sought. These findings of fact will be put before the divisional court, and will form the basis of the appeal on a point of law. Where there is a point of law of general public importance a final appeal may be allowed from the divisional court of the Queen's Bench Division to the House of Lords. Secondly, an appeal may be made by way of case stated directly to a divisional court of the Queen's Bench Division on a point of law only and thence, as has been mentioned above, to the House of Lords.

The Crown Court

Prior to the passing of the Courts Act 1971, less serious indictable cases were tried by quarter sessions, which were courts manned by magistrates, and which met quarterly. The quarter sessions also heard appeals from magistrates' courts. The 1971 Act, which abolished the assizes and quarter sessions, set up in their place the Crown Court which it made part of the Supreme Court of Judicature. Although the Crown Court is a single court, is has court buildings all over the country, and may sit anywhere in England and Wales.

Crown Court composition

The jurisdiction of the court may be exercised by a High Court judge, a circuit judge (all existing county court judges are now circuit judges). New circuit judges can be appointed from barristers of ten years' standing or recorders in office. Such recorders had previously to obtain five years' experience to enable them to become circuit judges, but under the Administration of Justice Act 1977 the period was reduced to three years. A recorder is a part-time judge appointed from the ranks of either barristers or solicitors of ten years' standing. When appeals are being heard from magistrates' courts, the Crown Court consists of one professional judge and two, three or four lay justices. The court thus constituted exercises the former domestic, betting, gaming and licensing jurisdiction of quarter sessions.

When sitting in the City of London the Crown Court is known as the Central Criminal Court with the Lord Mayor and Alderman of the City being entitled to sit with the professional judge.

Jurisdiction of the Crown Court

All criminal business above the level of the magistrates' court lies within the jurisdiction of the Crown Court. Jurisdiction is exercised at various centres within one of the six circuits established in 1970. (The circuits are: North Eastern; Northern; Midland and Oxford; South Eastern; Wales and Chester; Western.) All indictable offences are tried by a judge and jury of 12 in the Crown Court. High Court judges hear the most serious cases, while circuit judges and recorders hear the less serious cases. Circuit judges may also sit in county courts to hear civil cases.

Appeal may be made from trial in a magistrates' court against conviction or sentence or excess of jurisdiction. On appeal the Crown Court may confirm or allow the appeal against conviction, and on appeal against sentence may confirm, reduce, vary or even increase the sentence within the limits allowed to the court below. A further appeal by way of case stated on a point of law lies to the High Court as before.

Solicitors and the Crown Courts

The Courts Act empowers the Lord Chancellor to direct that solicitors be given the right of audience in Crown Courts but only in matters specified in the direction. The Lord Chancellor has in fact directed that solicitors be given the right to appear in appeals to Crown Courts or on committals to Crown Court for sentence where the solicitor, his colleague or partner appeared in the case before magistrates.

Juries

The Lord Chancellor, acting through each court's administrator, is responsible for summoning persons liable for jury service. An incomplete jury may be completed by the court requiring any person in or near the court to become a member of the jury. Juries can no longer be sworn en bloc and may be challenged individually before they are sworn. The selection of jurymen to form a jury is by ballot taken in open court. An absentee juryman or one who attends unfit as a result of alcohol or other drugs is liable to summary proceedings in a magistrates' court as well as to committal for contempt.

The principle of majority verdicts extends to civil juries in the High Court and the county court.

Courts with criminal appellate jurisdiction

The Crown Court

Appeals lie from magistrates' courts to the Crown Court (see p 97).

Divisional Court of the Queen's Bench Division

Appeals lie from magistrates' courts and from the Crown Court to the divisional court.

Court of Appeal (Criminal Division)

The Criminal Appeal Act 1907 established the Court of Criminal Appeal. Appeals lay to this court against conviction at quarter sessions or assizes, but the prosecution could not appeal against an acquittal. An appeal could be made on a point of law as of right, and on a question of fact or mixed law and fact if the trial court or the Court of Criminal Appeal gave leave. An appeal against sentence could be heard only with the leave of the Court of Criminal Appeal. The members of the court were the Lord Chief Justice and the judges of the Queen's Bench Division. The quorum was three, and there was an uneven number sitting. The court could increase or decrease a sentence imposed in a lower court, and could quash a conviction if there had been a wrong decision. If an appellant succeeded in showing that the lower court had made a technical error, the Court of Criminal Appeal could let the conviction stand if there had been no substantial miscarriage of justice. Generally the court had no power to order a new trial, but the Criminal Appeal Act 1964 gave the Court of Criminal Appeal power to order a new trial on the grounds that the interests of justice required a new trial where fresh evidence had become available and it was not clear to the Court of Criminal Appeal how a jury would have acted. Where the court felt that the fresh evidence would have caused a jury to acquit, the court could allow the appeal, and where the court thought the fresh evidence was of so little weight that it would not have affected the jury the court could disallow the appeal. In other cases the court could order a new trial.

From October 1973, by virtue of the Criminal Justice Act 1972, the Attorney General may refer cases where the jury has acquitted an accused person to the Court of Appeal for its opinion on the point of law involved. However, this is not in the nature of an appeal by the prosecution and the jury's verdict of 'not guilty' is final.

The Criminal Appeal Act 1966 abolished the Court of Criminal Appeal and split the Court of Appeal into two divisions, the Civil Division, which carries on the work formerly done by the Court of Appeal, and the Criminal Division to which is allocated the work of the old Court of Criminal Appeal. More than one court may sit at any one time. The Criminal Appeal Act 1968 consolidates the relevant law. In most appeals the court will consist of three judges but appeals against sentence may be heard by two judges although where they disagree the case must be re-argued before at least three. The constitution of the court is now governed by s 55 of the Supreme Court Act 1981.

The House of Lords

Appeals to the House of Lords lie from both divisions of the Court of Appeal and the divisional court of the Queen's Bench Division. An appeal, which can be on a point of law only, may be instituted by the defendant or the prosecution. Neither side can appeal unless (a) the court below certifies that a point of law of general public importance is involved, and (b) either the court below or the House of Lords gives leave to appeal which it will do only where it considers it desirable that the House of Lords should hear the appeal. The court has the same membership as for civil appeals (see p 93, above). The Administration of Justice Act 1969 makes provision for appeals direct from the High Court to the House of Lords (see p 93, above).

Other criminal courts

Courts-Martial

Members of the armed forces are subject to naval discipline, military law, or air force law in addition to the ordinary law that applies to other citizens. Offences against the statutes that regulate the armed forces are dealt with by special courts known as courts-martial, and these are usually staffed by officers of the services. An appeal lies from the decision of a court-martial to the Courts-Martial Appeal Court.

The Courts-Martial Appeal Court

The Courts-Martial (Appeals) Act 1951 established the Courts-Martial Appeal Court to hear appeals from courts-martial held by the Navy, Army, and Air Force. The composition of the court was altered by the Criminal Appeal Act 1966 and now includes the judges of the Court of Appeal, and judges of the Queen's Bench Division, together with Scottish and Northern Irish judges. The Courts-Martial (Appeals) Act 1968, as amended, consolidates the relevant law.

Coroners' courts

Coroners have held office under the Crown since the twelfth century. A coroner must be a barrister, solicitor or doctor of at least five years' standing and is usually appointed by the local authority. The main duty of coroners is to hold inquests (inquiries). An inquest will usually be held by the coroner for the district in which any person is believed to have died a sudden or unnatural death, or where a person has been executed or had died in prison or in a mental hospital. A jury (see p 113, below) must be summoned by the coroner to assist him in certain cases, as, for example, where it is reasonable to suspect that the death was due to murder or a street accident. If the jury find that death was caused by murder or a similar crime, they had previously to name any person they found guilty but under the Criminal Law Act 1977, s 56, they must no longer do so. In these circumstances the coroner will normally adjourn the inquest until after the conclusion of the relevant criminal proceedings. If gold, silver or money is found buried, an inquest will be held to decide if it was deliberately hidden or not; if it was, it will be pronounced 'treasure-trove' and will belong to the Crown; otherwise the ownership will depend on various factors.

Superior and inferior courts

Courts may be classified as superior or inferior. There are three main differences between them. In the first place most superior courts have a wider jurisdiction than inferior courts. Secondly, the superior courts have the power to supervise the others. This supervisory jurisdiction is mainly exercised by the Queen's Bench Division as described above. In the third place superior courts have a wider power to punish for contempt of court than inferior courts. Contempt of court means the failure by somebody to carry out the order of a court, improper behaviour in court such as insulting the judge, or conduct prejudicing a fair trial. An example of the latter would be the publication of comments about a person accused of murder just before the trial. Whilst both superior and inferior courts can punish for a contempt committed in the face of the court, only superior courts can punish for other types of contempt. It is well to note the tremendous power given to a judge who can punish a person for contempt in the face of the court, e g insulting the judge. The judge becomes victim, prosecutor and judge in his own cause. Justice is not seen to be done and the contemnor committed to prison may with justification complain that he has not been judged by an 'independent and impartial tribunal' as required by Art 6 of the European Convention on Human Rights. Some examples of superior courts are the House of Lords, the Judicial Committee of the Privy Council, and the Supreme Court of Judicature. Among inferior courts are county courts, magistrates' courts and coroners' courts.

Legal aid

The Legal Aid Act 1974, Part II regulates the conditions under which legal aid may be granted in criminal proceedings. The purpose of legal aid is to help a person with insufficient means to pay for his defence. He may be given aid also to bring an appeal. The income of any person applying for legal aid is calculated and, depending on the outcome, he may be given the services of a solicitor, or a barrister or both as appropriate, each free of charge or for a reduced sum of money. The financial assistance given depends on the calculation of the applicant's disposable income and his disposable capital. As the income limits are raised so legal aid becomes more widely available. As inflation takes effect fewer people find themselves within the financial limits. In November 1983 the income limits were increased to make legal aid available to those with disposable incomes of not more than £4,925 a year and available without payment of a contribution to those with disposable incomes of £2,050 a year or less. The capital limits were increased to make the upper limit of disposable capital above which legal aid may be refused if it appears that the applicant could afford to proceed without legal aid, £4,500 and the lower limit of disposable capital, below which no contribution in respect of capital may be required, £3,000. In future years the financial limits will be reviewed in November to coincide with the review of Supplementary Benefit levels.

In November 1983 the income limits were increased to make legal advice and assistance available to those with disposable incomes of not more than £103 a week and available without payment of a contribution to those with disposable incomes of £49 a week or less.

The capital limit was increased to make legal advice and assistance available to those with disposable capital of not more than £730.

At the same time the limit on the Green Form Scheme under which a solicitor may give legal advice and assistance (but not representation), without obtaining prior approval of the appropriate authority, was raised to £50.

The legal aid scheme is open to serious criticisms. Its low financial limits mean that a new privileged class has appeared, the very poor. The rich can stand the cost of litigation etc., the poor are sustained by the state and the bulk of the population between these two extremes are disadvantaged. Another criticism is that legal aid is not more widely available. Although available for representation before the Lands Tribunal it is not available before the Industrial Tribunals; however, legal advice may be given by a solicitor under the Green Form Scheme to anyone appearing before an Industrial Tribunal (see also p 89, below).

Legal aid in civil courts is dealt with by the Legal Aid Act 1974, Part I. A system has been set up with the courts whereby there is a system of local legal aid committees to which application is made for financial assistance. The scheme is administered by the Law Society, and applicants, after having had their income assessed, are given the services of a lawyer if they appear to have a good reason for applying.

The major appellate courts

Showing the courts from which appeals lie

1 The House of Lords

Appeals lie from:

Court of Appeal (civil and criminal divisions)
Divisional Court of Queen's Bench Division (criminal cases)
Courts-Martial Appeal Court
Court of Session (Scotland) (civil appeals only)
Court of Appeal (Northern Ireland)
Court of Criminal Appeal (Northern Ireland)
High Court (Administration of Justice Act 1969)

2 *The Judicial Committee of the Privy Council*

Appeals lie from:

Prize Court (Queen's Bench Division of the High Court)
Provincial Courts of Canterbury and York
Channel Isles courts
Isle of Man courts
Certain Commonwealth courts
General Medical Council (and similar bodies)

3 *Court of Appeal (Civil Division)*

Appeals lie from:

High Court (all three Divisions including Bankruptcy Court of Chancery
    Division)
Restrictive Practices Court
Court of Protection
County courts
Mayor's and City of London Court
Patents Appeal Tribunal
Lands Tribunal
Employment Appeal Tribunal

4 *Court of Appeal (Criminal Division)*

Appeals lie from:

Crown Courts

5 *High Court of Justice*

(a) *Queen's Bench Division (Divisional Court)*

Appeals lie from:

Crown Court (appeals in summary cases)
Magistrates' courts (criminal matters)

Solicitors' Disciplinary Committee
Rent tribunals (and similar bodies)

(*b*) *Chancery Division (Divisional Court)*

Appeals lie from:

County courts (bankruptcy)

(*c*) *Chancery Division (single judge)*

Appeals lie from:

Commissioners of Taxes

(*d*) *Family Division (Divisional Court)*

Appeals lie from:

Magistrates' courts (matrimonial matters).

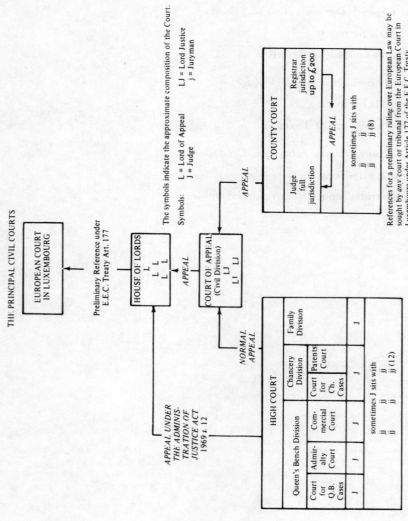

THE PRINCIPAL CIVIL COURTS

The symbols indicate the approximate composition of the Court.

Symbols: L = Lord of Appeal   LJ = Lord Justice
            J = Judge   j = Juryman

References for a preliminary ruling over European Law may be sought by *any* court or tribunal from the European Court in Luxembourg under Article 177 of the E.E.C. Treaty

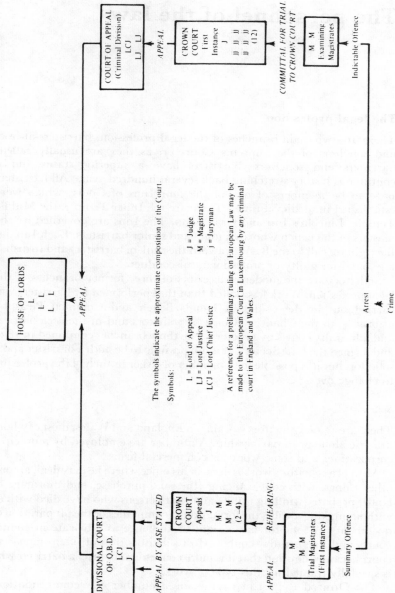

THE PRINCIPAL CRIMINAL COURTS

The symbols indicate the approximate composition of the Court.

Symbols:

L = Lord of Appeal   J = Judge
LJ = Lord Justice   M = Magistrate
LCJ = Lord Chief Justice   j = Juryman

A reference for a preliminary ruling on European Law may be made to the European Court in Luxembourg by any criminal court in England and Wales.

HOUSE OF LORDS
L
L L
L

APPEAL

COURT OF APPEAL
(Criminal Division)
LCJ
LJ   LJ

APPEAL

CROWN COURT
First Instance
J
JJ JJ JJ
JJ JJ JJ
(12)

COMMITTAL FOR TRIAL TO CROWN COURT

M   M
Examining Magistrates

Indictable Offence

Arrest

Crime

DIVISIONAL COURT OF Q.B.D.
LCJ
J   J

APPEAL BY CASE STATED

CROWN COURT
Appeals
J
M   M
M   M
(2–4)

REHEARING

M
M   M
Trial Magistrates
(First Instance)

APPEAL

Summary Offence

Chapter 7

The personnel of the law

The legal profession

There are two main branches of the legal profession, barristers-at-law, and solicitors of the Supreme Court or, as they are usually called, barristers and solicitors. Barristers have a superior status and a continuous history stretching back several hundred years. All barristers have to be members of one of the four Inns of Court, which were established in medieval times. These are the Inner Temple, the Middle Temple, Lincoln's Inn and Gray's Inn. The Inns are governed by the masters of the bench who are judges and senior barristers. Each Inn has the right to 'call to the Bar' (to award the rank of barrister) and to disbar any barrister guilty of professional misconduct.

Solicitors are the modern successors of three former branches of the legal profession. Work less skilled than that performed by barristers was carried out in the courts in King's Bench and Common Pleas by attorneys, in the Chancery Court by solicitors and in the ecclesiastical and admiralty courts by proctors. The three branches combined in 1831 and formed the Law Society. It is not possible to be both a barrister and a solicitor, but it is possible for a member of either branch of the profession to change over.

Solicitors

There are 43,000 solicitors working in England and Wales, most of whom practise alone or in partnership. A number are employed by municipal corporations and some work for commercial firms.

Most of a solicitor's work is done in his office where he may deal, among other things, with conveyancing (the sale, purchase, and mortgage of land), probate (winding up the affairs of persons who have died with or without making a will), the formation of companies or the preparation of documents. A solicitor has a right of audience as advocate in county courts and magistrates' courts. Most solicitors do not often appear in court because they find that it is more convenient to brief a barrister who is specially trained for this type of work.

The Ormrod Report of 1971 made a number of recommendations which included the proposal that a person who wished to qualify as a solicitor or a barrister should normally possess a law degree and then undergo a period of vocational training. This proposal has been only partially implemented. Thus law graduates must pass the Law Society's Final Examination and then serve a period of articles with a solicitor in order to qualify as a solicitor. Non-law graduates must pass the Common Professional Examination and then pass the Final Examination and serve articles as above. Solicitors are officers of the Supreme Court and there are statutory provisions regulating admission to the profession and standards of conduct. As a solicitor is an officer of the court he is subject to judicial discipline in the form of being ordered to pay compensation to an aggrieved party where the solicitor's conduct is inexcusable and merits reproof (*R & T Thew Ltd v Reeves* (1982) CA). The Law Society is the controlling body of the profession, and provides the members of the Disciplinary Committee that hears allegations of professional misconduct against solicitors. (The Disciplinary Committee is described on p 88, above.) The Solicitors Act 1974, s 45 allows for the appointment of a Lay Observer to examine any written allegations by a member of the public concerning the Law Society's treatment of a complaint by that person about a solicitor or his employee. Every practising solicitor must take out an annual practising certificate.

If a lay person (non-lawyer) is in need of legal advice he must go to a solicitor and not to a barrister. A rule of professional etiquette lays down that barristers must deal only with clients who are solicitors; it follows from this that everyone who employs a barrister must do so indirectly by having a solicitor as an intermediary. A person who has to sign some document and swear that it is true must go to a solicitor who is also a 'commissioner for oaths' and who is authorised to declare that he has witnessed the taking of the oath by the person concerned. Certain documents, and in particular some required for use in foreign countries, must be sworn before a solicitor who is also a 'notary public'. Solicitors' fees are generally regulated by law.

In June 1984 (at proof stage) the Council of the Law Society reversed an attitude of many years by deciding to allow solicitors to advertise. Faced with the government's announced proposals to remove by legislation the solicitors' conveyancing monopoly, this decision enables solicitors to compete with banks, building societies and others in the house transfer market. Solicitors may advertise prices charged for specific work or an hourly rate. Advertisements may appear in newspapers or on radio but not on television, because of the advantage given to larger firms, and not by direct mailing. In the United States advertising was introduced in 1977 yet only 13 per cent of lawyers advertise.

Legal executives

Solicitors employ in their offices staff who have not been admitted as solicitors; senior unadmitted staff are known as managing clerks.

Although managing clerks discharge heavy responsibilities they did not for many years enjoy a recognised professional status. This omission was rectified in 1963 by the establishment of the Institute of Legal Executives. Membership of the Institute (now over 14,000) is open to those employed by solicitors in private practice or otherwise. The first examination leads to associate membership, and holders of 'A' level GCE in 'General Principles of English Law' receive certain exemptions. The final examination consists of three papers of the same standard as the solicitors' final examination.

Barristers

There are approximately 4,800 barristers practising in England and Wales. They are also called 'counsel'. Each barrister works on his own account but groups of them employ a 'barristers' clerk' in common, and share 'chambers' (rooms in offices). A barrister's duties are divided between 'paper work', as it is usually called, and advocacy. Paper work consists mostly in giving opinions on specialised or difficult points of law to solicitors, and preparing documents to be used in the various stages of litigation. It is customary in London for many sets of chambers to specialise, and solicitors know, for example, which are the tax chambers or the criminal chambers.

In recent years because of shortage of accommodation in the Temple, some counsel have established chambers in other parts of London, for example in the buildings of the former Covent Garden Market.

Barristers have a right of audience in every court, and advocacy is counsel's special province. A member of the public requiring the services of a lawyer (which expression includes both solicitors and barristers) will ordinarily not know whether he needs a solicitor or both a solicitor and counsel. The solicitor will advise his client when a barrister ought to be consulted and will usually be expected to choose one, although the client, who has to pay, is entitled to make his own choice.

In the interests of his client the solicitor must choose a barrister who specialises in the appropriate work, who has had sufficient experience for the type of case in question, but who is not too expensive. The solicitor and the barrister's clerk will fix the fee payable, and the solicitor will send the barrister a 'brief', i e a bundle of the necessary documents together with written instruction as to the work required. A barrister cannot sue for his fees, the obligation to pay him being binding in honour only. Moreover, a barrister cannot be sued in negligence for his conduct of a suit in court. This immunity is based on the public interest and can be justified in view of the duty which a barrister owes to the court as well as to his client (*Rondel v Worsley* (1969) House of Lords). The court in *Rondel v Worsley* also indicated obiter that a similar immunity applied to solicitors.

In order to become a barrister it is necessary to join one of the Inns of Court. In addition to passing examinations a law student who is 'reading for the bar' must attend his Inn and dine on a specified number of occasions for two years before he is qualified to practise. After practising for a number of years an ordinary barrister who is called a 'junior' may apply to the Lord Chancellor to be appointed a 'Queen's Counsel' (QC). This is a promotion that is signified by his wearing a silk gown in court instead of a stuff gown and in practice it means that he will always have a junior briefed with him, and may usually expect higher fees. A Queen's Counsel is also called a 'leader' or a 'silk'.

Fusion of the profession

The suggestion is sometimes advanced that the professions of barrister and solicitor should be amalgamated in order to reduce costs. It is true that some types of legal work now being done by the employment of both a barrister and a solicitor could be carried out just as efficiently and more cheaply by employing only one man. For instance, undefended divorce petitions could well be presented in court by a solicitor instead of a barrister having the sole right of audience as at present. It is sometimes suggested that if fusion were to take place, larger firms would develop, overhead expenses could be reduced, more office machinery bought and costs to the client consequently reduced. On the other hand, some types of work demand the attention of specialists. In large firms there would still be general practitioners and specialists such as specialist company lawyers and specialist advocates who would handle difficult cases referred to them from within their own firm. The major disadvantage in taking specialist members of the Bar into large firms is that they would then cease to be available to other firms and their clients throughout the country. At present a solicitor may choose any barrister to advise his client or to appear for the client in court. With the current tendency to increasing technicality in the law there is a greater need for more specialists readily available to the public seeking their advice through a solicitor whose job is to deal with such matters as he can, and in other cases seek counsel's opinion. Also, as an argument against fusion it may be said that one person who meets the client and prepares the evidence becomes so personally involved that he loses the detachment which is necessary to the conduct of cases, particularly lengthy or difficult ones, in court. A comparatively small Bar engenders a trust between Bar and Bench which in turn enables many cases to be accelerated and in most countries where the profession is fused this valuable confidence does not exist. Complete amalgamation would have the effect of making every lawyer competent to act as advocate in all courts. However, the strength of traditional ideas, both at the bar and among solicitors, makes amalgamation a remote possibility.

The Benson Report of 1979 (the Royal Commission on Legal Services) noted the following criticisms of a split profession: (i) inefficiency, in that it encourages failures in communication and inadequate instructions by solicitors to barristers; (ii) delay; (iii) lack of time for preparation if a barrister is unable to take a brief and it has to be reallocated to another barrister; (iv) undermining of clients' confidence because of barristers' perceived 'detachment'; and (v) the employment of two people instead of one increases the cost of legal representation. The Report concluded, however, that fusion was against the public interest, principally because it was felt that fusion would cause a serious fall in the quality of both advocacy and the consequent judicial decisions. It was also thought that fusion would lead to a concentration of large firms who would provide a comprehensive legal service in the wealthier neighbourhoods but, as this would correspondingly diminish the provision of legal services in the poorer areas, smaller towns and rural areas, the public's freedom of choice would be adversely affected. It was further thought that fusion would disperse the available specialist service at a time when there is likely to be an increasing need for specialisation and that, on balance, fusion would not result in a saving in cost. Benson saw the objects of a two branch profession as being: (i) to ensure, through the barristers' right of audience rule, that advocacy in important matters is practised by specialists; and (ii) through the access via a solicitor rule, to free barristers from distraction and to encourage the sifting out by solicitors of irrelevant facts.

Other legal services

It is by no means uncommon for people to be overawed at the prospect of having to consult a solicitor. This feeling is often accompanied by the fact that solicitors have been reluctant to establish their practices in deprived urban areas because such areas do not provide them with their traditionally lucrative commercial and property conveyancing work. The result of this situation is that there is an unmet need for legal services.

These shortcomings in the provision of legal services have been remedied in various ways. Citizens' Advice Bureaux provide, country-wide, publicly-funded free general legal advice and information. A large number of trades unions provide their members with legal advice and representation and newspapers, radio and television often provide help with individuals' legal problems. America provided the stimulus for the development in this country of neighbourhood law centres, which are intended to provide a legal service in poor areas of the country. In America in the 1960s a major feature of the war against poverty was the desire to make legal services more readily available to the poor. This was done largely through the setting up of Neighbourhood Law Firms in deprived areas. From this developed the idea in England of law centres, set up in areas traditionally ignored by solicitors' firms, staffed by salaried solicitors who have obtained a waiver from the Law Society of professional rules relating to such matters as advertising and the provision of services to clients free of charge. The first law centre in England was set up in North Kensington, London, in 1970.

Law centres are variously funded, some by the local authority, others by charitable foundations and some by the Lord Chancellor's Department. For the proponents of law centres the inadequacy of their funding (some 2% of the money spent on legal services by central and local government) and the lack of any coherent government policy is a cause for concern. Their main areas of work are housing, social security, employment, race relations, immigration and consumer problems; the kind of matters with which the poor are more likely to have to grapple than other citizens.

Benson recommended the extension of Citizens' Advice Bureaux and the improvement of legal services in deprived areas by the establishment of some Citizens' Law Centres which would be publicly funded and by the provision of interest free loans to solicitors who set up practice in such areas.

Laymen

A great deal of useful work in the administration of the law is done by persons who are not legally qualified. They work in various capacities of which the most important are detailed below:

Justices of the peace. Magistrates sit in a judicial capacity in petty sessions, the Crown Court, and juvenile courts. They also issue summonses and grant bail, besides granting licences for public houses and betting shops. The Justices of the Peace Act 1968, as amended, provides for a retirement age of 70 years.

Jurors. The function of a jury summoned to try a case is to follow the proceedings of the trial and then to return a verdict on questions of fact put to them by the court. The court assists the jury in its task by giving an explanation of the law. Certain persons such as doctors and clergymen are exempt from jury service. In the High Court and in criminal courts there are usually 12 jurors. The Juries Act 1974, s 17, provides that in criminal proceedings, the verdict of a jury need not be unanimous provided that ten out of eleven or twelve, or nine out of ten agree on the verdict. In the county courts there are eight jurors, and in coroners' courts, seven, nine or eleven. The majority principle was extended to the High Court and county courts by the Courts Act 1971.

Under the Juries Act 1974 a person is liable for jury service if he or she is aged at least 18 but is not older than 65, is registered as an elector and has been resident in the United Kingdom, Channel Islands or Isle of Man for at least five years since the age of 13. Notwithstanding that these qualifications are satisfied, a person may be *ineligible*, e g judges, lawyers, policemen, *disqualified*, e g on the ground of having been sentenced to imprisonment for more than five years, or *excused*, e g members of Parliament, practising members of the medical profession and those who have served on a jury within the preceding two years.

Though the jury system is highly regarded in many quarters and has been praised by Lord Denning MR as being the 'bulwark of our liberties', it has not escaped criticism. The following are some of the criticisms which have been made:

1   Though s 2 of the 1974 Act governs the way in which jurors are summoned, it does not prescribe the criteria used to determine which particular voters are summoned. Although directions under s 5 of the Act lay down that selection should be on a 'random' basis, rarely does the composition of the jury reflect that of the community as a whole. This is a cause for concern in a multi-racial society when members of ethnic minorities are tried before predominantly white juries.

2   The rules for the disqualification of jurors are such that ex convicts may be eligible for jury service. The increase in 'jury nobbling' (the practice of bribing or threatening jurors in order to secure a particular verdict), which is often aimed at ex convicts, has led to several attempts to extend the scope of disqualification. Proposals to this effect were introduced to the House of Commons in April 1984.

3   As jurors are not selected on the basis of ability, cases involving complex facts may be beyond their competence.

4   Jurors' unfamiliarity with their role may lead them to be seduced by the eloquence of counsel and to acquit through misplaced sympathy.

5   The compulsory element in jury service is disliked by jurors, particularly when allied to the inadequate compensation for loss of earnings for the higher-paid.

6   Increasingly juries are being directed by judges that the meaning of so-called 'ordinary' words in statutes, e g 'dishonestly' in the Theft Act 1968, is a matter for them. This would seem to be a task for which juries were not designed and for which they are ill-equipped.

In view of the above, and the fact that in civil cases the jury has all but disappeared, it might be thought surprising that the jury still plays such an important role in criminal trials. The argument in favour of retaining the jury in such trials is that it protects the accused. It does this, so it is claimed, by redressing the balance in favour of the accused in the face of prosecution-minded judges, by introducing the views of the man-in-the-street as a counterbalance to the narrow socio-economic background of the judiciary and by providing a safeguard against legislation repugnant to the community.

Lay Members of the Restrictive Practices Court. see p 84, above.

Nautical Assessors.   Nautical assessors are experienced mariners who sit with Admiralty judges and give technical advice.

Judges

When considering the role of the judge it should be borne in mind that the background of the judiciary may predispose it towards a particular view of an accused's conduct and the appropriate sentence it should attract. A wide range of evidence shows that the judiciary is selected from experienced barristers who themselves represent a narrow social, economic and educational sector of society. There is also some evidence of a right-of-centre political bias which may well play an important role in such matters as those affecting trade unions.

These influences are particularly important when there is still some scope for the judges to make law. The most striking example of this occurred in *Shaw v DPP* (1961) when the House of Lords disinterred the eighteenth-century crime of conspiracy to corrupt public morals on the pretext that in the absence of statutory intervention the courts are guardians of public morality. Even in more recent times many cases in the Court of Appeal (Criminal Division) and the House of Lords have exhibited a propensity on the part of the judges to make law under the guise of statutory interpretation of provisions in the Theft Acts of 1968 and 1978.

Although magistrates may also exhibit bias, it is the all-too-often wide disparity between sentences in different courts for broadly similar offences which causes public disquiet and reduces the confidence of the citizen in the administration. The fact that magistrates attend sentencing exercises seems not to have had the desired impact.

Legal officials

Attorney General. The Attorney General advises the government on points of law and represents the Crown in court. He must be a practising barrister and a member of Parliament who supports the government party. The Prime Minister appoints him.

Solicitor General. The Solicitor General is the deputy of the Attorney General. Like the Attorney General he must be a practising barrister and a member of Parliament supporting the government party. He is appointed by the Prime Minister. The Attorney General and the Solicitor General are called the 'law officers'.

Director of Public Prosecutions. The Director of Public Prosecutions is a civil servant who is a barrister or solicitor of at least ten years' standing. He and his department advise the police and others on prosecutions in serious cases. He prosecutes through his staff or treasury counsel (see below) in the following cases: all offences punishable by death, cases referred to him by government departments, important cases where he thinks this is justified.

Treasury Counsel.   Treasury counsel are barristers nominated by the Attorney General to receive briefs from the Director of Public Prosecutions at the Central Criminal Court.

Chancery Masters.   Chancery Masters are High Court officials who are solicitors of at least ten years' standing. They have certain judicial powers and deal with matters leading to the trial of cases in the Chancery Division.

Chancery Registrars.   Chancery Registrars are High Court officials who are solicitors of at least three years' standing. They draw up judgments and orders of the Court of Appeal and the Chancery Division.

Queen's Bench Masters.   Queen's Bench Masters are High Court officials who are barristers of at least ten years' standing. They have certain judicial powers and deal with matters leading to the trial of cases in the Queen's Bench Division. Judgments and orders in the Queen's Bench Division are drawn up by the solicitors concerned under the supervision of the Court.

The Official Solicitor.   The Official Solicitor is a civil servant who acts in litigation to protect the interests of mentally disordered persons, children being adopted and those imprisoned for contempt of court.

The Parliamentary Commissioner.   The Parliamentary Commissioner (or 'ombudsman') was appointed in anticipation of the passing of the Parliamentary Commissioner Act 1967. Under this Act his function is to investigate complaints in relation to actions by various departments and authorities in the exercise of administrative functions. Such an investigation will only be made at the request of a member of Parliament and so a member of the public who wishes to have a complaint investigated must first bring it to the attention of an MP.

The Advocates general.   Independent officials of the European Court, one of whom in every case delivers in open court an opinion as to how the case should be decided.

Chapter 8

The sanctions of the law

The expression 'sanctions', as far as civil law is concerned, covers the means by which the courts secure compliance with their decisions, and as far as criminal law is concerned, covers punishments that may be awarded.

Civil law

Although the civil courts have at their disposal coercive powers, the main object of their work is to redress harm and to restore injured parties to their former position. The following outline indicates the means used by the courts to achieve their objects:

1 *Damages*

There are two ways of classifying damages. The first way is based on the information that must be included in the statement of claim. From this point of view that are two types of damages:

(*a*) *General damages.* These are damages that the law will presume to be a necessary result of the harm alleged. Even though the plaintiff has suffered general damages he need not mention them in the statement of claim (see p 82, above), because, if he proves that the tort was committed, the court will automatically award him a sum as general damages. An example is damages for inconvenience and discomfort in actions for false imprisonment.

(*b*) *Special damages.* These are damages that the law will not presume to be a necessary result of the tort alleged. If the plaintiff has suffered damages of this type he must mention them specifically in the statement of claim. Examples are medical expenses and damaged clothing in cases involving personal injury.

The second way of classifying damages is based on the amount awarded. From this point of view there are four types of damages:

(*a*) *Nominal damages.* These are damages awarded to a plaintiff who has suffered no real pecuniary loss, although he has had some important right infringed. Nominal damages are awarded where a plaintiff proves that he has suffered from a tort actionable per se (see p 191, below) if he is unable to show any loss. The amount will be a small sum such as ten pence.

(*b*) *Compensatory damages* (also called 'real damages' or 'ordinary damages'). These are damages awarded to a plaintiff whose loss is substantial and are intended to compensate him. Their amount will, of course, depend upon the magnitude of the loss suffered.

Before mentioning the two other types of damages in this classification, it is necessary to say that the law concerning them has been altered and clarified by the decision of the House of Lords in *Rookes v Barnard* (1964). This decision was followed in *Cassell & Co Ltd v Broome* (1972). The present law rests on the speech of Lord Devlin.

(*c*) *Aggravated damages.* These are damages intended to compensate a plaintiff who has suffered an injury that has been aggravated by the motives or conduct of the defendant. The judge or jury awards a round sum. As Lord Devlin said,

> 'There may be malevolence or spite or the manner of committing the wrong may be such as to injure the plaintiff's proper feelings of dignity and pride. These are matters which the jury can take into account in assessing the appropriate compensation'.

(*d*) *Exemplary damages.* These are damages awarded against a defendant in order to make an example of him and thus deter others from committing the same tort. Lord Devlin said that exemplary damages may be awarded in the following cases:

(i)   Where there has been oppressive, arbitrary or unconstitutional action by the servants of the government.

(ii)   Where the defendant's conduct has been calculated by him to make a profit for himself which may well exceed the compensation payable to the plaintiff. (In *Broome's Case* it was thought that the profits on the sale of a book highly defamatory of B would exceed any possible award of libel damages.)

(iii)   Where exemplary damages are expressly authorised by statute.

Having described the occasions meriting the award of exemplary damages Lord Devlin went on to express three considerations to be borne in mind whenever awards of exemplary damages are being considered. These are:

(i)   The plaintiff cannot recover exemplary damages unless he is the victim of the punishable behaviour.

(ii)   The power to award exemplary damages constitutes a weapon that, while it can be used in defence of liberty, can also be used against liberty.

(iii)   The means of the parties, irrelevant in the assessment of compensation, are material in the assessment of exemplary damages.

Allied to the subject of damages is the question of remoteness of damage. Remoteness of damage in tort is dealt with on p 148, below and in contract on p 338, below.

2 *Equitable remedies*

Both the High Court and county courts exercise equitable jurisdiction concurrently with their common law jurisdiction. If a plaintiff proves that a common law right has been infringed, the court must grant him damages and it has no discretion in the matter. Equitable remedies are discretionary. This means that even if a person seeking an equitable remedy can show he is suffering from the unlawful act of the plaintiff, he may not be granted an equitable remedy. He will be refused an equitable remedy if, for example, there is an adequate common law remedy (such as damages) or if his own behaviour has been wrongful.

(*a*) *Injunction.*   This is a court order that is granted to prevent a defendant from doing some wrongful act, such as breaking a contract or committing a tort. If the order requires the defendant to do something, such as pulling down a wall that he has built unlawfully, it is called a 'mandatory injunction'; if it requires him to refrain from doing something such as circulating a libel, it is called a 'prohibitory injunction'. An injunction will be granted only in cases where the following conditions are fulfilled: if money damages would not be sufficient compensation, if the order is one that the court could effectively enforce and, in the case of an injunction to restrain a breach of contract, if the threatened breach concerns an express negative stipulation (see p 350, below). An injunction granted at a trial is called a 'perpetual injunction' and may be unlimited in point of time. If a plaintiff fears that he may suffer damage while waiting for the case to come to trial he may apply for an injunction that will last until the date of the trial; this is called an 'interim injunction' or sometimes an 'interlocutory injunction'. In cases of great urgency an application can be made for an interim injunction 'ex parte' (in the absence of the defendant). An ex parte injunction will be granted only to protect the plaintiff for a short time until another application can be heard in the presence of the defendant.

(*b*) *Specific performance.*   This is an order of the court that commands the defendant to carry out the terms of a contract. In most cases it is used to enforce contracts for the sale of land (see p 350, below).

3 *Prerogative orders and habeas corpus*

These remedies have already been discussed at p 90, above.

Criminal law

English criminal law generally imposes a maximum sentence for a crime and gives the judge a discretion to impose a lesser sentence. In view of this and the multiplicity of facts which may influence the exercise of that discretion, sentencing is far from being an easy task. It may be thought that the qualitites required of a sentencer are not necessarily or solely those required of a person who presides over a trial, yet this assumption lies at the heart of the criminal trial.

Purpose of punishment

If an accused person is found guilty of a crime he will generally be punished. Punishments vary, and different punishments may have different objects, but in general it may be said that the purposes of inflicting punishment are as follows:

(i)   To express public condemnation of a criminal's behaviour.

(ii)   To prevent crime by making the criminal incapable of repeating the offence; this is done by imprisoning or executing him.

(iii)   To prevent crime through using the example of the punished criminal to deter others from criminal offences.

(iv)   To satisfy society's and the victim's desire to avenge the wrongful act of the criminal.

(v)   To reform the criminal.

Though retribution (see (iv), above) i e the crime committed attracts a proportionate sentence, is often the basis of sentencing in serious cases, this 'tariff' approach is sometimes discarded in favour of a sentence which is intended to deter by being *more severe* than the crime would normally warrant. This utilitarian approach may be justified on the basis that successful deterrence maximises the happiness of the majority but it is open to the moral objection that it subordinates the interests of the individual to those of the group. In any case, deterrence is a particularly troublesome objective because it is notoriously difficult to prove that a particular sentence has, in fact, deterred. Some of the participants in the 'Great Train Robbery' in the early 1960s were sentenced to 30 years' imprisonment but this has not prevented others from emulating their example for far larger sums of money.

In recent times the element of deterrence has become less important, while the element of reform has grown in importance. Youth custody, which is mentioned below, is aimed mainly at reforming criminals. Opinions differ as to the relative importance that ought to be attached to the deterrent value and the reformative value of punishment in modern society and much research on this and allied problems is being done by criminologists and psychologists.

Modern penal policy has begun to take account of the harm done by a criminal to his victim and this is seen in, for example, the court's power to make compensation orders and restitution of property orders (see below).

The punishment that has aroused the most controversy is the death sentence. This was imposed for a number of crimes, the most frequent of which was murder. At common law the only penalty that could be imposed for murder was death but this situation was altered by the Homicide Act 1957 which substituted a sentence of imprisonment for life except in certain cases. The Homicide Act was the outcome of a report presented to Parliament in 1953 by the Royal Commission on Capital Punishment that had been appointed to consider whether liability to suffer capital punishment should be modified. The Royal Commission examined the arguments advanced by those who wished to see the death penalty abolished and those who wished it to be retained. Those who supported capital punishment based their support on various grounds; the deterrent force of the death penalty was the factor most stressed. Other reasons put forward for retaining the sentence of death were: that through the use of it, the state could mark its disapproval of the breaking of its laws by a punishment proportionate to the gravity of the offence and that it enabled the state to satisfy the wronged individual's desire to be avenged. The abolitionists argued that in other countries the abolition of capital punishment had not led to an increase in the number of murders and pointed out that the deterrent effect of the death penalty is weakened by the fact that, for various reasons (such as that some murderers committed suicide or were found to be insane), there was only one execution for every twelve murders. The Royal Commission came to the conclusion that, although generally the death penalty is likely to be a stronger deterrent than any other form of punishment, there are many offenders on whom this deterrent has little effect.

The death penalty for murder was ended by the Murder (Abolition of Death Penalty) Act 1965, which was to continue in force only until 31 July 1970 unless renewed. The Act imposes a penalty of life imprisonment for murder and empowers a judge to recommend a minimum period of confinement (because life prisoners are often released under the Queen's prerogative of mercy before serving their full sentences). In 1983 on a free vote a Bill to re-introduce the death penalty was defeated in the House of Commons.

Sanctions which may be imposed

(*a*) *Death by hanging.*   The death penalty can be imposed only on persons aged 18 or over. The following offences carry the death penalty:

(i) treason (violation of allegiance owed to the Queen),
(ii) piracy with violence.

(*b*) *Death by beheading.*   Under the Treason Act 1814, the Queen, by a warrant countersigned by the Secretary of State, may order a person sentenced to death for treason to be beheaded.

Neither type of execution is now likely to be carried out in practice.

(c) *Imprisonment.*   Sentence of imprisonment can be imposed on persons aged 17 or over. Sentences vary from one day's imprisonment to life imprisonment according to the crime and other circumstances. Under the Royal Prerogative, exercised by the Home Secretary, many prisoners are released before the expiration of their sentences. This system of parole owes its existence to such factors as prison overcrowding, the promotion of internal prison discipline, the economic costs of maintaining a large prison population, the increase in the length of prison sentences and the need to rehabilitate prisoners.

The Criminal Justice Act 1967 established an independent Parole Board to advise the Home Secretary and it authorised him to release on licence prisoners who had served one-third of their sentence or a year, whichever is the longer. Under the Criminal Justice Act 1982 he has been given power to reduce below a year the minimum period of eligibility for release on licence. In the case of life sentences there are similar rules regarding early release provided by other legislation.

Under the Criminal Justice Act 1972 certain classes of prisoner may be released on the recommendation of a local review committee without the need for the Parole Board to be involved. By 1976 almost half the grants of parole were made on this basis.

Although the granting of parole is a discretionary matter for the Home Secretary, the present Home Secretary has indicated that parole will be refused until a sentence has been almost completed in the case of violent crimes and drug trafficking carrying sentences of more than five years, and that in the case of particularly heinous murders it will not be granted until at least 20 years of the sentence have been served.

Although parole may be regarded as an important feature of a humane penal policy it should not be forgotten that the very fact that the pre-release system is discretionary is likely to increase the tension in prisons because of the gap between prisoners' expectations and parole recommendations. Furthermore, parole removes the sense of urgency from the need to question the sentencing policy of the courts.

Where the defendant consents the courts have power under the Criminal Justice Act 1972, s 22, to defer the passing of sentence until as late as six months, after the conviction. This is to enable the court when passing sentence to take into account the offender's conduct after conviction, such as his help given to the victim of his crime.

(d) *Suspended sentence.*   The Criminal Justice Act 1967, since replaced by the Powers of Criminal Courts Act 1973, introduced a new concept into our penal system. Under the section a court which passes a sentence of imprisonment for a term of not more than two years, may order that the sentence shall not take effect unless, during a specified period, which must be between one and two years from the date of the order, the offender commits another offence punishable by imprisonment. The court that convicts the offender for a further offence within the stipulated period must order the suspended sentences to take effect, unless this would be unjust. Under the Criminal Justice Act 1972, s 11 the suspended sentence is to be given only where imprisonment is appropriate.

A court may also partly suspend not less than 28 days of a sentence of imprisonment provided the sentence is between three months and two years and the court thinks a wholly suspended sentence would be inappropriate.

(*e*) *Attendance centre order.*   A male juvenile, i e a person between the ages of 10 and 17, may be ordered to attend an attendance centre. In the case of a juvenile under the age of 14 the order should not generally be for less than 12 hours; in the case of a younf person (a person aged between 14 and 17) it should not generally exceed 24 hours.

In the case of persons aged 17 but under 21 an order may be made for up to 36 hours.

(*f*) *Detention centre order.*   Orders for detention and youth custody (see below) cannot be made in the case of persons under the age of 21 unless the court is satisfied that there is no other appropriate method of dealing with the offender because he is unable or unwilling to respond to non-custodial orders, or a custodial sentence is necessary to protect the public, or a custodial sentence is justified by the seriousness of the offence.

Male offenders aged 14 but not over 20 may be sentenced to detention where the offence is punishable with imprisonment. The period of detention must be between three weeks and four months.

(*g*) *Youth custody.*   Under s 6 of the Criminal Justice Act 1982 offenders aged 15 (17 in the case of a female) but not more than 21, convicted of an offence punishable with imprisonment, may be sentenced to youth custody provided the court is satisfied that a custodial sentence is the only appropriate way to deal with the offender.

The usual term of youth custody must exceed four months though in certain circumstances it may be no more than three weeks. The maximum term is the maximum term of imprisonment which may be imposed for the offence committed but it cannot exceed one year in the case of an offender under the age of 17.

(*h*) *Fine.*   A fine is an order that a convicted person must forfeit a certain sum of money to the Crown. Fines may be imposed for most offences either instead of, or in addition to, imprisonment. In some cases, e g treason, where there are fixed penalties fines cannot be imposed.

(*i*) *Probation.*   Criminal courts have the power, in cases they consider suitable, to make a probation order in respect of a convicted person, instead of fining him or sending him to prison. This power is often exercised in the case of first offenders. The order lasts for between six months and three years, and it may include a condition requiring the person concerned to live in a particular place, or that he attend a Day Centre for social education on not more than 60 days. The most important practical requirement of a probation order is that the probationer must keep in touch periodically with a probation officer, who is a court official. The duty of the probation officer is to help probationers in various ways such as helping them with employment difficulties and to inform the court about the progress of probationers allotted to him. If a probationer breaks a condition of the probation order he may be fined or may incur a period of community service (see below) or may be punished for the original offence.

(*j*) *Recognizance.*   This is a procedure whereby a convicted person agrees to pay a certain sum of money to the Crown unless he carries out stipulated conditions. This promise is known as a contract of record and the procedure is often described as 'binding over'. For example a person might agree to be bound over to keep the peace for a year or pay £20.

(*k*) *Compensation.*   A court that convicts an offender of an indictable offence, other than a motoring crime, or an offence against the person may order the offender to pay up to £1,000 compensation for each offence of which he is convicted.

The Criminal Injuries Compensation Board, which was set up in 1964, awards sums of money after investigation to persons injured by crimes of violence in cases it considers proper. In 1971 £2m was paid out to victims of crime and in 1976 the figure rose to £6m. By 1977 it exceeded £9½m.

In the working year 1975/76 there were some 16,000 applicants for compensation to the Board, but it is believed that many who would be entitled to make a claim do not do so. All enquiries and claims are dealt with at the Board's offices, which are at 10–12 Russell Square, London WC1B 5EN. The total of compensation paid out since 1964 is over £30m.

The Powers of Criminal Courts Act 1973, s 35, as amended, makes provision for Compensation Orders up to £1,000 for personal injury, loss or damage resulting from each offence for which a person has been convicted. This sum may be awarded by magistrates and in any subsequent civil proceedings based on the same facts the award made in the criminal proceedings is to be taken into account when assessing civil damages. An example of the working of the Act is to be found in its possible application to cases brought under the Trade Descriptions Act 1968 which makes provision for fines only. Under the 1968 Act the person who buys goods to which a false trade description has been applied receives no compensation. Under the Powers of Criminal Courts Act 1973, s 35 the buyer of the goods may be awarded compensation by the magistrates who try the criminal case under the 1968 Act.

(*l*) *Community service order.*   Under s 15 of the Powers of Criminal Courts Act 1973, as amended, a suitable offender aged 16 years or more who consents and who has committed an offence punishable by imprisonment may be made the subject of a Community Service Order. The hours spent on Community Service, such as tidying old people's gardens, public parks or youth club work, can vary between 40 and 240 but must be performed within 12 months of sentence. In the case of 16-year-olds the hours must not exceed 120.

(*m*) *Forfeiture of property order.*   A person may be deprived of his property where this has been used in the commission of a crime. This provision of the Powers of Criminal Courts Act 1975, s 43, coupled with the power to disqualify a person from driving where his car has been used in the commission of a crime, is most important. Thus a dock-worker who drives home with a stolen box of apples in the back of his car may lose his car and his driving licence on conviction for theft. Also, a person found siphoning petrol from another's car into his own may be fined for the theft *and* be deprived of his own car.

(*n*) *Restitution of property.*   A person convicted of an offence with reference to the theft of goods may be ordered under s 28 of the Theft Act 1968 to restore the goods to the person entitled to them. If the offender no longer possesses the goods, he may be ordered to pay to the person entitled to them a sum not exceeding their value out of any money found on him when apprehended.

(*o*) *Criminal bankruptcy.*   The Crown Court may make certain offenders bankrupt so that their assets may be distributed to benefit their victims. The court must be able to specify the amount of loss or damage suffered by identified individuals as a result of the offence, the loss or damage must not be attributable to personal injury and the loss or damage must not be below £15,000.

(*p*) *Absolute and conditional discharge.*   These involve a technical conviction being recorded against a person in circumstances where the court thinks it not expedient to impose punishment and a probation order is inappropriate. An absolute discharge involves no consequences but a conditional discharge is conditional on the offender not offending again for a period not exceeding three years or other maximum as ordered by the Secretary of State.

Chapter 9
The criminal process

The system of investigating and prosecuting crime in England and Wales has grown in a piecemeal fashion over the centuries. In 1978, some 150 years after the last comprehensive enquiry into the system, the Royal Commission on Criminal Procedure began its enquiry into such matters as the powers of the police, the prosecution process and complaints against the police. The Royal Commission reported in 1981 (Cmnd 8092) and many of its recommendations have been incorporated in the Police and Criminal Evidence Bill which is currently (April 1984) before Parliament.

In a democratic society any system of criminal justice must seek to strike a balance between the need to give the police sufficient powers to protect society and the need to be fair to the citizen who is suspected or accused of a crime. Though this is a difficult balance to achieve because these needs often conflict, the extent to which it is achieved is a useful yardstick by which to judge a system and any proposals for its reform.

The role of the police

1 Powers of investigation and prosecution

The police perform a dual function in the criminal process. Not only do they investigate a crime and arrest the suspected perpetrator, but they also prosecute him on behalf of the Crown, usually through the medium of their prosecuting solicitors' departments. This dual role has increasingly been criticised because it provides both an incentive and an opportunity, not always resisted, for the investigating policeman to ignore, or at worst fabricate, evidence in order to ensure that the police prosecution will secure a conviction. An obvious way of minimising this danger would be to separate the functions of the investigator and the prosecutor as is done in, for example, Scotland and British Columbia.

The Royal Commission proposed that there should be an independent Crown prosecution service. Under this system the police would be responsible for investigations up to the point when the decision to prosecute has been made. Thereafter the Crown prosecutor would take over the case. The majority view of the Royal Commission was that the proposal would allow the police to channel their energies into their main tasks of preventing, detecting and investigating crime.

The above proposal forms the basis of the government's White Paper, *An Independent Prosecution Service for England and Wales*, published in 1983 (Cmnd 9074). The service would be accountable to the Director of Public Prosecutions and the responsible Minister would be the Attorney General. Unlike the Royal Commission the White Paper sees no justification for restricting the existing right of individuals to bring a private prosecution, currently exercised in not more than 1% of cases.

Police investigations are often assisted by using informants and *agents provocateurs* (those employed to lead others to commit crimes), though empirical evidence of the extent of such use is hard to obtain. The former, who may or may not be accomplices of the person charged, have received notoriety in trials in Northern Ireland of alleged members of the IRA.

Informers obtain their bargaining strength from the fact that the law gives an accused person a general right to remain silent and a privilege against self-incrimination. If help in the fight against crime is to be obtained from persons with such immunities, it will usually be at a price. As informants almost invariably act from the motive of self-interest, a difficulty arises as to the kind of inducement which may be offered to a potential informer by the police or other authorities. Inducements may range from the legitimate offers of money and promises of immunity from prosecution to the improper promises to 'look the other way' when crimes are being committed.

In Northern Ireland the so-called 'supergrasses' have been promised immunity from prosecution in return for their testimony; in England both spies and those who are willing to testify before Government inquiries have been promised such immunity. The legal basis for this kind of immunity was set out in a statement made by the Attorney General in the House of Commons in November 1981. He pointed out that immunity may be granted only by the Attorney General or the Director of Public Prosecutions and the criteria used to decide whether immunity should be granted include: (a) whether in the interests of justice it is more valuable to have a suspect as a Crown witness or as a defendant; (b) whether in the interests of public safety the obtaining of information is more important than obtaining a conviction; and (c) whether it is very unlikely both that information could be obtained without an offer of immunity and that a prosecution could be launched against the person offered immunity. Though such immunity is an Executive decision against prosecution and is, therefore, revocable, revocation is unlikely to occur since it would discourage other potential informants. In practice a true immunity is provided where the Attorney General enters a *nolle prosequi* to indicate his unwillingness to proceed with an indictable offence. As he is not required to state his reasons for so acting the courts' ability to challenge the Attorney General's decision is severely curtailed.

It should be noted, however, that even the *nolle prosequi* has its limitations as it does not, for example, apply to summary offences or private prosecutions and a mere promise to enter it is not an effective protection against subsequent proceedings.

The practice of granting immunity has attracted criticism because it provides informants with an incentive to give false testimony in order to settle old scores or to escape prosecution for their own crimes, or both. This danger is recognised by the growing judicial practice of warning the jury about taking care before convicting on the uncorroborated evidence (evidence not supported by independent testimony) of a person who may have some purpose of his own to serve in giving evidence against an accused.

In *R v Turner* (1975) it was stressed that undertakings of immunity should never be given by the police; the Director of Public Prosecutions should give them most sparingly and, in cases of serious crime, it would be prudent of him to consult with the Law Officers. Home Office guidelines state that the police should never commit themselves to a course which would make them mislead the court in any subsequent proceedings in order to protect an informant. As regards the instruction to the Director of Public Prosecutions it is doubtful whether it is the proper function of a court to tell him how to do his job as he is under the supervision of the Attorney General.

The extent to which an informer's identity may remain secret involves a conflict between the need for secrecy between the police and their informers for effective police work and the legitimate demands for disclosure in an open society. In *D v National Society for the Prevention of Cruelty to Children* (1976) an informant made an unfounded allegation of mistreatment by a mother of her child. The mother brought an action to force the NSPCC to disclose the name of its informant so that she could sue him. The House of Lords, in holding that there was immunity from disclosure, drew an analogy with the rule in criminal cases whereby it is in the public interest to grant immunity to police informants.

As regards *agents provocateurs*, e g plain-clothes policemen buying drugs from drug pushers or buying obscene publications, it is likely that they would have a defence to a criminal charge, provided they were not the prime movers in the crime, although judges have expressed disapproval of such conduct. On the other hand, the person trapped by the police into committing a crime does not have a defence and the House of Lords in *R v Sang* (1980) emphasised that the judge's discretion to exclude relevant evidence merely because it was improperly obtained, and thereby to prevent a conviction, is severely restricted. In America and Canada the defence of 'entrapment' is available to a person who has been actively encouraged by the police to commit a crime. The Law Commission, in deciding not to recommend the creation of a similar defence in this country, has apparently placed greater weight on the need for effective law enforcement, notwithstanding that this may involve questionable conduct on the part of the police, than on an accused's claim to a defence to such conduct.

Allied to immunity from prosecution is the phenomenon of 'plea bargaining', This is an informal system whereby an accused person agrees to plead guilty in return for a changed or lesser charge. This system, which is a much more institutionalised feature of the criminal justice process in America than it is here, has obvious advantages. Thus, for example, it may save an accused from an unwarranted trial, as in the case of 'mercy killings' where an accused will often be charged with manslaughter in return for a guilty plea and thereby escape the injustice caused by the mandatory life sentence for murder. Again, a guilty plea to a lesser charge when the police feel that the graver charge is unlikely to stand up in court owing to the weakness of the evidence saves police time and taxpayers' money.

There are, however, disadvantages. The very informality of the system is the greatest disadvantage in that decisions are made without being subject to public scrutiny and to the right of appeal, both of which were regarded by the Royal Commission on Criminal Procedure as important features by which to judge the criminal justice system. Furthermore, an individual accused may be disadvantaged as the judge is not bound to honour any agreement struck between prosecution and defence.

In an attempt to regularise plea bargaining the Court of Appeal laid down four guidelines in *R v Turner* (1970). First, as counsel must be free to do his duty to his client this may include advice that a guilty plea is a mitigating fact which will allow the court to impose a lighter sentence. Second, the accused must have freedom of choice to accept or reject his counsel's advice. Third, any discussion as to a negotiated plea must take place between the judge and counsel for both the prosecution and the defence. Fourth, the judge should never indicate the sentence he is minded to impose, as a statement that a guilty plea would attract a lesser sentence would be regarded as undue pressure on the accused.

Notwithstanding the apparent contradiction between guidelines one and four, the guidelines are a welcome step in that they involve the judge in the bargaining process, though they leave open the exact scope of his role and the extent to which, if at all, he is bound by any promises which he made. Moreover, the rules seem impliedly to outlaw informal discussions between prosecution and defence before a trial begins, a practice which the American experience indicates has much to commend it.

Clearly *Turner* has made bargaining for a lesser charge, though not a lesser sentence, a respectable feature of our criminal justice system. The ethical doubts which centre on the lack of public accountability remain.

2 Powers of search and seizure

Two major defects exist in relation to the powers of the police to stop and
search persons in public places and to enter and search premises. First,
police powers vary from one part of the country to another and, second,
the existing powers are often uncertain and/or inadequate. The Royal
Commission recommended that there should be a single, uniform power
to stop and search, applicable to the whole of England and Wales, which
would replace the existing statutory powers. This proposal received
limited acceptance in the Police and Criminal Evidence Bill which gives
the police power to search any person or vehicle found in a public place
for stolen or prohibited articles and to detain a person or vehicle for such
a search, provided that there are reasonable grounds for suspecting the
presence of such articles. The Bill does not seek to replace the existing
statutory powers of stop and search.

As an example of the kind of anomaly which exists in relation to the
searching of premises the Royal Commission noted that the police may
search premises for wild birds' eggs yet may not enter and search the scene
of a murder. The Royal Commission's recommendations, largely
incorporated into the Bill, were that the police would be able to enter
premises without a warrant, using force if necessary, for such matters as
executing a warrant for arrest, recapturing an escaped prisoner and
saving life or limb. All the common law powers of entry, except those
relating to breaches of the peace, would be abolished.

As regards entry under a search warrant, the Royal Commission
thought that the existing powers to enter and search where there is a
reasonable suspicion that the items in question are on the premises should
be retained. It was also thought that, as a last resort, there should be a
compulsory power to search for *evidence* of a crime subject to stringent
safeguards, e g only a circuit judge would be able to authorise such a
search. The Bill departs from this proposal in that only in limited
circumstances will a magistrate be unable to approve an application for
such a search.

In order to discourage the arbitrary use of the powers of stop and
search and of entry and search, and in order to increase the
accountability of the police, certain procedural safeguards have been
incorporated into a code of practice, breach of which will lead to
disciplinary proceedings (see p 130, below). Thus, e g a police officer will
have to state his name, identify his police station and state his grounds for
the search before carrying out a search. Furthermore, police officers will
be under a duty to make a full record of the search and to tell the person
searched that he may obtain a copy of the record within the next 12
months.

One highly controversial aspect of the police quest for evidence of
a crime which is not touched upon by the Bill is the police interception
of a suspect's telephone conversations ('telephone tapping') and his

mail. Although the 1980 White Paper *The Interception of Communications in Great Britain* (Cmnd 7873) regarded telephone interception as an 'indispensable tool' in the fight against the rapid growth of organised and sophisticated crime, there is bound to be public disquiet over the fact that the courts are not free to challenge the issue of a warrant authorising interception granted by the Home Secretary.

Before a warrant is granted the Home Secretary must be satisfied that the suspected crime is really serious, that normal methods of investigation have unsuccessfully been tried or would be unlikely to succeed if tried, and that there is good reaon to think that interception is likely to lead to arrest and conviction. In 1979 the Home Secretary was so satisfied and granted 411 warrants for telephone interception and 52 in respect of mail.

In an attempt to redress the balance in favour of the citizen and to pre-empt the anticipated unfavourable judgment of the European Court of Human Rights in the *Malone* case (see p 68, above), the Government has accepted the need to subject interception to statutory controls along the lines suggested in the 1980 White Paper. Legislation would also provide for the issue of a Home Secretary's warrant authorising interception to be challenged through the courts.

In the case of unauthorised interception the individual citizen has little redress before the English courts owing to the failure of English law to recognise a general right of privacy.

3 Police powers of arrest

These are complex and unclear and are derived from three sources. First, the common law empowers anyone to arrest without warrant a person who is committing a breach of the peace or who is reasonably thought to be about to commit a breach of the peace. Second, the police have an unqualified power of arrest if they act in obedience to a magistrates' warrant of arrest. Third, a large number of statutes permit arrest without warrant but the most commonly used statutory provision is that contained in s 2 of the Criminal Law Act 1967. This section created the 'arrestable offence' which is defined as an offence for which the sentence is fixed by law (i e murder, treason and piracy with violence), or for which a statute imposes imprisonment on a first offender for at least five years, and attempts to commit these offences. Some offences, though not falling within the above definition, are expressly made 'arrestable' by statute, e g taking a conveyance without consent under the Theft Act 1968.

A police constable may arrest without warrant anyone he reasonably suspects of committing, or having committed, or being about to commit an arrestable offence. These powers are now contained in the Police and Criminal Evidence Bill. The Bill also gives the police a new general power of arrest for offences which are not normally arrestable where the service of a summons is likely to prove difficult because, e g the constable reasonably believes the name and address given are false, or there are reasonable grounds for believing that arrest is necessary to prevent particular types of social harm, e g physical harm or loss or damage to property. This general power of arrest renders unnecessary most statutory powers of arrest and the Bill consequently repeals such powers.

The Royal Commission recommended that the common law rule which requires the arrested person to be told that he has been arrested and the grounds of his arrest should be enacted. The Bill does this and adds that the information must be given notwithstanding that the fact of or the ground for the arrest is obvious. An arrest will still be lawful where the statutory requirement cannot be complied with because of the condition or behaviour of the person arrested.

The Royal Commission also recommended that persons arrested away from a police station should usually be taken there straight away so that their subsequent treatment by the police could become subject to the general measures proposed for the protection of detained persons. In order that the rights and duties of the suspect and the police contained in the Bill and the Code of Questioning may operate at the earliest practicable time, the Bill requires the person arrested to be taken to a police station 'as soon as practicable', though delay is possible if the arrested person's presence is necessary elsewhere for the effective investigation of an offence.

4 Police detention of a suspect

The Bill provides that detention by the police for more than 36 hours of a person who has not been charged with a crime is unlawful unless a magistrates' court hearing, attended by the accused, has sanctioned it. An extension of the 36 hours may be approved by the magistrates provided that the total period of detention does not exceed 96 hours. This provision has attracted criticism on several counts. There are no comparable provisions in other common law countries. It militates against the basic principle of English criminal law that a person is innocent until proved guilty and offends against the principle of openness.

In an attempt to protect an accused detained by the police for questioning the common law devised a series of rules, known as the Judges' Rules. These originated from the judges of the King's Bench Division in 1912 and 1918 and were revised by the Queen's Bench judges in 1964.

The Rules provide the framework for the conduct of police interrogations of suspects and they emphasise the importance of answers and statements by suspects being made voluntarily. They lay down rules for the cautioning of suspects and for the making of written statements but they do not affect such principles as the right of the person being interrogated to communicate and to consult privately with his solicitor and the inability of the police, other than by arrest, to compel a person to enter or remain in a police station (subject to the provisions mentioned above). A failure to comply with the Rules may result in answers and statements being rendered inadmissible as evidence in any subsequent trial.

The Royal Commission thought that the Rules were so vague that they should be replaced by a code of practice which would have legal effect. This has been implemented by the Bill which provides that a failure to observe a provision of the code will not result in civil or criminal proceedings but will render a police officer liable to disciplinary proceedings (see p 138, below). As under the Judges' Rules, whether a breach of the code will render evidence inadmissible will be at the discretion of the trial judge.

The code covers such matters as:

(a)   the need to deal expeditiously with suspects;

(b)   the entering by the custody officer into the custody record of the relevant details of the detention, e g the time detention began, the suspect's signature acknowledging his receipt of notice of his rights and any complaint by him about his treatment, and notification to the suspect before his release of his right to obtain a copy of the custody record;

(c)   the need to make a written record of any interviews with the suspect even if the interviews are tape-recorded;

(d)   the requirement for the custody officer, before the suspect is questioned, to inform the suspect of the reason for his detention and to tell him, both orally and in writing, of his right to legal advice and to have someone informed of his detention;

(e)   the rules relating to the cautioning of suspects. In particular, if questioning is interrupted a caution must be given each time it is resumed;

(f)   the conduct of interviews as regards rest periods, meal breaks, the heating and ventilation of interview rooms etc;

(g)   the questioning of the mentally disordered, children and young persons, the deaf and those who cannot understand English.

An additional protection, not only for the suspect but also for the interrogator, is provided by modern technology. One of the elements of police investigation which has attracted considerable criticism is the opportunity, which the lack of any independent scrutiny of interrogation allows, given to the police to fabricate incriminating statements purporting to have been made by the suspect the so-called 'verbals'). Proposals to remedy this have largely centered on the tape-recording of police interviews at police stations. Though experiments along these lines were suggested by the Criminal Law Revision Committee in 1972, the Royal Commission recommended a less ambitious scheme because of the costs involved. This recommendation, which was to tape an oral summary of the interview, has been rejected by the Government in favour of taping the entire interview.

The Bill provides that it will be the Home Secretary's duty to issue a code of practice regarding the tape-recording of police interviews at police stations and to make an order by way of statutory instrument requiring such tape-recording in accordance with the code.

In order both to establish the practicability of a nationwide scheme of tape-recording and to ascertain the likely costs field trials have been started in six police areas. A steering committee has drawn up guidelines for the conduct of these two-year trials and, after the results of the trials have been evaluated, it is expected that a national scheme will come into existence some time after 1987. By that time, of course, the tape recorder may well have been supplanted by the video recorder.

Although this is a welcome development for the protection of both suspect and police officer, the fear has been voiced that there may be an increase in unrecorded police questioning outside the police station as has happened in some Scottish forces where tape-recording has been used.

The trial of the accused

Under the Bill a person who has been charged with an offence and is being held in police custody must be brought before a magistrates' court as soon as is practicable.

In the case of an adult a magistrates' court's role differs according to the type of crime charged:

(a) where the crime is triable only summarily the actual trial takes place in the magistrates' court;
(b) where the crime is triable only on indictment (i e the formal, written accusation of a crime to be tried before a jury) the magistrates may only hold a preliminary inquiry (often called 'committal proceedings'). The trial takes place in the Crown Court;
(c) where the crime is triable either way it may be tried either in the magistrates' court or in the Crown Court.

As regards committal proceedings, if the prosecution makes out a prima facie case against the accused he will be remanded to the Crown Court for trial. It should be noted that the prosecution does not have to prove the guilt of the accused 'beyond reasonable doubt', as will usually be the case at the trial.

Where the magistrates' court remands the accused it may do so on bail or in custody. Bail is governed by the Bail Act 1976, as amended by the Criminal Justice Act 1982. The accused is no longer required to enter into a recognizance (an obligation to pay a sum of money in the event of the accused's non-appearance as and when required by the court), though he may be required to provide a surety (a person who is willing to enter into a recognizance for the accused's appearance). Bail now essentially involves releasing the accused and placing him under an obligation to surrender to custody at an appointed time and place and a failure to do so without reasonable cause is a crime.

A person has a right to bail unless, e g the court is satisfied that he should be kept in custody for his own protection or there are substantial grounds for believing that he would fail to surrender himself. The Lord Chancellor has criticised the vagueness of the 1976 Act because it provides for the possibility of persons facing serious charges being released on bail and repeating offences. He has recommended that magistrates should be slow to grant bail in cases of murder, rape and wounding with intent. The only crime to which bail does not apply is treason.

An accused may be required to comply with certain conditions (e g to report to a specified police station or surrender a passport), or provide a surety or give security for bail, if the court thinks this necessary to ensure that he surrenders to custody, does not commit an offence while on bail, does not obstruct the course of justice or makes himself available for further enquiries. In considering a surety's suitability the court may have regard to such matters as his financial resources, his character and any previous convictions and his relationship to the person for whom he is to be a surety. The Act makes it an offence for a person to indemnify a surety in criminal proceedings against any liability he may incur as a surety. Security, e g a deposit of money, may be required if the court thinks an accused is unlikely to remain in Great Britain until the time appointed for his surrender to custody.

A record of the bail decisions of the court, or of a police constable entitled to grant bail where a warrant for arrest has been so endorsed, in the prescribed manner and containing the prescribed particulars, must be made and a copy given to the accused. Where bail is refused, or conditions are imposed or varied, the reason for the decision must be given and recorded and a copy thereof must be given to the accused. Such reasons as the accused's previous record, his lack of accommodation or the strength of the evidence against him may be given. Where bail is refused or conditions imposed the magistrates must inform an accused who is not legally represented of his right to apply for bail to the High Court or the Crown Court.

The Criminal Justice Act 1982 allows the Crown Court to grant bail to anyone remanded in custody by a magistrates' court in criminal proceedings provided that court certifies that it has heard full argument on the application for bail before refusing it.

The alternative to remand on bail is remand in custody. Remand in custody has attracted criticism because it is seen as a form of imprisonment before trial and this offends against one of the basic principles of English criminal justice that an accused is innocent until proved guilty. Concern is also felt over the length of remands, it being estimated that at any one time there are some 1,200 accused in prison who have been awaiting trial for up to four months. This has prompted the National Association of Probation Officers to call for a statutory limit on the period of remand as already exists in Scotland. A further criticism is that a large number of those remanded in custody are subsequently acquitted or given a non-custodial sentence. It has been estimated that in 1982 of some 48,500 accused remanded in custody, 2,000 were acquitted and more than 16,000 were given non-custodial sentences. Figures like these obviously raise questions about the way in which magistrates refuse bail and highlight the injustice in the fact that there is no right to compensation on an acquittal after remand in custody.

When an accused is brought before magistrates it is vital that his interests are protected. This is done by ensuring that legal aid and advice is available to him should he request it, by the duty solicitor scheme which exists in many magistrates' courts and by the help given to unrepresented accused by the clerk of the court.

If an accused cannot afford to pay for legal representation, the court may make a legal aid order under the Legal Aid Act 1974 if it appears desirable in the interests of justice to grant it. In deciding whether it is so desirable the court will apply the criteria laid down in the Report of the Departmental Committee on Legal Aid in Criminal Proceedings (Cmnd 2934, 1966). These are the likelihood of the accused losing his liberty or suffering serious damage to his reputation; whether the charge raises substantial questions of law; the accused's inability to conduct his case; the complexity of the defence and the desirability of legal representation in the interests of some person other than the accused. The Royal Commission on Legal Services recommended a change whereby, instead of grounds having to be found for granting legal aid, it would be necessary to find grounds for refusing it.

Where the court grants legal aid the accused may be required to make a contribution depending upon his resources and this contribution may be ordered to be paid in a lump sum or by instalments.

The duty solicitor scheme, first established in England and Wales by the Bristol Law Society in 1972, is a scheme under which solicitors in private practice make themselves available on a rota basis to assist accused persons appearing before a magistrates' court. Until recently the schemes, available in about 130 of the 700 or so magistrates' courts, depended upon the initiative of local law societies and co-operation between local solicitors, magistrates' courts and the police. As the schemes depended upon local ad hoc arrangements, there was no national coverage and the quality of the service given differed from place to place. The Royal Commission on Legal Services found variations of practice in the manner in which initial contact between the duty solicitor and the accused was made; the manner in which the schemes were publicised; the extent to which the service was available to accused who were not in police custody; the extent and nature of the service offered to juveniles; and, probably more disturbing, it found variations in the competence of the solicitors on the duty solicitor rota.

While the Royal Commission wanted to see the scheme continue because it thought that this would be in the public interest, it was concerned both at the lack of uniformity in the scheme and the absence of any mechanism to ensure acceptable standards of service. Both these defects could be cured, it was thought, if the Law Society took over responsibility for the scheme and drew up a code of practice for its operation. In response to this suggestion the Legal Aid (Duty Solicitor) Scheme 1983 has been made under s 1 of the Legal Aid Act 1982. This scheme divides England and Wales into 24 duty solicitor regions, each with its own regional committee responsible for the operation of the scheme in its own region. The scheme also lays down criteria for the selection of duty solicitors and defines the scope of the services to be provided by them.

The advice given to an accused by a solicitor under the above scheme is funded by way of the Green Form Scheme (so named after the original colour of the Law Society form; in fact it is now pink). This allows for out-of-court advice to be given free to persons whose means qualify them. The court may also allow legal representation before it to be funded under the Green Form Scheme and cases where this would be appropriate are often determined on the same criteria used for granting a legal aid order (see above). Whichever use is made of the Green Form, the solicitor's claim for fees is limited to a present maximum of £50.

Police accountability

It is of prime importance, if the citizen is to have confidence in his police, for the police to be accountable for their conduct. This accountability is achieved by virtue of the fact that the police officer is accountable under the ordinary law and he is also accountable for breaches of police discipline. As regards the hearing of complaints against the police, one of the consistent criticisms levelled at the present sytem is the absence of a system completely independent of the police themselves. It should not, however, be forgotten that justice also requires that the police officer is dealt with fairly when a complaint against him made by a member of the public is being heard. This is not always felt to be the case as the right to legal represenation at such hearings is limited.

The present machinery for dealing with complaints against the police is contained in the Police Acts of 1964 and 1976. Allegations of a criminal nature must be referred to the Director of Public Prosecutions (DPP) (see p 115, above) and those of a disciplinary nature go to the Police Complaints Board (PCB) established by the 1976 Act.

The PCB, which is concerned only with complaints involving members of the public, comprises not less than nine members appointed by the Prime Minister. It cannot include any present or past constable in the United Kingdom. Appointment is for three years and a member may be removed on grounds of unfitness, conviction of a crime or incapacity. It is an independent body which is not subject to directions from the Home Secretary although he may give it guidance which it is not bound to accept.

Where there is a complaint against a member of his force the chief officer of police must record it and cause it to be investigated by one of his own senior officers or one from another force and the report of such investigation will be considered by the deputy chief constable. Every report of an investigation must be sent to the PCB unless:

(a)   it shows a possible crime, in which case it must be referred to the DPP;

(b)   the officer is above the rank of superintendent, in which case it must be referred to a person selected from a list nominated by the Lord Chancellor;

(c)   the accused is charged with and admits a disciplinary offence, in which case the matter is dealt with by his chief officer; or

(d)   the complaint is withdrawn.

In all other cases the PCB decides whether disciplinary action is to be taken and, if so, whether the hearing is to be by the chief officer alone or a disciplinary tribunal. The tribunal consists of a chief officer of police as chairman and two members of the PCB.

The PCB may bring disciplinary proceedings against police officers notwithstanding that the DPP has decided that there is insufficient evidence for criminal proceedings to be brought or that they have been acquitted in criminal proceedings. Disciplinary proceedings will be restricted to breaches of police procedures, e g conduct likely to bring the service into disrepute or a failure to report to a superior officer.

The Police and Criminal Evidence Bill amends the procedure for dealing with breaches of police discipline and it replaces the PCB with a Police Complaints Authority, the chairman of which will be appointed by the Queen. The Government's proposals relating to this Authority are contained in a White Paper published in 1983 (Cmnd 9072) and they indicate that it will supervise complaints involving death or serious injury and it may supervise others if it so wishes.

The Bill requires the chief constable to have regard to the guidance issued by the Home Secretary for the hearing of discipline charges whereby hearings are to be held in accordance with the principles of natural justice and an officer has a right to be represented by a member of his staff association (note, not a lawyer). However, on appeal he will have the right, as at present, to be legally represented at the tribunal hearing. If there is no tribunal hearing of an appeal, the Home Secretary will give reasons for his final decision.

In some cases informal resolution of a complaint is allowed. This may occur where the member of the public consents and the chief officer is satisfied that the conduct complained of will not amount to a crime or a disciplinary charge. The Bill provides that the result of an informal resolution must be recorded for inspection by the relevant police authority and by Her Majesty's Inspectorate of Constabulary.

N.B. No separate chapter on the civil process appears in this book. As the book is for the large part based on civil law it has been possible to deal with issues involving the civil process to be dealt with in the context in which they arise. See, for example, the discussion of the burden of proof in civil cases at p 165, below.

Chapter 10

The law of torts

One of the functions of the civil law is to regulate and defend the rights of individuals. An infringement of a right recognised by the civil law is known as a civil wrong. Civil wrongs may be divided into two main classes, (i) those which arise purely from a breach of contract or a breach of trust and which are not torts, and (ii) those which arise from the breach of some other duty enforceable by the civil law, and which are known as torts. It is with the latter class that we are here concerned.

The nature of a tort

Definition of tort

The main difficulty in defining tort lies in the fact that one and the same physical act may be simultaneously a tort and a crime, a tort and a breach of contract, a tort and a breach of trust or even a combination of all three.

For example, if a carrier contracts to carry goods and does so in a negligent manner so that they are damaged, he will be liable to be sued for breach of contract or for tort. Since it is not possible to differentiate between tort and other civil wrongs simply by referring to particular acts or omissions, it becomes necessary to define tort by referring to the origin of the rule that has been broken and to the legal consequences of the breach. There is no authoritative definition of tort although several writers have put forward suggestions. The best definition is probably that formulated by the late Professor Winfield; it is as follows:

> 'Tortious liability arises from the breach of a duty primarily fixed by the law: such duty is towards persons generally and its breach is redressible by an action of unliquidated damages'.

Professor Winfield meant that the duty to refrain from committing a tort is imposed by the law, not by the parties involved in the tort, and that the duty is owed to everybody. In the last part of his definition he points out that if a civil wrong is to rank as a tort, the legal consequence must be that an action for unliquidated damages is available to the person harmed. An action for unliquidated damages is one where the amount awarded to a successful plaintiff is fixed by the court. Although every tort is redressible by an action for unliquidated damages, additional remedies are available in certain torts. Thus a plaintiff in an action for nuisance will probably be more anxious to obtain an injunction restraining the defendant from making vibrations or noises than to get damages. Another remedy available in some torts is self-help; if a man is wrongfully dispossessed of land, he is permitted to re-enter it and resume possession if this can be done without force.

Torts distinguished from other wrongs

A tort differs from a crime in that a crime is not a civil wrong at all. The object of criminal proceedings is to protect the community by punishing the offender whereas the object of proceedings in tort is to compensate the plaintiff for his loss.

A tort differs from a breach of contract because liability in contract can come into existence only by the agreement of the parties concerned, whereas liability in tort is imposed by the law.

A tort differs from a breach of trust because the common law, which gives remedies for torts, has never recognised the existence of trusts and actions for breach of trust may be brought only in equity.

General conditions of liability

A topic that has been much canvassed by writers is whether there exists a rule of common law that all unjustified harm is tortious, or whether only certain types of harm are tortious. If there were a rule that all unjustified harm is tortious, then the courts would be justified in inventing new torts to cope with new forms of harm whenever this is necessary. If there is no such rule, the courts must be content in the main to give remedies for existing torts only. Another way of putting the question is to ask whether there is a law of *tort* (in which case all unjustified harm is tortious) or a law of *torts* (in which case only certain types of harm are tortious). In the past two centuries very few torts have been created by the courts and, although the question remains unresolved, it seems unlikely that there is any rule that all unjustified harm is tortious. It is possible to name all the torts that exist today, and the probability is that it would be more accurate to say that there is a law of torts rather than a law of tort.

Although the information has little value in practice, it is possible to say in general terms what must be proved before a person can be held liable in tort. The reason why the general conditions of liability have little practical value is that each tort has its own particular rules as to liability which must be known, and which are more detailed than the general conditions. To establish that the general conditions are present the plaintiff must prove all the following: (i) That the alleged tortfeasor has done an act, or has failed to do an act that he should have done; (ii) That he acted intentionally, or was negligent, or failed to comply with some strict duty laid upon him by the law; (iii) In the case of certain torts, that the act caused some damage to the plaintiff.

The expression 'negligent' referred to in condition (ii) has a different meaning as used here from that attributed to it in connection with the tort of negligence. Here it means that the person in question had his mind wholly or partly diverted from what he was doing.

In condition (ii) we mentioned that one of the facts that may be proved is that the defendant failed to comply with some strict duty laid upon him by the law. This refers to certain torts where a person who has done something potentially dangerous is saddled with the responsibility if the danger materialises whether or not he acted intentionally or negligently; an example is the rule in *Rylands v Fletcher* (1868 (see p 199, below).

It is necessary to mention that condition (iii) is applicable to certain torts only, because torts are divided into two categories: torts which are actionable only if the plaintiff can prove that he has suffered some harm as a result of what the defendant did, and torts where all the plaintiff need do in order to succeed in his action is to show that the defendant did the act forbidden by law. In torts of the latter type the plaintiff will be awarded a small sum of money, known as nominal damages, even though he has not suffered any loss at all. Torts of this type are said to be 'actionable per se' (by their very nature). Of the torts considered in this book, trespass, and certain forms of defamation are actionable per se.

It should be borne in mind when considering the question of harm that a distinction is drawn between harm actually suffered by a person, which is termed *damnum*, and harm that is actionable as a tort, which is termed *injuria*. For some types of harm the law offers no redress, e g where a trader loses money as a result of trade competition. In cases such as these there is said to be *damnum sine injuria* (harm which is not actionable as a tort). In most torts the plaintiff has to show both *damnum* and *injuria*, but in torts which are actionable per se there is said to be *injuria sine damno* (harm that is recognised by the law without actual loss being incurred by the plaintiff). The torts that are actionable per se all protect interests that the law regards as particularly important.

Malice

In the law of torts malice means acting from a bad motive. Generally speaking, the presence or absence of malice is irrelevant in tort, so that a wrongful motive will not turn a lawful act into an unlawful one. Similarly in most torts, it is unnecessary for the plaintiff to prove malice in order to succeed. There are, however, exceptions to both these rules.

The leading case on the proposition that malice is generally irrelevant in tort is *Bradford Corpn v Pickles* which was decided by the House of Lords in 1895. Pickles wanted to force the corporation to buy his land at a high price so he made excavations on his land and abstracted some of the water that would ordinarily have flowed into the nearby reservoir of the corporation through undefined channels in the soil. The corporation sued in nuisance and contended that although the action of Pickles would have been lawful in normal circumstances, his malice made it unlawful. This contention failed, and Lord Macnaghten said: 'It is the act, not the motive for the act, that must be regarded.' Exceptional cases are as follows:

(i)   In order to succeed in his action a plaintiff must prove malice in the following torts: malicious prosecution and malicious falsehood.

(ii)   In the tort of defamation, if the plaintiff can prove malice, this will destroy a defence of qualified privilege or fair comment.

(iii) In the tort of nuisance, although malice is not an essential element, there are situations where the plaintiff will succeed if he shows that the defendant acted maliciously. This is so where the malice turns what would otherwise be reasonable acts into unreasonable ones. For example, in *Hollywood Silver Fox Farm Ltd v Emmett* (1936), the defendant, who had a farm near the plaintiff's silver fox farm, had a dispute with the plaintiff. Following this the defendant arranged for guns to be fired on his own land, but near the plaintiff's land during the foxes' breeding season. He did this maliciously to interfere with the breeding and an injunction to restrain him from making noises was granted against him, together with damages. (See also p 188, below.)

General defences to an action in tort

Defences to an action in tort are of two kinds, those available in respect of more than one tort and which are known as general defences, and those available only in respect of one particular tort. General and particular defences may be raised together in any action to which they are appropriate.

The following are the general defences:

1 Volenti non fit injuria (assumption of risk – sometimes known as 'consent')

If a person suffers harm after having consented expressly or impliedly to either of the following, he cannot afterwards sue in tort in respect of that harm:

(a)   If he agrees to somebody doing an *intentional act* that would otherwise be a tort.

(b)   If he agrees to *run the risk* of *accidental harm* that would otherwise entitle him to sue for the tort of negligence.

If a man entered hospital to have his appendix removed, this would be an example of (a), for he would be agreeing impliedly to an act that would otherwise amount to the tort of battery. If he went to watch a dangerous sport such as motor racing, this would be an example of (b). The difference between (a) and (b) is that in the former the person gives his consent to harm that he knows *will* occur, while in the latter he gives his consent to harm that *may or may not* occur; he goes to hospital in order to be cut with a scalpel but he does not go to a motor race in order to be hit by a crashing car.

It should be noted that no consent will legalise a criminal act, such as the infliction of a wound in the course of a duel with swords.

Accidents on the highway

In *Holmes v Mather* (1875) it was held that, although persons using the highway impliedly consent to the risk of harm arising from road and traffic conditions, they do not consent to the risk of negligent harm. The result is that a person on the highway who suffers injury to himself or to his goods must sue in negligence if he is to succeed: similarly if premises adjoining the highway are damaged by a traffic accident, the owner must sue in negligence.

Knowledge of the risk distinguished from consent to run the risk

In order to substantiate a defence of volenti non fit injuria a defendant must show not only that the plaintiff knew of the risk, but that he freely consented to run the risk at his own expense. This principle is illustrated by two cases. In *Smith v Baker & Sons* (1891) the plaintiff, a quarryman, continued to work for the defendants although he knew that they were negligently using a crane to swing stones above his head. He sued when a stone fell on him and his employers pleaded the defence of volenti non fit injuria. Although the employers were able to establish that Smith knew of the risk, the House of Lords held that their defence failed because they could not show that he meant to consent to the risk of injury to himself. In fact he probably worked on through fear of losing his employment. In *Bowater v Rowley Regis Corpn* (1944) the Court of Appeal rejected the defence of volenti non fit injuria where the defendants had made a carter in their employment take out a horse they knew to be unsafe. Although the carter agreed to take out the horse his consent to do so was not freely given. Goddard LJ remarked that this defence can hardly ever be applicable where an employer is sued by an employee, unless the employee is engaged in dangerous work. The payment of danger money would be evidence that the employee had consented to run the risk of injury from his work (see also *Imperial Chemical Industries Ltd v Shatwell*, at p 158, below).

Rescue cases

If a man acts negligently with the result that some other person is placed in danger and a rescue is made or attempted, then if the rescuer is injured or killed the man who acted negligently will be liable to the rescuer or his personal representatives. The defence of volenti non fit injuria has in the past been raised by negligent individuals when sued by injured rescuers but the attitude of the courts has been that, when the rescuer risked his life, he was not really agreeing to run the risk but rather acting in response to the call of duty. It makes no difference whether the rescuer was under a legal duty or only a moral duty to try to effect a rescue. In *Haynes v Harwood* (1935) the servant of the defendants left his horse van in a street unattended. The horses dashed away when a boy threw a stone at them and a policeman was injured when stopping the runaway horses from causing injury to persons in the street. The Court of Appeal would not accept the defence of volenti non fit injuria, since Haynes was acting under a duty and did not consent to run a risk at his own expense.

Another interesting aspect of *Haynes v Harwood* is that there was little English law on the point at issue and in the Court of Appeal an article by an eminent lawyer, Dr Goodhart, concerning the American cases was referred to. In his judgment Greer LJ cited part of the articles as representing English law. This incident illustrates how on occasions the common law may be influenced by legal writers (see p 61, above).

In *Chadwick v British Railways Board* (1967) there was negligence causing a collision between two trains at Lewisham in which 90 persons were killed, and others injured. The deceased husband of the plaintiff spent an entire night helping in rescue operations. His experience caused anxiety neurosis which necessitated hospital treatment and in an action for negligence the court held, rejecting the defence of volenti, that it was reasonably forseeable that strangers might try to effect rescues in the circumstances and suffer nervous shock. The defendants were held liable notwithstanding that the deceased's shock was not caused by fear for his own or his children's safety.

If the negligence causes inconvenience but no real danger, a person intervening to prevent the consequences of the negligence will be acting voluntarily and a defence of volenti non fit injuria may successfully be raised against him. Thus in *Cutler v United Dairies* (1933) the plaintiff was injured while trying to calm a horse that had bolted into a field and his action against the owners of the horse failed.

It is necessary to show that the defendant has been negligent. Where a man living opposite a building site climbed a fence to enter the site and attempt to put out a fire he could not recover damages or compensation for injuries sustained when a gas cylinder exploded as there was no evidence that the building company occupying the site had been negligent (*Sims v L Goodall & Sons Ltd* (1966)).

2 Mistake

Generally a mistake, whether of law or of fact, is no defence to an action in tort but the following exceptional cases should be noted:

(*a*) *Malicious prosecution*.   If the defendant commenced the prosecution under the mistaken belief that the plaintiff was guilty, this will be a defence to an action for malicious prosecution.

(*b*) *False imprisonment*.   If a policeman without a warrant arrests somebody who in fact has not committed an arrestable offence, but whom he mistakenly believes on reasonable grounds to have committed one, he will not be liable for false imprisonment.

(*c*) *Defamation*.   Under the Defamation Act 1952, s 4, if the defendant did not intend to publish the words of and concerning the plaintiff and did not know of the circumstances by virtue of which they might be understood to refer to him, he may make an offer to publish a suitable correction and apology. This offer may act as a defence (see p 193, below).

3 Inevitable accident

An inevitable accident is one that cannot be prevented by using ordinary care and skill because it arises from some very unusual occurrence. The defence succeeded in *Stanley v Powell* (1891) where the defendant accidentally shot the plaintiff. The defendant had fired his shotgun at a pheasant and, by complete mischance a pellet had ricocheted from a tree and struck the defendant who was working for a shooting party. Consequently it was held that the plaintiff had failed to establish that the defendant had been negligent. In *National Coal Board v Evans* (1951) the predecessors of the NCB had laid an electric cable under some land they did not own without telling the occupiers of the land what they had done. When the landowners instructed a firm to excavate the land the cable was damaged. The defendants successfully resisted the action brought by the NCB by raising the defence of inevitable accident and showing that they could not have known of the presence of the cable.

4 Act of God

A definition of Act of God was formulated by Lord Westbury and approved by the House of Lords in *Greenock Corpn v Caledonian Rly Co* (1917). He said that the defence was available in 'circumstances which no human foresight can provide against, and of which human prudence is not bound to recognise the possibility'. The defence is of most importance in connection with the rule in *Rylands v Fletcher* (see p 199, below). The effect of the defence in this connection is that if a person brings on his land anything likely to do mischief if it escapes, he will not be liable for damage caused by any escape brought about by an Act of God such as an extraordinarily violent cloudburst or an earthquake. The defence of Act of God was pleaded successfully in *Nichols v Marsland* (1876) where the defendant's artificial lakes burst their banks and swept away four bridges because of an extraordinarily heavy rainfall. Despite its name this defence has no theological meaning. The defence is probably available against actions in nuisance and actions for the escape of dangerous animals. An event can be an Act of God only if it is caused solely by natural forces without human intervention. It is this that distinguishes it from the defence of inevitable accident which is available where one of the factors bringing about the event is human intervention, as in *Stanley v Powell*.

5 Self-defence

A person may use reasonable force to defend himself or anybody else against unlawful force. Whether the force used is reasonable will be a question of fact that depends on the circumstances of the case. It will not be reasonable if it is unnecessary or excessive.

Reasonable force may also be used to defend chattels. In *Cresswell v Sirl* (1948) where the defendant was sued for shooting the plaintiff's dog that had been attacking the defendant's sheep, the Court of Appeal held that such a shooting would be lawful only if he could show either that this was the only way of defending the sheep or that, in all the circumstances, he acted reasonably.

An occupier of land may defend it by reasonable means such as barbed-wire but not by something, such as a spring-gun, that is very dangerous. Reasonable force may be used to prevent a trespasser from getting in or to eject him if he refuses to go.

6 Necessity

This defence may be used where loss has been inflicted on an innocent plaintiff in order to prevent an even greater loss to the defendant. The difference between the defences or self-defence and necessity is that the former is used against a plaintiff who was a wrongdoer, while the latter is used against a plaintiff who was not a wrongdoer. In *Cope v Sharpe* (1912) the defendant was a gamekeeper who was sued for trespass to land. His employer had shooting rights over some land where there were some nesting pheasants. A fire broke out on some adjoining land, the defendant went on to it and set fire to some heather to make a firebreak in order to prevent the spread of the fire to the place where the birds were. It turned out afterwards that what he did had been unnecessary. The defence of necessity succeeded, as the threat of fire had been a real one and he had acted reasonably. This meant of course that in the circumstances the innocent owner of the adjoining property had no remedy for the trespass to his land. In *Leigh v Gladstone* (1909) a suffragette who was in prison went on hunger-strike and was forcibly fed. She sued the warders for battery, but failed because they successfully pleaded that their actions were necessary to prevent her death.

7 Statutory authority

A statute authorising something to be done may give authority which is absolute or which is only conditional. In the former case if anybody suffers as a result of the doing of the authorised act he will be unable to sue in tort. In the latter case a person adversely affected may sue because conditional authority granted by statute permits only such actions as may be performed without causing any damage. In the event of a dispute the court will decide whether the authority granted is absolute or conditional.

The same principles apply where the thing done is authorised by delegated legislation.

8 Remoteness of damage

If, in the eyes of the law, there is not a sufficiently close connection between the behaviour of the defendant and the damage suffered by the plaintiff, the defendant will not be liable. In such a case the damage will be said to be 'too remote' a consequence of the defendant's act. Remoteness of damage is not strictly speaking a defence but if it can be established by the defendant he will escape liability. An example is furnished by *Hobbs v London and South Western Rly Co* (1875). The plaintiff took tickets for himself and his family to travel late at night. Through the negligence of a porter employed by the defendants they were put on the wrong train and had, in consequence, to walk four miles home in the rain. The plaintiff's wife contracted a cold and required medical attention. In an action against the railway company it was held that there was a sufficiently close connection between the negligence of the porter and the inconvenience of walking home to support an award of damages but that there was no sufficiently close connection between the porter's negligence and the doctor's bill, so that the damage suffered in respect of the doctor's bill was too remote.

The test of remoteness

A difficult question in relation to remoteness of damage is the test to be applied so as to decide whether or not the damage is too remote. In 1961 the Judicial Committee of the Privy Council held, in *Overseas Tankship (UK) Ltd v Morts Dock and Engineering Co Ltd*, that the test should be one of *reasonable foreseeability*, and that the defendant should be liable only for all the consequences of his act which a reasonable man would have foreseen.

This case, on appeal from Australia, is usually called by the shorter name of *The Wagon Mound*, after a ship involved in the case. In *The Wagon Mound* the defendants' servants carelessly spilt oil into Sydney harbour. The oil spread alongside the plaintiffs' wharf where welding operators were causing sparks to fall into the water. The oil caught fire, damaging the plaintiffs' wharf and ships alongside. At first instance it was held that a reasonable man would not have foreseen that the type of oil in question would have caught fire in those circumstances. The Privy Council applied the test of reasonable foreseeability, so that the defendants were not liable for the damage to the plaintiffs' wharf. In *Hughes v Lord Advocate* (1963) the House of Lords in a Scottish case made a pronouncement elucidating the idea of foreseeability. In this case, Post Office workmen negligently left a lighted warning paraffin lamp near a manhole covered by a tent in a street in Edinburgh. A boy of eight years knocked the lamp over and was injured by an explosion. It was held that although only a fire, and not an explosion, would normally be expected to result from such an accident, yet, nevertheless, the two were not different types of accident, and therefore the defendant was held liable for the result of the explosion, which must be considered reasonably foreseeable in the circumstances.

Although the decision of the Judicial Committee of the Privy Council was an Australian decision and not strictly binding in England it has been followed by Court of Appeal in *Doughty v Turner Manufacturing Co Ltd* (1964). In this case a workman was injured when a fellow worker carelessly caused an asbestos cement cover to slide into a cauldron of very hot molten liquid. After a minute or two the liquid erupted and injured the workman. Such an accident had not been known to occur previously and it appeared to have been caused by a chemical change in the cover. The accident, although the direct result of the act of the defendants' servant, was not reasonably foreseeable, and the defendants were held not liable. Harman LJ said: 'I take it that whether *The Wagon Mound* is or is not binding on this court we ought to treat it as the law'. It therefore appears to follow that henceforth the test of remoteness in England ought to be *reasonable foreseeability* so that a defendant will be able to escape liability even for his wrongful act if he can convince the court that the damage suffered by the plaintiff was not reasonably foreseeable.

There is an exceptional class of cases to which the test of reasonable foreseeability laid down in *The Wagon Mound* will not be applied by the courts. These cases are usually called the 'thin skull' cases. The rule of the common law has always been that the tortfeasor (defendant) 'takes his victim as he finds him'. This means that, provided the defendant is found liable, he must pay whatever damages have been suffered by the plaintiff. If, for example, the defendant commits the tort of battery by hitting the plaintiff on the head and the plaintiff suffers greater injury than an ordinary man would, because he happens to have a thin skull, then the defendant will have to pay him more than he would have to pay a man with a normal skull. The same principle would apply in the case of a man with a weak heart or other infirmity. It is obvious that a person striking the skull of a stranger would not know about the thinness of it, and that the extra damage would not be reasonably foreseeable. This rule of the common law, which conflicts with the test of remoteness of damage laid down in *The Wagon Mound*, was followed in *Smith v Leech Brain & Co Ltd* (1961). Here a workman was injured by the negligence of the defendants' servant when molten metal hit him on the lip. He contracted cancer and died, since his body was already liable to cancer, and the burn brought it on. It was not reasonably foreseeable that the workman would die from such a small burn since his condition was not known, and accordingly this case comes within the 'thin skull' category. Lord Parker CJ indicated that, although in an appropriate case he would be prepared to follow *The Wagon Mound*, he was quite satisfied that the Judicial Committee of the Privy Council did not intend to alter the rule concerning thin skull cases and that the rule remains in force.

Novus actus interveniens

In many cases where a defendant does a wrongful act this does not at once damage the plaintiff, but instead starts off a series of events which lead to the damage being suffered. An example of this is seen in *Haynes v Harwood* (p 145, above). Horses were left unattended; this was the original wrongful act and it led to the horses running away. This in turn led to the policeman being injured in stopping the horses. A series of events of this nature is often called a 'chain of causation'. It is this chain of causation that connects the original wrongful act to the damage suffered by the plaintiff and makes the defendant liable. If the defendant can prove to the court that the chain of causation was broken by some event caused by another person that occurred between the original wrongful act and the damage being suffered, he will have established that the damage is too remote and will not be liable. In effect he will have proved that it was not his original act but the subsequent act that caused the injury.

An incident that changes the course of events is called a 'novus actus interveniens' (new act coming in between). There have been many cases where some event has happened between the original act and the damage being suffered but not all of these have made a sufficient difference to the course of events to break the chain of accusation. A novus actus interveniens that could reasonably have been foreseen by the defendant never breaks the chain of causation. The following are some examples.

(i) In *Scott v Shepherd* (1773) the defendant threw a lighted squib into a crowded market place. The squib fell on a stall, from which it was picked up and thrown to another stall, from whence it was thrown into a man's face injuring him. It was held that when the original wrongful act of throwing the squib was done, it was the natural consequence that somebody would be injured, therefore the person who first threw the squib was liable. The onward throwing of the squib was not a novus actus interveniens and did not break the chain of causation, so that the damage was not too remote.

(ii) In *Haynes v Harwood* (1935), the facts of which are mentioned above, it was pleaded by the defendant that the action of the policeman in trying to stop the horses amounted to a novus actus interveniens but this was rejected by the court which held his action to be reasonably foreseeable.

(iii) In *Davies v Liverpool Corpn* (1949), an appeal to the Court of Appeal from the former Liverpool Court of Passage, the defendants' servant, a tram conductor, negligently remained on the upper deck of the tram at a stop. As the plaintiff was getting on a passenger wrongfully rang the starting bell and the plaintiff was injured. It was held that the act of the passenger did not break the chain of causation between the wrongful act of the conductor and the damage suffered by the plaintiff, and the defendants were held liable.

9 Limitation of actions

A right of action in tort can be discharged in three ways:

1   Consent of the parties – by accord and satisfaction or by release under seal (see p 317, below).
2   Judgment by a court of competent jurisdiction.
3   Lapse of time.

It is with the last of these with which we are concerned under the heading 'Limitation of Actions'. It will be a defence if it can be shown that the plaintiff has not commenced his action within the period laid down by law which can now be found in the Limitation Act 1980, which is a consolidatory statute. There are various periods laid down for different actions. Some of the more important are as follows:

(i) Actions for the recovery of land where the plaintiff is out of possession must be brought within 12 years.

(ii) Actions in tort must in general be brought within six years of the date when the cause of action accrued. In torts actionable per se time begins to run when the act constituting the tort is committed, e g the publication of a libel. In cases where damage must be proved, e g slander, time begins to run on the occurrence of the damage. Negligence is a tort involving proof of damage, which often gives rise to particular problems of discovering the date of the occurrence of the damage in order that it might be determined exactly when time begins to run. (For problems involved where there is latent damage see the Law Reform Committee's *Final Report on Limitation of Actions*, 1977 Cmnd 6923.) The House of Lords in *Pirelli General Cable Works Ltd v Oscar Faber and Partners* (1983) held that the cause of action in tort for negligence in the design or workmanship of a building accrued at the date when physical damage occurred to the building, as by the formation of cracks, whether or not the damage could have been discovered with reasonable diligence at that date. The defendant had designed a chimney for the plaintiff in 1969. By April 1970 cracks had formed at the top of the chimney and were unseen. In 1977 the plaintiff discovered the cracks. His action, commenced in 1978, was time-barred as being brought more than six years after 1970. Following this case the court in *Dove v Banham Patent Locks Ltd* (p 160, below) held that the cause of action accrued when the burglary occurred not when the defective security work was carried out. In *Anns v London Borough of Merton* (1977) plans had been approved and the foundations of a building negligently inspected by the local authority in 1962. By 1970 cracks began to appear in the walls of the building owing to the defective foundations. Lessees of the owner-builder sued the local authority in 1972. The House of Lords held that they were not time-barred. The cause of action accrued at the time when the damage occurred as a result of the negligent act. In this case that meant the date (in 1970) when the state of the building became such that there was a present or imminent danger to the health and safety of people occupying it.

(iii) Actions in tort for personal injuries or death (e g arising from negligence, nuisance or breach of duty) must ordinarily be brought within three years of the date on which the cause of action accrued.

(iv) In certain circumstances actions for personal injuries may be brought outside the normal three-year period. This possibility was introduced as a result of the unfortunate case of *Cartledge v Jopling* (1963) in which the widow of a workman failed to recover damages for the death of her husband due to pneumoconiosis because he had not realised that he was suffering from the disease until after the statutory period (which began to run when he first contracted it) had expired, so that he was unable to sue within the time laid down by statute.

Under the Limitation Act 1980, s 11, an action for damages for personal injuries caused by negligence, nuisance or breach of duty may be brought by a plaintiff outside the three-year limitation period within three years of his 'date of knowledge'. The 'date of knowledge' (by s 14) is the date on which he first had knowledge of the following facts –

(a)   that the injury in question was significant, and
(b)   that the injury was attributable in whole or in part to the act or omission which is alleged to constitute negligence, nuisance or breach of duty, and
(c)   the identity of the defendant, and
(d)   if it is alleged that the act or omission was that of a person other than the defendant, the identity of that person and the additional facts supporting the bringing of an action against the defendant.

and knowledge that any acts or omissions did or did not, as a matter of law, involve negligence, nuisance or breach of duty is irrelevant.

Under s 33 of the Act, if it appears to the court trying the case that it would be equitable to allow an action to proceed, it may direct that the time limits shall not apply. The court is given a wide discretion in the matter and s 33(3) gives six guidelines to be considered in coming to a decision. These include the length of delay in bringing proceedings and the reason for that delay, the conduct of the defendant and the duration of the disability of the plaintiff. It appears that there is now little fear of a new *Cartledge v Jopling*.

An application of the above provisions can be seen in *McCafferty v Metropolitan Police District Receiver* (1977). McCafferty had worked as a police officer, and later as a temporary officer, in the ballistics section of the police authority since 1948. He carried out tests which involved firing guns in a room 22 feet by 6 feet. The room was not equipped with sound absorbant walls and for many years he was not given ear muffs. In 1967 McCafferty consulted a specialist about a persistent ringing in his ears, which was diagnosed as a defect caused by the loud bangs experienced in the course of his work. He did not view this seriously and did not tell his employers. By 1973 routine tests were introduced on all personnel in ballistics as a result of which McCafferty was advised to stop work immediately. His employment was, soon after, terminated. In January 1974 he began his action alleging negligence. The Court of Appeal held that, although McCafferty knew his injury was significant in 1967, having regard to his concern over the temporary nature of his job and the small detriment to the defendant resulting from the delay, it would be equitable to hold that he was not statute-barred by the passing of three years since the date of knowledge in 1967. He recovered damages.

(v) Actions relating to personal injuries or damage to goods suffered on a ship must usually be commenced within two years of the cause of action arising, by virtue of the Maritime Conventions Act 1911. The same Act applies to damage to the ship.

(vi) Actions arising out of injury to passengers or damage to goods in transit in civil aircraft must be brought within two years. For international flights the authority is the Carriage by Air Act 1961 and for other flights it is a statutory instrument.

Parties to an action in tort

As a general rule anyone who is over 18 and of full capacity may sue in tort. There are a number of special cases with their own particular rules and these should be noted.

Parties to whom special rules apply

The Crown

The Sovereign in her private capacity cannot be sued at all. The Crown Proceedings Act 1947 provides that the Crown in its public capacity shall be liable in tort as if it were a private person of full age and capacity, in respect of the torts of its servants or agents. Actions are brought against the government department concerned or, in case of doubt, against the Attorney General. The Crown is not liable for torts committed by the police or by the employees of local authorities or nationalised undertakings.

Foreign Sovereigns

The heads of other sovereign states are immune from actions in tort except as provided in the State Immunity Act 1978. The immunity would extend, for example, to the Grand Duke of Luxembourg and the President of Chile but not to the Governor of the State of California because, although California has its own legislature, it is not independent. If there is any doubt as to the status of a foreign sovereign, the matter will be settled by a certificate supplied to the court by the Foreign Office. A foreign sovereign may waive his immunity and take part in legal proceedings.

Ambassadors

The ambassadors of Commonwealth countries are called high commissioners and they, together with foreign ambassadors and the representatives of certain international organisations, cannot be sued in tort during their term of office because they derive immunity from the state or organisation they represent. As the immunity is not personal to the individual concerned, however, his state or organisation may withdraw it from him and leave him in the position of anyone else. The law relating to diplomatic immunity is governed mainly by the Diplomatic Privileges Act 1964. Immunity is not confined to ambassadors and high commissioners but extends also to some members of their families and to some of their employees. Only such persons as are included in lists maintained by the Foreign Office or Commonwealth Relations Office are entitled to this extension or immunity. Certain employees of international organisations and their families are also included in the lists. As soon as a person with immunity has come to the end of his term of office and has had reasonable time to pack and leave the country he becomes liable to be sued for any tort he committed during his term of office, and the Limitation Act 1980 begins to run in his favour from the moment his immunity ceases.

Unborn children

Under the Congenital Disabilities (Civil Liability) Act 1976, if a child is born disabled as a result of such an occurrence as to affect either parent in his ability to have a normal healthy child, or such an occurrence as to affect the mother during her pregnancy, so that the child is born with disabilities, then the child's disabilities will be regarded as damage resulting from the wrongful act of the person responsible for the occurrence. The child when born may sue in tort for damages.

Minors

In itself minority is not a defence to an action in tort but it may be relevant in torts where a certain mental element must be shown by the plaintiff. For example, a child may be so young that it is impossible to show that he was actuated by malice. If a minor is in breach of a contract through performing it wrongfully he cannot be sued in tort for this breach but if the wrongful act, although done in connection with a contract, is really independent of it the minor will be liable to an action in tort. A case which illustrates this point is *Fawcett v Smethurst* (see p 248, below).

In the tort of negligence there are special rules relating to minors. The father of a tortfeasor who is a minor will not be liable as such for the tort of his child but may be liable in negligence if he has permitted the child to do something dangerous to others. If the minor works for his father, the latter may be liable as employer for any torts which the minor may have committed in the course of the employment. Even if the father pays the minor nothing for the work done he may still rank as an employer.

A minor may sue in tort but must do so through an adult who will normally be his father. This adult is called his 'next friend'. There is nothing to prevent a minor from suing his father; if a minor is injured by his father's negligent driving and brings an action against his parent, both are likely to benefit because payment will be made by the father's insurance company.

Persons suffering from mental disorders

Insanity is not a defence to an action in tort but, like minority, it may prevent the defendant from forming the intention required to constitute some particular tort. In *Morriss v Marsden* (1952) the defendant was held liable to trespass to the person although he was suffering from mental disorder.

Bankrupts

Theoretically a bankrupt may be sued in tort but it would not be worth suing him because all his property would have vested in a person appointed by the court. If a bankrupt suffers injury to his reputation or his person he may sue in tort and keep the proceeds but if he succeeds in an action for damage to his property the proceeds must be paid to his creditors.

Husband and wife

If a husband or a wife suffers from the tort of a third party, or commits a tort against a third party, and sues or is sued, the other will not become involved simply because of being the spouse of the one affected. Some aspects of the law relating to the liability of husbands and wives in tort were altered by the Law Reform (Husband and Wife) Act 1962. Before the Act a husband could not sue his wife in tort at all, while a wife could sue her husband only for the protection of her own property. Section 1 of the Act provides that either spouse may now sue the other in tort as if they were not married, but that the court may stay the action if it appears that no substantial benefit would accrue to either party from a continuation of the proceedings. If the dispute is one concerning the ownership or possession of property, instead of staying the action the court may deal with it under another statute, the Married Women's Property Act 1882, s 17. It is open to a spouse to bring a property dispute before the court under s 17 of the 1882 Act in the first place.

Corporations

A corporation must act through individuals and is liable for the torts of its servants and agents committed by the servant or agent in the course of his employment.

Joint torts

If two or more persons commit a tort jointly they will be liable both 'jointly' and 'severally'. This means that each may be sued with some or all of the other persons in the same action or may be sued alone. It means, further, that if judgment is obtained against all jointly, the plaintiff may execute the judgment in full (e g by fi fa (see p 82, above)) against any one of them.

If one joint tortfeasor has had to pay the plaintiff the whole amount due from all the joint tortfeasors, or if he has had to pay more than his fair share, then by virtue of the Civil Liability (Contribution) Act 1978 he may sue the others to recover a contribution from them. The court will award whatever sum is just and equitable having regard to the extent of the responsibility of the other tortfeasor for the damage.

A person may be a joint tortfeasor without having committed any tort himself. This is so in the case of the vicarious liability of a master for the torts of his servant discussed below; the master is jointly and severally liable with his servant for the torts of the servant which are committed in the course of the servant's employment. The special rule whereby employers are liable for the torts of their servants exists for the benefit of injured third parties. The reason for this is that a third party would be more likely to obtain satisfaction from the employer who would have the means to pay damages rather than from the servant who would probably not have the necessary means. However in *Lister v Romford Ice and Cold Storage Co Ltd* (1957) it was held that in such a case the employer may obtain an indemnity from the servant for breach of an implied contractual duty of care to his employer.

The circumstances which will give rise to the employer's liability are discussed more fully below.

Vicarious liability

As we have seen, vicarious liability means the responsibility of one person for the torts committed by another. This liability may arise by a contract of insurance but apart from this there is a common law rule which imposes it on employers in respect of torts committed by the employees in the course of their employment.

In this connection it is important to bear in mind the two categories into which employees may be divided. These are servants and independent contractors. The general rule, to which there are various exceptions, is that an employer is liable for the torts of his servants committed in the course of their employment but not for the torts committed by his independent contractors in the course of their employment. If, then, an employee commits a tort in the course of his employment it becomes necessary to know whether he is a servant or an independent contractor.

There is no agreed and precise way to distinguish a servant from an independent contractor but the best test is whether or not the employer retains control of the actual performance of the work. If he does, the employee will probably be a servant; if not, he will be an independent contractor. In 1952 Lord Denning expressed the difference in another way saying that it lay between an employee with a *contract of service* (a servant) and an employee with a *contract for services* (an independent contractor). If an employee works on the premises of his employer and is shown how to do the work for which he is employed he is likely to be a servant. If he is a professional man, such as an accountant who works on his own premises and decides himself how best to do his work, he is likely to be an independent contractor. An employer of a servant is usually termed a master; he will be liable for a tort committed by his servant in the course of his employment even though the servant has been doing his work negligently or mistakenly. Thus in *Bayley v Manchester Rly Co* (1873) the defendants were held liable when their porter made a mistake as to the destination of a train and, meaning to be helpful, dragged a passenger out of his correct train.

Even if the servant is doing something forbidden by his employer he will still be acting in the course of his employment if he is doing his authorised work but in an improper way. So in *Limpus v London General*

Omnibus Co (1862) an omnibus driver who had been forbidden to race other omnibuses did so and caused a collision. His master was held liable because he was doing work, but in an improper way. This case should be contrasted with *Beard v London General Omnibus Co* (1900) in which at the end of a bus route a conductor attempted to turn the bus round, and became involved in an accident. Since the conductor was not employed to drive at all it was held that he had not been acting in the course of his employment and therefore his master was held not liable for the damage suffered by the plaintiff. In *Lloyd v Grace Smith & Co* (1912) a solicitor's clerk defrauded his master's client of her property by means of getting her to sign false documents and, even though he intended to benefit himself, the House of Lord held that he was acting within the scope of his employment so as to make his master liable. In *Imperial Chemical Industries Ltd v Shatwell* (1964) the defendants, who would ordinarily have been vicariously liable for a servant's tort, were able to escape liability by availing themselves of the defence of volenti non fit injuria which was open to that servant.

If the tort is quite unconnected with the servant's work, the master will not be liable for it. Thus in *Warren v Henlys Ltd* (1948), where a garage attendant assaulted a customer out of personal spite, his master was held not liable. However in *Rose v Plenty* (1976), where contrary to orders a milkman employed a boy of 13 to help him deliver milk and collect empty bottles, and injured the boy by driving his milk float negligently, the boy succeeded in an action both against the milkman and his employer. The Court of Appeal held that the instructions forbidding the milkman to employ children affected only his mode of conduct and what he had done remained within the scope of his employment.

Although the general rule is that the employer of an independent contractor is not liable for torts committed by the latter, there are some exceptions to the rule, the more important being as follows:

(i)   Where the independent contractor creates a danger in a highway;
(ii)   Where the independent contractor has committed a tort under the rule in *Ryland v Fletcher* (see p 199, below).

Negligence

At the outset we must distinguish between *negligence as a state of mind* which accompanies an act and makes it tortious, and *negligence as a tort*. In this section we are concerned with the latter meaning of the word. It is perhaps the most important tort at the present time as it covers so many areas of activity; for example, it embraces road accidents, factory accidents and injuries caused by dangerous premises.

The elements of negligence

As a tort negligence involves three elements or ingredients as they are sometimes called. These are:

1 A legal duty of care owed by one person to another.
2 Breach of duty by the person owing it.
3 Damage to the person to whom the duty is owed which is caused as a result of the breach.

All three elements must be established to the satisfaction of the court before the court will hold that the tort of negligence has been committed. Thus, a driver of a motor car, which potentially is a dangerous weapon, owes a duty of care to other road users. If he drives without due care, as where he ignores traffic lights, fails to signal when turning or drives at excessive speed in a busy street, he will not commit the tort of negligence *unless* he injures someone. He owes a duty of care, which duty he breaks, but until someone is injured as a result the three essentials of negligence are not present and the tort has not been committed.

We will now consider in more detail what a plaintiff who is suing in negligence must prove before he is able to win his case. He must prove *all three* elements of negligence.

1 *Duty of care*

The plaintiff must satisfy the court that a legal duty of care is owed by the defendant to him (the plaintiff).

By 'legal duty of care' we mean such duty of care as is recognised by law. The well-known test of duty of care is the so-called 'neighbour test' formulated by Lord Atkin in the famous case of *Donoghue v Stevenson* (1932, HL). He said that we owe a duty of care to our neighbour and in law our neighbour is anyone who we can *reasonably foresee* would be likely to be injured by our acts or omissions. That is to say

> 'persons who are so closely and directly affected by my act that I ought reasonably to have them in contemplation as being so affected when I am directing my mind to the acts or omissions which are called in question'.

The facts of the case are that a manufacturer made and bottled ginger beer in which a snail was later discovered by the eventual consumer. The ginger beer was sold to a retailer who in turn sold it to a person who gave the ginger beer to a friend. As the bottle was opaque it was impossible for anyone other than the eventual consumer to discover the partly decomposed snail. The friend discovered the snail on drinking the beer and was made seriously ill thereby. The House of Lords held that the manufacturer owed a duty of care to anyone he could reasonably foresee would be likely to be injured by drinking his ginger beer, if he failed to take sufficient precautions against harmful matter entering the bottle. He, therefore, owed a duty of care to the friend. In allowing the snail to enter the beer he had broken this duty and damage had clearly resulted from the breach.

The following three cases dealing with the question of the existence of the duty of care show the approach of the courts.

(i) A crane manufacturer sold a crane to certain builders whose expert was under the obligation of assembling the crane. The expert, finding that a cogwheel was inaccurate, marked it to show the inaccuracy but proceeded to use the crane. As a result of the discovered fault he was killed. His widow brought an action under the Fatal Accidents Act 1846 alleging negligence by the manufacturers of the crane. The Court of Appeal held that as the defect was discoverable on a reasonable examination the manufacturer owed no duty of care to the expert (*Farr v Butters Bros* (1932)).

(ii) A motor-cyclist, while driving at an excessive speed, was involved in an accident with a car. Some distance away, and in a position of safety behind a tram, a fishwife heard the sound of the crash which frightened her and made her ill. She was then eight months pregnant and her child was later still-born. She sued the personal representative of the motor-cyclist in negligence and lost her action. The House of Lords held that she was beyond the area of foreseeable danger so that no duty of care was owed to her (*Bourhill v Young* (1943)).

(iii) A taxi-driver carelessly reversed his taxi in the road and ran over a little boy's tricycle, whereupon the little boy screamed. His mother, who was in an upstairs room of a nearby house, heard him scream, ran to the window and saw the tricycle under the taxi. The sight caused her shock and made her ill. In an action in negligence the court held that when reversing his taxi the driver owed a duty to such persons as he could reasonably foresee would be injured by his act, in this case people on the road in the immediate vicinity of the taxi. Thus, no duty was owed to the mother and she failed in her action (*King v Phillips* (1952)).

In a number of cases involving the construction of buildings the local authority, which has a statutory duty as well as a common law duty in connection with inspection of the work at various stages of construction, has been held liable to the owner or subsequent owner. In *Dutton v Bognor Regis Urban District Council* (1971) builder's plans were approved by the local authority and the foundations were examined during the course of building. In these circumstances the Court of Appeal held that the local authority owed a duty of care to subsequent owners of the property. In 1977, the House of Lords, in *Anns v London Borough of Merton*, applied *Dutton's* case to circumstances where the local authority failed to detect that the depth of the concrete foundations was less than on the approved plans. In *Dove v Banhams Patent Locks Ltd* (1983) a security firm, which installed a security system in 1967, owed a duty of care to a subsequent owner of property, which was burgled in 1976 as a result of defective workmanship.

NB In *Dutton's* case an action would also lie against the builder.

However, it does not necessarily follow that there is always a duty of care when damage is reasonably foreseeable from the defendant's act. Nevertheless such a duty will always arise in cases where the damage is *physical* injury to persons or property, whether such injury is the result of the defendant's act, in the strict sense of the word, or the result of a careless statement or representation by the defendant. There are a number of examples of the latter type of case. Thus in *Sharp v Avery and Kerwood* (1938, CA) a motor-cyclist undertook to guide another motor-cyclist carrying a pillion-rider along the road to Margate. The first motor-cyclist carelessly drove off the road and the second, relying on the first's representation as to the correct route, followed him as a result of which the pillion rider was injured. It was held that the pillion rider could recover damages from the first motor-cyclist. In *Clay v A. J. Crump & Sons* (1963, CA) the defendant, an architect, stated that a wall on a demolition site was safe and could be left standing. In fact it was unsafe and eventually collapsed injuring the plaintiff. It was held that the plaintiff could recover damages from the architect for his negligent statement.

The question whether damages are recoverable for a careless statement resulting in *financial* injury has been, however, a very vexed one. Until 1963 the law was that, except in very exceptional circumstances or in cases where there was a contractual relationship, damages could *not* be recovered for such injury. This principle was laid down in the case of *Candler v Crane, Christmas & Co* (1951, CA). The decision of the Court of Appeal in *Candler's Case* was much criticised and in 1963 the House of Lords, in *Hedley Byrne & Co Ltd v Heller & Partners Ltd* approved of the dissenting judgment of Denning LJ and unanimously agreed that *Candler's Case* was wrongly decided. The facts of the *Hedley Byrne Case* are as follows: H bank was approached by N bank who were making enquiries as to the financial stability of E Ltd. N bank were making their enquiries at the request of *Hedley Byrne & Co Ltd*, one of their customers. The case was argued on the basis that the reply by the H bank was negligently prepared. The reply by H bank was communicated to Hedley Byrne who, in reliance thereon, entered into a contract with E Ltd and lost money due to that company's financial instability. The H bank headed their reply with the words 'For your private use and without responsibility on the part of this Bank or its officials'. In view of these words disclaiming liability the House of Lords held that no duty of care was accepted by H bank and none arose. Therefore, the claim by Hedley Byrne against the H bank for damages to compensate for the financial loss they had suffered by the negligence of the H Bank failed. But the House also considered what the legal position would have been if no words of disclaimer had been used and here the speeches of their Lordships constitute the most persuasive of obiter dicta (see p 43, above). All five Lords of Appeal in Ordinary opined that *Candler v Crane, Christmas & Co* was 'wrongly decided' and that, in appropriate circumstances, a duty of care would arise where an innocent, as opposed to a fraudulent, misrepresentation was made and the fact that the sole damage was a financial loss did not affect the question of liability. The circumstances in which a duty of care will arise when a person makes a statement is expressed by Lord Morris as follows:

> 'if, in a sphere in which a person is so placed that others could reasonably rely on his judgment or his skill or on his ability to make careful inquiry, a person takes it on himself to give information or advice to, or allows his information or advice to be passed on to, another person who, as he knows or should know, will place reliance on it, then a duty of care will arise'.

The characteristic difference between the type of negligence recognised by the House of Lords in this case and the more usual type of case, say, for example, *Donoghue v Stevenson*, are firstly, that here the damage was caused by a negligent *statement* and not a negligent *act* and secondly, that here the damage was a *financial* damage and not physical. It must remembered that those parts of the judgments dealing with *Candler's Case* are obiter dicta and that that case was 'disapproved' rather than 'overruled'. However, as the House was unanimous, it would seem that no lower court would beg to differ and, should the principle come before the House for decision, then there appears little doubt that the House of Lords will follow its own highly persuasive voice.

In *Esso Petroleum Co Ltd v Mardon* (1976) a petrol company induced a tenant to take a lease of a petrol station by representing negligently that 200,000 gallons would be sold from it annually whereas in 15 months only 78,000 gallons were actually sold. The Court of Appeal held the petrol company liable in negligence under the principle of *Hedley Byrne & Co Ltd v Heller & Partners Ltd* (1964).

2 Breach of duty

Once the duty of care has been established the plaintiff must show that the defendant has broken his duty of care.

The duty is broken when the defendant fails to do what the reasonable man would do or does what the reasonable man would *not* do in all the circumstances of the case. The principle is well-illustrated by the case of *Roe v The Ministry of Health* (1954). A man was paralysed from the waist downwards as a result of an injection of a drug called nupercaine given to him in one of the ministry's hospitals in 1947. Ampoules of nupercaine were kept in a phenol solution. Unknown to the *then* existing medical science very fine cracks could, and did, appear in the ampoules through which the phenol solution seeped and mixed with the nupercaine. The court held that *in the circumstances* all reasonable care was taken and the anaesthetist responsible for giving the injection had not been negligent. But, the court pointed out, in the light of the experience gained from the events of 1947, in a future case such an act would constitute negligence by the anaesthetist, unless he took reasonable steps to ensure that there were no cracks in the ampoules containing the nupercaine.

Whether an action or omission amounts to a breach of the duty of care is always a question of fact depending on the circumstances of each particular case. In his well-known work on *Torts* Salmond suggested the following test which subsequently was judicially approved. He proposed that

(a) the magnitude of the risk of injury (which consists of a combination of the *seriousness* of the possible injury and the *likelihood* of its being caused) should be balanced against

(b) the importance of the object to be achieved by the defendant's action which is alleged to be negligent and the measures to prevent injury.

How the above suggestion of Salmond has been applied can be seen from a consideration of the following cases in which it has been approved.

(i) The plaintiff was struck by a cricket ball which had been hit over a 17 foot fence 78 yards from the batsman. Such hits were most unusual at that ground. The magnitude of the risk was not great as the likelihood of its happening was so slight. To prevent injury an extremely high fence or even a dome over the whole ground would be necessary and in view of the slight risk involved the House of Lords held that there had been no negligence (*Bolton v Stone* (1951)).

(ii) A garage hand, who, to the knowledge of his employers, had only one good eye, injured this eye at work underneath a vehicle. No protective goggles had been supplied to him nor was it usual in the trade to supply such goggles. The likelihood of the eye being injured was not great but the consequences of injury were very great; therefore, the magnitude of the risk was considerable. The measures necessary to prevent injury were slight (the provision of goggles) so it is not surprising to find that the House of Lords held the employers liable in negligence for failing to supply protective goggles. However, if the employers had not known of the incapacity of their workman it is suggested that this circumstance would have been material so that the employer's failure to supply goggles would not have been unreasonable in the circumstances of the case (*Paris v Stepney Borough Council* (1951)).

(iii) Exceptionally heavy rain caused flooding in a factory and the water, normally carried away in open channels, lay about the factory floor in patches. Sawdust was used to cover most of the patches but not enough was available and a worker slipped on an uncovered area. The likelihood of injury through slipping was clearly present but the danger was obvious and, by the exercise of care in movement, could have been avoided. The only way to prevent injury would have been to take the drastic measure of closing the factory and sending all the workers home. It was held that the risk was not so great as to demand such extreme measures and the employer had not failed to take reasonable care, in all the circumstances of the case, for his employee (*Latimer v AEC* (1952)).

3 Damage

The plaintiff must show that as a result of the breach of duty he has suffered some damage. Negligence is a tort which is only actionable on proof of damage. Damage resulting from the breach is an essential element of the tort. In *Barnett v Chelsea and Kensington Hospital Management Committee* (1968) a night watchman was taken to hospital complaining of vomiting. The casualty officer sent him to see his own doctor. A few hours later the man died of arsenic poisoning. The court held that the action in negligence failed. The casualty officer had been negligent in not examining the night watchman but as the night watchman would have died from the poison in any event the death was not a result of the doctor's negligence. For a discussion of the circumstances in which the damage may be too remote to create liability, see pp 148–151, above.

Measure of damages

In *Anns v London Borough of Merton* (p 160, above) where the defective foundations in turn caused damage to buildings, the House of Lords held that the amount of damages recoverable (known as the *quantum* of damages) included all loss which foreseeably could arise from the breach of the duty of care including personal injury as well as damage to property. Included in the compensation for damage to property are damage to the building structure and possibly expenses arising from necessary displacement during rebuilding work. The building structure must be restored to a condition in which it is no longer a danger to the health or safety of people living there.

The extent to which the courts will allow a plaintiff to recover all loss, including purely economic loss, consequent upon the tort of negligence is not at all clear. In *Dutton's* case Lord Denning MR said that the plaintiff would not be precluded from recovering compensation on the ground that the loss was solely economic. In *Dove v Banhams Patent Locks Ltd* (1983) the owner of the house recovered the value of property stolen as a result of faulty security work undertaken by the defendant for a previous owner of the house which had been burgled, i e the economic loss consequent on the defective workmanship. The court applied the decision of the House of Lords in *Junior Books Ltd v Veitchi Ltd* (1982) where consequential loss was allowed as a head of compensation to a factory owner who claimed against a sub-contractor in respect of a defective floor which had to be replaced. During the period when the replacement work was being carried out the factory owner expended money on moving machinery, closing the factory, payment of wages and overheads and suffered a loss of profit. The House of Lords held that the damage caused to the owners of the factory was a direct and foreseeable result of the sub-contractor's negligence in laying a defective floor. (NB There was no privity of contract between the factory owner and the sub-contractor.)

Burden of proof in negligence

The expression 'the burden of proof' has two meanings. First, it refers to the obligation to prove the case and, second, to the standard of proof (amount of evidence) required before it can be said that the case has been proved. In civil cases the general rule is that he who asserts must prove and which is the asserting party can only be gathered from the pleadings. In the majority of cases it is the plaintiff who is obliged to prove. He must prove the act of negligence and the damage resulting from it. He proves his case when he adduces sufficient evidence of his assertions to satisfy a jury. If a negligence action is tried by a judge and a jury, a preliminary question the judge must ask himself is whether there is sufficient evidence of negligence (ignoring any evidence of the defence) on which reasonable men might conclude that the damage was caused by the fact negligence has been committed. If the answer is 'No' then the judge asks himself is 'Yes' then he leaves the case to the jury to decide whether in fact negligence has been committed. If the answer is 'No' then the judge withdraws the case from the jury and the plaintiff has lost his action. When the judge withdraws a case in this way his action does not amount to a finding of fact that there has been no negligence but that in his opinion no reasonable man (or jury of reasonable men) could think that negligence had been proved. On the other hand, it may be that in the opinion of the trial judge there was no negligence but, in view of the fact the evidence is such that reasonable men may reasonably differ, he will leave the question of negligence to the jury. The relationship between the judge and jury has been expressed thus:

> 'The judge has a certain duty to discharge, and the jurors have another and different duty. The judge has to say whether any facts have been established by the evidence from which negligence may be reasonably inferred; the jurors have to say whether from these facts, when submitted to them, negligence *ought to* be inferred. . . . It would . . . place in the hands of the jurors a power which might be exercised in the most arbitrary manner, if they were at liberty to hold that negligence might be inferred from any state of facts whatever' (per Lord Cairns in *Metropolitan Rly Co v Jackson* (1877)).

Today almost all negligence cases are in fact tried by a judge sitting alone.

A decided case illustrating the circumstances in which a case may justifiably be withdrawn from the jury is the case of *Wakelin v London and South Western Rly Co* (1886). The plaintiff's husband had been found, at night, dead on a railway crossing. The evidence showed that a train which had passed over the crossing had carried a light but had failed to give warning of its approach by sounding a whistle in accordance with normal practice. The House of Lords held that, assuming the evidence revealed negligence by the defendant company's train-driver, no evidence had been given to show the connection between this negligence and the death. Thus there was no case to go to the jury. The plaintiff had not brought any evidence to prove the third element of the tort of negligence. If, as is usually so, the case is being tried by a judge alone, he must perform the functions of both judge and jury.

The rule which places the obligation of proving the negligence on the plaintiff can work hardship in cases where the plaintiff can prove the damage but cannot show the cause of the damage because the events leading up to the damage are exclusively within the knowledge and control of the defendant. To assist the plaintiff in these circumstances there has been evolved a rule of evidence known as res ipsa loquitur (the facts speak for themselves). Under this rule, where the only reasonable explanation of the events is that the defendant was negligent, the judge is justified in leaving the case to the jury and the jury is justified in finding negligence proved in fact. The rule has no application where all the facts are known and it only says that the jury *may* find negligence not that they must find negligence in a res ipsa loquitur situation.

From the cases it would appear that there are *three* requirements of the rule:

1   The defendant must have means of *knowledge* denied to the plaintiff.
2   The defendant must have *control* over the events which are alleged to be the cause of the damage (sometimes referred to as control over the 'vehicle of mischief').
3   The damage must be such that would not normally have happened if proper care had been shown by the defendant. Where there is an alternative reasonable explanation the doctrine will not apply and the plaintiff will be left to prove in the ordinary way all the ingredients of negligence. There will be no inference of negligence in his favour. Once the plaintiff has established a res ipsa situation any reasonable alternative explanation must be consistent with the absence of negligence in the defendant and the defendant must show that he has taken reasonable care. In a case where oxygen exploded in a pipeline the occupier of the premises failed to show that he had inspected the pipeline and was thus unable to rebut the inference of res ipsa loquitur. (*Colvilles Ltd v Devine* (1969), HL.)

A well-known illustration of the application of the res ipsa loquitur rule is to be found in the case of *Byrne v Boadle* (1863). A barrel of flour rolled out of an upper doorway of the defendant's warehouse and injured the plaintiff who was walking in the street below. If anyone knew what caused the flour to roll out, it would be the defendant (or one of his servants for whom he would be responsible in tort). The flour was in the control of the defendant. The only reasonable explanation of the flour descending on the plaintiff in this way was that the defendant had failed to take reasonable care. Although the plaintiff could not adduce any evidence of the defendant's negligence, other than proof of his injuries caused by the falling flour, it was held that the res ipsa loquitur rule applied and the jury was entitled to find negligence proved.

The following two cases form an interesting contrast. In *Mahon v Osborne* (1939) a swab was left in a patient's body after an operation and subsequently was the cause of considerable pain. The only reasonable explanation was that the person responsible for the supervision of the operation was negligent. Such person would know what went on and would be in a position to control the situation. The patient, who would wish to sue in negligence, would be unconscious at the material time and unable to give any evidence as to the negligent acts complained of, other than evidence as to his consequent suffering. Consequently it was held in this case that the doctrine applied. In *Fish v Kapur* (1948) a patient's jaw was found to be fractured after a dentist had extracted a tooth. The doctrine did not apply here because the dentist's negligence was not the only reasonable explanation of the fracture – quite possibly the plaintiff had a weak jaw. As the doctrine did not apply the patient was under the obligation of proving all three ingredients of the negligence.

Contributory negligence

Contributory negligence is said to exist where one party is in part the cause of the damage of which he complains. Before the Law Reform (Contributory Negligence) Act 1945 came into operation the rule was that a person who was in part the cause of his own injury could not recover in negligence. If the fault of both parties contributed to an accident neither could recover from the other for the damage done so long as there was some negligence on the part of both of them which could to some extent be said to be the cause of the accident. Thus contributory negligence of the plaintiff was a complete defence in an action based on negligence. This rule was altered by the Law Reform (Contributory Negligence) Act 1945. Under the Act the damages recoverable by a plaintiff who has negligently contributed to his own injury will be reduced in accordance with his own degree of fault. The court is to find and record the total damages recoverable if there had been no contributory negligence and then to award that sum to the plaintiff less the estimated proportion due to his own fault (s 1 (2)). Thus if A, driving his car in a westerly direction at night on the left hand side of the road but with his lights *off*, is involved in a collision with B who is travelling at great speed in the opposite direction and on the wrong side of the road and A is injured then A will be deemed to be guilty of contributory negligence. If, for example, his responsibility is assessed at one-third, and damages for his injuries are assessed at £1,200, the situation before the coming into operation of the 1945 Act would have been that B could have raised A's contributory negligence as a complete defence. The situation after the Act is that A will recover £800 as compensation for his loss. The actual words of the Act are as follows:

> 'Where any person suffers damage as the result partly of his own fault and partly of the fault of any other person or persons, a claim in respect of that damage shall not be defeated by reason of the fault of the person suffering the damage, but the damages recoverable in respect thereof shall be reduced to such extent as the court thinks just and equitable having regard to the claimant's share in the responsibility for the damage. . . .'

The Act has been held to apply only to cases where it can be shown that the contributory negligence accounted for at least 10% of the damages.

Another case illustrating the working of the contributory negligence rule is *Baker v Willoughby* (1969). A motor car struck a pedestrian who was walking across the road. For the last 200 yards travelled by the car the pedestrian had a clear view of the road. Neither the pedestrian nor the motorist took any evasive action. The trial judge held that the motorist was 75% to blame. On appeal against the apportionment of liability the Court of Appeal held that the parties were equally blameworthy.

In *Owens v Brimmell* (1976) it was held that a person is liable to be found guilty of contributory negligence if he travels as a passenger in a car with a driver he knows to be drunk.

Defences to an action in negligence

From the preceding discussion it will be seen that the defences to an action in negligence are: (i) volenti non fit injuria, (ii) that no duty of care was owed, (iii) that there was no breach of the duty of care, (iv) that even if there was a breach of the duty of care, this was not the cause of the injury, and (v) contributory negligence on the part of the plaintiff.

Difficulties in obtaining evidence

A major difficulty inherent in the tort system, particularly in relation to personal injuries caused by negligence, is that the scales are weighted against the plaintiff when it comes to establishing the necessary fault on the part of the defendant. Thus, it may be impossible to obtain the necessary evidence because, for example, witnesses cannot be traced or they have genuinely, or conveniently, forgotten relevant details or science is insufficiently developed to be able to detect the link between the defendant's conduct and the plaintiff's injuries. Another difficulty is caused by the emotional distress which often accompanies negligently inflicted injuries and which may dissuade the plaintiff from maintaining an action. A further weakness is based on the economics of the system. It may be prohibitively expensive for the individual to fight large commercial or state organisations. On the other hand, even though a plaintiff could succeed in an action the defendant might have no money and no insurance cover (the so-called 'man of straw') with which to satisfy a claim for damages. Furthermore, the need to engage the judicial system greatly increases the cost involved in recovering compensation.

To some extent these defects are mitigated by the existence of the social security system, private insurance and schemes like that operated by the Motor Insurers' Bureau whereby the victim of an uninsured or unidentified driver may obtain compensation from the Bureau. However, recognition of the grave defects of such a mixed compensation system has led to a more ambitious solution being adopted in New Zealand. There the Accident Compensation Acts of 1972 and 1973 established a no-fault, earnings-related, compensation scheme for persons suffering personal injuries caused by accident. The scheme is funded from various sources, levies being charged on motor vehicles, drivers' licences, employers and the self-employed. The 1972 Act abolished the tort action in respect of injury and death but the accident compensation scheme remains separate from New Zealand's social welfare system.

In 1974 the Royal Commission on Civil Liability and Compensation for Personal Injury under the chairmanship of Lord Pearson was established to review the United Kingdom system of compensation based upon a mixture of tort liability and social welfare provision. Its report, published in 1978 (Cmnd 7054), made almost two hundred specific recommendations but did not recommend the abolition of the tort system because it was thought just to make those at fault pay and there was a lack of evidence as to the likely cost of a social welfare scheme. In the event the government indicated its unwillingness to implement the recommendations and it seems likely that for the foreseeable future we shall have to continue with an inefficient and unjust method of compensating the victims of negligence.

Breach of statutory duty

A breach of statutory duty which results in injury to another person may be a tort actionable in damages at the suit of the person injured. At a time when statutory duties are being more frequently imposed upon us this aspect of our law is increasing in importance. Whether a breach of duty causing injury will in any particular case give rise to an action in damages is a question of interpretation for the courts to determine in the light of the normal rules of statutory interpretation. (See above, p 54.) Although a decision of the courts cannot be predicted with certainty the following considerations will usually apply in determining the intention of the legislature.

(i) Where the duty appears to be imposed for the benefit of the public as a whole it is usually the case that *Parliament did not intend to benefit any particular individual in damages.* The duty is here usually enforced by criminal proceedings. An example of this is to be found in the Trade Descriptions Act 1968, where a false trade description can be made the subject of a fine while the Act gives no civil remedy to a person who has bought goods in reliance on a false trade description.

(ii) *Parliament may intend an individual to have no remedy by way of damages.* A pecuniary penalty may be imposed as the sole remedy for breach of the duty. Thus where a penalty was imposed on a fire-fighting authority for failure to maintain adequate water pressure and a house was burnt out as a result of the fire authority's failure the house owner could gain no compensation (*Atkinson v Newcastle and Gateshead Waterwords Co* (1877)).

(iii) *Where a civil remedy in damages is available.* It is less likely that an action for breach of statutory duty will be held to exist.

(iv) *No action on a statute will lie unless the injured person is able to show that he belongs to the class of persons the statute was intended to protect and that the injury he suffered was what the statute intended to guard against.* In *Gorris v Scott* (1874) the plaintiff was able to show that his injuries were what Parliament intended to guard against. The plaintiff's sheep were swept overboard as a result of the defendant's failure to provide sheep pens aboard a ship. The purpose of the statutory requirement of sheep pens was to minimise the spread of disease among animals. The plaintiff failed to recover damages for the loss of the sheep.

Absolute statutory duties

It is always a question of construction whether the person on whom a statutory duty is imposed is to be liable absolutely for its breach (that is to say without fault on his part), or is to be liable only where he has himself been in some way negligent. In *Groves v Wimborne* (1898) a 15-year-old boy, employed in a factory, was injured when his hand became caught between two cogwheels in a machine. The relevant statute provided that the machine should have been fenced. It had not been fenced and the defendant on whom the duty had been imposed was liable for breach of statutory duty, without the plaintiff being obliged to show negligence by the defendant. The liability was absolute. This case is also interesting because a fine was imposed by the relevant Act for breach of the duty to fence and the court was empowered to order the fine to be paid to the boy. Nonetheless the court felt that Parliament had intended the person injured to be benefited and so gave damages for breach of statutory duty. (N.B. This term is sometimes referred to as 'statutory negligence'. This expression is a misnomer because, as *Groves v Wimborne* shows, the defendants' liability may be absolute). The Health and Safety at Work etc. Act 1974, s 15 gives power to the Secretary of State to make regulations to promote health and safety and s 47 indicates that, subject to anything to the contrary in such regulations, an action for breach of statutory duty will lie for failure to comply with such regulations.

Defences

It is the duty of the plaintiff to show that he was injured as a result of the breach of a statutory duty and that the breach of duty is actionable as a tort. Once this has been done it is then up to the defendant to raise any relevant defence. Where the duty is not absolute the defendant may show that he took reasonable care and thus discharged his duty. However, where the duty is absolute certain general defences, normally available, cease to be available to the defendant. The defence volenti non fit injuria is not available because no one can consent to the breach of an absolute statutory duty, for this would be to go contrary to Parliament's expressed will. Delegation to another is also no defence.

The contributory negligence of the plaintiff is, however, relevant as can be seen in *Uddin v Associated Portland Cement Manufacturers Ltd* (1965). A workman, who was injured by machinery that was unfenced contrary to s 14 of the Factories Act 1961, had left his work to catch a pigeon for his meal and was injured in so doing. Although his action for breach of statutory duty was successful, the defence of contributory negligence was also successful, the court holding the workman to be 80% responsible for his own injuries.

Occupiers' liability

This branch of the law is concerned with the duties owed by occupiers of premises to those who come on them, so far as the condition of the premises is concerned. The law used to divide entrants on land into two categories, 'visitors' (those who enter on land with permission) and 'trespassers' (those who enter without permission), prescribing the degree of care to be exercised by the occupier in respect of each category. The rules relating to visitors are mainly statutory, while those concerning trespassers were to be found in the common law until the Occupiers'

Liability Act 1984 included them in the new category of 'persons other than visitors'. We will consider first the law relating to visitors.

The Occupiers' Liability Act 1957 superseded a complicated set of common law rules. After the Act 'occupiers' of premises owe a duty to 'visitors' who are on the occupier's land with permission. The term 'visitors', therefore, has a very wide scope and would cover, for example, all the following persons present in a theatre: the actors and usherettes who are paid to be there, members of the audience who have paid to enter (i e those present under a contract), as well as people in the entrance hall enquiring about the price of tickets. Bus passengers, workmen on scaffolding, people examining or buying goods in shops, and friends invited to tea are all visitors too. Section 2 (1) lays down that ordinarily the occupier shall owe the same duty to all his visitors and it gives to this standard of behaviour the name of 'common duty of care'. This duty is defined in s 2 (2), which is the most important part of the Act, in the following terms:

> 'The common duty of care is a duty to take such care as in all the circumstances of the case is reasonable to see that the visitor will be reasonably safe in using the premises for the purposes for which he is invited or permitted to be there.'

Section 1 (3) defines 'premises' so as to include not only land and buildings, but even 'any fixed or moveable structure, including any vessel, vehicle or aircraft'. This means that, for example, if a passenger in an aeroplane is injured by falling through the defective floor while taking his place at an airport, he will be able to bring an action under the Act, although the Act will not extend to an accident caused, say, by a mistake of the pilot during flight. Section 2 (3) gives further guidance as to the degree of care required in two particular instances. Section 2 (3) (a), which is dealt with below, calls for extra care towards children, but s 2 (3) (b) indicates that an occupier may expect a person entering premises 'in the exercise of his calling' will beware of dangers inherent in it. This means, for example, that it would not normally be necessary to warn a plumber to beware of burst pipes, although it would be necessary to warn an electrician.

It will be observed that the common duty of care requires reasonable care of the visitor; there are two ways in which the occupier can carry out this duty; that is to say either by making the premises safe, or by giving warning of the danger. The effect of s 2 (4) (a) is that the warning must be an effective one if it is to absolve the occupier from liability for injury to a visitor who has ignored it. A notice in morse code or Provençal would be ineffective, and the same would apply to a warning given too late to be acted on. Before the Act an occupier was automatically liable for any tort of his independent contractor (see p 157, above) that caused injury to an invitee, but now s 2 (4) (b) has the effect of allowing the occupier to escape liability if he has 'acted reasonably in entrusting the work to an independent contractor', and has done what he could (if anything) to be sure the work was properly done. Thus in *O'Connor v Swan and Edgar Ltd* (1963), the plaintiff, who was working as a demonstrator on the premises of the first defendants who were not her employers, sued them when she was injured by a fall of plaster from the ceiling. The first defendants pleaded that they had employed the second defendants, a firm of plasterers, to do the work as independent contractors and were not guilty of any misconduct. They said that they were therefore entitled to escape liability by reason of s 2 (4) (b), and they succeeded in this defence. The second defendants who had been guilty of faulty workmanship were held liable in negligence. Section 2 (5) extends the principle of volenti non fit injuria (see p 143, above) to occupiers' liability. In *Bunker v Charles Brand & Son Ltd* (1969) main building contractors on the new Victoria underground line were occupiers of the tunnel and a machine in it. An employee of the sub-contractor was injured when he fell and was injured in trying to cross certain dangerous rollers on the machine which was at rest. It was held that ss 2 (4) and 2 (5) must be read together and that he was 50% to blame for the accident, the occupiers being also 50% to blame. He was awarded half the damages he had sustained. If a contract provides that the occupier is bound to let in persons who are 'strangers to the contract', eg if the occupier of a hall contracts with the Joint Matriculation Board for its use as an examination centre for the General Certificate of Education, then under s 3 (1) the occupier owes to these strangers (who are visitors) the common duty of care. The parties to the contract can include a provision entitling the strangers to a higher degree of care than the common duty of care, but that they cannot by their contract reduce the strangers' entitlement to anything less than the common duty of care.

Exclusion of liability

Since the Unfair Contract Terms Act 1977, ss 1 and 2, liability for negligence, including breach of the common duty of care under the Occupiers' Liability Act 1957, causing death or personal injury, cannot be excluded or restricted. Liability for other loss or damage can be excluded or restricted but only to the extent that such provision is reasonable.

Liability of landlords

Where a landlord is under an obligation to repair or maintain the premises let he owes a duty to all persons, visitors and others, who might reasonably be expected to be affected by defects in the premises. His duty is to take reasonable steps to ensure that such persons and their property are reasonably safe. A landlord will be liable for such defects as exist at the time the tenancy commences or arise later and which result from a failure by him of his obligation to repair or maintain the premises (Defective Premises Act 1972, overruling s 4 of the Occupiers' Liability Act 1957).

Child visitors

The cases establish that an occupier is liable if he fails to protect visitors from being lured towards some attractive object on his land, where the child is likely to be harmed by a hidden danger. An object of this kind such as a railway turntable is known as an 'allurement'. If the object is an obviously dangerous one, such as a pond, it will not be regarded as an allurement. An occupier is entitled to assume that very young children will be accompanied by those who will look after them, and he does his duty if he gives a warning sufficiently clear to be understood by somebody competent to look after them. This was decided in *Phipps v Rochester Corpn* (1955) where a boy of five years accompanied by his sister aged seven fell into a hole and broke his leg. He failed to recover damages because the occupier was entitled to assume that such young children would be in the charge of some competent person.

Liability to persons other than visitors

The Occupiers' Liability Act 1984 covers the situation where the person on land is not there as a visitor, e g he is a trespasser or a burglar. Generally the Act lays down a test of reasonableness. It defines an occupier and a visitor as in the 1957 Act and goes on to provide that an occupier owes a duty of care to a person other than a visitor where the occupier is

> 'aware of the danger or has reasonable grounds to believe that it exists; (ii) knows or has reasonable grounds to believe that the other is in the vicinity of the danger concerned or that he may come into the vicinity of the danger (in either case, whether the other has lawful authority for being in that vicinity or not); and, (iii) the risk is one against which, in all the circumstances of the case, he may reasonably be expected to offer the other some protection.'

The duty is not an absolute one but is to take such care as is reasonable in all the circumstances of the case to see that he does not suffer injury on the premises by reason of the danger concerned. The occupier of premises will be able to carry out his duty, and thus will not be liable to an injured person, 'by taking such steps as are reasonable in all the circumstances of the case to give warning of the danger concerned or to discourage persons from incurring the risk'.

The duty is expressly negatived in respect of persons who consent to run the risk. The Act imposes no duty in respect of highway users.

Exclusion of liability

The Unfair Contracts Terms Act 1977 places restrictions on the extent to which the liability of occupiers for death or personal injury may be excluded or limited (ss 1 and 2). The Occupiers' Liability Act 1984 negatives the application of ss 1 and 2 of the Act to the educational or recreational use of premises unless such use is part of the business use of the occupier of the dangerous premises which cause injury.

Trespass to the person

Trespass to the person may take the form of battery, assault or false imprisonment.

Battery

A battery is the intentional, or possibly negligent, application of force to another person without lawful justification. To constitute a battery the act of the defendant must be direct in the sense that the application of force must be a direct consequence of it. In *Fowler v Lanning* (1959) it was held that a plaintiff must prove either intention or negligence on the part of the defendant in an action for battery. The following are examples of battery: wounding a person with a sword or pistol, hitting somebody with the fist or a stick, throwing water or a stone at a person, pulling off a person's shoe, and probably shining a powerful beam of heat on him or a beam of light in his eyes; there is, however, some doubt about the two last-named examples. In *Nash v Sheen* (1953) a lady asked her hairdresser for a permanent wave but he applied a tone rinse to her scalp and this caused a skin complaint. It was held that the hairdresser was guilty of battery. Battery is actionable per se and substantial damages may be recovered even though no physical injury has been caused.

The defences to an action for battery include: (i) volenti non fit injuria, eg as in the case of participants in a boxing match; (ii) self-defence, provided that no more force than is reasonably necessary is used; (iii) necessity as in the case of *Leigh v Gladstone* (1909) where a prisoner on hunger strike was forcibly fed by warders to save her life; the warders were not liable for battery; (iv) lawful chastisement such as the punishment of a child by a parent or teacher; (v) inevitable accident, as in *Stanley v Powell* (see p 146, above); (vi) the ejection of a trespasser from land with only reasonable force; (vii) a battery committed while upholding the criminal law as, for example, where a citizen assists a constable to arrest a criminal; (viii) it is not a battery to touch a person merely to attract his attention.

The remedy for battery is an action for damages.

Assault

An assault is an act which intentionally or negligently creates in a person's mind a reasonable fear that he is about to suffer a battery. To constitute an assault there must be some movement. Therefore in the case of *Innes v Wylie* (1844) where a policeman stood still and acted as a closed door so that the plaintiff could not pass, there was held to be no assault. Words alone cannot constitute an assault but they can prevent an act that would otherwise be an assault from amounting to one, as in *Turbervell v Savadge* (1669) where a man reached for his sword and said 'if it were not assize time, I would not take such language from you'. Since it was assize time the words prevented the act from being an assault. It is an assault to point a loaded pistol at someone, and it is probably an assault to point an unloaded pistol where the victim does not know that the gun is not loaded. (*R v St. George* (1840).) There may be an assault even though the defendant in trying to commit a battery is prevented from doing so. This was the case in *Stephens v Myers* (1830) where the defendant, who tried to get at the plaintiff in a meeting to hit him but was stopped by others present, was held liable for assault.

An assault and a battery often occur in the same incident, as in the usual case where a person sees another lift his hand and then feels the blow. This is not always the case for there may be an assault alone, as in *Stephens v Myers*, or a battery alone as, for example, where a person receives a blow from behind without any prior warning to operate on his mind.

The defences to an action for assault include (i) volenti non fit injuria, (ii) self-defence, and (iii) necessity. The remedy is an action for damages.

False imprisonment

False (wrongful) imprisonment is committed when, without lawful justification, a person is intentionally or negligently restrained from going wherever he wants to. There are various ways in which this tort can be committed. Thus in the absence of any legal right it is false imprisonment to lock a person in a room, to make him stay in an open field by threatening him with a rifle or to compel him by force or threats to walk along a street. The threat may be express or implied. A wrongful arrest is a false imprisonment. There is no false imprisonment unless all ways out are barred. Thus in *Bird v Jones* (1845) on a bridge overlooking the river Thames the defendants wrongfully fenced off a part of the footpath before a boat race and made a charge for admission. The plaintiff climbed into the enclosure and walked along the fenced off footpath but was prevented from leaving by the route he wished to use, although he was told that he could take another way out. It was held that the defendants had not committed false imprisonment. In *Robinson v Balmain New Ferry Co Ltd* (1910) there was a ferry that was approached by a wharf. A penny was charged to persons using the ferry when they entered or left the wharf. The plaintiff paid a penny to enter but, as he had just missed a ferry, he wished to leave the wharf, and the defendants refused to let him out unless he paid another penny. He sued for false imprisonment, but the Judicial Committee of the Privy Council held that the defendants were not obliged to let him out free of charge, since he had entered under a contract that envisaged that he would leave by the ferry and a penny was a reasonable sum to ask in return for letting him out. The action failed. In *Herd v Weardale Coal Co Ltd* (1915) a miner went down a mine to work but, in breach of his contract with the defendants, refused to do certain work and, with others, asked to be taken to the surface before the end of his shift. The defendants refused to let him come up for 20 minutes. In an action for false imprisonment the House of Lords held that the principle of volenti non fit injuria was applicable and the action failed.

It was held in *Meering v Grahame-White Aviation Co Ltd* (1919) that a man may be falsely imprisoned without knowing it and that this might happen while he is sleeping, drunk or a lunatic, or if, while he is in a room, the key is turned in the lock without his knowing it. In *Herring v Boyle* (1834) knowledge was held to be irrelevant.

Powers of arrest. The law on this subject is complicated and somewhat uncertain. Although most arrests are made by policemen, there are, under the Criminal Law Act 1967, 'arrestable offences' (those for which the sentence is fixed by law (i e murder, treason, and piracy with violence), or for which a statute imposes imprisonment on a first offender for at least five years, and attempts to commit these offences), for which anybody may effect an arrest (see p 18, above). Any unlawful arrest amounts to a false imprisonment. An arrest may become a false imprisonment if the person arrested does not receive proper treatment after the arrest. It was held by the House of Lords in *Christie v Leachinsky* (1947) that normally a person who is arrested must be told the true ground of the arrest at the time he is taken into custody. If no reason, or an untrue reason, is given there will be false imprisonment. It is not necessary to give a reason where this is impracticable, as when the person arrested is fighting or running away. A man arrested by a private person must be brought before a magistrate or a police officer within a reasonable time, but not necessarily at once. This was decided in *John Lewis & Co Ltd v Tims* (1952). In this case the plaintiff and her daughter went into the defendant's shop and when the daughter was seen stealing both were arrested by the defendant's store detectives. They were detained for between 20 and 60 minutes while the managing director heard an account of what had passed and decided to prosecute. The police were then called. It was held by the House of Lords that there had been no false imprisonment as the defendants had acted reasonably.

Defences.   The defences to an action for false imprisonment include, (i) volenti non fit injuria, as for example, if a prison visitor agrees to be locked in a cell with a prisoner, and (ii) mistake. The defence of mistake is not available to everybody who effects an arrest by mistake, but it may be set up by a policeman who makes an arrest for a crime which has not been committed if he acts honestly in the reasonable belief that the person arrested had committed the crime.

Remedies.   False imprisonment is said to be 'actionable per se' which means that an action may be brought against the person who has committed the tort even though no actual damage can be proved. In such a case nominal damages would be awarded (see p 117, above). The remedies are, (i) self-help, in the sense of breaking out, (ii) application for a writ of habeas corpus, and (iii) an action for damages.

Trespass to goods

The Torts (Interference with Goods) Act 1977 collectively describes torts causing damage to goods as 'wrongful interference with goods' though it neither replaces nor redefines most of them. Thus, trespass to goods may be defined as an intentional physical interference with the possession of goods without lawful justification. The interference must be direct and forcible and the tort is actionable per se. This tort takes three principal forms. These are, (i) taking the goods out of possession of the person entitled to them, (ii) damaging or otherwise altering the physical condition of the goods and, (iii) intermeddling with the goods, as for instance by moving them about. It is the tort of trespass to goods to scratch a car door, to throw a stone at a dog or to tear a book. Although the interference will usually have to be direct and forcible to constitute trespass to goods, there are certain cases that differ from the majority in this respect. It has been held to be trespass to chase cattle even though the defendant has not actually touched them. If somebody puts poison into a cat's milk it is undecided whether this will be merely trespass to the milk or trespass to the cat as well. The argument against it being trespass to the cat is that there was no direct and forcible interference with the animal.

If goods are damaged in a highway accident the plaintiff will be assumed by the law to have consented to run the risk of damage to his goods arising from pure accident due to highway conditions. This is an application of the maxim volenti non fit injuria (see p 143, above). If the plaintiff is to recover, therefore, it will be necessary for him to prove negligence on the part of the defendant. This is the effect of the decision in *Holmes v Mather* (1875), a case of trespass to the person, and subsequent decisions.

In order to sue, a plaintiff must show either that he was in possession of the goods or that he was in a position equivalent to that of a possessor (i e that he had 'constructive' possession). In *Bailiffs of Dunwich v Sterry* (1831) the plaintiffs were entitled to take possession of the goods from wrecked ships and in an action against a defendant who had taken a barrel of whisky from a wreck it was held that the plaintiffs were in constructive possession of the wreck and entitled to sue in trespass to goods.

The defences to an action for trespass to goods include, (i) volenti non fit injuria which applies where a possessor agrees to his goods being moved or used, (ii) self-defence, e g if a person being attacked by a dog injured it, and (iii) inevitable accident. The defence of inevitable accident was first upheld in *National Coal Board v Evans* (1951). In this case an electric cable belonging to the plaintiffs was buried in land occupied by the local authority, and had been placed in position without the knowledge or consent of the local authority. A mechanical excavator owned by the defendants which was digging on the land of the local authority damaged the cable. Since neither the local authority nor the defendants knew of the cable and because there had been neither an intention to damage the cable nor any negligence, the defendants were held not liable, the damage being an inevitable accident.

The remedy for trespass to goods is an action for damages.

Trespass to land

Trespass to land may be defined as the intentional or negligent interference with the possession of land of another without lawful justification. Since this is a tort against possession and not against ownership, an owner who is not in possession cannot sue a trespasser. Thus if A owns the fee simple and leases his land to B, then if C walks across the land without permission, B only can sue him because he is the person in possession. Indeed B may also sue A if he enters the land without B's permission. Trespass to land is actionable per se, which means that an action may be brought against a trespasser even though he has not caused any actual damage to the land. In such a case the person in possession would be awarded nominal damages (see p 117, above).

The forms of trespass to land

To constitute trespass the interference must be forcible and direct which means that it must be physical interference. The interference may take one or more of the following three forms:

1 *Entering on land*

It is a trespass to enter on land in the possession of another without lawful justification.

It is therefore a trespass to walk on to the land of another without permission even if this is done in ignorance. It is no defence to show that the trespasser crossed an unmarked boundary or that he thought that he owned the land. If, however, the person who found himself on the land of another had not intended to go there at all, as for example if he were thrown on, he would not be liable.

Trespass by abuse of right of entry.   If a person is allowed to go on a certain part of some land and goes on another part, or if he is allowed to go on for a certain purpose and does something outside that purpose, he will become a trespasser by abusing his right of entry. Thus in *Harrison v Duke of Rutland* (1893) the Duke owned certain moors and the road that led across them. He used the moor for grouse shooting and permitted members of the public to use the road for travelling on from one place to another. The plaintiff, to annoy the Duke, went on the road and by waving his umbrella frightened away the grouse that the Duke and his party were about to shoot. The Duke's servants then held the plaintiff on the ground for a while because he would not stop his tactics. In an action for trespass to the person the Duke successfully pleaded that the plaintiff, because of his actions, was a trespasser on the road.

Trespass ab initio (from the beginning).   This is a form of trespass that was originally made available to those who needed a remedy against abuse of authority. The rule is that if a person enters on land by authority of the law and while there does an act which is an abuse of his right to enter, he will be regarded as having been a trespasser, not merely from the time he did the wrongful act, but from the beginning of his being on the land. The two distinctive points about this type of trespass are, (i) that the entry must have been made originally by authority of the law, as in the case of members of the public entering an inn under their common law right to do so or of a constable entering premises by authority of a search warrant, and (ii) that the wrongful act must have been something positive and not a mere omission. This is illustrated by the *Six Carpenters' Case* (1610) where six carpenters who had entered an inn and consumed a quart of wine and some bread refused to pay the price of eightpence. It was held that they were not trespassers ab initio because they were guilty only of an omission.

2 *Remaining on land*

It is a trespass to remain on land in the possession of another after permission to stay has ended.

A person who is lawfully on land in the possession of another and who refuses to go when the permission is withdrawn becomes a trespasser. If, however, a man has obtained possession of land by the grant of a lease and will not leave when the lease expires, he does not become a trespasser.

This is so because, by refusing to go, the tenant retains possession and the landlord cannot sue anybody in trespass until he regains possession himself. The landlord will nevertheless be able to regain possession by an action for the recovery of the land and may sue for mesne profits (see p 182, below).

3 *Placing objects on land*

It is a trespass to put any object on land in the possession of another without permission.

In the ordinary case of trespass where a person walks across land or digs a hole on land in the possession of another, the plaintiff is entitled to bring only one action. If, on the other hand, a person remains on land or wrongfully puts something on land, this is said to be a 'continuing trespass' and a fresh cause of action arises each day while the intrusion lasts. If therefore a trespasser dug a hole on the land of A and put the soil on the land of B, A would be entitled to bring only one action against the trespasser in which he would have to claim all his damages but B could bring successive actions against the trespasser until the soil had been removed.

Trespass above and beneath the surface of the land

Possession of land carries with it possession of the subsoil and possession of the airspace above. If therefore a man tunnels horizontally from his land under the land of the National Coal Board to take coal, this will be trespass. Similarly it was held in *Kelsen v Imperial Tobacco Co Ltd* (1957) that to erect an advertising sign projecting into the airspace above the plaintiff's land was a trespass. As far as aircraft are concerned, the Civil Aviation Act 1982, s 76 which applies to all civil aircraft, provides that no action shall lie in respect of trespass or nuisance for flights over any property at a reasonable height. In considering whether the height is reasonable or not, regard must be had to weather and other circumstances. The same section makes the aircraft owner liable for all damage caused by it, or by anything falling from it, while it is taking off, flying or landing. The plaintiff need not prove that the aircraft owner was negligent or acted intentionally, and the owner will be liable as if what happened had occurred through his wilful act, or default.

In *Lord Bernstein of Leigh v Skyviews and General Ltd* (1977), where the defendant's aircraft flew a few hundred feet over the plaintiff's house and took a photograph, a copy of which was offered for sale to the plaintiff, there was held to be no trespass to land.

Remedies for trespass to land

There are a number of ways in which this tort can be committed, and therefore a variety of remedies are needed. The following are some of the types of interference that constitutes trespass to land: entering land and then leaving; entering land and remaining; entering land and remaining after having ejected the person in possession; throwing things on land; removing doors from a building; taking plants from the ground; flying unreasonably low; tunnelling under land; letting cattle go upon another's land.

The possible remedies are as follows:

1 *Action for damages.*   If the defendant goes on land without doing any damage, as for example by walking on a concrete path without permission, nominal damages will be awarded (see p 117, above). If he does damage, compensatory or exemplary damages may be awarded (see p 118, above).

2 *Action for mesne profits.*   Any person who has been debarred from enjoying possession of his land may bring an action to recover his loss. Such an action, which is called an 'action for mesne profits' may, for example, be brought by a person who has been wrongfully ejected by force from his land.

3 *Injunction.*   In appropriate cases an injunction may be obtained restraining a named person from trespassing.

4 *Action for the recovery of land.*   This is an action by means of which any person wrongfully dispossessed of land may sue for its return to him. If the court orders the land to be returned to the plaintiff and the defendant refuses to carry out the order of the court, the plaintiff can apply to the court to direct its officers to remove the defendant forcibly. This action is sometimes conveniently, but incorrectly, called the action of ejectment, which was the name of the writ used before the abolition of the old forms of action.

5 *Ejection of a trespasser.*   The person in possession of land on which a trespasser has made a peaceable entry may, after he has requested the trespasser to go and allowed him time to get out, remove the trespasser if he fails to go. The occupier must not use more force than is reasonably necessary; if he does use too much force this will be the tort of trespass to the person of the trespasser. Alternatively, he or his servants may control the trespasser's movements as in *Harrison v Duke of Rutland* (p 180, above). If a trespasser is entering or has entered by force, he may be immediately forced out.

6 *Forcible entry and ejection.*   A person wrongfully dispossessed of land or prevented from entering land to which he has a right of possession may enter with no more force than reasonably necessary and may eject the trespasser (or other person in possession including a tenant who has refused to go at the end of the tenancy) together with the goods of the trespasser. This was decided in *Hemmings v Stoke Poges Golf Club* (1920)

where the plaintiff who was the tenant of a cottage owned by the defendants refused to go when his tenancy was lawfully ended by a notice to quit. The defendants, without unnecessary force, removed the plaintiff and his furniture and were held not liable for trespass to land or trespass to the person of the plaintiff (a person acting nowadays like the defendants might however be liable to criminal proceedings under the Criminal Law Act 1977). In respect of premises let as a dwelling, the law has been changed by the Protection from Eviction Act 1977, s 3. This provides that tenants who remain in possession after the expiration of a lease may be turned out only by means of court proceedings.

Defences to an action for trespass to land

In considering the defences to trespass to land, or any other tort, it is necessary to differentiate between general defences (see p 143, above), which are those available in respect of a number of torts, and the particular defences which relate only to one tort. The general defences which are available in respect of trespass to land are volenti non fit injuria, self-defence, necessity, and statutory authority. The most important statute affording a defence is the Civil Aviation Act 1982, s 76 mentioned above. Some of the particular defences have already been alluded to. For example it is a defence to an action for trespass to land to prove that the entry was made by a person entitled to possession peaceably or with reasonable force only, as in *Hemmings v Stoke Poges Golf Club* (above). Similarly it is a defence to prove that a highway was being used for lawful transit; the defendant in *Harrison v Duke of Rutland* (p 180, above) could not prove this. The following particular defences must be especially noted:

1 *Entries justified by law.* These include entry by a court bailiff to seize goods, entry by a policeman into a public house to end a breach of the peace, and many other similar entries.

2 *Jus tertii.* There is a rule that a person claiming land from another, who is in possession of it, can succeed only by showing that his title is stronger than that of the person in possession. If it is shown by the person in possession, or if it appears from the evidence at the trial, that the land rightfully belongs neither to the person in possession nor to the person claiming the land (but to a third person), this will be a good defence. This was decided in *Doe d. Carter v Barnard* (1849) where the evidence put forward by Mary Carter, who had been turned out of certain land by Barnard, was held by the court to indicate that neither of them was entitled to the land. Therefore Barnard was allowed to retain the land as against Mary Carter. This rule, which is called the doctrine of *Doe d. Carter v Barnard*, has an exception. If a tenant has taken a lease and it turns out that the landlord had no right to grant the lease, the tenant is not permitted to set up the defence of jus tertii against his landlord.

3 *Licence.*   It is a defence to an action in trespass to land to show that the land is being used under a lease or under a licence. A lease gives the right to exclusive occupation of the land, while a licence is a less extensive right that permits a person to go on land without giving him any interest in it. The person granting the licence is known as the licensor and the person receiving it is the licensee. A licence is best described in a negative way by saying that it is a permission to do something that would otherwise be a trespass. The following are examples of licensees: students in a classroom, a theatre audience and a hotel guest. If a licence is validly terminated and the licensee refuses to go he becomes at once a trespasser (in this, as we have seen, he differs from a tenant who refuses to go). Licences may be of two types, bare licences, which are those granted without consideration (see p 225, below) and contractual licences. It is settled that bare licences may be revoked at any time by the licensor but there is some uncertainty as to whether contractual licences may be revoked or not. It would appear from *Winter Garden Theatre (London) Ltd v Millennium Productions Ltd* (1948) that this will depend on the terms of the contract and the circumstances of the case.

Nuisance

There are two types of nuisance, public nuisance and private nuisance, and they have little in common.

Public nuisance

In *A-G v P.Y.A. Quarries Ltd* (1957) a public nuisance was described as an act or omission which materially affects the reasonable comfort and convenience of life of a class of Her Majesty's subjects. The requirement that a class of people must be affected means that if what is done will affect only one or two people, it cannot be a public nuisance. It is not possible to say exactly how many persons there must be to constitute a class; this will depend on the circumstances of the case. There are many types of public nuisance and there is only one feature that they all have in common, namely that every public nuisance is a crime. It is this fact that constitutes one of the main differences between public and private nuisances, for private nuisances are never crimes as well. Examples of public nuisances are selling impure food, obstructing a public highway or public right of way and carrying on an offensive trade. The importance of public nuisance in the law of tort lies in the fact that if any member of the public can show that a public nuisance exists, and that he has suffered some special loss beyond the discomfort or inconvenience suffered by the public at large, he can succeed in an action in tort against the person creating the public nuisance. Thus in *Campbell v Paddington*

Corpn (1911) the defendants were held liable in public nuisance when they wrongfully obstructed the highway by a stand on the occasion of Edward VII's funeral procession so that the view from the plaintiff's windows was blocked and she was unable to make a profit by letting spectators view the procession from her premises. In most cases of public nuisance there is an interference with public rights that continues for a considerable length of time, and it is sometimes suggested that an isolated incident cannot constitute a public nuisance, but the better opinion appears to be that this is not so. This in *Midwood & Co Ltd v Manchester Corpn* (1905) a sudden explosion caused by the fusing of an electric main was held to be a public nuisance.

Many cases of public nuisance arise in connection with highways. It has long been the rule that if a local authority, which is charged with the responsibility for maintaining a highway, carried out its work badly, it may be held liable in public nuisance for damage arising from its workmanship (misfeasance). On the other hand, if a highway authority let a highway get into a dangerous condition and caused damage by doing nothing (nonfeasance), it was not liable. This rule affording immunity to highway authorities for nonfeasance was abolished by the Highways (Miscellaneous Provisions) Act 1961, s 1, now replaced by the Highways Act 1980, s 58. A highway authority is now liable for damage arising from the non-repair of a highway but under the Act it may plead as a defence that it has taken reasonable care to secure that the highway was not dangerous, taking into account various matters, such as the character of the highway and the traffic expected to use it. Not every obstruction of a highway amounts to a public nuisance and if the highway is obstructed for such a purpose as building a house or repairing a gas main, then there will be no public nuisance provided that the amount of the obstruction and the length of time for which it lasts is reasonable. If something projects above the highway from land adjoining the highway, this will not constitute a public nuisance if no obstruction is caused. In *Noble v Harrison* (1926) the branch of a tree that overhung the highway suddenly fell and damaged a passing motor coach. The owner of the land on which the tree stood was held not liable because the defect in the tree could not have been discovered by a reasonably careful examination. In *British Road Services Ltd v Slater* (1964) the defendant occupied land adjoining the highway. A tree stood on the land and protruded over the highway for a distance of two feet at a height of 16 feet. The plaintiff's lorry was carrying a load, the top of which was 16 feet 4 inches from the ground and, while trying to pass another lorry, this load hit the tree causing damage. It was held that although the tree constituted a nuisance the defendant was not liable because he was not aware that it was a nuisance and could not in the circumstances have been expected to realise that any nuisance existed.

There are two sets of remedies for public nuisance. In its criminal aspect, public nuisance may give rise to a prosecution or to an application for an injunction by the Attorney General to restrain the defendant from committing the crime. In its civil aspect public nuisance may be remedied by an action for an injunction or damages, or both, by the person suffering damage.

Private nuisance

This tort was defined by Professor Winfield as unlawful interference with a person's use or enjoyment of land, or of some right over or in connection with it. There are the following important differences between a public and a private nuisance: (i) a private nuisance is not a crime, (ii) a private nuisance may be committed by interfering with only one person's rights, (iii) the unlawful act in private nuisance must be connected with land and (iv) there is some doubt in private nuisance whether damages for personal injuries are recoverable whereas there is no such doubt in public nuisance.

The essence of private nuisance is interference with the enjoyment of land. There are two ways in which land may be enjoyed. These are, firstly, by occupying land and, secondly, by exercising some right over land occupied by another. A right over the land of another is known as a servitude and the mot important type of servitude is an easement (a right to cross the land of another). It follows that there are two types of private nuisance, interference with the enjoyment of land occupied by the plaintiff and interference with servitudes.

(a) Interference with servitudes

Although most of the law concerning private nuisance deals with interference with the enjoyment of land occupied by the plaintiff, it should be borne in mind that interference with any of the following servitudes constitutes a private nuisance: the use of a private right of way, a right to light flowing through a window, a right of support, i e a right to have one's land held in place by adjoining land.

(b) Interference with the enjoyment of land occupied by the plantiff

For an action to succeed in respect of this type of nuisance, three essentials must be established by the plaintiff. These are as follows:

(i)   There must be an indirect interference with the enjoyment of the land by letting any of the following enter the land of the plaintiff, namely, branches or roots of trees, smells, smoke, gas, heat, vibrations, noise, germs of disease or water. The courts may extend this list.

(ii)   There must be actual damage to the plaintiff consisting of either physical injury to the land or interference with the use of the land

causing discomfort or inconvenience to those in possession.
(iii)   The interference must be unlawful.

The three essentials will be examined separately.

(i) With regard to the first essential it will be noticed that the type of interference required to constitute nuisance will generally be harm done by something intangible or harm caused by a known process of nature.

(ii) With regard to the second essential, an example of interference consisting of physical injury to land is furnished by the case of *St. Helen's Smelting Co Ltd v Tipping* (1865) where the owners of a copper-smelting works were held liable to the owner of land whose crops were damaged by fumes from the works. An example of interference with the use of land may be seen in *Bliss v Hall* (1838) where an action in nuisance succeeded against a candle maker whose trade caused noxious vapours, fumes and stenches to invade the plaintiff's land.

(iii) The third essential, that of unlawfulness, is more difficult to establish than the other two because, in order to decide whether or not an interference is unlawful, a court may have to take into consideration one or more of the following factors: (i) reasonableness, (ii) sensitivity, (iii) locality, (iv) duration, (v) malice.

With regard to reasonableness the law seeks to preserve a proper balance between the right of a landowner to use his property as he likes and the right of his neighbours to freedom from interference. The standard the law aims at preserving is that of reasonable comfort judged by the views of ordinary people. With regard to sensitivity, the position is that a person who is more likely than others to suffer cannot, because of his vulnerability, impose an extra burden on others. Thus a person with a keen sense of smell or acute hearing cannot succeed in an action in nuisance if an ordinary person in the same circumstances would have remained undisturbed. In *Robinson v Kilvert* (1889) the plaintiff was unsuccessful in his action when he claimed damages because his unusually sensitive brown paper diminished in value when stored in premises above a cellar heated by the defendant to a temperature that would have been harmless to most goods. Locality is an important factor in determining the question of reasonableness. In *Sturges v Bridgman* (1879) it was said that what would be a nuisance in Belgrave Square would not necessarily be so in Bermondsey. A person in a town cannot expect country air or silence, and the standard of comfort protected by the law varies from place to place. If the interference is of short duration it is less likely to amount to a nuisance than if it continues for a long time. Malice is not an essential ingredient in nuisance but it may be relevant to the question of reasonableness. Thus in *Christie v Davey* (1893) the plaintiff taught music and held musical parties in his house which adjoined that of the defendant. The defendant, acting maliciously, blew whistles, beat trays, shrieked and hammered on the wall separating the houses while lessons and parties were going on. An injunction was granted to restrain interference by the defendant because of the way in which the nuisance arose. See also *Hollywood Silver Fox Farm v Emmett* (1936) (p 143, above).

Persons who may sue in nuisance

Only a person in *possession* of land can sue in nuisance, although a reversioner (a person entitled to possession at a future time) can sue in respect of a nuisance that permanently injures the land and reduces the value of his future interest. A tenant could sue for nuisance, but a licensee (see p 184, above) could not.

Persons who may be sued in nuisance

Depending upon the circumstances there are various persons who may be liable to be sued in respect of the creation of a nuisance. In most cases a nuisance originates on land near to that of the plaintiff and the plaintiff will usually be able to sue one or more of the following persons:

(i) *The creator of the nuisance.*   This would include a person who starts a nuisance on land he is occupying and then gives up possession of it before he is sued.

(ii) *The person in possession of the premises when the nuisance comes.*   He may be liable not only for his own wrongful acts but also for the acts of certain categories of persons coming on his land. These include the following: (a) acts of his servants, (b) acts of his licensees (see p 184, above), (c) acts of a trespasser provided that he knew or should have known of them. This was laid down in *Sedleigh-Denfield v O'Callagan* (1940) where a trespasser entered the defendants' land and put a pipe in a ditch. The entrance to the pipe was protected by a grating laid by the trespasser, but this grating was unsatisfactory and after three years the pipe became blocked so that the land of the plaintiffs was flooded. The defendants were held liable for the act of the trespasser because they knew of the pipe and ought to have realised that the adjoining land might be flooded.

(iii) *The landlord of the person in possession.*   The landlord will be liable if he permits his tenant to commit a nuisance or if he lets premises knowing that a nuisance originates from them.

Defences to private nuisance

It is no defence to an action in nuisance that the defendant is carrying on a trade that benefited the public or that the land from which the nuisance emanated is suitable for the purpose which led to the nuisance. Neither is it a defence that, despite all the skill and care of the defendant, the nuisance was unavoidable; because the rule is that, if something cannot be done without causing a nuisance, then in the absence of statutory authority or the consent of those suffering damage, it may not be done at all. It is not a defence to show that the plaintiff came to the nuisance. Thus in *Sturges v Bridgman* (1879) a confectioner had for more than 20 years, by using pestles and mortars in the course of his trade, caused noise and vibrations in the adjoining garden of a physician. This did not cause the physician any damage until he built a consulting room at the end of his garden. The physician succeeded in an action for an injunction despite the fact that after a nuisance has been in continuous existence for 20 years a right to continue it is acquired (see below). The point was that although there had been an interference for 20 years, this interference did not amount to a nuisance until damage was caused in respect of the new consulting room. A similar defence was raised in *Miller v Jackson* (1977), below.

The defences to an action in nuisance are as follows: (i) volenti non fit injuria, (ii) statutory authority, (iii) that the nuisance was due to the act of a stranger and that the defendant neither knew nor could be expected to know of it, (iv) that the nuisance was caused by an unobservable process of nature such as a subsidence of land, and (v) that the nuisance had been in continuous existence for 20 years (Prescription Act 1832).

Remedies for private nuisance

The usual remedy sought is an injunction to restrain the defendant from continuing the nuisance. However, an injunction will not be given in all cases where nuisance is proved. In *Miller v Jackson* (1977) a cricket club had used their ground for over 70 years; from time to time balls were hit for six onto nearby farmland. A house was put up on an estate on the farmland and cricket balls sometimes smashed its windows. The tenants could not use the garden while cricket was played. Although the Court of Appeal held the club liable in nuisance and negligence it refused, in the exercise of its equitable discretion, to grant an injunction against the playing of cricket. The public hardship of losing cricket weighing more than the private hardship of not being able to use the garden during games of cricket. In *Kennaway v Thompson* (1980) the Court of Appeal, refusing to follow *Miller v Jackson*, rejected the public interest argument.

It is possible to sue instead, or in addition, for damages. The other remedy for nuisance is called abatement. This is the ending of the nuisance by the party affected. It is lawful for an occupier of land to cut roots and branches that cross his boundary without giving any previous notice to the owner of the tree. It is also lawful to enter the land of the party causing the nuisance to remove an obstruction to a right of way, to take away a fence shutting out light to which the party affected is entitled, or to extinguish a fire than threatens the property of the abator (as the person carrying out an abatement is called). In some of these cases of entry on the land of another, however, prior notice must be given.

Nuisance contrasted with trespass to land

Nuisance	Trespass to Land
A tort against enjoyment of land	A tort against possession of land
The injury done must be indirect	The injury done must be direct
Actionable only on proof of actual damage	Actionable per se
Usually consists of more than one act	Consists of one act only – each new act is a new trespass
Public nuisance is a crime at common law	Trespass to land is not a crime at common law

Defamation

The most widely accepted definition of defamation is the one formulated by Professor Winfield who said:

> 'defamation is the publication of a statement which tends to lower a person in the estimation of right-thinking members of society generally; or which tends to make them shun or avoid that person'.

Only a false statement can amount to defamation. The word 'statement' in the definition has an extended meaning and includes words, visual images, gestures, and any other methods of signifying meaning.

Libel and slander

Defamation takes two forms, libel and slander. The differences between them are, firstly, that libel is a defamatory statement published in a permanent form, while slander is a defamatory statement published in a transient form. The following types of publication are classified as libel: (i) writing, (ii) printing, (iii) pictures, (iv) the placing of a wax figure of a person near similar figures of convicted murderers in a 'chamber of horrors' (*Monson v Tussauds Ltd* (1894)), (v) making a defamatory statement in a sound film (*Youssoupoff v Metro-Goldwyn-Mayer Pictures Ltd* (1934)).

The following types of publication are classified as slander: (i) word of mouth, (ii) gestures. The following types of publication resemble both libel and slander and it is not possible to say, in the absence of a precedent, under which heading they should be classified, although it seems more likely that they amount to libel: (i) gramophone records, (ii) a parrot that is taught to say defamatory words in public. It should be noted that mere insults or abuse do not amount to defamation since, although they may hurt a man's feelings, they do not affect his reputation.

The second difference between libel and slander is that some libels amount to a crime, where they tend to provoke a breach of the peace, but slander can only be a tort.

The third difference between libel and slander is that libel is actionable per se (without proof of actual damage) but slander is actionable only on proof of actual damage except in certain cases, e g an imputation that the plaintiff has committed a crime punishable by imprisonment or that he is suffering from a disease likely to make others avoid him socially.

At common law it has not been settled whether defamation published by radio or television is libel or slander. The Defamation Act 1952 provides that words and visual images broadcast for *general* reception are to be treated as publication in permanent form (i e as libel). This covers BBC and ITV broadcasts but not such transmissions as messages from police cars to one another.

The Theatres Act 1968, s 4, provides that in general, the publication of words in the course of a performance or play shall be treated as publication in permanent form.

The proof of defamation

In order to establish that the tort of defamation has been committed against him, the plaintiff must prove the existence of the following essential elements of the tort: (i) that the statement is untrue in fact, (ii) that the statement was defamatory, (iii) that the statement referred to him, (iv) that the statement was published by the defendant, (v) in appropriate cases, that he suffered damage. These points are dealt with in order.

(i) *Untrue in fact.* Although a true statement may be defamatory in the sense outlined below it cannot constitute the tort of defamation.

(ii) *Proof that the statement was defamatory.* In many cases defamation actions are tried by a judge and jury and both must be convinced in different degrees. The function of the judge is to decide whether or not the statement could be regarded as defamatory. If he decides that it could, the function of the jury is to say whether or not the statement is in fact defamatory. Words may be defamatory in their ordinary meaning but in some cases words that seem on the face of them to be innocent may be defamatory because they have some secondary or hidden meaning. A defamatory statement conveyed by a secondary or hidden meaning is called an innuendo. It is for the jury to decide whether or not the statement was defamatory by reason of an innuendo. In *Tolley v J. S. Fry & Sons Ltd* (1931) an amateur golfer who was not allowed to accept money for advertising found that the defendants, without his knowledge, had published an advertisement containing a caricature of him together with a verse praising their chocolate. The plaintiff succeeded in proving that the advertisement amounted to a defamatory statement by way of innuendo; the secondary meaning of the advertisement was that Tolley had accepted money for appearing in it and had thereby prostituted his amateur status.

The requirement that the plaintiff be lowered in the estimation of right-thinking members of society generally is illustrated by *Byrne v Deane* (1937). The police raided a golf club and removed an illegal gambling machine and on the club notice board there appeared a verse that included the words 'But he who gave the game away may he byrnn in hell and rue the day'. The plaintiff sued the club alleging that the verse imputed that he had informed the police about the machine and further that such a statement was defamatory. It was held that although the statement might lower him in the estimation of the club members, it would no do so in the estimation of right-thinking members of society and the action failed.

(iii) *Proof that the statement referred to the plaintiff.* The plaintiff may be named in the statement. If there is only a description, the plaintiff must prove that it refers to him; thus in *J'Anson v Stuart* (1787) a newspaper spoke of a swindler and described him by saying that he 'has but one eye, and is well known to all persons acquainted with the name of a certain noble circumnavigator'. It was held that the plaintiff was entitled to prove that the statement referred to him by showing that he had one eye and a name like that of a famous admiral. A class of persons cannot be defamed so that if it were said that all politicians are rogues no individual politician could sue. If a class is so small, however, that the statement can be taken as referring to each and every member, then all will be able to bring an action. If the defendant has made a defamatory statement intending that it shall refer to a fictitious character or to another person than the plaintiff, he will be liable for defamation of the plaintiff if a reasonable person would think that the statement referred to the plaintiff. Thus in *Newstead v London Express Newspaper Ltd* (1939) the defendants stated that Harold Newstead, a 30-year-old Camberwell man, had been convicted for bigamy. This was true of one Harold Newstead but not of the plaintiff who bore the same name and also lived in Camberwell. The reporter had sent the newspaper the address and occupation of the criminal, but this had been deleted from the published account by the sub-editor, so that the mistake arose. The defendants were held liable. In some instances of unintentional defamation a special defence is available under the Defamation Act 1952, s 4 (see below).

(iv) *Proof that the words are published.* The plaintiff must prove that there has been a publication for which the defendant is responsible. Publication is the communication of the defamation to some person other than the plaintiff or the defendant's wife (although it does include communication to the plaintiff's wife). A plaintiff will be liable for any publication he has made himself or which he has asked others to make. In some cases liability will depend on whether or not the defendant ought to have foreseen that his actions would lead to publication. Thus in *Huth v Huth* (1915) the defendant was not liable for the publication of defamatory matter that took place when a butler without authority opened and read an unsealed letter. In *Theaker v Richardson* (1962), however, the defendant addressed a defamatory letter to the plaintiff but her husband opened it without looking at the envelope and the defendant was held liable for this publication. There is a legal presumption that a postcard has been read in the course of its journey, but this does not apply to a letter. A repetition of defamatory matter is a new publication. The result is that a libel which is printed will bring liability not only to the author but also to the printer and publisher. On the other hand a person engaged only in distributing the document containing the libel will not be liable if he did not know of the defamation in the document and his ignorance was not due to negligence on his part.

(v) *The proof of damage.* Damage, i e financial loss, is necessary in slander except in the exceptional cases mentioned earlier. It is not necessary in libel actions, although a plaintiff who has suffered actual damage will be put into a stronger position in his claim for damages if he can prove this. Damage here means financial loss.

Unintentional defamation under the Defamation Act 1952, s 4

Section 4 of the Defamation Act 1952 makes provision for a special defence in cases where there has been a defamation that was unintended. The defence is available if a person *innocently* publishes 'words' alleged to be defamatory and has *exercised all reasonable care* in relation to the publication. 'Words' includes pictures, visual images (e g on a television screen) and gestures. Publication is treated as being innocent only if one of the following conditions is fulfilled: (i) if the publisher (or his servants or agents who were concerned with the contents) did not intend to publish the words of and concerning the plaintiff and did not know of circumstances by virtue of which they might be understood to refer to him, or (ii) if the words were not defamatory on the face of them and the publisher did not know of circumstances by virtue of which they might be understood to be defamatory of the plaintiff. Where the above conditions are fulfilled the publisher of the defamatory statement may make an 'offer of amends', which must be accompanied by an affidavit (a sworn statement) of the facts on which he relies. An offer of amends means (a) an offer of a suitable correction and apology, and (b) in addition, in cases where copies of the defamatory statement have been distributed, an offer to take reasonable steps to notify those who received the distributed copies that the words are alleged to be defamatory.

If the offer of amends is accepted, this is an end of the matter. If it is rejected, it may be pleaded as a defence in any action brought in respect of the defamatory statement.

Defences

Justification

It is a defence in an action for defamation to prove that the statement, although defamatory, was true. This defence is called 'justification'. It is not necessary to prove that every detail in the statement was true. It will be sufficient if the statement is accurate as a whole. Thus in *Alexander v North Eastern Rly Co* (1865) the defence of justification succeeded where the defendants said that the plaintiff had been fined with an alternative of three weeks' imprisonment when in fact the alternative was two weeks' imprisonment.

The Defamation Act, s 5 provides that in respect of words containing two or more distinct charges against the plaintiff, it *shall not be necessary to prove the truth of every charge* if the words not proved to be true do not materially injure the plaintiff's reputation having regard to the remaining charges. This provision is of considerable advantage to defendants.

If the plaintiff pleads that the statement complained of is defamatory by reason of an innuendo (hidden meaning), it is open to the defendant to prove that the innuendo is true.

Fair comment

If a statement can be shown to be a fair comment on a matter of public interest this will be a defence to an action for defamation. In order to establish the defence various elements must be present. These are as follows:

(i) *The subject matter of the statement must be of public interest.* This defence is not available for example in a case of defamation concerning only a private individual not in the public eye, in a matter relating to his mode of life. If a man holds a public office, however, the conduct of his private life will be a matter of public interest if it has a bearing on his fitness or otherwise to hold the office. Matters of public interest are numerous of course, and include the conduct of politicians, generals, judges, clergymen and others who exercise functions affecting the community. The judge must decide whether a matter is of public interest or not.

(ii) *The comment must be about some facts which are either stated truly or stated untruly with privilege.* Thus if the defendant said 'Smith stole from Jones and is unfit for his job' the second part of the sentence is a comment on the first. Ordinarily the defence of fair comment will succeed only if the defendant can show that Smith did steal from Jones. But the defence will also be available if the defendant can show, for example, that at the trial of Smith the magistrate found him guilty of stealing from Jones, even if the magistrate had made a mistake, since here the comment would be made on a statement uttered on a privileged occasion.

(iii) *The words must be a comment and not a statement of fact.* It may not at once be obvious into which category the words fall, and it is for the jury to make the decision.

(iv) *The comment must be fair, in the sense that it is an honest expression of the defendant's opinion.* The fact that the comment is couched in violent language will not automatically make the comment unfair. The test is whether any honest man however prejudiced he may be would have said the words in question.

(v) *The comment must not be malicious.* Malice has the same meaning here as in the case of qualified privilege (see p 198, below).

Absolute privilege

This defence is available in a limited number of cases where the public interest demands it. Where the defence is applicable it exempts from liability no matter how falsely and maliciously the statement has been made. The defence of absolute privilege is available in the following cases:

1 *Any statement made in Parliament by a member of either House.* This was laid down by the Bill of Rights 1688, s 1.

2 *Parliamentary papers (including Hansard) published by the order of either House of Parliament.* The authority for this is the Parliamentary Papers Act 1840, s 1. This absolute privilege is available also to a person who republishes *in full* any document published by order of either House (see p 197, below, as to qualified privilege for publication of extracts of such documents.)

3 *A statement made by one officer of state to another in the course of his duty.* This was decided in *Chatterton v Secretary of State for India* (1895) where absolute privilege was held to apply to a communication from the defendant to the Parliamentary Under-Secretary for India stating that the Government of India recommended that the plaintiff be placed on the half-pay list. It is uncertain how high a rank the defendant must have before he can claim this privilege; in any event if it were decided that the officer of state had too low a rank to claim absolute privilege, he would certainly have qualified privilege as far as his communication with other officers of state are concerned.

4 *Any statement made by one spouse to another.* Such statements are absolutely privileged because they do not constitute publication.

5 *Statements made in the course of judicial proceedings.* This applies to a statement made by a judge, juryman, witness, party or advocate provided that the statement refers to those proceedings. Utterly irrelevant remarks are not privileged.

6 *Newspaper reports of public judicial proceedings.* Such reports must be *fair, accurate and contemporaneous.* This class of absolute privilege stems from the Law of Libel Amendment Act 1888, s 3. The section states that it does not authorise the publication of any blasphemous or indecent matter. This privilege will not apply if any of the requisite elements are missing. Thus it will not apply if the report concerns proceedings held in camera, or if it is biased or inaccurate or if it is published long after the court proceedings. A 'newspaper' is

> 'any paper containing public news, intelligence, or occurrences, or any remarks or observations therein printed for sale, and published in England or Ireland periodically . . . at intervals not exceeding twenty-six days'.

Thus, daily, weekly and fortnightly publications are 'newspapers' for this purpose but monthlies are not. The Defamation Act 1952, s 9 has extended this type of privilege to cover reports broadcast for general reception from radio and television stations in the United Kingdom.

7 *Officials and other servants of the EEC.* Under European law these persons shall be immune from legal proceedings in respect of acts performed by them in their official capacity, including words spoken or written. European law has thus, in this detail, set foot in the English law of tort.

Qualified privilege

There are some occasions where the public interest does not demand the complete immunity of absolute privilege but when, nevertheless, some extended right of freedom of speech is desirable. On such occasions the law admits of qualified privilege. A statement to which qualified privilege attaches will not render its author liable in defamation unless either the defendant is actuated by malice in making the statement or the defendant publishes the statement more widely than he need. The defence of qualified privilege is available in the following cases:

1 *Legal or moral duty.* Where the person making the statement is acting under a legal or moral duty to do so *and* the person to whom the statement is made either has a legal or moral duty to receive it or has an interest in receiving it. It is for the judge to decide, in the light of all the circumstances, whether the defendant had a duty to make the statement. Even though the person to whom the statement is made has an interest in receiving it, there will be no privilege if the person making the statement

has no duty or interest in making it. Thus in *Watt v Longsdon* (1930) the defendant received a letter alleging that the plaintiff was, among other things, a blackguard, a thief and a liar, and asserting that he lived exclusively to satisfy his own passions and lust. The plaintiff was working abroad for the company of which the defendant was a director. The allegations were false. The defendant showed the letter to the chairman of the board of directors and to the plaintiff's wife. It was held that when the defendant communicated the statement to the chairman this was an occasion of qualified privilege because he was under a duty to tell the chairman. On the other hand the court held that the communication to the plaintiff's wife (who instituted divorce proceedings) was not an occasion of qualified privilege because, although the wife had an interest in receiving the statement, the defendant had no duty or interest to make it.

2 *Protection of an interest.* Where the person making the statement is acting for the protection of an interest *and* the person receiving the statement has a duty or an interest in receiving it. The interest to be protected may be any of the following: (a) the interest of the person making the statement; (b) the public interest; (c) a common interest affecting the person making and the person receiving the communication.

3 *Solicitor and client.* Where the statement is contained in a professional communication between a solicitor and a client, there is some doubt as to whether the privilege is absolute or qualified. Nevertheless such a communication will certainly receive qualified privilege.

4 *Reports of proceedings in Parliament.* Fair and accurate reports of proceedings in either House of Parliament receive qualified privilege. This privilege is not limited to newspapers.

5 *Extracts from parliamentary papers* (see p 195, above). The authority for this qualified privilege is the Parliamentary Papers Act 1840, s 3.

6 *Reports of judicial proceedings.* At common law qualified privilege is afforded to fair and accurate reports of judicial proceedings that are open to the public. This privilege is available to all and it matters not what form the publication takes as long as there is no malice. This privilege will be available to a newspaper report that does not qualify for absolute privilege under the Law of Libel Amendment Act 1888, s 3 (see p 196, above).

7 *Reports of public meetings.* Reports of public meetings published in newspapers and by United Kingdom radio and television stations within the Defamation Act 1952, s 7 are entitled to qualified privilege. This privilege is extended by s 7 to newspapers and radio and television stations in the United Kingdom broadcasting for general reception. The

expression 'newspaper' here has a special meaning different from the meaning in respect of absolute privilege (see p 196, above). It includes monthly publications. The definition is contained in the Defamation Act 1952, s 7 (5) and lays down that 'newspaper' means

> 'any paper containing public news or observations thereon, or consisting wholly or mainly of advertisements, which is printed for sale and is published in the United Kingdom . . . at intervals not exceeding thirty-six days'.

The qualified privilege is conferred in respect of reports of public meetings and certain other matters. The meetings and other matters to which s 7 relates are set out in the schedule to the Defamation Act 1952.

If a defendant pleads that he is protected by qualified privilege the plaintiff is permitted to counter this, if he can, by showing that the defendant was actuated by malice. Malice here means a wrongful motive such as personal spite. If the plaintiff can prove malice the defence of qualified privilege will be destroyed. In *Egger v Viscount Chelmsford* (1964), it was held that if a plaintiff proves malice against some only of a number of co-defendants who have pleaded qualified privilege, the others remain protected by their qualified privilege.

Apology and mitigation

A defendant in an action for defamation may be able to assist himself by taking action in respect of the following two matters:

Apology.   An apology is not in itself a defence but it may reduce damages. Section 2 of the Libel Act 1843 (also called Lord Campbell's Act), as amended by the Libel Act 1845, provides that in an action against a newspaper for libel the defendant may plead that the libel was inserted in the newspaper without actual malice or gross negligence and that before the commencement of the action or as soon as possible afterwards he inserted a full apology in the newspaper or, if the newspaper is published less frequently than weekly, that he offered to publish the apology in any newspaper selected by the plaintiff. Any plea of this type must be accompanied by a payment of money into court by way of amends.

Mitigation of damages.   Section 1 of Lord Campbell's Act, which is not confined to newspapers, provides that in an action for defamation, if the defendant gives notice to the plaintiff at the time he serves his defence, he may give evidence in mitigation of damages to the effect that he made or offered an apology before the commencement of the action or as soon as possible afterwards. There need be no payment into court. Evidence may be given by the defendant of the plaintiff's general bad reputation before the defamation was published.

Remedies for defamation

The remedies available are damages, or an injunction to restrain repetition of the defamation. The damages may be compensatory or exemplary. In *McCarey v Associated Newspapers Ltd* (1964), following *Rookes v Barnard* (see p 118), it was held that exemplary damages should be awarded only where the defendant's conduct is calculated by him to make a profit exceeding the compensation payable to the plaintiff.

Rylands *v* Fletcher

This tort received its name from a famous action in 1868. The defendant employed an independent contractor (see p 157, above) to construct a reservoir on his land. The work was done so negligently that the independent contractor did not discover or stop up an old shaft that led from the reservoir to the plaintiff's coal mine. When the reservoir was filled the water escaped and flooded the mine. There were several hearings and the case eventually went to the House of Lords. The most important judgment was, however, delivered in the Court of Exchequer Chamber (see p 27, above) by Blackburn J who said:

'We think that the true rule of law is, that the person who for his own purposes brings on his lands and collects and keeps there anything likely to do mischief if it escapes, must keep it in at his peril, and, if he does not do so, is prima facie answerable for all the damage which is the natural consequence of its escape'.

The House of Lords accepted what had been said by Blackburn J and added a proviso which was expressed in the speech of Lord Cairns, the Lord Chancellor, to the effect that the rule would apply only if there had been a 'non-natural' use of the land. The defendant was found liable for damages in tort.

The 'things' to which the rule applies were stated by Blackburn J in his judgment to include beasts, water, filth and stenches. In subsequent decisions the rule has been extended to cover the escape of explosions, vibrations, gas, electricity, and in *A-G v Corke* (1933) even the escape of caravan dwellers who broke fences and did other damage on the land in the neighbourhood of the field where they were permitted to live. In *Matheson v Northcote College Board of Governors* (1975), a New Zealand case, the owners of a dwelling sued the governors of a secondary school in the Auckland Supreme Court. They complained that the defendants had failed to prevent the children from stealing apples, hitting golfballs, throwing firecrackers, leaving rubbish and trampling on flower beds on their land. The court held that these facts could constitute an actionable private nuisance, but were not a *Rylands v Fletcher* escape.

The requirement that proof of escape is necessary means that only a person who suffers damage by reason of the dangerous thing crossing the boundary of the land from which it comes can succeed in an action. Therefore in *Read v Lyons* (1947) an inspector of munitions who was injured in an explosion while on the actual premises where the explosion took place, was unable to succeed in an action based on *Rylands v Fletcher* because there was no escape. The plaintiff could not have succeeded in an action for the tort of negligence, since there was none, and neither could she have succeeded in an action for trespass to the person because the defendants had not acted intentionally or negligently with respect to the explosion.

'Non-natural' use is interpreted more restrictively than formerly and covers, for example, storing water, gas and electricity in bulk and the operation of a chair-o-plane.

The defences to an action under the rule in *Rylands v Fletcher* are (i) volenti non fit injuria, (ii) that the escape was due to the fault of the plaintiff, (iii) that the escape took place as the result of an unexpected act done by a stranger, thus in *Rickards v Lothian* (1913), the plaintiff's stock in trade which was kept on the second floor of a building was damaged by the overflow of water from a wash basin in a separate apartment on the fourth floor. The fourth floor tenant was held not liable because some person unknown had blocked up the waste pipe and turned on the tap, (iv) Act of God (see p 146), and (v) statutory authority.

The remedy for injury suffered as the result of a *Rylands v Fletcher* escape is an action for damages. To be successful a plaintiff must have an interest in the land affected by the escape. If so, he may recover damages for personal injuries but not for mere financial loss.

Part two

The law of contract

Summary

Chapter 11

Introduction

The law of contract is that branch of our civil law which tells us when a promise or set of promises is legally binding. A contract may be defined as an agreement which the law will enforce. There are many agreements which, for various reasons, the courts will not enforce. Where a contract does exist, the parties to it have rights and obligations which have arisen by their agreement and are personal to themselves. Generally the contract cannot give the parties rights against outsiders (strangers or third parties, as lawyers call them) and the rights of the parties are confined to each other.

Many of the modern rules of contract were developed in the atmosphere of the nineteenth-century economic doctrine of laissez-faire (freedom). In consequence, the underlying theory is that the parties to a contract represent two equal bargaining powers who enter into the agreement of their own free will and as a result of negotiations in which each of them is free to accept or reject the terms of the other. For a time there had been little legislative interference with this position with the result that in the present century of monopolies, large-scale business and standard form contracts which an individual accepts or goes without, great injustice could be caused to an individual who may be forced to deal with a large organisation. An instance of this is to be found in the law relating to the sale of goods. Unless they were specifically excluded by the contract several terms were implied by statute in the sale for the benefit of the buyer. But when, for example, an individual bought a car from a garage he would almost certainly have had to buy the car on the basis of a contract drafted for the benefit of the garage proprietors by their federation and which would have *excluded* all the benefits which would otherwise have been given by the implied terms. If the individual did not agree to this form of contract, the probability is that the garage would not have sold the car to him. However, for several years now the tide has been slowly turning. Statute does now intervene more forcibly with the freedom to contract as is evidenced by the Misrepresentation Act 1967, the Unfair Contract Terms Act 1977 and the Sale of Goods Act 1979.

The basis of a contract is agreement which, in most cases if not all, may be analysed into an offer made by one party to another and an acceptance by that other of the offer made to him.

This basic idea is often expressed in Latin as *consensus ad idem* (consent to the same thing) which means that both parties must assent to all the terms of the agreement. Agreement may be signified by oral or written words of the parties and may even be deduced from their conduct. In any situation, whether there is an offer and an acceptance and consequently an agreement is a question of *construction* (interpretation) for the courts. When considering this question the courts adopt what is known as the objective test, i e they decide what are reasonable inferences to be drawn from the words used by, and the conduct of, the parties. This test is applied rather than the subjective test of the mental intention of the parties concerned, because an outward agreement could otherwise be nullified by the mental reservations of one party.

Before considering in detail the features of offer and acceptance in the next chapter, students should note that an agreement will be enforceable only when certain other requirements of a valid simple contract (i e a contract not under seal) are present. The essentials of a simple contract are:

(i)   agreement,
(ii)   consideration.
(iii) intention to enter legal relations,
(iv)   capacity to contract,
(v)   reality of the consent, and
(vi)   lawfulness of the object.

Chapter 12
Offer and acceptance

Offer

1 *An offer must be firm.* The offer must be made with a definite intention to adhere to its terms. In some situations it is clear that a firm offer has been made. In others, for example where negotiations are protracted or complicated, it may be a difficult question of construction to determine whether there has been a firm offer by one party.

Where a person merely makes a *declaration of intention* this will not amount to an offer in law but will simply be a statement by him indicating the state of his mind. In *Re Fickus, Farina v Fickus* (1900) a father wrote to the man who was about to marry his daughter stating that his daughter would derive a benefit under his will. This letter was held to be an expression of intention and not a firm offer capable of acceptance.

In other circumstances a person may make a statement which the court will interpret as being a call to others to start negotiations, an invitation to others to make offers. Technically this is known as an *invitation to treat*. An invitation to treat frequently appears very similar to an offer but the legal distinction between them is vital. An offer which is accepted forms an agreement which is the basis of contract, and if all the other essentials of contract are present, the agreement will be enforceable. The so-called acceptance of an invitation to treat cannot give rise to an agreement as the invitation to treat is not an offer. There are many illustrations of the importance of this distinction in practice and the following cases are merely examples.

In 1970 Manchester City Council wrote to one of its tenants saying the Council 'May be prepared to sell the house to you . . . If you would like to make a formal application to buy your Council house please complete the enclosed application form'. The tenant completed the form and returned it to the Council. In 1971 there was a change in the political outlook of the Council, after the May election, and the Council refused to proceed with the sale. The tenant sought a decree of specific performance. The House of Lords held against the tenant on the ground that the correspondence from the Council was no more than an invitation to treat which was not capable of being accepted by any action by the tenant. As the Council had changed its intentions before any formal documents had been signed there was no enforceable contract in respect of which a decree of specific performance could be issued. The tenant's completed form amounted to an offer, not an acceptance. (*Gibson v Manchester City Council* (1979)).

At an auction sale the call for bids by an auctioneer is an invitation to treat and the bid itself is the offer. The acceptance is completed by the fall of the auctioneer's hammer. Thus, when a bid has been made no contract is then concluded and the bid (offer) may be withdrawn. (The common law rules embodied in a late nineteenth-century statute, are now to be found in the Sale of Goods Act 1979, s 57.) Also, an advertisement which states that an auction will be held is merely an invitation to treat incapable of acceptance. If the auction is cancelled anyone attending the place where the auction was to be held cannot claim successfully that by his conduct he has accepted an *offer* to hold an auction. There is no contract here (*Harris v Nickerson* (1873)). Where an auction is held 'without reserve', which means that the highest bidder is to be the buyer of the lot auctioned no matter how low that bid may be, a difficult question of construction arises. In normal circumstances at an auction, where the auctioneer calls for bids for a valuable painting worth about £2,000 and the highest bid is £120, the auctioneer may withdraw the painting from the auction. In accordance with the Sale of Goods Act 1979 the contract of sale is not concluded till the fall of the hammer (acceptance) and therefore, the painting could be withdrawn from the sale. But there is authority for the view that where the auction is held 'without reserve' the call for bids by the auctioneer amounts to a firm promise to accept the bid of the highest bidder and this promise is accepted by the person making the highest bid (*Warlow v Harrison* (1859)).

Marked prices on articles displayed for sale in shop windows will almost invariably be construed as invitations to treat and not offers to sell at the stated price. A young lady who sees a dress marked at £3 and who tries on the dress and decides to buy it will receive a nasty surprise if she is told that the price ticket should read £50. If she has already decided to buy the dress she may well want to know whether she can insist on having it for £3. If the marked price were an offer she could accept the offer and insist on having the dress for £3 but in fact it is not an offer and any acceptance does not conclude an agreement. When she says that she will have the dress she makes an offer to buy, and is then told the price of £50 which she can agree to or not as she pleases. This principle has been upheld in the Court of Appeal in *The Pharmaceutical Society of Great Britain v Boots Cash Chemists (Southern) Ltd* (1953) in which the facts were as follows. By statute it is an offence to *sell*, other than under the supervision of a qualified pharmacist, drugs which are on the Poisons List. Boots opened a self-service store in which certain drugs were for sale on a counter with the price marked on them. A customer picked up drugs at the counter and took them to the cashier near the exit to pay for them. No pharmacist supervised the counter but a pharmacist did supervise the cashier. The question was whether the sale had taken place at the counter, in which case an offence had been committed, or whether it had taken place at the cashier's desk. It was held that the sale had taken place at the cashier's desk because the display of the drugs on the counter was merely an invitation to treat. The offer was made by the customer taking the drugs to the cashier and the acceptance (and therefore the sale) took place when the cashier accepted the customer's money.

Catalogues and circulars which offer goods for sale and time-tables which offer transport at a particular time and place are in most cases mere invitations to treat. In order to protect themselves further, persons responsible for the issue of catalogues and time-tables usually insert (albeit in small print) a clause to the effect that they do not bind themselves to sell or to provide transport on time or at all, as the case may be.

Where the subject matter of a proposed sale is land the courts are always reluctant to find a firm offer to sell unless this is clearly expressed in a formal document. The law does not say that contracts for the sale of land cannot arise in an informal way but in view of the many and complicated questions involved in sales of land the courts are in practice most careful not to find a firm offer wherever there is the slightest doubt. In *Clifton v Palumbo* (1944) C offered to sell a large estate for £600,000. He wrote, 'I am prepared to offer my estate for £600,000 and also agree that sufficient time shall be given to you to complete a Schedule of Completion'. When interpreting these words, even though the word 'offer' had been used, the court held that they amounted to a preliminary statement as to price and not a firm offer to sell. The Schedule of Completion was taken as referring to a contract by which the parties intended to be bound. In another case (*Harvey v Facey* (1893)) H telegraphed F, 'Will your sell us Bumper Hall Pen? Telegraph lowest cash price'. F replied by telegraph, 'Lowest cash price for Bumper Hall Pen, £900'. H then telegraphed, 'We agree to buy Bumper Hall Pen for £900 asked by you. Please send title deeds'. This case came before the Privy Council for decision on the question of whether there was a contract. The Privy Council advised that the first telegram asked two questions and the reply in the second telegram answered the second question only by saying what the price would be if F were prepared to sell. It was not an offer to sell and therefore the acceptance by H in the third telegram did not conclude an agreement.

2 *The terms of the offer must be certain.*   The terms of a contract must be certain. Unless the terms of the offer are certain, the acceptance of that offer will give rise to a vague agreement and not to one that is enforceable. However, the rule that the offer must be certain is subject to the qualification that anything which is capable of being made certain is to be regarded as certain for this purpose – *id certum est quod certum reddi potest*

(that is certain which can be made certain). There are many illustrations of terms which have been held to be uncertain:

A bought a horse from B and promised to pay a further sum if the horse were 'lucky' to him. The court held the term 'lucky' to be too vague to be enforceable (*Guthing v Lynn* (1831)).

R engaged an actress for a play at 'a West End salary to be mutually arranged between us'. The court held that the provision as to the salary was too vague (*Loftus v Roberts* (1902)).

S sold a motor-van on the 'usual hire-purchase terms'. The House of Lords held that this term was too vague and the agreement could not be made certain. There were no usual hire-purchase terms in the trade, there was no previous course of dealings between the parties, there was no statutory implied term and the agreement contained no machinery for rendering vague terms certain (*Scammell v Ouston* (1941)). Again, in an agreement concerning the development of land for use as a motel and filling station, an agreement 'to negotiate fair and reasonable contract sums in respect of' the work was held to be too vague in the absence of any provision for the method by which the price was to be calculated (*Courtney and Fairburn Ltd v Tolaini Brothers (Hotels) Ltd* (1975)).

Generally, the courts will examine the wording used by the parties and while it is not the function of the courts to make agreements for them they will not be too keen to find uncertainty and thus frustrate the intentions of the parties. In an agreement for the sale of $51\frac{1}{2}$ acres of land at £500,000 it was provided that payment was 'to be phased as to £250,000 upon first completion, as to £125,000 twelve months thereafter and as to the balance of £125,000 a further twelve months thereafter', and 'On the occasion of each completion a proportionate part of the land shall be released forthwith' to the purchaser. A dispute arose and the vendor argued that as the provisions of the agreement were vague it was not an enforceable contract. However, the court held that the contract was not void for uncertainty. The court attempted to achieve the intention of the parties by holding that the words 'proportionate part' meant in proportion to the purchase price (*Bushwall Properties Ltd v Vortex Properties Ltd* (1975)).

From a consideration of *Scammell v Ouston* it is clear that there are various ways in which a vague term could possibly be made certain. We will now consider these in turn although some of them are considered again in a later part of the book where they will be dealt with in more detail:

(a)   An uncertainty may be cured by a term implied by trade usage (see p 360, below).

(b)   The previous course of dealing between the parties to a vague contract may clarify the vagueness. If A contracts to supply B with a definite quantity of machine tools over a period of two years in accordance with a schedule setting forth a detailed specification of the tools, then, should B place an order after the two years have elapsed for 200 particular tools as named in the specification and A delivers such tools, there will be a contract between A and B which is explicable by reference to the previous course of dealings. If the tools delivered by A are not of the standard required by the specification he will be in breach of contract. In *Hillas v Arcos* (1932) the parties had agreed a contract for the sale of softwood timber in 1930. The contract gave the buyers an option to purchase further timber in 1931. No details were given as to the size, quantity and date of shipment of the timber referred to in the option. The House of Lords held that the option was not an agreement to negotiate a further contract but was a definite offer to sell timber in 1931 on the terms of the 1930 agreement where all such details were settled.

(c)   Terms may also be implied by statute, either to add a provision not agreed expressly by the parties or to clarify some doubt. For example, the Sale of Goods Act 1979, s 8, may impose an obligation to pay a reasonable price in a contract for the sale of goods (see p 309, below).

(d)   The contract may contain some provision by which vague terms are to be clarified, e g by express reference of disputes to arbitration in accordance with the Arbitration Act 1950. In *Foley v Classique Coaches* (1934) there was an agreement for the sale of petrol 'at a price to be agreed by the parties in writing and from time to time'. This was obviously a vague term but the contract went on to provide that in the event of dispute reference should be made to arbitration in accordance with the Arbitration Act 1889 (see now the Arbitration Act 1979). The court interpreted this as meaning that the sale was at a reasonable price and where there was a dispute about this the dispute was to be referred to arbitration. Maugham LJ said,

> 'An agreement to agree in the future is not a contract; nor is there a contract if a material term is neither settled nor implied by law and the document contains no machinery for ascertaining it.'

(e)   A term may be implied by applying the 'officious bystander' test as explained in *The Moorcock* (1889) (see p 360, below).

Moreover, in extreme cases where a subsidiary term is not only vague but also *meaningless* it can be struck out and the remainder of the contract enforced. Thus in *Nicolene v Simmonds* (1953, CA) P ordered from D specific iron bars at a definite price and wrote 'I assume we are in agreement and the *usual conditions of acceptance apply.*' A dispute arose as to the quality of the iron delivered and D argued that there was no enforceable contract because the words 'usual conditions of acceptance' were too vague. The court held that the words were vague *and meaningless* and, as they involved a *subsidiary* matter, could be ignored; otherwise, it was pointed out, a vague minor term would allow a party to escape his liabilities. The principle in *Nicolene v Simmonds* has since been recognised and applied by the House of Lords in *Hunter v Fox* (1964). Where all the terms of an agreement have been negotiated and agreed upon, the words 'subject to contract' appearing at the end of a contractual document may be regarded as meaningless and may be ignored. In this situation a contract exists (*Michael Richards Properties Ltd v Corpn of Wardens of St. Saviour's Parish Southwark* (1975)).

3 *The offer must be communicated to the offeree*.   Where a firm and certain offer is made it will be legally effective only when brought to the notice of the person to whom it is made. An offer cannot be accepted by the offeree until brought to his notice. This is illustrated by the type of situation where an offer of reward is made for the return of lost goods such as an item of jewellery or a dog. If *in response* to the offer a person returns the goods lost he will be deemed to have accepted the offer by his conduct and will be entitled to the reward. If, however, he returns the goods *in ignorance* of the offer he will be unable to claim the reward (see p 214, below).

4 *Offer to a class of persons*.   An offer which is made to a class of persons or even to the whole world will not fail for uncertainty. This and other principles of law are illustrated by the interesting case of *Carlill v Carbolic Smoke Ball Co Ltd* (1892). The company advertised its smokeball as a preventive against influenza and in the advertisement said that it would pay £100 to anyone who caught the infection after using the smokeball as prescribed for a period of 14 days. They also stated that as earnest of their good faith they had deposited £1,000 with the Alliance Bank to meet possible claimants. Mrs C bought a smokeball from a shop, used it as prescribed and caught influenza. When the £100 was refused to her she sued in contract for its recovery. The company raised several points in its defence. First, it alleged that the so-called offer in the advertisement lacked sufficient certainty to be an offer in the legal sense. It was made to no one in particular and therefore could not be accepted by anyone. To hold otherwise, the company argued, would be to make them liable in contract to the whole world. The court answered this line of defence by saying that a general offer was valid and could be made to a class or even the whole world; but this did not automatically make the offeror liable in contract to the whole world. He would be liable only to those offerees who accepted his offer. A general offer, such as the one in this case, might be improvident but it was not one unknown to the law. Another defence raised by the company was that even if the advertisement were construed as a certain offer it was not a firm offer. It was a mere boosting of its products known in the commercial world as 'mere business puff' and was not capable of acceptance so as to conclude an agreement. Here the court

agreed that the majority of advertisements were not firm offers but *each adverisement was to be construed on its merits and in the light of surrounding circumstances*. In this advertisement the words stating that £1,000 had been set aside to meet possible claimants evidenced an intention to abide by the promise. This was what a reasonable man would infer from the words of the advertisement. Yet another defence raised was that even assuming the advertisement was a valid offer in law it was never accepted by Mrs C who had never communicated with the company and of whom the company knew nothing at the time the alleged contract was formed. This defence was rejected by the court on the grounds that, although as a general rule the acceptance must be communicated to the offeror before it would be complete so as to form a binding agreement, there were exceptions to this rule. Where an offer stated, expressly or impliedly, that performing an act was to be the mode of acceptance, the acceptance would be completed by the performance as requested and did not have to be communicated to the offeror. If an offer takes the form of a promise in return for an act, the performance of that act is in itself an adequate indication of assent.

5 *Termination of the offer.* As a general rule an offer may terminate or be terminated at any time before the acceptance is complete.

In most cases an acceptance is not complete until communicated to the offeror. There are several ways in which an offer may come to an end. It may be *accepted*, in which case it is merged into the agreement, or it may be *rejected*, in which case it ceases to exist and can be revived only by the act of the offeror. However, there are other not so simple ways and these require further discussion.

Revocation. An offer can be withdrawn so long as it is withdrawn before the acceptance is complete. In *Payne v Cave* (1789) it was held that a person who had made a bid at an auction was entitled to withdraw it before the fall of the hammer. The revocation must be *communicated* to the offeree to be effective in law although it need not be conveyed by the offeror himself. Provided there are reasonable grounds for believing in its accuracy, a communication made by any person to the offeree will suffice for this purpose. Thus in one case O offered to give I an option on a house, which was for sale at £800, but changed his mind and sold to A. B told I of this sale and the next day I sought to exercise the option by accepting O's offer. The court held that the intention of O not to sell to him had been effectively communicated to I and there was therefore no offer for him to accept (*Dickinson v Dodds* (1876)).

Where the offeror promises to leave the offer open for a certain time (i e gives the offeree an option) he is under no obligation to abide by his promise. As we shall see later, the English law of contract enforces a promise only where it is 'bought' by the promisee (offeree) in the sense that he has given something of value (known as 'consideration') in return for the promise. In the absence of consideration the offer can be withdrawn. Therefore, if A offers to sell his car to B for £200 and to give him seven days to think it over, it is advisable for B, if he wants time to consider the offer, to pay A a small sum (say 50 pence) as consideration for his promise to leave the offer open.

A problem arises in relation to the revocation of an offer which may be accepted by the performance of an act. Is it possible to revoke the offer while the act is being done? For example, Billy Bee offers £1,000 to the winner of a race from Land's End to John O'Groats. When the runners have covered over 900 miles can Billy Bee revoke his offer? In accordance with the authority of *Carlill's Case* (p 210, above), the acceptance of the offer is the performance of the act – in this case the act of winning – and Billy Bee would seem to be able to revoke. However, the Sixth Interim Report of the Law Revision Committee (1937) suggested that this was not so. It drew a distinction between the actual acceptance and the performance of the act which was to be done in return for the promise. Once a person had entered the race, or at least once he had started, the offer would have been accepted and therefore Billy Bee could not revoke it. But only one person would be entitled to the £1,000 because only one person could win and thus provide the consideration.

Lapse. Where an offer is expressed to be open for a definite period of time it will automatically terminate at the end of that period. Where it is made without any reference to the period of time during which it is to remain open it will lapse at the end of a reasonable time. What amounts to a reasonable time is a question of fact to be determined in the light of all the circumstances of the case. In one case where a person offered to buy shares in June and the offer was accepted in the November of the same year the court held that there was no contract because the offer had lapsed as a result of the unreasonable delay in making the acceptance (*Ramsgate Victoria Hotel Co v Montefiore* (1866)). Also an offer will lapse where it is made on the basis of a condition or state of affairs which ceases to exist. If an offer is made to buy a car and before the offer is accepted the car is seriously damaged the offer to buy the car lapses and is incapable of being accepted (*Financings Ltd v Stimson* (1962), CA).

The death of the offeree causes the offer to lapse and on his death it cannot be accepted by his executors (*Duff's Executors' Case* (1866)). The death of the offeror will cause the offer to lapse in all cases where the death is known to the offeree when he accepts. However, where the offeree does not know of the death when he accepts and the contract is one which does not require personal service from the offeror, it appears that the death will not affect the offer and its acceptance concludes a valid agreement. Thus, if A, a well-known singer, offers to sing at B's concert and then dies before B accepts in ignorance of A's death, the offer will die with A as its performance depends on his personal co-operation. But if A had merely promised to sell a book to B then, if B accepts in ignorance of his death, it is suggested that A's executors would be obliged to sell the book to B and B would be obliged to pay the price to the executors.

Acceptance

Once the person suing on the contract has proved an offer he must show an acceptance of that offer by the person to whom it was made. *An acceptance is the unconditional assent to all the terms of the offer.* The whole agreement – offer and acceptance – is to be deduced from the words spoken and written by the parties as well as from their conduct. The court when interpreting the words used and acts done looks not so much at the state of mind of the parties as at a consideration of the *inferences to be drawn from their conduct by a reasonable man*; for instance, where a person boards a bus he impliedly promises to pay the fare. This test is known as the objective test, as opposed to the subjective test which is based on an examination of the state of mind of the parties rather than the inferences from conduct when reasonably construed.

Once the offeree has decided to accept the offer an agreement is not necessarily present in the eyes of the law. For an acceptance to be legally complete, or effective in law, it must be *communicated* to the offeror. We may thus draw a distinction between the actual acceptance and the *communicating* of acceptance. If A, talking on the telephone to B, makes an offer which B accepts, but immediately before B speaks his words of acceptance the line goes dead, B will have accepted but the acceptance will not have been communicated. For the purposes of reaching an agreement which is recognised in law as the basis of a contract there is no agreement here because the acceptance has not been completed by communication to the offeror. Moreover, the communication is not valid unless it is made by a person having authority to effect the communication (*Powell v Lee* (1908)).

An acceptance is *effective* in law, therefore, when the unconditional assent of the offeree to all the terms of the offer is communicated to the offeror.

The remaining pages of this chapter are devoted to a study of the situations where the above rules are modified or give rise to difficulty in their application to certain types of case.

1 *Mode of acceptance prescribed by offeror.* In some cases the offer may prescribe a mode of acceptance which does not result in communication of the acceptance to the offeror.

'There can be no doubt that where a person in an offer made by him to another person, expressly or impliedly, intimates a particular mode of acceptance as sufficient to make the bargain binding, it is only necessary for that other person to whom such offer is made to follow the indicated method of acceptance; and if the person making the offer expressly or impliedly intimates in his offer that it will be sufficient to act on the proposal without communicating acceptance of it to himself, performance of the condition is a sufficient acceptance without notification' (per Bowen LJ in *Carlill's Case*).

In *Carlill's Case* (see p 210, above), the advertisement impliedly stated that acting on its terms by taking the smokeball as prescribed would be sufficient acceptance without communication.

This form of acceptance can give rise to difficulty in cases where the acceptance is performed in ignorance of the offer, as where the finder of a lost dog returns it to its true owner, without knowing that the owner has made an offer of reward for its safe return. The problem is whether an offer can be accepted by a person who does not know of it. It seems unjust that a person should not be able to claim a reward when he has done the act for which the reward was offered but it is suggested that this is the law and that an inference of agreement cannot be drawn from two independent acts. The act of Mrs Carlill was done with knowledge of the offer and in the earlier case of *Williams v Carwardine* (1833) a similar situation existed. W made a statement, to ease his conscience, giving information leading to the discovery of certain murderers and for which information a reward had been offered. W recovered the reward as the court was satisfied that he knew of the offer and his actual motive for giving the information was irrelevant. The Australian case of *R v Clarke* (1927), on its facts, is an even stronger case in favour of the view put forward. A reward was offered for information leading to the conviction of certain murderers together with a promise that if it was given by an accomplice he would receive a free pardon. C, an accomplice, panicked and gave the information required but he was held not entitled to the reward. C admitted that in his state of panic the question of the reward had passed out of his mind and all he intended to do was to obtain the pardon. His acceptance was directed to an acceptance of the offer of a pardon and he was not thinking of the reward when he accepted. This was not a case of performance in ignorance of an offer but because he had forgotten the offer at the time of performance there could be no intention to accept.

From the above discussion it is clear that where the offeror prescribes the performance of an act as sufficient acceptance a person *knowing* of the offer and *performing the act* accepts the offer. However, there is little judicial authority to assist with the difficulties which arise where the prescribed mode of acceptance is *not* followed, but acceptance is in fact communicated to the offeror. It is clear that where the offeror prescribes a method of acceptance and insists that it shall be followed that method must be followed unless the offeror waives his right to insist on the prescribed mode being complied with. But where it is not so stipulated it is *suggested* that if the altered mode of acceptance results in no less advantageous communication to the offeror the acceptance is valid. An example would be where the altered mode of acceptance results in earlier communication. (*Manchester Diocesan Council of Education v Commercial and General Investments* (1969)). This principle was applied in a case where the vendor provided that an option should be exercised by 'notice in writing . . . to be sent registered or recorded delivery'. The purchaser sent his acceptance by ordinary letter post. Here the court held that the words used were to be construed as only directory and not mandatory and the substance of the requirement of *written notice* had been fulfilled. The requirement of registered or recorded delivery was more advantageous to the sender rather than the recipient of the letter (*Yates Building Co Ltd v R. J. Pulleyn & Sons (York) Ltd* (1975)).

Although the offeror can stipulate how the acceptance is to be made he cannot by his own act stipulate that silence shall amount to acceptance. If provisions to this effect were enforceable then the offeror would be capable of imposing contractual liability on the offeree without his consent. In *Felthouse v Bindley* (1863) F wrote to J offering to buy his horse for £30 15s, and adding, 'If I hear no more about him I consider the horse mine at that price'. J did not reply to this letter but told an auctioneer, who had been commissioned to sell the horse, not to put it up for auction. In error the auctioneer sold the horse to X, and F, claiming to be the owner, sued the auctioneer for the tort of conversion alleging that the auctioneer had sold his (F's) property. The court held in favour of the defendant as the silence of J did not amount to an acceptance of F's offer. In the absence of a contract of sale between F and J ownership of the horse did not pass to F.

The following general rules about the communication of acceptance should be noted:

The acceptance must be communicated before an agreement is concluded except in the following cases:

(i)   Where the offer expressly or impliedly states that performance of the terms of the offer shall be sufficient acceptance *(Carlill's Case)*.

(ii)   Where the 'post rules' apply the acceptance is complete on the posting even though the acceptance is never communicated in fact (see p 220, below).

(iii)   Under s 57 (2) of the Sale of Goods Act 1979, a sale by auction is complete on the fall of the auctioneer's hammer. It would, therefore, appear that communication of the acceptance is not necessary.

      (N.B. An *offer* and a *revocation* are never complete until *communicated* to the party to whom they are made.)

2 *Offer and acceptance uncertain.*   There are cases where it is very difficult to find an offer and an acceptance, if at all. Where the negotiations

between the parties have taken place over a long period of time and there have been many stages in the negotiations it may be difficult, and even impossible, to say with certainty wherein lies the offer and the acceptance and, hence, precisely when agreement was reached. In the case of *Brogden v Metropolitan Rly Co* (1877) the facts were as follows: B had for several years supplied the company with coal without any formal agreement. The parties decided to have a formal agreement drafted and the company's agent sent a copy to B who inserted the name of an arbitrator and then returned the copy approved to the company. The company's agent put the agreement in a drawer, doing nothing to indicate his assent to the arbitrator selected by B. After the negotiations, the parties carried on business with each other in accordance with the terms of the agreement. A dispute arose and B denied that there was a binding contract. The House of Lords found an agreement but could not say precisely when it was formed. The House held that the subsequent conduct of the parties could be explained only on the assumption that they had both approved the terms of the draft and that a contract came into existence *either* when the company placed its first order for coal from B upon those terms *or* at least when B supplied it.

Another situation of difficulty is where several people enter a competition and agree to abide by the rules of the competition. There is clearly an offer and an acceptance between each competitor and the organisers of the competition but it is very difficult to find a contract between the competitors. Thus, if in a yacht race the rules make provision for the payment, or otherwise, of compensation for damage caused by fouling it is difficult to find an agreement *between the competitors* to abide by the rules. In this type of situation the House of Lords has held (*Clarke v Dunraven*, *The Satanita* (1897)) that there is a contract between the competitors on the basis that

> 'a contract is concluded when one party has communicated to another an offer and that other has accepted it *or when the parties have united in a concurrent expression of intention to create a legal obligation*'.

3 *Difficulties of construction.* Where the words used in reply to an offer are not clearly an acceptance of the offer a difficult question of construction (interpretation) arises. If R offers to sell his only car to E for £500 and E accepts, R is then under contract to sell to E. If E rejects R's offer, R is free to sell to someone else. If the reply by E to R's offer is neither an acceptance nor a rejection of the offer, it will still be open but may be revoked. Moreover, if E 'accepts' at £450 he is not assenting to all R's terms so there will be no acceptance. E's acceptance will be termed a counter-offer (i e an offer to buy at £450) and is in law a rejection of R's offer to sell at £500. In this case R will be free to sell elsewhere. It is, therefore, vital for R to know what interpretation to place on E's reply to his offer to sell his car to him for £500. The type of difficulty which can

arise and the necessity of distinguishing between a counter-offer and an invitation to treat are well illustrated by the case of *Hyde v Wrench* (1840). On 6 June W offered to sell his estate to H for £1,000. On the 8th, in reply, H offered to buy it for £950, which offer W refused. Without withdrawing the offer W sold the estate elsewhere and on the 29th H accepted the offer to sell at £1,000. H sued W for breach of contract. The court held that the counter-offer of 8 June rejected the original offer which could be revived only by the original offeror (W) and not by the offeree (H) changing his mind and accepting it.

A more recent example of the problems involved in contracts arrived at by commercial correspondence, or 'battle of the forms' as it is sometimes phrased, is to be found in *Butler Machine Tool Co Ltd v Ex-Cell-O Corpn (England) Ltd* (1979). Here the Court of Appeal considered the frequently occurring situation where each party communicates with the other on letter-headed paper on the reverse side of which appears a set of standard conditions of sale. As each set differs from the other, the problem of which set is to apply in the event of a dispute arises. In this case the seller claimed that the machine tool being sold was priced at £75,535 and was subject to a clause saying that it is 'a condition of acceptance of order that goods will be charged at prices ruling on the date of delivery'. The seller's offer also made it clear that the seller's conditions were to prevail over any conditions in the buyer's order. The buyer accepted the offer on his own official stationery which included conditions which made no provision for a variation in price. The seller acknowledged the order and said that it was being entered in their order book in accordance with the seller's earlier quotation. When, after several months, the machine was delivered, the seller claimed an extra £2,892 under the terms of the price-variation clause. The buyer refused to pay and were sued for payment.

If the court took the view that the seller had made their position clear at the outset, and therefore the buyer knew he was contracting on the seller's terms and no other, then the seller would succeed in the claim based on the price-variation clause. On the other hand, the buyer argued tha his reply to the offer, being on different terms, was a counter-offer which destroyed the seller's offer and constituted an offer to buy the machine on the buyer's terms which did *not* include a price-variation clause. If this argument were accepted by the court, the buyer's defence would succeed.

The unanimous view of the Court of Appeal (reversing the trial judge) was that the ordinary rules of contract were to be the guide. The seller made an offer which the buyer did not unconditionally accept. Therefore, there could be no contract on the seller's terms. The buyer's reply was a counter-offer on the buyer's terms and these were accepted by the seller. The seller's reply in which it was said that the order was booked in accordance with the earlier quotation was interpreted by the Court of Appeal as referring back to the identity and price of the machine tool and not to the terms on the reverse of the seller's document. The plaintiff seller's action failed.

In some cases the reply to an offer may be neither an acceptance nor a counter-offer but a mere seeking after further information. Thus in one case M made an offer to sell iron to S at '40s. nett cash per ton' and S replied by asking whether delivery could be over two months. M subsequently sold the iron elsewhere but before the revocation of this offer had been received by S, S accepted on the terms proposed by M. The question arose whether the offer had been rejected by S's reply. If the reply was a counter-offer M was free to sell elsewhere. If it was not a counter-offer but a mere seeking after information, M ought to have revoked it before selling elsewhere. As he had not revoked it the acceptance by S was held to be a valid acceptance in law and M was in breach of contract (*Stevenson v McLean* (1880)).

4 *Contracts for the sale of land.*   Contracts for the sale of land in many respects have distinctive features. One requirement – that they be evidenced in writing – is discussed below at p 255. The sale of land involves many complications not found in other types of sale. The purchaser will probably need a mortgage. The property bought may be subject to a claim by the local authority for road charges. (Local authorities have the right to make up roads and seek payment from the owners of property abutting on the road made up.) The vendor, who appears to be the owner, may offer to sell the freehold yet in fact be the owner only of a lease. These are just three of the difficulties which have to be clarified before the purchaser hands over his purchase money in return for the transfer to him of ownership. Very briefly the stages in the sale of land are as follows:

P (the purchaser) and V (the vendor) agree in outline upon the house and land to be sold and any fittings which are to be included in the sale. Both parties will almost certainly intend to consult a solicitor before being finally bound. Any written note of their agreement must therefore be signed 'subject to contract'. This will have the effect of making the agreement conditional and not binding. The solicitor for P will make the necessary inquiries before contract (e g from the local authority as to liability for road charges) and will agree with V's solicitor upon the precise terms of the formal contract. Both V and P will sign a copy (known as a part) of the contract and return it to his solicitor. The solicitors will then arrange for the exchange of the parts. It is in most cases impossible to find an offer and an acceptance and there is no judicial authority where contracts (i e the parts) are exchanged by post to state when the contract is completed – on the posting or delivery. When contracts are exchanged in this manner the parties are in a contractual relationship with each other. One is bound to sell and the other to buy. Rights in personam exist. If V sells to a third party, he will be liable to P in damages for breach of contract but as P's rights were in personam against V he will have no claim against the property in the hands of the third party. Where only one copy of the agreement is prepared, as where the same solicitor acts for V and P, the second party to sign may be taken as accepting the offer of the other (*Smith v Mansi* (1962)). After the parties become bound in contract the purchaser's solicitor makes further inquiries (e g as to the title of the vendor) and finally the ownership of the land and house is transferred to P by means of a document under seal known as a transfer, where the land is held under registered title, or by conveyance in other cases. The transfer or conveyance acts to pass to P rights in rem – rights of ownership in the land as against the whole world. At this stage P pays the balance of the purchase price to V having in all probability paid the customary 10 per cent of the purchase price to V on exchange of contracts.

From the point of view of our present study, we shall concentrate on the difficulties which arise before and at the exchange of the contracts. Where the parties sign a written document 'subject to contract' then, in the normal case, there is clearly no legal obligation created (*Tiverton Estates Ltd v Wearwell Ltd* (1975)). But where they use other words which are not so clear the court has to determine *as a matter of construction* whether the so-called agreement is conditional upon some event taking place (e g preparation of a formal contract), in which case it will not be binding, *or* whether there is a present unconditional agreement coupled with a statement that the agreement should later be embodied in a formal document. In this latter case the unconditional agreement will be binding and continue to be binding until a later formal document is prepared. If this later document is not prepared the earlier agreement will continue to bind and regulate the conduct of the parties. The words 'I accept your offer and have asked my solicitors to prepare a contract' have been held to bind the parties immediately even though no formal contract is ever prepared (*Rossiter v Miller* (1878)). In another case concerning the sale of a mushroom farm the agreement was expressed to be 'provisional agreement'. Here the court emphasised that questions of construction must each be resolved on the basis of their own facts and in this case the word 'provisional' was interpreted to mean presently binding until a later document was drawn to bind the parties (*Branca v Cobarro* (1947)). In contrast to the decisions on the above words, an agreement to take a lease 'subject to the preparation and approval of a formal contract' has been held not to have any binding legal effect and that no contract would come into existence until the formal contract had been prepared and approved (*Winn v Bull* (1877)). A case concerning the sale of land by exchange of contracts is *Eccles v Bryant* (1947). The parties had signed an agreement 'subject to contract' and then consulted solicitors. Their solicitors agreed upon a draft contract. Each party signed his part and the purchaser forwarded his to the vendor's solicitor for the purpose of exchange. The vendor notified his solicitor of his change of mind and the vendor's solicitor informed the purchaser's solicitor that the vendor had sold the property to another purchaser. The court held that the negotiations were subject to formal contract, so no contract existed during the preliminary negotiations. The means by which the parties intended to be bound was by exchange of contracts and until this took place no binding obligation arose. The court did not say when in law, apart from agreement, the exchange would take place – on the posting or on receipt. Where the contract incorporates the Law Society's Conditions of Sale the exchange is complete when both parts are exchanged, and where the post is used when the second part is actually delivered to the other party.

It cannot be stressed too emphatically that *it is always a question of construction for the courts to determine* whether in any given case the words used by the parties are conditional and not binding upon them *or* unconditional and giving rise immediately to contractual rights and obligations.

5 *Acceptance by post.*   Where according to the ordinary usage of mankind the post may be used as the means of communication between the parties, an acceptance is complete on posting. It thus follows that a communication is not necessary to complete the acceptance. The fact that the acceptance is delayed in the post, or even lost, will not affect the validity of the agreement which is concluded on the posting. However, for this rule to apply it must be clear from the circumstances of the case that the post is to be used as a means of communication and the acceptor must do nothing to contribute to a possible delay in, or failure of, communication of the acceptance to the offeror. Thus the letter of acceptance must be prepaid and correctly addressed. A letter is 'posted' when it is put into the control of the Post Office in the normal manner not, for example, when it is handed to a postman authorised to *deliver* letters (*Re London and Northern Bank ex p Jones* (1900)). As the 'post rule' is an *exception* to the general rule that the acceptance is not complete until communicated to the offeror, it must be strictly applied and not extended to other means of communication. In *Brinkibon Ltd v Stahag Stahl und Stahlwarendels GmbH* (1982) the facts of the case raised the question whether an acceptance by Telex in London and sent to Vienna was made in London or Vienna. The House of Lords said the foundation of the 'post rule' lay in convenience and it is logical to say the *place* as well as the *time* of the acceptance should be *where* and *when* the acceptance was put into the charge of the Post Office. As in this case communication between principals was instantaneous or reasonably so the general rule would apply. The acceptance by Telex would be complete *where* and *when* it had been *received*. That was in Vienna and not within the jurisdiction of the English courts. However, there is authority (*Cowan v O'Connor* (1888)) for the

proposition that the post rules may be extended to telegrams – but no further. An acceptance by telegram is complete when the acceptance is put into the hands of the telegraph service. Students should note that the Post Office no longer offers a telegram service. However, the legal principles established in cases involving telegrams will generally remain valid.

The following three cases are authoritative illustrations of the working of the post rules.

In *Henthorn v Fraser* (1892) F made an offer to sell land to H at £750, the offer to remain open for 14 days. At 3.50 pm on the day after he received the offer H posted a letter accepting F's offer. This letter arrived at 8.30 pm on the day it was posted. At 5.30 pm on that day H received a letter which was posted at mid-day cancelling the offer. It was held that F was under a binding obligation to H as the acceptance was complete on the posting before H received notice of the revocation of the offer.

In *Byrne v Van Tienhoven* (1880) T wrote to B in New York on 1 October offering goods for sale. B received the offer on the 11th and accepted by telegram on the same day, and by letter on the 15th. On the 8th T wrote to B withdrawing the offer and this revocation reached B on the 20th. The court held that, as the offer had been accepted (on the posting) before the revocation had been communicated (on the 20th), there was a binding contract.

In *Household Fire Insurance Co v Grant* (1879) G had applied for (i e offered to buy) shares in the plaintiff company. The shares were allotted to him (i e the offer was accepted) and his name was placed on the register of shareholders. A letter of allotment was posted to G but never received by him. When the company went into liquidation the liquidator made calls upon G to contribute, as a shareholder, the balance owing on the price of his shares. The court held that G was bound to pay the balance as the contract had been completed on the posting of the letter of allotment (acceptance). The following observations were made by the court: (i) the 'post-rules' should be limited to cases where acceptance by post is expressly or impliedly authorised, and (ii) the offeror may protect himself by stipulating that the acceptance is complete only if and when actually received by the offeror on or before a certain date.

An interesting example of a situation where the 'post rules' do not operate is as follows. Under an agreement HS Ltd were given by H an option to purchase land. The agreement provided that the exercise of the option, which would constitute the acceptance of an offer, 'shall be exercisable by notice in writing to' H within six months. HS Ltd posted a letter accepting H's offer (option) to sell but this letter was never delivered. HS Ltd sought specific performance of the contract under which H was to sell the land to HS Ltd. The court held that there was no contract in existence as the post rules do not apply in a case where the offeror clearly requires 'notice' i e *communication* to him of the acceptance

(*Holwell Securities Ltd v Hughes* (1973)). It is well to note that where an offer requires 'notice in writing' of the acceptance, the offeror is not stipulating the post as the means of *communicating* the acceptance. He is stipulating *writing* as the form (or mode) the acceptance shall take. A written note delivered by hand would be sufficient.

By way of summary the following formulation of the 'post rules' may be considered:

Where, expressly or impliedly, by custom or course of dealing between the parties the post may be used as a means of communication, the acceptance is complete on posting, whether the letter of acceptance be delayed or even lost, provided that the letter is prepaid and correctly addressed. This principle may not be extended to acceptance by Telex.

(NB. The 'post rules' deal with '*acceptance*' made through the post and to *offers* and *revocations* which are posted. These two are *never* complete until communicated to the party to whom they are made.)

The reason for the post rules is one of convenience. If the normal rule as to communication of the offer and acceptance applied to postal acceptances such acceptances would be complete only when communicated to the offeror. The acceptor (offeree) would then know in his own mind that he had accepted but would *not* know whether he was bound. If the rule is that the acceptance is complete on posting where the post is the normal means of communication the acceptor (offeree) knows he has accepted and knows he is bound. But here the offeror does not know that a binding contract exists until he receives the acceptance. Whichever rule is adopted either the offeror or the offeree is in the dark. English law favours, in this instance, the offeree by making the acceptance complete on the posting under the circumstances explained above. The rule is based on convenience rather than logic.

6 *Tenders.*   Where a large undertaking, such as a hospital authority or the Ministry of Transport, wants to consider various offers for the supply of goods or the provision of services, such as the supply of vegetables or the building of motorways, it will advertise for tenders. A tender is an estimate submitted *in response to a prior request*. Exactly what is the legal effect of the acceptance of a tender is often a difficult *question of construction*. Where the tender is certain in its terms and is accepted then it constitutes an offer which is accepted and as a result an agreement is reached. If A tenders for the supply of '100 tons of potatoes to the National Hospital to be delivered between 1 January and 31 December 1985' the words of the tender are certain and its acceptance will complete an agreement. Even if the words continued 'as and when required' the agreement would still be for the supply of a definite quantity of potatoes between certain dates. On the other hand, if the tender is for the supply of 'potatoes, if and when required between 1 January and 31 December 1985. Estimated quantity 100 tons', the tender is by no means certain. There is no definite quantity

only an estimated one and if the National Hospital does not require any potatoes there will be no sale. This type of tender is at the best an invitation to treat so acceptance can never conclude a contract but does have the effect of converting it into a *standing offer*. The interpretation placed on such a tender is that it is an offer to supply such quantities as may be required by the National Hospital. Because it is a standing offer it may be withdrawn at any time *before* it is accepted by the placing of a definite order for a specific quantity, but once a specific order is placed the maker of the standing offer must supply the goods ordered within the terms of his standing offer. The order is an acceptance and must be supplied. Revocation thus ceases to be possible in relation to the quantity of goods ordered but revocation may be made for the future – the placing of an order prohibits pro tanto (to that extent) the possibility of revocation. It is possible, of course, to promise consideration for the standing offer in which case there will be a definite contract to keep it open and it cannot be revoked other than in breach of contract. The leading case on the problem of tenders is *Percival v LCC* (1918). P submitted a tender to the LCC for the supply of certain goods 'in such quantities at such times and in such manner as the Committee' shall from time to time require. P's tender was accepted. Estimates of the requirements were given but actual orders were placed elsewhere. P claimed damages for breach of contract. The court held that the LCC were under no obligation to order goods but on the other hand P who had made a standing offer was under the obligation to supply goods which were ordered so long as the offer remained open. P therefore lost his action.

7 *Identical cross-offers.*   Where X offers to sell his car to Y for £500 and at the same time Y offers to buy X's car for £500 a difficult problem arises on which there is little authority. To the layman it would seem that the parties are in agreement but for the lawyer, because there is no offer made by one party to the other and accepted by that other, difficulties arise. Strong obiter dicta of the Court of Exchequer Chamber in 1873 suggest that no contract would result from identical cross-offers (*Tinn v Hoffman*). Brett J said, 'cross-offers are not an acceptance of each other, therefore there will be no offer of either party accepted by the other'. Blackburn J the greatly respected common law judge, said that where there is a contract

> 'there are two assenting minds, the parties agreeing in opinion, and one having promised in consideration of the promise of the other – there is an exchange of promises; but I do not think exchanging offers would, upon principle, be at all the same thing. . . . The promise or offer being made on each side in ignorance of the promise or the offer made on the other side neither of them can be construed as an acceptance of the other'.

All told, five judges gave as their opinion that *no* contract would result from identical cross-offers and two judges opined that there would be a contract. However, both parties are undoubtedly of the same mind on all the important terms – the parties, the property and the price. Each is prepared to offer his own promise as consideration for the promise of the other. On this basis there appears to be a contract. The question has yet to be decided by an English court.

Chapter 13
Consideration and intention to create legal relations

Consideration

It has already been pointed out there are several essential elements of a valid simple contract. Where there is an offer and acceptance there is agreement but the agreement is not enforceable as a contract unless the other essential elements are also present. One such element is consideration. The doctrine of consideration, as it is called, is peculiar to English law. It is based on the view that our law enforces bargains not promises. A firm promise is not enforceable unless bought by some consideration provided by the party seeking to enforce it. Consideration may be an act of forbearance or a promise to act or forbear but whatever form it takes it must be something of value in the eyes of the law. In *Dunlop v Selfridge* ((1915) HL, p 266, below) Lord Dunedin adopted the definition of consideration given by Pollock in his book on *Contracts* where he wrote,

> 'an act or forbearance of one party, or the promise thereof, is the price for which the promise of the other is bought, and the promise thus given for value is enforceable'.

A simple illustration will show how the definition is applied in practice. B contracts to buy coal from S, payment to be made on delivery. S fails to deliver the coal. B, therefore, sues S for breach of his promise to deliver. As plaintiff B will have to prove the contract by showing that all the necessary elements – offer, acceptance and consideration etc – are present. B's consideration will be his *promise* to pay on delivery. This promise is the *price* for which the promise of S to deliver the coal is *bought*. However, the plaintiff must also prove that this consideration and the promise the defendant gave were part of the same bargain. If the promise of one party is given subsequently to the promise, act or forbearance of the other, there will be no contractual relationship between the two. The plaintiff must show that when the promise of the defendant, which is sued on, was made the plaintiff *then* did something in return or promised to do something in the future. If the alleged consideration of the plaintiff had *already been performed* at the time of the promise by the defendant the plaintiff could not claim that he did something *in return* for the promise. The rule may be simply expressed as follows: past consideration is no consideration. In *Roscorla v Thomas* (1842) T sold R a horse and *after* the sale promised him that it was free from vice. Some time later it became apparent that this was not so and R sued T on his promise. R was unable to show that, at the time T promised that the horse was free from vice, he (R) did anything in return or promised to do anything in the future. R's act of paying for the horse had already been performed. Another case is *Re McArdle* (1951). Under a father's will the mother was to live in the family house for her life and thereafter their five children were entitled to the house equally. One of the children and his wife lived with the mother and during her lifetime effected certain improvements to the house which were paid for by the son's wife. Later the five children signed an agreement promising to pay the son's wife the cost of the repairs when the property was distributed on the death of the mother. When in fact the son's wife claimed the money after the death of the mother the children (apart from the married son) refused to sanction the payment. In these circumstances the court held that the alleged consideration – the doing of the repairs – had already been done and was past at the time the promise to pay was made. Therefore, the son's wife failed in her action to recover the cost of the repairs.

There are said to be *two* exceptions to the rule that past consideration is no consideration in law. First, where the consideration was induced by the previous request of the party promising, the subsequent promise is related back to the request and the consideration is then subsequent to the promise. In this case the exception is apparent rather than real. An illustration is the old case of *Lampleigh v Brathwait* (1615). B had killed M and asked L to obtain a pardon for him, L received the pardon *then* B promised to pay him £100 for his trouble. B failed to pay £100 and when sued by L pleaded lack of consideration. The court held that the previous request and subsequent promise were to be treated as part of the same transaction. The subsequent promise is taken as the fixing of the sum to be paid under an *implied promise in the previous request to pay a reasonable sum*. The second exception is to be found in s 27 (2) of the Bills of Exchange Act 1882, where it is stated that a bill of exchange may be supported by an 'antecedent debt or liability'. (For a discussion of the nature of a bill of exchange see p 273, below.)

Promisor and promisee

In any contract each party is a promisor and a promisee and because of this difficulties may arise when a textbook or a judge talks of a promisor or a promisee. If A contracts to build a house for B for £3,500 A is the promisor of the promise to build a house and B is the promisee, the person to whom the promise is made. On the other hand B is the promisor of the promise to pay £3,500 and A is the promisee, the person to whom the promise is made. There is a rule that consideration must move *from* the promisee though *not necessarily* to the promisor. This rule means that the defendant in an action in contract cannot successfully claim the absence of consideration as a defence merely by showing that *he* has received no benefit. In an action based on a contract the person sued on his promise is the defendant, the promisor. So long as consideration moves from the plaintiff he has furnished consideration and it is not necessary for him to show that the defendant received the consideration. Thus where a young man orders flowers to be sent to his fiancée the contract is between the young man and the florist. If the florist is forced to sue the young man for payment for the flowers delivered to his fiancée, so long as the florist (the person to whom payment was promised, i e the promisee) has provided consideration (delivery of the flowers), it does not matter that the young man (the person who promised to pay, i e the promisor) has not received any flowers himself. Consideration must move from the promisee though not necessarily to the promisor. Thus the young man will not be able to plead lack of consideration from the florist as a defence. The act of delivering the flowers was done at his request and this was the consideration given by the florist to him.

It follows from what has been said above that only a person who has provided consideration may derive any enforceable rights under a contract. In the above example the young man has rights against the florist but if the flowers are not delivered the fiancée will not be able to sue for breach of contract because she has not furnished consideration. (Also she is not a party to the contract: see p 262, below.) This principle is illustrated by the well-known case of *Tweddle v Atkinson* (1861). It is particularly noteworthy because here the third party who was to receive a benefit under the contract was expressly given a right to sue to enforce this benefit. Tweddle entered into an agreement with Guy whereby each of them was to pay a certain sum by a specified date to the plaintiff, who was Tweddle's son and who had married Guy's daughter. The agreement gave the plaintiff 'full power to sue the said parties in any court of law or equity for the aforesaid sums hereby promised and specified'. Guy failed to pay any sum to the plaintiff and on his death an action for damages for breach of contract was brought against his executors. Judgment was given for the defendant on the basis that the plaintiff had not provided consideration under the agreement on which his action was based. He had not provided consideration for the defendant's promise.

Executed and executory consideration

Executed consideration is the performance of an act *in return for* a promise. Where, for example, coal is ordered on 'cash with order terms' the payment of the cash is considered as executed consideration. If the coal is not delivered and the coal company is sued for breach of contract the plaintiff proves the payment which *he has in fact made* as support for the defendant's promise to deliver. The reward cases are an example of executed consideration (see p 214, above). Executory consideration arises when the promise of one party is made in return for the promise of the other. Where coal is ordered 'cash on delivery' one party promises to pay in the future in return for the promise of the other to deliver. If the coal is not delivered the plaintiff relies on his *promise* to pay as consideration for the promise of the coal company to deliver the coal.

Past and executed consideration

Consideration is past when at the time the promise of the other is made the act allegedly supporting it has already been performed (see p 225, above). The past act and the later promise are *not* connected as part of the same bargain. Executed consideration is valuable consideration which supports a promise made by another person since either it has not been carried out until after the promise was made or is carried out simultaneously with it. Both are part of the same bargain.

Consideration is something of value in the eyes of the law

To be recognised by the law as consideration the act or forbearance or promise must be some, though not necessarily of fair or equal, value for the promise of the other party. If A promises to give B his car the promise of A will not be enforceable. But if A promises to give B his car in return for B's pencil then, as a pencil is of value in the eyes of the law, albeit of little value when compared with the value of a car, A's promise will be bought by consideration furnished by B and will be enforceable by him. Where the law recognises the consideration it is said to be 'sufficient' or 'real'. Consideration must be sufficient in law but it need not be adequate commercially, i e of equal value from the point of view of the commercial man. For instance, in the above example, in the popular sense A has not struck a favourable bargain because the consideration he receives – a pencil – is totally inadequate. The court does not concern itself with the commercial adequacy of the promises of the parties. The following few pages will be devoted to showing various situations where the law finds a consideration, even though it is of exceedingly little value, and other situations where the law fails to recognise the act alleged to be consideration as *sufficient in law*.

(a) *Cases where the consideration is of little value.*   1. A compromise made in good faith of a claim is sufficient consideration though the claim may not be sustainable at law. If R trespasses on the land of S, he will be liable to S for the tort of trespass. If S forbears to sue for damages his forbearance will support a promise by R to pay compensation. However, it may subsequently turn out that R and S were mistaken and that the land belonged to R and so his act was no trespass. Even in these circumstances the forbearance of R will be consideration. In the words of Bowen LJ (in *Miles v New Zealand Alford Estate Co* (1886))

'The reality of the claim which is given up must be measured, not by the state of the law as it is ultimately discovered to be, but *by the state of the knowledge of the person who at the time has to judge and make the concession*. Otherwise you would have to try the whole cause to know if the man had a right to compromise it'.

2. The case of *De la Bère v Pearson* (1908) is often said to be a case where the court stretched the doctrine of consideration to its limits in order to find consideration and so provide a remedy where there ought to have been one. B read an advertisement in the financial section of a newspaper where the proprietor offered financial advice. B wrote up for the name of a reliable stockbroker through whom he could safely invest in stocks and shares. P, in reply, supplied B with the name of an undischarged bankrupt and as a result B lost money on his investments. At this time the general belief was that there was no liability in law for an innocent misstatement (see p 162, above) and B's only hope for a remedy lay in contract but he had to show a consideration for P's promise to give the name of a good stockbroker. The court found such a promise in P's *option* to publish B's letter of enquiry in whole or part. Thus B received damages for breach of a contract to provide sound financial advice. As P did not know that the stockbroker was an undischarged bankrupt he was not liable in fraud (a tort) but Pollock suggested that liability should be regarded 'as arising from default in the performance of a voluntary undertaking independent of contract'. The opinion appears particularly cogent in view of the *Hedley Byrne Case* (1963) (p 161, above).

3. In the case of *Alliance Bank Ltd v Broom* (1864) B, who had an overdraft of £22,000, was asked by the bank to furnish some sort of security. He promised to do this but failed to do so and was sued by the Bank on his promise to provide security. The court held that the Bank had given consideration in their forbearance to sue even though after a short time they brought their action. A forbearance to sue is valuable consideration even where it is only for a short time. In this type of case the courts take the view that the forbearance is at the implied request of the debtor. If this were not so the Bank, in the above case, would not have been able to show that they had furnished a consideration in return for the promise to provide security for the debt.

4. In *Thomas v Thomas* (1842) a deceased had left his house to his sons and before he died he had expressed a desire that his wife should be allowed to live in the house for her life. On his death the executors entered into an agreement with the widow to give her a life interest for £1 per year. When sued on this agreement the executors pleaded lack of consideration but were unable to deny that the payment of the rent of £1 per year was sufficient (real) consideration in law.

5. In situations where, as part of a sales promotion, a retailer offers something in addition to the goods offered at the advertised price, difficulties often arise. The Nestlé Company Limited advertised a rock music record for sale at 1s 6d plus three wrappers from their 6d milk chocolate bars. Subsequently a claim was made for royalties to be paid on the retail price of the record. Was the true retail price 1s 6d or 1s 6d plus three wrappers? Nestlé Company Ltd argued that the wrappers were useless to them and were thrown away when received, therefore the royalty should be based on 1s 6d. The House of Lords said that consideration was not limited to a single payment or single act but could involve two or more requirements. Here the Nestlé Company Limited required *cash* plus *wrappers* and both formed part of the consideration, it being irrelevant that the wrappers were of little or no value to the Nestlé Company Ltd. The company received what it had requested as part of the bargain (*Chappell and Co Ltd v Nestlé Co Ltd* (1960)).

(b) *Cases where the law considers the sufficiency of the consideration.*   Before the law will recognise an act of forbearance or promise as consideration it must be of some economic value to the promisee.

1 If a person does no more than he is bound to do by virtue of a duty imposed by law he will not have furnished consideration. Where a person on subpoena (under a penalty) attends court as a witness he does not furnish consideration for the promise of another party to pay the expenses of his attendance (*Collins v Godefroy* (1831)). But if more is done than the legal obligation requires consideration is given in return for a promise to pay for the act. A similar situation exists with regard to contractual duties. If A is under contract to act as a member of a ship's crew, a promise to pay him more than agreed if he continues his services after two crew members have deserted is not consideration. He does no more than he is obliged to do (*Stilk v Myrick* (1809)). On the other hand, where the crew is so depleted in number on account of desertion and death that the journey becomes inherently dangerous, continuing in service is consideration for a promise to pay above the agreed wage. In these circumstances continued performance of the contract could not be enforced as the contract would be discharged by frustration (see p 319, below) (*Hartley v Ponsonby* (1857)). However, where the person to whom a promise is made is in a contractual relationship, not with the promisor but with a third party, any promise by the promisee to perform, or the performance of his

contract with the third party, will be sufficient consideration to support the promise made to him by the promisor. In one case S, a young barrister, was engaged to Ellen Nichol. His uncle promised him on his marriage a yearly sum during his uncle's life until S's income at the bar should reach six hundred guineas. On the uncle's death, S sued his executors for the arrears and the court held that his performance of the promise to marry Ellen Nichol was a real consideration for the promise of the uncle and he recovered the arrears (*Shadwell v Shadwell* (1860)).

2 At common law there is a simple rule that the payment of less than the sum which is due to a creditor will not be sufficient consideration to support his promise not to sue for the full debt. If A is indebted to B and B gratuitously promises not to sue A for the debt or promises not to sue if A pays half the debt, B may go back on his promise. In neither case has A provided consideration as in one case A gave B nothing at all and in the other he gave him only half of what he had the right to insist on. This rule can be illustrated by reference to *Pinnel's Case* (1602). P sued Cole in debt for £8 10s 0d, payable on a bond (a promise under seal to pay money) which became due on 11 November. Cole's defence was that *at P's request* he had paid him £5 2s 6d on 1 October and P had accepted this in full satisfaction of the debt. Judgment was given for the plaintiff on a technical fault, otherwise, it was said

> 'payment of a lesser sum on the day ... cannot be any satisfaction for the whole but a change in time or mode of payment, or the addition by the debtor of a tomtit, or canary or the like will suffice to constitute consideration for the plaintiff's (the creditor's) promise to forgo his debt'.

Thus, as a general rule, at common law a creditor could go back on his promise to accept less than the full debt unless:

(i) At the creditor's request the debtor made an earlier payment. This gives the creditor something to which he is not entitled and, therefore, is consideration. A later payment of less will not be sufficient as after the due date the creditor is entitled to the full sum.

(ii) There is an altered mode of payment. The normal method of payment is in cash. If this is not followed, or if the originally prescribed method, being other than by cash, is not followed, the payment by any other mode will be sufficient, e g where £10 cash is due, the handing over of a book worth only £5 will discharge the obligation to pay £10 cash.

For several years it was thought that the payment of a cheque for less than the sum of money which was due was sufficient alteration of mode to discharge the full debt. However, following *D and C*

Builders Ltd v Rees (1965, CA) this argument will be held to be wrong unless the defendant can show (a) that payment by cheque was made at the specific request of the creditor, and (b) that it would be inequitable for the creditor to go back on his agreement to accept a lesser sum. In this case D & C Builders Ltd pressed for the payment of £482, owed to them by Rees for work done. The builders were being pressed by their own creditors. Mrs Rees, knowing this, offered them a cheque for £300 in full settlement, which offer was accepted. Later the builders sued for the balance. The Court of Appeal held that there was no true accord here as Mrs Rees had put pressure on the builders, which she was able to do in the circumstances, to accept the cheque; nor was the alleged accord binding in law as it was not supported by consideration. The payment *by cheque* was not sufficient alteration of mode to amount to consideration as it was not done at the request of the builders. It was held, in addition, that there was no equity in the defendant to warrant any departure from the due course of law.

(iii)   Something of value in the eyes of the law is added. If A owes B £50 and pays only £10, so long as he gives B consideration for his promise not to sue for the balance of £40 B will not be able to sue for the balance. Thus if A gives B a canary he will be considered as having bought the forbearance to sue for £40 by the payment of a canary. B could not have insisted on A giving him the canary so he has received something of value.

In each case the change in time of payment, mode of payment or addition of something of value must be done at the request of the creditor and in return for his promise not to sue.

The harshness of this common law principle was applied by the House of Lords in *Foakes v Beer* (1884). Mrs B had obtained a judgment against Dr F ordering him to pay her £2,090. Judgment debts bear interest from the date of the judgment. Dr F could not pay and, by a written agreement (not under seal), he agreed to pay £500 immediately and the balance by instalments. In return for this promise Mrs B promised to forego proceedings on the judgment (she could have obtained a court order ordering the seizure and sale of Dr F's property). Once the balance had been paid, Mrs B demanded payment of interest due. The House of Lords reviewed the existing *common law* and held that, in the absence of consideration, Mrs B's promise to forego proceedings on the payment was not enforceable. Dr F had not *bought* her promise not to sue for interest.

Equitable estoppel.   The harshness of this common law rule has to a limited extent been mitigated in equity by the principle of promissory estoppel, also known as the principle of *High Trees Case* (1947). The principle may be stated thus: If A, a party to a legal relationship, intending legal consequences, promises B, the other party to the relationship, that he (A) will not insist on his full rights under the relationship provided that B does, or refrains from, some act and B relying on this promise, does so act to his detriment, B may use the promise as a defence to an action by A to enforce A's original rights. The principle aroused great controversy when reported in 1947 as it was merely obiter dicta and was in contradiction to *Foakes v Beer*, a House of Lords' decision; moreover, it seemed to strike at the roots of the doctrine of consideration. The facts of the *High Trees Case* are as follows: In September 1939, A leased a block of flats to B at a rent of £2,500 per annum. As a result of the war conditions in 1940 B could not readily get tenants for the flats and he was carrying on the lease at a loss. The parties in this year agreed in writing on a reduction in the rent to £1,250 per annum, i e a promise by A to accept less than the sum due in *future* years. No time limit was expressed for the operation of this reduction. By 1945 the flats were again fully let at a rent to the individual tenants of B far higher than that contemplated in 1939. A, in 1945, claimed the full rent for the last two quarters of that year. In the course of his argument counsel for A, the plaintiff, said that if he had wished he could have claimed the full rent back to 1940 on the principle that payment of less than the full sum due is never a discharge of the whole debt though so agreed. Denning J gave judgment for the plaintiff. He held that implied in the agreement of 1940 between A and B was a term to the effect that the agreement was to operate only so long as the shortage of tenants created by the war existed. In 1945 conditions had changed and A was entitled to the full rent. That decided the case, but Denning J went on to consider (obiter) the suggestion of counsel that he could validly have claimed the arrears of rent. He held against the plaintiff on this point. Estoppel is a rule of evidence which prevents a person from denying the truth of some statement previously made by him. For the rule to apply *at common law* the statement must be one as to existing fact (e g *Jorden v Money* (1854)) whereas the statement by A in 1940 was as to his future conduct. Common law estoppel was thus not applicable here. Denning J, however, found authority for the view he expressed in the case of *Hughes v Metropolitan Rly Co* (1877, HL) where it was pointed out that the rule applies where it would be *inequitable* to allow a person to go back on his promise. The facts of the case are that under a lease the landlord could give his tenant six months' notice to repair the premises let and if the tenant failed to effect the necessary repairs in the time the landlord could forfeit the lease. The landlord gave the tenant notice to repair then opened negotiations with him for the sale of the property to the tenant. During these negotiations the tenant neither did repairs nor sought alternative accommodation. The sale fell through and the landlord sought to enforce the forfeiture at the end of six months from the giving of the original notice. The House of Lords held that he could not do this as he had, during the negotiations, impliedly suspended the notice. He could, however, give notice again and enforce the forfeiture at the end of six months.

> 'It is the first principle upon which all Courts of Equity proceed, that if parties who have entered into definite and distinct terms involving certain legal results . . . afterwards by their own act . . . enter upon a course of negotiations which has the effect of leading one of the parties to suppose that the strict rights arising under the contract will not be enforced . . . the person who otherwise might have enforced those rights will not be allowed to enforce them where it would be inequitable, having regard to the dealings which have thus taken place between the parties.' (*per* Lord Cairns LC).

In 1888 the case was followed in the Court of Appeal.

The principle of promissory estoppel has been severely criticised on many grounds, most of them based on misunderstanding. The following points should be noted:

(1) The principle can be invoked only where a promise is made with the intention that it should be acted on and the promisee did so *act to his detriment*. It is this latter point which was stressed by Lord Tucker in his judgment in the *Tool Metal Case* (1955, HL) in which the principle of promissory estoppel was referred to as the principle in *Hughes v Metropolitan Rly Co*, not as an undesirable invention of Denning J. For example, where S owes R £100 due on a contract and R tells S that he will accept £10 in full satisfaction of the debt, at common law R may go back on is promise and in equity promissory estoppel will not apply if all S does is pay the £10. S will have to show that he acted to his *detriment*, e g buying a tape recorder for £50 in reliance on R's promise and thus making himself less able to pay the debt if called upon to do so by R. In these circumstances it would be inequitable to allow R to go back on his promise.

Although the idea that the promisee must act to his detriment is not free from doubt, it can hardly be inequitable to allow a promisor to go back on his promise unless the promisee has acted in some way to his detriment or refrained from acting as he would otherwise have wished as a result of the promise. However, what amounts to 'detriment' is not at all clear.

(2) The effect of the equity is *suspensory* except where it is no longer possible to restore the promisee to his original position, that is to say, the obligation is not extinguished nor is the right to sue extinguished but the right to sue is in effect suspended by the equitable defence. If the promise is made for an express period of time or by reference to special circumstances the promise comes to an end at the end of the time or on the alteration of the circumstances as in the *High Trees Case*. In appropriate circumstances, reasonable notice must be given before the promisor can withdraw his promise and revert to the original position.

(3) The principle acts as a *defence* – a 'shield and not a sword'. If a husband promises his wife an allowance and in reliance on this promise she forbears to sue for an order for maintenance payments in a divorce action against him, she cannot sue on his promise if he fails to make the payments as promised. This was held to be the position in *Combe v Combe* (1951, CA) where Denning LJ, as he was by then, took the opportunity of restating and explaining the principle behind the equity. The principle could be used, he pointed out, only where the party who was suing had made a promise, had gone back on it and was bringing the action against a person who had acted in reliance on the promise. This was the position in both *Hughes' Case* and the *High Trees Case* where the landlords had made promises and then went back on them. In *Combe v Combe* the *husband* had made the promise and his *wife* sued on it. The real distinction is that in the cases such as *High Trees* where the equitable principle applies, a contract or legal relationship of some kind already exists between the parties and A merely promises to *refrain* from enforcing his full contractual rights so that B may use this promise as a *defence* against an action brought to enforce the original rights. In *Combe v Combe*, on the other hand, there was no existing contract and A's promise was to *do* something. Because this promise had not been bought by consideration on her part B could not enforce it. She could sue neither at common law nor in equity on her husband's promise because it was unsupported by consideration.

(4) Thus, a point also made clear in *Combe v Combe*, is that the principle of promissory estoppel *does not strike at the roots of the doctrine of consideration*. Consideration is essential to the formation of contract though not necessarily to its variation. The principle applies only where there is an existing contract, with its attendant agreement plus *consideration*, which is varied by one of the parties promising not to insist on his strict rights under the agreement. In *Hughes' Case* and *High Trees Case* there was an existing contract (a lease) a term of which was varied by the landlord. In *Combe v Combe* there was, as we have seen, no existing contract varied by the husband's promise to make maintenance payments to the wife.

Lord Hailsham, the Lord Chancellor, has suggested that the whole concept of promissory estoppel is in need of review (*Woodhouse A.C. etc. v Nigerian Produce Marketing Co Ltd* (1972)).

3 A particular type of situation where payment of less than the sum due can effectively discharge the whole debt is where a person who cannot pay his debt in full makes a composition arrangement with his creditors. Under such an arrangement the debtor and all his creditors reach an agreement whereunder the debtor pays each creditor so much in the pound on the debt owed to him. Where this agreement is reached and each creditor is paid in proportion it would be a breach of contract for

one creditor to go back on his promise not to sue the debtor for the full debt which he made to the other creditors in return for a similar promise by them. There is clearly consideration between the creditors inter se (amongst themselves). But where is the consideration by the debtor to support a creditor's promise not to sue him for the full debt? If none can be found a perfectly reasonable and desirable practice could be made ineffective. However, the courts will not allow a creditor to go back on his promise as this would amount to permitting him to commit a fraud on the other parties – an argument of convenience rather than of legal principle.

A similar argument of convenience is the basis of decisions similar to that in *Hirachand Punamchand v Temple* (1911). The father of Lieutenant Temple, who was indebted to the plaintiffs, wrote to them offering a sum less than the debt in full satisfaction of their claim against his son. The plaintiffs cashed the draft sent by the father and began proceedings against the son. The court concluded that by accepting the draft, the plaintiffs had assented to the terms on which it was offered. But would this avail the son when sued on his debt? The implied promise not to sue was made to his father and in any case the son had not furnished consideration for the plaintiffs' implied promise not to sue him. The court held in favour of the son saying that it would be a fraud on the father and an abuse of the process of the court to allow the plaintiffs to succeed. Fletcher Moulton LJ also put forward another argument which is perhaps more satisfactory – that the payment by the father extinguished the obligation of the son to pay. Thus there was no longer a debt on which the plaintiffs could sue. Where A pays B £50 in return for B's promise to release C from his obligation to pay B £100, the payment of the £50 extinguishes the debt of C.

History of the doctrine of consideration

The origin of consideration as an essential element of a contract is obscure. Some writers suggest that its origin lies in the requirement of the old Writ of Debt that the plaintiff had to show that he had passed something of value (the quid pro quo) to the defendant in return for the defendant's promise to pay. Others suggest that it originates from the tort action of Assumpsit where a person undertakes (assumes an obligation) to carry out an obligation in return for a promise. Salmond argues that its origin is not English at all and that consideration came from outside the common law. He regards it as an importation by the Lord Chancellor who would require consideration by one party as the justification for enforcing the promise of the other. *If* this is so, there would appear to be little doubt that the idea is borrowed from the Roman Law of Contracts where there was no general law of contract but a series of special contract-type situations. Each situation would involve a promise which was enforceable because of some additional element known as a causa. Salmond suggests that consideration is the causa of English law.

Whatever may have been its origin it is clear that by the seventeenth century consideration was required in English law but its exact nature was yet to become a source of argument. In *Pillans v Van Mierop* (1765) Lord Mansfield CJ said that consideration was only *evidence* of an agreement and that if other evidence were present (e g writing) then the absence of consideration would not render the agreement unenforceable. This was the view of consideration taken by equity. But in 1778, in *Rann v Hughes*, the Lord Chancellor, acting on the advice of the judges, overruled this view and laid down the rule that consideration was an essential *element* of a contract and not merely *evidence* of a contract which exists independently of consideration. Thus a simple promise by A to pay B £10 is not enforceable by B as he does not provide consideration for A's promise.

Lord Mansfield, convinced of the evils of a requirement of consideration, framed his definition of consideration so widely as to cover most situations. He accepted a moral obligation as consideration and its validity was accepted without argument by Gibbs J in *Lee v Muggeridge* (1813). The view effectively destroyed the doctrine of consideration because as every promise involves a moral obligation to perform it so every promise was supported by consideration. However attractive this view may have been to Lord Mansfield, it did not commend itself to common lawyers without his zeal for reform and in *Eastwood v Kenyon* (1840) it was overruled and expressed to be wrong.

The result is that we now have a law of contract which will only enforce bargains – contracts where something is given in return for something. Not all promises are enforceable; the doctrine of consideration tells us which promises are.

As an exception to this rule it is important to note that *where a promise is in the form of a deed it will be enforceable on account of its form and will not require to be supported by consideration* (see p 252, below).

Intention to create legal relations

Even when the parties have reached an agreement and each has furnished consideration for the promise of the other there is not necessarily a contract in being. English law demands also that there be an intention to enter into a legal relationship. Without this intention there will be no contract, only an agreement. An invitation to dinner may result in an agreement plus consideration. The invitor impliedly promises to pay for the meal and the invitee incurs the expense of travelling to the place of dining but such an arrangement is unlikely to be intended to have legal consequences. As a general approach to problems of intention to enter legal relations it may be said that where the arrangement is a social one the courts incline strongly against any legal consequences being intended and where the arrangement is of a business nature the courts presume the necessary intention (*Edwards v Skyways* (1964)). This intention is to be gathered from what the parties say or do and in many cases where a firm promise is made and consideration given the courts will assume the presence of the intention to enter into a legal relationship without any argument on the point, so long as the absence of the intention is not pleaded by way of defence. As a result of this readiness by the courts to find the required intention there is little learning in English law on this element of a contract. There are situations where an agreement supported by consideration will fail to be a contract because the intention to enter legal relations is lacking. Whether the intention to enter legal relations exists is always a matter of construction for the courts to determine. In a case where a garage advertised a free coin depicting a world cup football star with every four gallons of petrol sold the House of Lords held that the coins were *given* as a free gift with every four gallons, and they did *not* pass to the buyer under a contract for the sale of petrol (*Esso Petroleum Co Ltd v Customs and Excise Commissioners* (1976)).

1 Intention expressly negatived

In certain cases the intention will be expressly negatived. Where an agreement is reached and the parties wish to avoid the jurisdiction of the courts arising they can specifically provide that there shall be no legal consequences as a result of their agreement. In effect they deny the intention to enter legal relations. This is done most frequently in business contracts where the courts would be ready to presume the existence of the intention if it were not expressly negatived. In football pool 'betting' the agreement (between the 'investor' who backs his selections by stake-money in return for a promise made by the football pool company to pay prize-money if his selections are correct) is invariably expressed to be 'binding in honour only' and 'not subject to the jurisdiction of the courts'. Thus in the event of an investor claiming his winnings in a legal action based on the 'contract' made with the football pool company he will be met with the successful defence that there is no contract on which to sue as the intention to enter legal relations is expressly negatived (*Jones v Vernon's Pools Ltd* (1938)). Another well-known illustration is the case of *Rose and Frank Co v Crompton & Bros Ltd* (1925, HL). The defendants, English manufacturers of paper tissues, entered into an agreement with an American firm, the plaintiffs, constituting them sole agents for sale in the United States of their tissues supplied by the English firm. The agreement ran, 'This arrangement is not entered into . . . as a formal legal agreement, and shall not be subject to legal jurisdiction in the law courts'. While the agreement was still in existence between the parties the plaintiffs placed several orders which were accepted but before they were executed the defendants withdrew from the agreement. In an action by the plaintiffs for breach of contract the defendants pleaded that there was no agreement enforceable by law. The House of Lords held that the agreement was unenforceable because at its creation it lacked an essential element of a valid contract. But the placing of the orders which were accepted resulted in an enforceable contract because here the House of Lords found an intention that the normal legal consequences should follow. Under the agreement 'there was no obligation on the American Company to order goods or upon the English conpanies to accept an order' but

> 'any actual transaction between the parties . . . gave rise to the ordinary legal rights; for the fact that it was not an obligation to do the transaction did not divest the transaction, when done, of its ordinary legal significance.' (*per* Lord Phillimore).

The 'subject to contract' cases are examples of situations where the parties reach agreement without intending to give rise to any legal obligation (see p 219, above, particularly *Eccles v Bryant*).

2 Relationship of the parties

In other cases the relationship of the parties will be evidence of the absence of any intention to create a legal obligation. In social situations the courts will be loth to find that a binding intention exists. An invitation to dinner does not invite litigation nor does an invitation to a young lady to take her to the theatre involve legal consequences if the young man inviting her fails to turn up. However, where the circumstances are such as to show an intention to be legally bound the courts will enforce the agreement even though it has a social as opposed to a business background. If A and B agree to dine together on the basis that A pays for the meal and B for the drinks there will probably be a contract. Also, where a husband and wife enter an agreement expressly stating that their agreement is to be legally binding the courts will probably apply their intention.

An interesting case where a contract was found to exist is the case of *Simpkins v Pays* (1955). S was a lodger with P, an elderly woman, and her granddaughter. S was very keen on entering competitions to be found in Sunday newspapers and on going to lodge at the home of P, was joined by P and her granddaughter in entering for various competitions. S drew up the forms in the name of P and the expenses of entry fees were shared. P promised to share any winnings obtained. One entry in a fashion competition won a prize of £750 which P refused to share. The Court held that there was an intention to enter a legal relationship. S had for years been a competitor and only combined efforts with the others on the basis of their entries being a joint effort, each sharing expenses and each having the benefit of any prize-money. Again in *Peck v Lateu* (1973) the Court found an intention to enter legal relations where two ladies entered an agreement to share winnings made by either of them when playing bingo.

A very well-known case where a promise was unenforceable is *Balfour v Balfour* (1919, CA). A husband went to India leaving his wife in England for the benefit of her health and promising to pay her £30 per month as maintenance. Later the wife obtained a divorce and the husband refused to make any further payments. When sued on his promise he argued that his promise was meant to fulfil a moral not a legal obligation. (Note also the wife provided no consideration.) The Court of Appeal accepted the argument of the husband and the wife failed in her action. But this case must not be taken as authority for the view that no contract can arise between husband and wife. In circumstances where each promises a definite consideration for the other and both intend to be bound by the agreement the courts will enforce their contract. Where the parties are separated or are about to separate the presumption of fact against an intention to enter legal relations as between husband and wife does not arise Thus an agreement between the husband and wife living apart to the effect that if the wife completes the mortgage repayments on the matrimonial home the husband conveys the house to her is enforceable (*Merritt v Merritt* (1969)).

The daughter of a resident in Trinidad was persuaded by her mother to give up her salaried employment and study for the Bar in England. In return for this the mother agreed to pay maintenance to the daughter and later to provide her with a house in England instead of the maintenance. After a while, when the daughter had passed some of the Bar examinations but not all, the mother sought possession of the house. The house had been conveyed to the mother. The Court of Appeal held that throughout the agreement was no more than a family arrangement having no intention to enter a legal relationship. The mother was entitled to possession of the house (*Jones v Padavatton* (1969)).

Where one of the parties is a public body under a statutory duty to supply what is 'contracted for' the courts have held, rather surprisingly, that there is no intention to enter into legal relations by the public body but only an intention to carry out its statutory duty. If the electricity supply, which is provided under an agreement with an electricity board, fails, so that a farmer's chickens die, the board will not be liable for breach of contract (*Willmore v South Eastern Electricity Board* (1957)). In another case it was held that no contract existed with the Postmaster General for the carriage of postal packets (*Triefus v Post Office* (1957)).

Chapter 14

Capacity of the parties

The law does not allow every person to enter into contracts freely. In some cases the law denies to a person contractual capacity in order to protect him. The study of capacity as an essential element in a valid simple contract involves a study of those classes of persons whom, for one reason or another, the law protects. The classes we shall consider are persons still in their minority (formerly known as infancy), persons suffering from mental incapacity or drunkenness and corporations.

A. Minority

Minors have long been protected by the law on account of their tender years though at the upper end of the age limit they may be as cunning as anyone. A minor is a person under the age of 18 years and he attains the age of 18 at the first moment of time on the eighteenth anniversary of his birth (Family Law Reform Act 1969).

At one time this branch of the law was particularly important. The age of majority, the age at which the law recognised a person as being able to contract freely, was fixed as 21 years. Today the age is 18 years. Fewer people are, therefore, in the section of society which the law seeks to protect. In the nineteenth century and earlier, it was usual for infant (now minor) defendants to be the sons of wealthy fathers.

The law aims to protect minors but not to prevent them entering contracts at all. Thus the basic common law is that minors' contracts are *enforceable by* minors but *not against* them. It is said that they are *voidable*, i e *void* as against the minor but *enforceable by him*. Such contracts are clearly one-sided. (Students should note what is said here most carefully because the word 'voidable' also has another meaning in relation to minors' contracts.) Where a minor enters into a contract voidable in this sense, he may avoid his obligations under it at any time – under or over the age of 18 – and it will become binding on him only when he ratifies it after attaining his majority. It will not bind him unless there is ratification after full age.

This is the basic nature of minors' contracts out of which the other three classes we shall refer to are carved. There are certain classes of contract on which a minor may be sued and statute has provided a class which is 'absolutely void'.

Contracts on which a minor may be sued

1 *Contracts for necessaries.* A minor *at common law* is liable to pay a reasonable price for necessaries (not, note, necessities). Necessaries here are goods *or services* suitable to his station in life and actual requirements at the time of sale and delivery. The expression is wider than the basic necessities of food and clothing and embraces different things in relation to different minors. It is clearly a flexible concept which will vary considerably with the minor's social status, his employment and his income among other factors.

As far as goods are concerned the rules are now in statutory form. The Sale of Goods Act 1979, s 3 provides that a minor shall be obliged to pay a reasonable price for necessaries sold *and delivered*. If goods are sold but before delivery the minor decides not to have them there is no obligation on the part of the minor to pay for them. Necessaries are defined by the Act as goods suitable to the condition in life of the minor and to his actual requirements at the time of sale *and* delivery. Neither at common law nor under the statute is the minor obliged to pay the contract price – only a reasonable price.

When considering whether a contract is one for necessaries the courts have first of all to determine whether the goods or services are capable of amounting to necessaries in law and then to consider whether they are in fact necessaries in the particular case. How the rules work can best be illustrated by reference to the facts of several decided cases. In *Nash v Inman* (1908), perhaps the best-known case on this topic, an under-graduate minor was supplied with several items of clothing including fancy waistcoats. His father gave evidence that he was already adequately supplied with clothing and the minor's tailor lost the case against him for payment for the goods delivered. In one case the court held that a pair of jewelled solitaires costing £25 could not in law be necessaries for a minor with an annual income of £500 (*Ryder v Wombwell* (1868)). In another case it was held that a gold watch and chain could be necessaries for an undergraduate minor (*Peters v Fleming* (1840)). In *Chapple v Cooper* (1844) Alderson B, discussing what necessaries were in law said,

> 'Articles of *mere* luxury are always excluded, though luxurious articles of utility are in some cases allowed'.

In this case an undertaker sought to recover the cost of a funeral carried out at the request of a widow for her husband, where the widow was still a minor. The minor was here held liable to pay for the services rendered as being necessary to the minor's station in life. If a lavish funeral had been provided for a family of humble means and social position it is suggested that nothing would have been recoverable by the undertaker as the services he provided would not have been suitable to the station in life of the family and therefore would not constitute necessaries.

However, a contract which appears to be for necessaries – goods or services – will not be enforceable against a minor where it contains an onerous term. Whether a term is sufficiently onerous to have this effect will depend on the circumstances of each case. In *Fawcett v Smethurst* (1914) a minor was held not liable for the hire of a car, which was a necessary service in this case, because it contained a term making him liable for damage to the car in any event, which would, of course, include the fault of another person.

2 *Beneficial contracts of service.* Contracts of service connected with apprenticeship, for education or closely analogous thereto which are for the benefit of a minor may be enforced against him as well as by him. The type of contract here envisaged is one under which a minor gains some training or experience or instruction in his future career. Mere trading contracts, which involve buying and selling, may undoubtedly be for the benefit of the minor, but will not fall within this category and contracts within the category will not be enforceable *against* the minor unless, when construed as a whole, at the time of the making of the contracts they were for his benefit.

In *Clements v L. and N.W. Rly Co* (1894) an agreement whereby a minor gave up his right to personal injury benefit under the Employers' Liability Act 1880 was held to be a valid contract of service for the benefit of the minor because it also gave him rights under an insurance scheme to which his employers contributed and his rights under this scheme were more beneficial. Thus, on balance and even though the contract took away certain rights it was for the minor's benefit. In *Doyle v White City Stadium Ltd* (1935), a minor boxer contracted to fight for £3,000, the contract being expressed to be subject to the rules of the British Boxing Board of Control. One of these rules provided that on a disqualification a boxer's purse should be withheld. The minor was disqualified but claimed the £3,000 from the promoters and Board. As the minor was a young boxer, a profession in which apprenticeship in the usual sense is not possible, it was said that this type of contract was analogous to a contract of apprenticeship. The contract would be enforceable against him if it was for his benefit when read as a whole. The minor argued that this could not be for his benefit as it deprived him of his purse-money. The court held that he could not recover the money withheld. The contract looked at as a whole was beneficial and even the offending clause was one which was designed to encourage clean fighting and thereby protect the young and inexperienced against the wiles of the older and experienced.

Because this type of contract is confined to contracts of service or those closely analogous thereto (see *Doyle's Case*, above), trading contracts are not enforceable against a minor, nor can he be made bankrupt on account of trading debts. In *Cowern v Nield* (1912) a hay and straw dealer who was a minor was held not bound to repay the price of hay he had failed to deliver.

In *Roberts v Gray* (1913) a minor was held liable on an executory contract. The minor had contracted to go on a world tour with a professional billiards player and to receive instruction from him. Before the minor had received any instruction under the contract he changed his mind and refused to go on the tour. The minor was held liable for breach of contract.

The nature of the minor's liability is sometimes most important. Is it a liability on the contract or is it a liability in 'quasi-contract' to pay a reasonable sum for a need satisfied? Quasi-contract means literally 'as if contract' and refers to situations where an obligation exists as if arising from contract although in fact there is no contract (see further p 308, below). In *Roberts v Gray* (1913) the courts enforced a contractual liability against the minor but if they had held that his liability was quasi-contractual then the minor would not have been obliged to pay damages because no need had been satisfied under the executory contract. However, support for the view that a minor's liability is quasi-contractual is to be found in the obiter dictum of Fletcher Moulton LJ in *Nash v Inman* (above) where he said,

> 'The foundation of the action . . . is not in contract, it is the obligation the law imposes on an infant to make a fair payment in respect of needs satisfied'.

3 *Voidable contracts.* We now come to our *second* use of the word voidable. Here it means *valid and binding on a minor unless and until avoided by him while he is a minor or within a reasonable time of his reaching the age of 18.* Such contracts bind a minor automatically with the passing of time. Ratification on full age is not necessary. When a minor avoids a contract of this type he is liable on the contract up to the time of the avoidance but no longer thereafter. Money paid by the minor before the avoidance by him is irrecoverable unless there has been a total failure of consideration. Contracts which fall within this category are those which involve an interest in permanent or continuing property such as shares, land, partnerships and trust deeds. An excellent illustration of the position is the case of a minor who takes a ten year lease of a flat at the age of 16 at a rent of £1,000 p.a. At 17 he avoids the lease. Between 16 and 17 he is liable on the covenants of the lease and to pay the rent and arrears, if any. From 17 onwards he is not obliged to pay rent or to keep up with the covenants. The lease is at an end. (It is well to note that under the Law of Property Act 1925, s 1 (6) a minor cannot own a legal estate in land with the result

that when he 'takes' a lease his interest is recognised by equity only.)

The following are decided cases which illustrate the rules relating to minors' voidable contracts. In *Steinberg v Scala (Leeds) Ltd* (1923) a female minor had bought shares in a company and later calls were made upon her. (A call is a demand by a company for the payment of the balance of the purchase price of its shares.) The minor avoided the contract and tried to recover the money she had already paid. The court held that the minor would not be liable for future calls and from the date of avoidance the minor ceased to have any liability on the shares but it was also held that the minor could not recover money paid because there had been no total failure of consideration. The minor had attended no meetings and had received no dividend but she paid money for the shares to be allotted to her and this they were. A case to contrast with *Steinberg v Scala* is *Corpe v Overton* (1833) in which a minor agreed to enter a partnership to be formed in the future and paid £100 by way of advance. He repudiated this agreement and was allowed to recover the £100 as there had been a total failure of consideration.

The avoidance of the contract entered into during minority may be made while the person avoiding is still under eighteen years of age or within a reasonable time thereafter. What amounts to a reasonable time is not laid down specifically but is always a question of fact depending on the circumstances of each case.

4 *Void contracts.*   This is a class specifically created by statute, namely the Infants' Relief Act 1874. Section 1 provides that

(a)   contracts for the repayment of money lent or to be lent,
(b)   contracts for goods *not* necessaries supplied or to be supplied, and
(c)   accounts stated,

made by an infant (i e a minor) shall be absolutely void. Class (a) needs no explanation. Class (b) is not confined to sales but will also cover exchanges. Class (c) refers to admissions that money is due (e g an IOU) and is of little importance in practice because such admissions are only prima facie evidence.

The word 'void' normally means of no legal effect and 'absolutely' would seem only to emphasise this. However, as before this Act was passed minors' contracts within s 1 were voidable in the sense of being enforceable *by* but *not against* minors, it seems strange that a Relief Act should put them in a worse position, for neither party can sue on a truly void contract. The courts have not always followed the same line of approach to this problem and as a consequence there are different views. *Coutts & Co v Browne-Lecky* (1946) is a case in which the word void was given its strict meaning of 'no legal effect'. In this case the guarantee (see p 253, below) of a minor's bank overdraft was not enforceable against the guarantor because his promise as guarantor was a promise to pay the 'debt' of another and here, as the other was a minor, there was no 'debt' under the Infants' Relief Act.

Moreover, if a minor's contract within the section is *void* then any property a minor takes under such a contract and then resells cannot result in ownership passing to the third party. But it has been suggested that the goods are in fact irrecoverable by the owner who supplied them to the minor (see *Stocks v Wilson* (1913) below).

Ratification

Section 2 of the Infants' Relief Act 1874 presents far more difficulties of interpretation than s 1. In this book one view only of s 2 is given.

First, a distinction must be drawn between a promise and a ratification. A promise is meant here to be some *new* promise and to be enforceable, whereas ratification is merely the re-affirmation of something which already exists. Section 2 provides that no action shall be brought whereby to charge any person upon (1) any *promise* made after full age to pay any *debt* contracted during minority and (2) any *ratification* made after full age of any *promise or contract* made during minority. Thus, a promise made by an adult to pay a debt contracted during minority will not be actionable. No ratification by an adult of a promise or contract made during minority is valid. A new promise supported by new consideration made by an adult is valid if it relates to any obligation other than the obligation to pay a debt.

The problem is to determine whethere there is a fresh promise or merely a ratification. The question is one of fact depending on the intention of the parties and in general the mere recognition of a previous contract will be a ratification but the addition of new terms to supplement or vary the previous promise made during minority will be a new promise. In an old case a minor servant on attaining his majority continued in service at an increased salary and this was held to be a new promise by which he was bound to serve (*Brown v Harper* (1893)).

Minors and tort

As a general rule a minor can be made liable in tort whenever he is old enough to know the nature of what he is doing. Thus a 17-year-old can be liable in trespass but a two-year-old cannot. An exception to this rule is where the action to make a minor liable in tort is merely an indirect way of enforcing against him a contract on which he would not be liable. A minor cannot be made liable in a tort which is *directly connected* with any contract which could not be enforced against him. Thus in the well-known case of *Leslie Ltd v Sheill* (1914, CA) a minor misrepresented his age in order to borrow money. He committed the tort of deceit as a result of his fraudulent misrepresentation. The moneylender brought an action, not in contract to recover the money lent, but in tort to recover damages or alternatively to recover the money in quasi-contract. The Court held that either way would be to attempt to enforce a contract on which the minor would not be liable and the action failed. In *Fawcett v Smethurst* (p 244, above) the minor hired the car to drive it to a station to pick up his baggage. He drove beyond the station and the car was damaged. Because of the onerous term in the contract it could not be enforced against the minor and so the minor was not liable in tort either.

Equity and minors' contracts

Equity does give some relief to those who contract with minors but as equity also seeks to protect minors the relief is of necessity very limited.

1 *Specific performance.*   This equitable decree (see p 350, below) is not allowed to minors on the principle of mutuality. As the contract cannot be enforced *against the minor* so equity will not allow the *minor* this remedy to enforce his contract *against the other party* (*Flight v Bolland* (1828)).

2 *The doctrine of subrogation.*   Under the doctrine of subrogation the maker of a loan which is made to enable a minor to spend money on necessaries and which is *actually* spent on necessaries may stand in the shoes of the person who supplied the necessaries and take over his rights. Thus if A lends £1 to a minor for him to spend on food and the minor spends 75p on food and gambles 25p A may sue to recover the 75p as if he had been the unpaid supplier of necessaries.

3 *Restitution.*   Restitution means restoration. Where a minor by fraud induces another to contract with him and so obtains an advantage, equity may compel the minor to restore his ill-gotten gains and to release the other from his obligations under the contract. The equitable remedy of restitution will be available only where the minor still has in his possession the ill-gotten gains, e g the chattels or the money. In *Leslie Ltd v Sheill* (1914) the minor borrowed £400 by fraudulently misstating his age but as he did not have the same money in his possession he could not be compelled to restore it.

In the case of *Stocks v Wilson* (1913) a minor, who obtained furniture on credit by fraudulently misrepresenting his age and then sold it for £30, was ordered to pay the £30 to the seller. This suggests that the court can order the repayment of the proceeds of sale of goods where the court could have ordered the restitution of the goods sold. This view was not approved of by the Court of Appeal in the later case of *Leslie Ltd v Sheill* (1914) and may be taken to have been overruled.

Reform.   It is generally agreed that the law relating to minors is out of date. Most of the law was settled before this century in cases involving persons aged 18 years or older. Young people are now more aware of the world around them than ever before and modern rules giving protection to the consumer also protect minors. An interesting and simple suggestion for reform has been put forward by the Law Commission (1982). All contracts should be binding on minors aged 16 years or more. Below 16 years the minor's contract should be *enforceable by but not against him*. An adult defendant should be able to raise any defence he could raise if sued by another adult. A minor who misrepresents his age in order to induce a contract should be liable in tort for deceit but in other cases of fraud a minor under 16 years should not be liable if the effect would be to make him liable indirectly on an otherwise unenforceable contract.

B. Mental incapacity

The law in relation to this topic is now to be read in the light of the Mental Health Act 1983. This Act recognises a wide range of types of mental incapacity and the name applied to the person concerned differs from case to case, the word most frequently used being 'patient'. However, the expression 'person of unsound mind' better conveys the idea which concerns us here.

If the person of unsound mind is one whose property is subject to the control of the court under Part VIII of the Mental Health Act 1983, he can never make a valid contract, for to allow him to do so would interfere with the court's right of control. His alleged contracts are void. Judges of the Chancery Division of the High Court sit as a Court of Protection and supervise and administer the property of persons of unsound mind.

In other cases contracts entered into by persons of unsound mind are prima facie valid but will be *voidable* at the option of the party subject to the disability if he can show that, at the time of the contract, by reason of mental disorder he did not know what he was doing *and* the other party knew of this. Such contracts will cease to be voidable if ratified during a lucid interval.

However, in cases where the person of unsound mind is not bound by his contract he will be obliged to pay a reasonable price for necessaries sold and delivered, as is the case with minors (Sale of Goods Act 1979, s 3). (See generally p 243, above.)

C. Drunkards

Where a person is so drunk at the time of contracting as not to know what he is doing and the other party is aware of this the contract is voidable at the drunk person's option. The rules relating to ratification and liability for necessaries are the same as with persons of unsound mind (Sale of Goods Act 1979, s 3).

D. Corporations

A group of two or more people may be recognised by the law as a person for many purposes including the capacity to form a contract.

Corporations may be classified as of three types according to their mode of creation: by charter, by statute or by registration under the Companies Act 1948.

1 *Chartered corporations.*   A corporation so created at common law by the grant of a Royal Charter can enter into any contract at all, but if its activities offend against the spirit of the charter its charter may be withdrawn. Charters are usually used to create charitable and educational corporations, e g the Queen Victoria University of Manchester.

2 *Statutory corporations.*   These are corporations created for a particular purpose by a special statute. Such corporations are limited in what they can do, and this involves contract, to that range of activities laid down in the creating statute. This type of corporation is usually created to carry out some sort of public utility undertaking such as an electricity, gas or water board or the National Coal Board.

3 *Companies registered under the Companies Act 1948.*   Since 1862 registration after complying with certain formalities has been a means of creating a corporation of a particular kind, usually a trading company. One of the documents which must be registered when corporate status is sought is the memorandum of association. This document tells outsiders most of the matters they want to know about a company such as its name, the situation of its registered office, its authorised capital and the objects clause. The objects clause in the memorandum of association lays down the permitted range of activities which the company can follow. Any act or contract outside the objects clause is beyond the powers of the company – ultra vires – and is not in law the act of the company at all. Where a company is sued on a 'contract' which is outside the scope of its objects clause the company may plead the doctrine of ultra vires in its defence, as such a 'contract' is no real contract at all. *It is void.* Formerly, a person contracting with a company was *deemed* to know the contents of a company's objects clause and was bound by them. However, since the United Kingdom's entry into the European Economic Community, any transaction with a company in good faith is *deemed* to be one within the contractual capacity of the company. The powers of the directors to bind the company are deemed to be free of any limitation under the memorandum or articles of association: s 9 (1), European Communities Act 1972. The result of this provision is that directors' powers are still confined by the objects clause but the company can no longer rely on the doctrine where it is dealing with a person who has acted in good faith.

At one time there were complicated rules governing the situations in which corporations were obliged to contract under the corporation's seal, i e situations in which a corporation's contract had to be written and the corporation's seal affixed. Now, the combined effect of the Companies Act 1948 which governs companies registered thereunder, and the Corporate Bodies' Contracts Act 1960 which applies to all other corporations, is to enable a company to contract in any form in which a natural person can contract. Thus a corporation's seal is now necessary only where a natural person would have to employ a seal, e g to transfer the legal estate in land.

For a further discussion of writing and contract see p 252, below.

Chapter 15
Writing and contract

As a general rule a contract may be in any form – word of mouth, writing or conduct or any combination of these. However, certain statutes require a particular form in certain cases and other statutes require writing as *evidence* of an existing contract. This chapter will be devoted to a discussion of these particular cases.

Deed

A document is sealed where a person places his finger on wax, a wafer or merely on the document provided that there is an *intention* to seal. A deed is a written promise under seal. A deed is enforceable on account of its form (writing under seal) quite apart from the presence, or absence, of consideration. To make a bare promise unsupported by consideration enforceable, it *must* be made in the form of a deed. The essentials of a deed are:

(i)   writing,
(ii)   seal,
(iii)   delivery, and a
(iv)   signature, if created after 1925.

A contract, which essentially consists of a *set* of promises and consideration, may be made under seal, in which case it is known as a contract under seal or a contract by deed. Documents in this form are essential to convey or transfer a legal estate in land (except for leases of three years or less) or to create a legal mortgage of land (see Law of Property Act 1952, ss 52 and 85). Where a deed is required but is not used by the parties the transaction will have no legal effect. Thus if A 'transfers' his land to B by a written document not under seal the legal ownership of the land will not pass to B.

The essential feature, from our point of view, about a deed is that it is binding on account of its form, as opposed to a simple contract which requires consideration before it will be enforced at law. Also, the period of time for the purposes of the Limitation Act 1980 within which actions on the deed must be brought is 12 years, and not six as is the case with simple contracts.

Writing

In some instance statute requires that a particular contract be *in writing*. In the exceptional case where this is so, the writing is as much an essential element of the contract as any other element. If there is no acceptance, there is no contract; if there is no consideration, there is no contract; if there is no writing, there is no contract. Examples of contracts which must be *in writing* are the transfer of shares in a limited company (Companies Act 1948), bills of exchange, cheques and promissory notes (Bills of Exchange Act 1882: see p 272, below) legal assignments of choses in action (Law of Property Act 1925: see p 269, below) contracts of hire-purchase within the Hire-Purchase Act 1965 and regulated consumer credit agreements under s 60 of the Consumer Credit Act 1974.

Writing as evidence

Under the preceding two headings we were concerned with the *form* a contract must take. In the first it must be in the *form of a deed* and in the second in the *form of writing*. However, there are statutes which require writing as *evidence* of the contract. Even without the writing the contract will have all its essential elements but all contracts must be proved to the satisfaction of the court and in these cases statute says that there must be written evidence. Thus, the effect of non-compliance with the statutes requiring writing is that the contract is unenforceable in a court of law.

The requirement of written evidence was introduced to our law in the seventeenth century when, under the then rules of procedure, the parties to an action could not themselves give evidence. To avoid fraud being committed by the perjured (false on oath) testimony of witnesses, the Statute of Frauds was passed in 1677 and it laid down that a wide range of contracts within the statute could be enforced only where written evidence of the contract between the parties existed. The old rules of procedure have been replaced and the parties to a contract may now give evidence. Standards of morality have also improved. As a result the reason for the existence of the statute has largely disappeared. Many sections of the Statute of Frauds have been repealed, others repealed and re-enacted in later statutes but cases which interpret the meaning of words used in earlier Acts will be a guide as to the meaning of similar words in later Acts. Therefore, in the discussion below many of the cases are based on contracts formerly covered by the Statute of Frauds 1677 or Sale of Goods Act 1893 (repealed on this point in 1954) but which no longer need writing as evidence of their existence. There are two main types of contract which today need to be *evidenced* by writing. They are contracts of guarantee and contracts for the sale of land.

1 *Contracts of guarantee*

In the words of the Statute of Frauds 1677, any 'promise to answer for the debt, default or miscarriage of another person' must be evidenced by writing. There are several points which must be noted about this definition.

(i) *'Debt, default or miscarriage'*. 'Debt' and 'default' are generally understood to refer to obligations arising out of contract but the word 'miscarriage' has been taken to mean liability arising out of a tortious act. For example, A wrongfully rides B's horse and kills it. C promises to pay B a sum of money as compensation if B will refrain from suing A in tort. C's promise is a promise to answer for the 'miscarriage' of another, is within the statute and will be enforceable only if there is written evidence of it (*Kirkham v Marter* (1819)).

(ii) *Parties to the contract.* There must be *three* parties to a contract of guarantee where a promise is given to answer for the obligation of another. These are the *debtor* (called the principal debtor), the person to whom the debt is owed (the *creditor*) and the *guarantor*, who promises to pay the creditor if the debtor does not. There is thus a contract between the debtor and the creditor with the guarantor joining in as a collateral (subsidiary to and depending on) matter to give greater security to the creditor. If A (principal debtor) contracts to buy goods from B (creditor) and C (guarantor) promises to pay B if A does not, there is a contract of guarantee which must be *evidenced* by writing if B is to succeed in an action against C on his promise to pay. If the guarantor (C) makes his promise to the debtor (A) there will not be a contract of guarantee (*Eastwood v Kenyon* (1840)). Nor will there be a contract of guarantee where the guarantor (C) takes over the liability of the debtor (A) as where C says to B, 'Give him a receipt for the money he owes you and I'll pay you' (*Goodman v Chase* (1818)). In both these cases the guarantor is not promising the creditor to pay the debt of another if he fails to pay his debt. If the apparent obligation is void the guarantee of it will also be void (see p 246, above). Confusion sometimes arises where there are three people involved in the events which happen but only two of them are *parties* to the contract. Here there cannot be a contract of guarantee. A simple illustration of this type of contract is where a man buys flowers from a florist to be sent to his wife. The man is not promising to pay *if* his wife does not. He assumes primary liability to pay and, as explained elsewhere (p 227, above), the wife has no enforceable rights and no obligations under the contract. This type of contract is called a *contract of indemnity* and must be distinguished from a *guarantee* because the former does *not* require *written evidence* for its enforcement. Thus a distinction is to be drawn between the situation where two people enter

'a shop and one buys, and the other to gain him credit, promises the seller "If he does not pay you, I will". This is a collateral undertaking and unenforceable without writing by the Statute of Frauds. But if he says "Let him have the goods, I will be your paymaster", or "I will see you paid", this is an undertaking for himself, and he shall be intended to be the very buyer'.

and the contract will not be within the statute (*Birkmyr v Darnell* (1704)). A well-known House of Lords' case is *Mountstephen v Lakeman* (1874). A local board intended to connect the drains of certain houses to the main sewer and the board's chairman (L) told the plaintiff (M), who was a builder, to do the work. When M asked how he was to be paid, L said, 'Do the work M and I'll see you paid'. There was no written note of the arrangement. M did the work, the local board refused payment on the ground that they had not authorised M to connect the drains and M sued L in contract. L's defence was that his promise was a guarantee of the debt of another and in the absence of written evidence of the promise it could not be enforced against him. The House of Lords, however, accepted M's argument that as the local board had never authorised M to do the work there was no primary liability on its part which could be guaranteed by L. Therefore, L's words were a contract of indemnity for the enforcement of which written evidence was not necessary. As M had sufficient oral evidence of witnesses to prove his case he was able to enforce L's promise.

In view of the fact that on occasions the statute enables a person to go back on a promise which he has made intending it to be binding, the courts have recognised, as exceptions, certain situations where the statute does not apply. Two examples of these exceptions will suffice:

(a) Where the promise made forms part of a wider transaction between the so-called guarantor and the so-called creditor the statute will not apply. Thus, where G undertakes to introduce clients to a stockbroker on terms that he should receive half of the stockbroker's commission and be liable for half of the losses (caused by default of the clients introduced), the statute does not apply to G's promise to answer for half of the default of another (*Sutton & Co v Grey* (1894)).

(b) The other example is where the so-called guarantor gives his promise in order to secure the release of a claim of another person which affects his property rights. Thus, the statute does not apply where A sells linseed to B who resells to C under such circumstances that A still has a lien (claim), as an unpaid seller, over the linseed in his possession, and C promises to pay A if B does not in return for the release of the linseed by A. A will succeed in an action against C even though there is no written evidence (*Fitzgerald v Dressler* (1859)).

2 *Contracts for the sale of land*

The authority for the requirement of written evidence in this case is to be found in the Law of Property Act 1925, s 40 (1) which includes contracts 'for the sale or other disposition of land or any interest in land'. The section covers sales of the fee simple, terms of years and minor interests in land such as easements (rights over the land of another). Difficulty arises where produce of the soil is sold. The common law distinguishes between *fructus industriales* (fruits of industry) which are produce grown as a result of cultivation of the soil by man and *fructus naturales* (fruits of nature) which grow without the intervention of man. Examples of *fructus industriales* are corn, carrots, peas, and potatoes; examples of *fructus naturales* are trees and grass. At common law the sale of *fructus industriales* was always a sale of *goods* but the sale of *fructus naturales* was a sale of goods only if the grass, trees etc. were to be severed from the land before contract or immediately after the contract was made. If the severance was to take place some appreciable time after the contract was made the sale of *fructus naturales* would be regarded as the sale of an interest in the land.

The requirement of writing

Both the Statute of Frauds and the Law of Property Act require a written note or memorandum of the agreement signed by the party to be charged on the promise contained therein or by his duly authorised agent. Certain points about this requirement must be noted.

(a) *Contents of the note.*   The note must contain all the material terms other than the actual consideration in the case of a contract of guarantee (Mercantile Law Amendment Act 1856, s 3). A material term is any important term, though there is no clear test for determining what is material. It will in general include the parties, the property, the consideration (not necessary in a guarantee) the date of commencement and the duration of a lease. In one contract where the written memorandum did not contain the date stipulated for vacant possession the court found that there was no note in writing and the party suing on the memorandum failed in his action (*Hawkins v Price* (1947)). In another case the written evidence failed to record that the parties had agreed that the purchase price should be paid in instalments. The court held that there was no sufficient memorandum (*Tweddell v Henderson* (1975)). However, where a term is omitted from the written evidence required by s 40 and the term is to the detriment of the person seeking to enforce the contract specific performance may be decreed if he is willing to perform the missing term. This was stated to be the law in *Scott v Bradley* (1971) where the plaintiff had agreed to buy the defendant's house and to pay half of her legal costs. The receipt for the deposit signed by the defendant contained all the material terms except the promise to pay half the legal costs. When the defendant refused to complete the contract the plaintiff sought and obtained the decree of specific performance, even though one term was missing from the receipt as a memorandum, on the understanding that he would pay half of the defendant's legal costs involved in the transfer of the house.

(b) *Form of the note.*   The document need not be prepared as a written agreement. All that is necessary is that at the trial of the action there should be written evidence of the agreement. It is not essential to have a formal document but merely some written evidence against the party charged (*Buxton v Rust* (1872)). (See also the case of *Turner v Hatton* (1952), below.)

(c) *Signature.* The document must be signed by the party charged or his duly authorised agent. A signature is any mark inserted by a person signing at the beginning, in the middle or at the end of the document with the *intention* of giving his authority to the document. An agent may sign on behalf of someone else (known as a principal) with that other's authority. The authority need not be given expressly to the agent to sign the particular document so long as the agent is one who has authority to sign documents on behalf of his principal. Authority to act as an agent may be given by word of mouth. Whether this authority exists or not depends on all the circumstances of each case. An auctioneer has authority to sign a document as agent for both the seller and the buyer (*Leeman v Stocks* (1951)). In the case of *Davies v Sweet* (1962, CA) an estate agent signed a receipt for a deposit on certain land. The purchaser knew the person signing was an agent but he did not sign as such. The purchaser sought specific performance. The court held that the agent was contractually bound even though he signed in his own name and was known to be an agent. The receipt was signed by a duly authorised agent of the vendor and the decree was therefore granted.

(d) *More than one document.* The written evidence may be contained in more than one document but for this rule to apply one document must refer expressly or inferentially to another. In *Long v Millar* (1879) L was allowed to link a written agreement to buy land, which he signed, with a receipt for the deposit, which M had signed. In his judgment Thesiger LJ said, 'If it appears from the instrument itself that another document is referred to, that document may be identified by verbal evidence'. In *Pearce v Gardner* (1897) a letter which began with the words 'Dear Sir' was linked with the envelope which contained it to identify the person to whom it was addressed. The facts of the case of *Turner v Hatton* (1952), referred to above, are as follows: H Ltd agreed to sell T 25 tons of goods. A document existed but was not signed by H Ltd. H Ltd wrote to their suppliers, 'Booked 25 tons with our customer, please send goods', and signed the letter. The court held that the letter to the suppliers referred to the sale to T and the full details of the transaction were in the document. The two could be linked together thereby providing a memorandum containing all the material terms and signed by the party to be charged.

A case in which two documents could not be linked because sufficient reference was lacking is *Timmins v Moreland Street Property Co Ltd* (1958, CA). V agreed to sell land to P. P paid a deposit by cheque made payable to V's solicitor and was given a receipt signed by V which identified the property, the parties and the price. The Court of Appeal refused to link the two documents together so as to form one memorandum because they could not link the receipt by V with a cheque payable *not* to V but to his solicitor. V, therefore, failed for want of written evidence in his action against P. Jenkins LJ said,

> 'it is still indispensably necessary, in order to justify the reading of documents together for this purpose, that there should be a document signed by the party to be charged, which, while not containing in itself all the necessary ingredients of the required memorandum, does contain some reference, express or implied, to some other document or transaction. Where any such reference can be spelt out of a document so signed, then parol evidence may be given to identify the other document referred to, or, as the case may be, to explain the other transactions, and to identify any document relating to it. If by this process a document is brought to light which contains in writing all the terms of the bargain so far as not contained in the documents signed by the party to be charged, then the two documents can be read together'.

Timmins' Case has been applied by the Privy Council in *Elias v George Sahely & Co (Barbados) Ltd* (1982). A vendor and purchaser agreed the sale of land over the telephone. The same day the *purchaser's* lawyer sent confirmation of the contract and a cheque for the deposit to the vendor's lawyer. The latter sent a receipt for the cheque to the purchaser's lawyer but did not acknowledge receipt of the letter. The vendor failed to complete the contract. The Privy Council held that an oral contract for the sale of land was not void but merely unenforceable. Also, the trial judge had been right in allowing the oral evidence of the purchaser's lawyer to be admitted to explain the transaction to which the signed receipt related and to identify his own letter as a document relating to the transaction. The letter and the receipt set out the terms and between them were a sufficient memorandum. An order for specific performance of the contract was made.

Effect of non-compliance

Both the Statute of Frauds and the Law of Property Act provide that 'no action shall be brought' whereby to charge (sue) a person on his promise unless there is a note or memorandum in writing duly signed as explained above. The Acts do not say there will be no contract. A contract does exist and rights and obligations do arise but the court will not assist in their enforcement. The contract is merely *unenforceable*. Thus if A pays a deposit on a house in accordance with an oral contract with B and then fails to complete the purchase, B cannot bring an action against A on the contract because there is no written evidence. If the contract were void in law A would be able to recover his deposit *but* he cannot do this as B has a right to it under a valid contract with A. In retaining the deposit B is not trying to enforce the contract by court action (*Monnickendam v Leanse* (1923)). That the requirement of written evidence is purely procedural is illustrated by *Leroux v Brown* (1852) where an oral contract for the hire of a servant for more than a year, which was made according to French law, was sued on in England. English procedure only is applicable in English courts but they will sometimes enforce foreign contracts which are valid according to their foreign law. In 1852 that part of the Statute of Frauds which required written evidence also applied to contracts for the hire of servants for more than a year. The contract in this case was valid according to French law and would have been enforceable in England but for the requirement of English procedure which demanded written evidence of it. The action on the contract therefore failed.

Doctrine of part performance

However, equity would not allow the Statute of Frauds to be used as an 'engine of fraud'. It was clearly contrary to good conscience that a man should be allowed to go back on his promise merely because there was no written evidence of an agreement. Equity, therefore, evolved the doctrine of part performance, which is now expressly recognised by the Law of Property Act 1925, s 40 (2). Under this doctrine, where certain conditions are satisfied, equity will give the equitable remedy of specific performance compelling the promisor to carry out his promise. The conditions which must be satisfied are as follows:

1 *Performance referable only to contract.* The promisee must have done an act of part performance which is referable to a contract such as he alleges exists (*Steadman v Steadman* (1974)). The act must be such that in combination with the other circumstances it suggests that the parties entered into a contract of the kind alleged. The payment of money may be sufficient and the physical alteration of the land in pursuance of an agreement will generally suffice. Whether an act is exclusively referable or not is a question for the court in each case but a consideration of the following decided cases will help in the understanding of the doctrine:

(i) T made an oral agreement to take a lease of land from D. D's solicitor gave notice to two weekly tenants. T refused to complete. The court held that the act of D (through his solicitor) was exclusively referable to the type of contract he alleged to exist (*Daniels v Trefusis* (1914)).

(ii) In return for a man's promise to leave his house to her in his will, his housekeeper continued in service without wages. The man signed a will to this effect but it was not properly witnessed and so failed to have any legal effect. The man died intestate and his property went to his relatives.

The woman sought equity's aid to enforce the man's promise to let her live in the house after his death but the court held that her remaining in service was explicable without reference to such new contract as she alleged to exist – she could have been destitute or could have been his mistress. (*Maddison v Alderson* (1883).) In another similar but materially different case W moved into a house as a domestic servant on condition that she would have the house and contents on the owner's death. She agreed to pay for her own board and coal. As a term of the agreement W gave up her own flat. On the owner's death it was discovered that he had not left the house to W as promised. The court here granted specific performance to W because her acts in giving up the tenancy of her flat and moving in with the owner of the home were acts which were exclusively referable to the type of contract alleged to exist: *Wakeham v Mackenzie* (1968). See also *Rawlinson v Ames*, below.

(iii) Over the years the courts have been concerned with the problem of whether the payment of money can amount to a sufficient act of part performance. The view was often taken that the payment of money is open to so many explanations that it is almost always equivocal and that it does not necessarily point to the existence of a contract such as is alleged to exist. This question arose again in *Steadman v Steadman* (1974).

An oral agreement for the settlement of a matrimonial dispute included a provision that the wife should surrender her interest in the matrimonial home for £1,500 and that the husband should pay her £100 which was part of the arrears of maintenance he owed. This agreement was approved by magistrates. The husband paid the £100 to the wife, who failed to surrender her interest. By a majority the House of Lords held that the payment of money by the husband together with all the other circumstances amounted to a sufficient act of part performance to enable the oral contract to be enforced. The case is complicated on its facts and confusing in its judicial reasoning. Probably the payment of £100 alone would not have sufficed as an act of part performance (see Lord Salmon). However, against the background of the other conduct of the husband it did suffice. Lord Reid, explaining the legal position, said:

> 'You must first look at the alleged acts of part performance to see whether they prove that there must have been a contract and it is only if they do so prove that you can bring in the oral contract. . . . In my view, unless the law is to be divorced from reason and principle, the rule must be that you take the whole circumstances, leaving aside evidence about the oral contract, to see whether it is proved that the acts relied on were done in reliance on a contract: that will be proved if it is shown to be more probable than not.'

As a result of *Steadman v Steadman* it can no longer be asserted that the payment of money can never amount to an act of part performance.

2 *Element of fraud.* It must be in the nature of fraud for the promisor to go back on his promise and rely on the statute for his protection. This can be seen from the case of *Rawlinson v Ames* (1925). A agreed orally to take a 21-year lease of R's flat. At A's request R carried out structural alterations. A changed her mind and refused to take the flat. The court held A to her agreement because R would never have carried out the alterations unless some contract such as he alleged did in fact exist.

3 *Specific performance possible.* The contract must be one of the type of which the court can grant its equitable remedy of specific performance. It will be recalled that this remedy is not available in all types of contract, notably where one of the parties is a minor and where the contract involves personal services or supervision (see p 350, below). In practice, today the application of the doctrine of part performance is confined to contracts within s 40 (1) of the Law of Property Act 1925.

4 *Oral evidence.* There must be adequate oral evidence of the contract. The act of part performance will not prove the contract but it will let in oral evidence which otherwise would have been excluded. In the absence of written evidence the oral testimony of witnesses must be relied on to prove the terms of the contract which the court is asked to enforce.

Hire-purchase and credit-sale

Under the Hire-Purchase Acts 1964 and 1965, as amended, contracts for the hire-purchase of goods (a contract of hire with the option to purchase by the payment of the last instalment) and credit-sale of goods (contracts of sale where the price is payable by five or more instalments) where the total price does not exceed £5,000 are *unenforceable by the owner against the hirer* unless there is an agreement in writing, signed by the hirer personally (not his agent) and by other parties, which is delivered to the hirer within seven days of the making of the agreement. The Act implies certain conditions for the protection of hire-purchasers and is designed to protect them against salesmen who may wish to persuade them to enter into contracts they do not understand.

The Act also provides that any guarantee by a third party of a debt due under an unenforceable hire-purchase contract shall also be unenforceable. This provision is necessary because the absence of writing does not make the hire-purchase contract void.

Chapter 16
Privity of contract and assignment of choses in action

Privity of contract

'The legal effects of a contract' wrote Pollock 'are confined to the contracting parties. Therefore, strangers to the contract ought to be immune from obligations imposed by the contract and unable to enforce benefits conferred on them by the contract.' Under any contract rights and obligations are created. According to the doctrine of 'privity of contract' only the parties to a contract can enforce the rights or be subject to the obligations which arise under it. However, it does not follow that a person who is a party to an agreement may necessarily sue on it. A simple contract consists of an agreement plus consideration but a person may be a party to an agreement without furnishing consideration, in which case he will not be allowed to sue on the contract.

As contract is based on agreement, it is easy to see why a person not a party thereto is not affected by obligations arising under the contract but where a contract is made for the benefit of a third party it may seem unreasonable that he should have no rights under it. The *facts* of the case of *Tweddle v Atkinson* ((1861) p 227, above) illustrate this type of situation. An important modern case on the doctrine of privity of contract is *Scruttons Ltd v Midland Silicones Ltd* (1962, HL). A shipping company agreed to carry certain chemicals belonging to the plaintiffs and in the bill of lading their liability for negligence to 500 dollars per drum. The shipping company hired a firm of stevedores to unload the ship and the stevedores negligently damaged the chemicals to the value of 1,800 dollars per drum. The plaintiffs sued the stevedores in tort and were successful. The stevedores in their defence attempted to obtain the benefit of the limitation clause in the contract between the plaintiffs and the shipping company, but the House of Lords applied the doctrine of privity of contract and would not allow them to take the benefit of any contract to which they were not a party. Even though they had a contract with the shipping company under which they were to receive the benefit of the limitation clause, the right to limitation arose under the contract between the *plaintiffs* and the *shipping company* and to this they were not a party.

The principle of privity of contract was upheld by the House of Lords in *Beswick v Beswick* (1967). The facts are as follows:

B entered into an agreement with N whereby N was to take over B's coal business in return for (i) £6 10s payable weekly to B as consultant, and (ii) the payment of an annuity of £5 weekly to Mrs B on the death of B. On B's death his widow sued to enforce the annuity payable to her under a contract to which she was not a party. Mrs B sued both as administratrix of B and in her own personal capacity. The House of Lords held that she could not succeed in her own personal capacity but could succeed as administratrix of her husband's estate and as such she was awarded a decree of specific performance against N.

A *possible* major inroad on the doctrine of privity of contract can be seen in the case of *Jackson v Horizon Holidays Ltd* (1975). By a unanimous decision the Court of Appeal held that a father who had booked a holiday in Ceylon for himself, his wife and three-year-old twin sons, could recover damages to compensate for his loss and the loss of his family when the holiday turned out to be very different from that described by the defendant. The Court of Appeal said that the father could not be said to be trustee for the others as there was no trust property, nor could it be said that he was acting as agent for his sons as principals. In the event of breach of contract by the defendants the father could sue to recover compensation for discomfort, vexation and disappointment suffered by all persons for whom he had booked. However, a considered obiter dictum of the House of Lords clearly states that the reasoning of the Court of Appeal in *Jackson's* case was wrong. Three of their Lordships also indicated that there was a need for the review of this area of the law (*Woodar Investment Development Ltd v Wimpey Construction UK Ltd* (1980)).

In modern society the doctrine can work considerable inconvenience so it is not surprising to find that there are several important exceptions. Before dealing with these it is well to note that other European systems do not have a doctrine of privity of contract.

(a) Cases where benefits may be conferred on strangers

1 *By statute*

Under the Married Women's Property Act 1882 a man may insure his life for the benefit of his wife or children and a woman may insure her life for the benefit of her husband or children and a trust will be created for the benefit of the persons intended to be benefited by the insurance. Thus, if Mr Jones enters into a contract of insurance with the Life Insurance Co Ltd whereunder on his death £10,000 is to be paid to his wife, under the doctrine of privity of contract Mrs Jones is a stranger to the contract between her husband and the insurance company. She cannot sue for the money due to her on her husband's death. Under the Act of 1882 the company becomes a trustee of the moneys due and she can sue to recover them.

Under the Road Traffic Acts it is obligatory for a motorist to insure against possible liability for injury caused to other road users by reason of his driving a motor car. The Acts allow third parties (i e strangers to the contract between the insured motorist and the insurance company) rights under the motor insurance policy and in certain cases they may proceed directly against the insurance company. The present Act is the Road Traffic Act 1972, s 149.

Under the Third Parties (Rights against Insurers) Act 1930, where a person incurs liability to a third person and is covered for that liability by an insurance policy then in certain events the third party has rights against the insurers (i e the insurance company) on the policy. These circumstances are, in the case of an individual, when he goes bankrupt or makes a composition or arrangement with his creditors, and, in the case of a company, when it goes into liquidation and in certain other circumstances. An example would be as follows. A is insured against liability to B. A injures B and A becomes bankrupt. B has a right of action against A's insurers.

Under the Bills of Exchange Act 1882 a third party may sue on a bill of exchange (including cheques and promissory notes). Thus if A buys a shed from B and pays for it by cheque which is made out to 'B or order' B can sue A on the cheque as it is part of his contract of sale with A. Later B indorses (signs) the cheque and hands it to C in payment for goods bought from C. Under the Act C may sue A on the cheque. Neither B nor C can sue A's bank because neither has a contract with the bank and the Act does not give B or C rights against the bank.

2　In equity

In certain cases the promisee may be regarded as a trustee for a third party. This idea of a constructive (imposed by equity) trust may be illustrated by reference to two well-known cases.

In *Gregory and Parker v Williams* (1817) Parker, being indebted to both Gregory and Williams, agreed with Williams to transfer the whole of his property to him if he would pay the debt due to Gregory. Parker transferred his property to Williams who failed to pay off Parker's debt. The common law doctrine of privity of contract forbade Gregory to sue on the agreement between Parker and Williams but Gregory and Parker successfully filed a bill in equity to compel performance of the promise, Parker being regarded as a trustee for Gregory. Where the trustee is not willing to sue as plaintiff he may be joined as co-defendant with the promisor.

The second case was decided by the House of Lords in 1919 and is known as *Walford's Case*. W, a broker, negotiated a charterparty (an agreement for the hire of a ship) between O, the owners of a vessel, and C, the company which wished to hire it. By a clause in the charterparty O promised C that he would pay the agreed commission to W. The House of Lords allowed C to sue as trustee for W.

However, there are many apparently inconsistent cases involving the trust concept as an inroad on the doctrine of privity and the courts seem most reluctant to find a trust. Such is the confusion that it is difficult to predict what the court's decision would be in a novel case, e g in *Beswick v Beswick*, at p 262, above, the court held that there was no trust. The Law Revision Committee in its Sixth Interim Report recommended the abolition of the trust concept in this connection and suggested that legislation should be introduced to enable a third party who is expressly given rights under a contract to sue to enforce those rights.

3 *At common law*

In the law of agency there is a rule known as the 'doctrine of the undisclosed principal'. Under this doctrine if A, acting as agent of B, enters into a contract with C, then A may drop out giving B the right to sue C. This is so even where C does not know that A is acting as an agent.

Under the rules relating to assignments a person not a party to a contract may derive benefits thereunder (see below).

(b) **Cases where liability may be imposed on strangers**

The general principle here is that strangers to a contract cannot be placed under any obligations by the parties to the contract. To this rule there are several exceptions although not as many as in the case of strangers obtaining benefits under a contract.

1. *Restrictions on use*

(i) *At common law.* Early in the development of the common law the position was reached whereby the assignee of a lease (the person to whom a lease was transferred) took the lease with the benefits (e g use or enjoyment) of, and subject to the burdens (obligation to pay rent and do repairs) of, his assignor. For example, if A, the fee simple owner, leases a house to B for 50 years and after two years B assigns the remaining 48 years to C, C takes the lease subject to the benefits and burdens of the lease between A and B. Between A and B there is privity of contract. Between A and C there is 'privity of estate'. Both A and C are interested in the house, A as owner of the fee simple and C as A's tenant, though no contract exists between them.

(ii) *In equity.* In the case of *Tulk v Moxhay* (1848) it was decided that in equity *restrictive* covenants may run with the land; that is to say, that where B buys land from A and promises *not* to build thereon and later sells such land to C, then C may also be bound by the covenant not to build. In *Tulk v Moxhay* T owned several parcels of land in Leicester Square and sold the centre garden to E taking a covenant from him *not* to build thereon. Over some years the land was sold a number of times until it was conveyed to M, who took the land knowing of the restriction, and who proposed to build on the centre garden. T could not sue M at common law for damages because there was no privity of contract between them so T sought an injunction in equity to restrain M from erecting the buildings. The court granted the injunction. As a court of equity is a court of conscience and M took with notice then in all good conscience he could not ignore the restrictive covenant. The principle of *Tulk v Moxhay* may be stated thus: a restrictive covenant voluntarily accepted by the purchaser of land as part of the contract of sale will bind persons who later buy the land with notice of the restrictive covenant.

The question has arisen whether the principle of *Tulk v Moxhay* can be applied to property other than land. In 1858 Knight Bruce LJ, in *De Mattos v Gibson* (1858) said, obiter, that the principle of *Tulk v Moxhay* could be applied to any property and in *Lord Strathcona SS Co v Dominion Coal Co* (1926) it was applied by the Privy Council to the case of a person who had bought a ship with notice that a previous owner had entered into a charterparty whereby the ship was let out on hire for a series of summer seasons. The Privy Council granted an injunction restraining the owner from using the ship inconsistently with the terms of the charterparty. However, this decision has been much criticised. In the years which followed 1848 it was decided that a person should rely on the *Tulk v Moxhay* principle only where he had retained land (property) to be benefited by the restrictive covenant. It is well settled that a charterparty gives the charterer no right of property in a vessel. In 1958 in *Port Line Ltd v Ben Line Steamers Ltd* Diplock J said that the *Strathcona Case* was 'wrongly decided' and in 1956 the Court of Appeal suggested that it should be limited to the special case of the charterparty of ships.

It would seem, therefore, that if the principle of *Tulk v Moxhay* is to be extended beyond restrictive covenants affecting land it will be extended only to the case of a ship under a charterparty.

2   *Restrictions on price*

In order to maintain the retail price of his goods a manufacturer would attempt to place a minimum retail price on his goods in such a way as to bind a retailer to sell at not less than this price. This is what happened in the case of *Dunlop v Selfridge* (1915) but the manufacturer who contracted with a wholesaler who in turn contracted with a retailer was unable to maintain any action against the *retailer* for breach of the price maintenance provisions which were contained in both the contract between the manufacturer and the wholesaler and in the contract between the wholesaler and retailer. The case of *Taddy v Sterious* (1904) is instructive in this context. The plaintiffs were tobacco manufacturers who sought to prevent retailers selling their products below a minimum price. On each packet of tobacco the plaintiffs attached a printed notice stating that the tobacco was sold on the express condition that it was not to be resold below the price indicated. The notice further stated that acceptance of the goods by the retailers would be deemed a contract between them and the plaintiffs to the effect that the retailers would observe these stipulations. In the case where the retailer bought through a wholesaler the latter would be deemed the agent of the plaintiffs. Under these terms the plaintiffs sold to a wholesaler who sold to a retailer, the defendants. The defendants, with notice of the terms of sale, sold below the minimum price. The plaintiffs sought a declaration to the effect that the defendants were bound by the terms. The court refused the declaration holding that the wholesalers in truth were not the agents of the plaintiffs so no contract between them and the defendants arose by the alleged agency of the wholesaler and that conditions as to price maintenance do not run with goods.

The Restrictive Trade Practices Act 1956 altered the above position. By s 24 the collective enforcement of price maintenance agreements was declared unlawful. By s 25 (1) individual price maintenance agreements might be enforced and damages obtained for their breach. Section 25 (1) provided:

> 'Where goods are sold by a supplier subject to a condition as to the price at which those goods may be resold, either generally or by or to a specified class or person, that condition may, subject to the provisions of this section, be enforced by the supplier against any person not party to the sale who subsequently acquires the goods with notice of the condition as if he had been party thereto.'

This provision applied only with regard to resale of goods by a person who acquired them for resale in the course of business. Thus, if a student buys a book, which is subject to a resale price maintenance agreement, for the purposes of studying for an examination and later wishes to sell the book, he may do so and will not be liable under the section. Nor does the section apply to goods let on hire nor, presumably, hire-purchase. (In these cases the principles illustrated in *Taddy v Sterious* apply.)

The word 'notice' in the section meant actual notice that there was a restriction but not necessarily knowledge of the terms of the restriction.

However, the provisions of s 25 became of very limited application because the Resale Prices Act 1964 provided that a resale price agreement in a contract between a supplier of and dealer in goods shall be void unless it was specifically exempted by the Restrictive Practices Court on one of the grounds mentioned in the Act, all of which serve to protect the public interest. Thus, orders may be made protecting fixed prices where this acts to maintain quality, variety of goods, or price, the number of places where goods are sold or necessary services provided in connection with them.

This area of the law is now covered by the Restrictive Trade Practices Act 1976 and the Resale Prices Act 1976 (see p 300, below).

Exclusion clauses and the privity rule

The established general rule was clearly expressed in *Scruttons Ltd v Midland Silicones Ltd* by Lord Reid when he said, 'Although I may regret it, I find it impossible to deny the existence of the general rule that a stranger to a contract cannot in a question with either of the contracting parties take advantage of provisions of the contract even where it is clear from the contract that some provision in it was intended to benefit him'. However, in the course of his judgment in *Scruttons' Case*, Lord Reid argued that he could see the possibility of a stevedore gaining the protection of a clause in a bill of lading between two other contracting parties where one of the others could be construed as an agent for the stevedores. Four conditions needed to be satisfied. They were (1) it must be clear from the bill of lading that the stevedore was *intended to be protected* by its provisions, (2) similarly it must be clear that the carrier was contracting both on his own behalf and *as agent* for the stevedore, (3) the carrier had *authority* to contract for the stevedore, and (4) any difficulties involving *consideration* by the stevedore must be resolved. On the facts of *Scruttons' Case* these requirements were *not* satisfied. Draftsmen learned from the lesson given by *Scruttons' Case* and, in 1974, the Privy Council did find the conditions present in *New Zealand Shipping Co Ltd v A M Satterthwaite Co Ltd*, a case which has since been followed by the Privy Council.

In the *New Zealand Shipping Co Ltd* case the bill of lading between the consignor and the carrier contained a clause which benefited the carrier and which . . . 'shall also be available and shall extend to protect every such servant or agent of the Carrier . . . and for the purpose of all the foregoing provisions of this Clause the Carrier is or shall be deemed to be acting as agent or trustee on behalf of and for the benefit of all persons who are or might be his servants or agents from time to time (including independent contractors . . .) and all such persons shall to this extent be or be deemed to be parties to the contract in or evidenced by this Bill of Lading'. In the events which happened the stevedores engaged by the carrier to discharge the cargo sought protection from a clause in the bill of lading. In *Scruttons' Case* Lord Reid had said that this was possible if the four conditions were present. Here Lord Wilberforce accepted that the conditions were present and considered the extent to which they applied on the facts before the Privy Council. On the facts it was clear that the stevedores were intended to be protected, that the carrier acted as agent and had authority so to do. As far as consideration was concerned one explanation of the facts was that a unilateral contract existed between the consignors and the stevedores and this became a full contract when the stevedores provided services by discharging the cargo. 'The performance of these services for the benefit of the shipper was the consideration for the agreement by the shipper that the stevedores should have the benefit of the exemptions and limitations contained in the bill of lading' (per Lord Wilberforce). (For exclusion clauses generally see p 367, below.)

Assignment of contractual rights and obligations

This section of the chapter on privity is set out separately from the general exceptions to the privity rules partly because of its importance and partly because as a topic it is so intricate that it cannot be conveniently dealt with as a mere exception to the privity rule.

Assignment of contractual rights

First we will consider how far contractual *rights* may be passed (assigned) from one person to another. As a major change in the law was brought about by the Judicature Act 1873, s 25 (6) the position will be considered as it was before that date and then after that date. Also, since the rules of equity differ from those at common law, there will, of necessity, be a further sub-division of our work.

1 *Before the Judicature Act*

At common law the rule was quite simple. Common law did not recognise the assignment of a chose in action. However, equity recognised two types of assignment. It recognised the assignment of an equitable chose in action, i e a chose in action which was enforceable before 1875 only in a court of equity. An example of an equitable chose in action would be the interest of a beneficiary under a trust fund. It also gave assistance to the assignee of a *legal* chose in action. The assignee of a legal chose in action had no rights at law but equity, basing itself on the intention to assign, compelled the assignor (the creditor) to bring an action at law against the debtor and to transfer his gain from the action to the assignee.

2 *After the Judicature Act*

(a) *At law.* The provisions of the Judicature Act 1873, s 25 (6) are now contained in the Law of Property Act 1925, s 136. The statutes do not make assignable any chose not assignable in equity before 1873 but merely make provision for a *legal* assignment of a legal chose in action. Under the Law of Property Act any debt or other legal chose may be assigned at law provided that:

(i)   The assignment is absolute and not by way of charge. An assignment is absolute where the whole interest of the assignor is transferred to the assignee. It will be considered as absolute even though the chose in action is only assigned for the time being, e g where a builder assigns to his bankers *all* money falling due to him in consideration of their allowing him an overdraft (*Hughes v Pump House Hotel Co* (1902)). An assignment will not be absolute where it attempts to assign *part* only of a debt or where it is conditional in the sense of becoming operative or ceasing to be operative on a certain event. Thus, if builders, in consideration of a loan to them, assigned to the lender part only of a sum due to them the assignment would not be absolute (*Durham Bros v Robertson* (1898)).

(ii)   It is in writing signed by the assignor.

(iii)   Written notice of the assignment must be given to the debtor. The notice will be effective on the date it is received by the debtor.

Assignment under the Act may be voluntary or for value and where the Act is complied with the assignment has the effect of transferring to the assignee the legal right in the chose in action assigned. Thus, the assignee gets all the legal rights of the assignor, including the right to sue in his own (assignee's) name and to give a good discharge, without the consent of the assignor. However, the assignee takes subject to equities. This means that the assignee receives no better right than his assignor had and, in any action by the assignee against the debtor, the debtor may set up against the assignee any defence which he could have set up against the assignor if sued by him before the date on which he received notice of the assignment, e g if the debtor had a set-off (a cross claim) against the assignor he may raise the set-off in an action by the assignee.

(b)   *In equity.*   As before the Act, equity recognises the assignment of an equitable chose and now recognises an assignment of a legal chose which does not comply with the statutory requirements, so long as it does comply with equitable principles. The basic requirement of equity is that there should be an *intention* to assign. Where this is present generally equity will recognise the assignment. A completed equitable assignment requires *no* consideration, though an agreement for a future assignment does need to be supported by consideration.

An *equitable* assignment of an *equitable* chose in action must be in writing to comply with s 53 of the Law of Property Act 1925. The requirement of writing is not a requirement of equity itself so that an invalid *legal* assignment may take effect in equity where there is no writing.

In equity where the assignment is absolute the assignee may sue in his own name but where the assignment is non-absolute equity requires the assignee to join the assignor as a party – usually as a co-plaintiff. Also where there is an equitable assignment of a legal chose the assignee must join the assignor as a party – either as a co-plaintiff or, if he proves difficult, as a co-defendant with the debtor.

Notice to the debtor is not necessary to complete an equitable assignment. As stated above the emphasis in equity is on the intention to assign. However, even in equity, it is highly desirable on practical grounds that the assignee should give notice of the assignment to the debtor. If the debtor does not receive notice of the assignment, payment of the debt by him to the assignor will discharge his (the debtor's) liability and there will be no obligation left for the assignee to enforce. Moreover a rule, known as the rule in *Dearle v Hall* (1828), says that where there are successive equitable claims they rank according to the date of notice given to the person obliged to meet the claims. Thus, if T holds certain income in trust for B and B assigns his equitable interest (in writing under s 53 of the LPA) to X, X should give notice to T so that T will know that he is to pay X and not B. Also B may further 'assign' the *same* interest to Y, and if T pays the income to Y without notice of X's claim he will be under no obligation to X. Notice is desirable in equity, therefore, to prevent the trustee paying the assignor and to preserve the priority of the first assignee.

It is not surprising that the assignee in equity, as well as at law, takes subject to equities.

Other rights assignable by statute. Certain statutes have made particular rights assignable. Examples are as follows: negotiable instruments, copyrights, patents, bills of lading, shares in a company and policies of life and marine insurance.

Rights not assignable. Rights which cannot be assigned include bare rights of action, such as the right to sue for a breach of contract or the right to sue in tort, or contractual rights of a personal nature, such as contracts for a personal service or involving a personal skill. Thus, a promise to supply all the eggs required in a business in a particular year could not be enforced by the person to whom the business was transferred, because the latter's requirements might be far greater (*Kemp v Baerselman* (1906)).

Assignment of contractual liabilities

In English law the liabilities under a contract cannot be assigned either in law or equity. The actual transfer of a liability, which cannot be achieved by way of assignment, can be achieved by a *novation*, i e where all three parties meet together and agree to the transfer of an obligation (for a discussion of assignment and novation see p 274, below). Consideration is given in a completed novation (see p 274, below) but when the novation is not completed some consideration additional to the promises must be given to make the agreement binding.

However, vicarious performance of a contract is allowed unless the contract is a personal one. This is sometimes expressed *qui facit per alium facit per se* (he who does through another does for himself – or, more accurately, he who performs through the agency of another discharges his obligation to perform). This is not a case of assignment because it does not involve the substitution of one debtor for another. Vicarious performance is possible only where there is nothing in the contract to show that it is to be performed by the parties alone. Examples of factors which would indicate that vicarious performance is not possible are the presence of a set-off and the possession of a special skill. Thus, a painter who is under contract to paint a portrait could not procure another painter to paint the portrait on his behalf.

Involuntary assignments

In the above discussion of assignments we have considered the transfer of rights and obligations effected by the parties or one of them. There are, however, certain cases where the law regards assignment as having taken place automatically on the occurrence of certain events. This is known as assignment by operation of law.

On the *death* of a party, as a general rule, contracts are enforceable by or against the deceased's personal representatives, who are termed executors or administrators. (If the deceased leaves a will the people who distribute his property in accordance with his wishes are called executors. If the deceased dies without leaving a will (intestate) the people who distribute his property in accordance with the intestacy provisions laid down by statute are called his administrators.)

On a man becoming bankrupt all his property vests, by operation of law, in his trustee in bankruptcy. The object of *bankruptcy* proceedings, which are taken when a man cannot meet his financial obligations, is to collect in all a man's assets and to distribute them rateably (in proportion to their claims) to his creditors. Rights of action for breach of contract vest in the trustee in bankruptcy who can sue on such contracts and who can also be sued on any contract broken by the bankrupt. (An exception to this general rule provides that a trustee in bankruptcy has no right to perform a contract which is of a personal nature.)

Note on negotiable instruments

A negotiable instrument is a chose in action in written form which possesses the characteristics of negotiability. This means that

(i)   it can be transferred by mere delivery, and
(ii)   the transferee takes free from the defects in title of the transferor.

There are several types of negotiable instruments and the rules relating to bills of exchange, cheques and promissory notes, which are all negotiable instruments, are to be found in the Bills of Exchange Act 1882. A bill of exchange is a written order by one person (drawer) to another (drawee) to pay a sum of money to him (drawer) or another person. The payee is the person to whom the money is to be paid. A cheque is a bill of exchange drawn on a banker and payable on demand. A promissory note is an unconditional promise by the maker (who is in the position of drawer and drawee) to pay a sum of money to the person named as payee. A bank note is a promissory note issued by a banker and payable to the bearer on demand.

A situation which could give rise to a bill of exchange being drawn (drafted) is as follows. W is a wholesaler who sells shoes on credit to R. Now if all W's customers want credit W will have no cash with which to buy shoes from M the manufacturers. W, therefore, draws a document known as a bill of exchange containing a promise to pay M a sum of money six months after the date on the document. R is the person on whom the document is drawn and he accepts the obligation to pay by placing his signature on the bill. W can then use this document, known as a bill of exchange, to pay his debts to M. M may allow W £97 for a £100 bill. W will then receive £97 worth of shoes from M and M will receive £100 after a wait of six months. In the above case the bill of exchange could look like this:—

12th April 1985

£100

Pay M the sum of one hundred pounds six months from date, for value received.

Signed

W.

To R.

Payee	= M
Drawer	= W
Drawee	= R
Acceptor	= R

If the bill is made payable 'to bearer' it may be assigned by mere delivery; if payable to 'M or order' and M wishes to assign the bill, M must sign (endorse) it and then deliver. In the latter case M is termed the endorser and the person to whom it is delivered is called the endorsee.

The holder of the bill at its maturity (the date on which it is payable) has the right to sue on the bill. So a person not a party to the original contract may derive a right of action under the bill of exchange. In the case of negotiable instruments consideration is presumed but it is necessary that consideration should have been given by someone, i e by the acceptor, payee or one of the subsequent endorsees. An antecedent debt or liability will be sufficient to support a promise in a bill of exchange.

Where a cheque or other negotiable instrument payable to 'X or order' is marked 'not negotiable' the marking does not mean that it cannot be negotiated in the sense of being transferred from X to Y by endorsement and delivery but that it cannot pass from X to Y or anyone else as a negotiable instrument. Placed on a cheque, the words destroy the negotiability of the cheque. A person who holds such a cheque takes it 'subject to equities'.

Assignability and negotiability

The rules relating to negotiable instruments make special provision for the transfer of certain specific choses in action. Generally a chose in action can be assigned in accordance with a particular statute such as shares in a company under the Companies Act 1948 or under the *general* provisions contained in s 136 of the Law of Property Act 1925. The special provisions relating to negotiable instruments apply *only* to *particular* types of chose in action which are recognised as possessing the characteristic of negotiability by statute, or to a lesser extent by precedent or custom.

The following points of difference between the transfer of a negotiable instrument and the assignment of a contractual right should be noted:

(i)   In the case of the transfer of a negotiable instrument it is not necessary to give notice to the debtor (i e the acceptor of a bill or the banker in the case of a cheque).

(ii)   The transferee of a bill, including a cheque, who takes in good faith and for value takes free from equities.

(iii)   Writing is not necessary for the transfer of a negotiable instrument.

Assignment and novation

Assignment involves one *contracting party* transferring his rights under the contact to a third party without the consent of the other contracting party. The rights of one party are assigned and the contract is not discharged. Novation can take place only with the consent of *both the contracting parties* and the new party. The old contract is destroyed and a new one created. By assignment only rights can be transferred; by novation obligations may be transferred as well (see p 318, above).

Chapter 17

Vitiating factors

Where there is an offer and acceptance, with consideration furnished by both parties who are of full age, there is an apparent contract, yet this may have no legal effect at all on account of the presence of some additional factor. Factors which have the effect of denying validity to an otherwise effective contract are known as 'vitiating factors'. Under this heading we shall deal with the effect of mistake, misrepresentation, duress and undue influence, non-disclosure in contracts of 'utmost good faith' and illegality.

1 Mistake

As contract is based upon agreement it might reasonably be thought that the presence of mistake as to the facts would destroy the agreement and hence the contract. However, this straightforward view does not represent the law. *As a general rule it can be said that the common law does not recognise mistake as affecting a contract, but to this rule there are exceptions.*

Mistake not affecting contract

First, the general rule of the common law is *caveat emptor* (let the buyer beware). It is the obligation of the buyer to see that he protects himself by making all necessary enquiries and any private misapprehension on his part will have no legal effect. The test of agreement is objective, so that if a reasonable man would believe agreement had been reached between two negotiating parties then the parties will be bound as if they had intended to agree to each other's terms, no matter how mistaken they may be. Thus in one case B bought new oats from S believing them to be old oats. This mistaken belief was in no way induced by the conduct of S and the court took the view that there had been no mistake sufficient to vitiate the contract (*Smith v Hughes* (1871)). The buyer ought to have taken more care and asked that the description 'old' be made a term of the sale. In another case a company bought the resignation of a salaried director when, unknown to the company at the time of the agreement as to the resignation, the company could have dismissed the director for irregular conduct without making any payment. The House of Lords (by a bare majority) held that the contract was valid (*Bell v Lever Bros Ltd* (1932)).

Mistake affecting consent

However, in certain cases the common law does recognise mistake as affecting consent. In these cases the mistake is said to be *operative* and renders the contract void from the beginning, i e there never has been a contract (void ab initio). The consequences of the contract being void on the ground of mistake are that no rights of ownership pass under the so-called contract and property which has physically passed may be recovered. The following are the situations in which mistake is operative at common law:

1 *Mistake as to the identity of the subject matter of the contract.*   Here there is no contract because there is no agreement on the thing to be sold or work to be done, i e no *consensus ad idem*. This is clearly illustrated by the case of *Raffles v Wichelhaus* (1864). S sold to B a cargo of cotton 'ex *Peerless* from Bombay'. Unknown to the parties there were two ships carrying cotton at Bombay and both were named *Peerless*. S was thinking of one ship and B of the other. The court held there was no *consensus ad idem*.

A mistake as to the value or quality of the subject matter of the contract will *not* be operative. This is an obvious application of the rule that the buyer should protect himself by inserting an appropriate term in the contract. The rule is *caveat emptor* (let the buyer beware). Although in some situations the distinction between quality and identity is clear, in others it is not. For instance, if a person buys particular tablecloths, which he believes to be the genuine property of Charles I but which in fact are not, is this a mistake of identity or quality? It has been suggested that this is a mistake as to identity (or essential nature). In another case where a person bought a painting believing it to be by Constable but which in fact was not, counsel for the buyer did not argue the point of mistake in the Court of Appeal and the court approved of this course thereby implying there was no mistake as to identity but only one of quality (*Leaf v International Galleries* (1950)).

2 *Mistake as to the existence of the subject matter.*   This will occur when, for example, the subject matter has ceased to exist. The contract is said to be for *res extincta*. It is entered into on the basis of a state of affairs which at the time of the contract no longer exists. Thus a separation deed entered into by a husband and wife was declared a nullity when it was found that the parties were never validly married (*Galloway v Galloway* (1914)). The sale of an annuity on the life of a person was declared void when it was later discovered that the person was already dead (*Strickland v Turner* (1852)). A frequent illustration of this type of operative mistake is the case of *Couturier v Hastie* (1852). The sale concerned a cargo of corn which both parties believed to be at sea. Unknown to both parties the corn had begun

to ferment and the captain of the vessel carrying the corn had already sold it as a precautionary measure at the nearest port. The House of Lords held that there was no contract here. One view of this case is that the House of Lords found that the agreement had been entered into on the understanding that the corn existed and was subject to its being in existence at the time the contract was formed; in brief, the contract was subject to an implied condition precedent, that is an implied term which must be true before liability will arise (see p 319, below).

The common law rules about *res extincta* are now subject to s 6 of the Sale of Goods Act 1979 which provides that

'Where there is a contract for the sale of specific goods, and the goods without the knowledge of the seller have perished at the time when the contract is made, the contract is void'.

3 *Mistake as to identity.* A mistake as to the identity of one of the parties to a contract in circumstances where the identity is fundamental to the formation of the contract will render the contract void. This situation arises where A intends to contract with B but in fact contracts with C and C knows, actually or inferentially, of A's mistake. Where A makes an offer to C there is a presumption of fact that A intends to contract with C and it is up to A to rebut the presumption by showing that in fact he intended to contract with B. This is a general principle to be applied to the facts of each particular case and, of course, views of facts differ widely. *Cundy v Lindsay* (1878) is a clear case on its facts. A rogue, Blenkarn, ordered goods on credit from L and signed his name in such a way as induced L to believe that the goods were ordered by Blenkiron & Co, a reputable firm with whom L regularly dealt. The goods were never paid for and Blenkarn sold them to C who bought in good faith. L brought an action in conversion (a tort involving a denial of ownership) against C. However, the liability of C in tort depended on the validity of the contract between L and Blenkarn. If this were valid Blenkarn would have made C the true owner by the sale to him. The House of Lords held that there was no contract between L and Blenkarn. The House took the view that as L never knew of Blenkarn and never intended to contract with him there could not have been a contract. There was no agreement as to who were the parties. There was no *consensus ad idem*, the contract was void ab initio and consequently L succeeded in his action against C. Another illustrative case is *King's Norton Metal Co v Edridge, Merrett & Co Ltd* (1897) the facts of which are as follows: W, for the purpose of cheating, established a business under the name of Hallam & Co, which company had business letter paper showing a large factory and stating that there were several depots. Using this paper, W bought goods from K. After a while W ordered goods on credit which he later resold to E who took in good faith. W never paid for the goods and K brought his action against E. Again the validity of the contract became material. The court here

held that as K knew of W, K intended to contract with him, even though he would not have contracted with him if he had known that Hallam & Co was a sham company.

In *Phillips v Brooks Ltd* (1919) the mistake as to identity was not operative. N, a rogue, went into P's jewellery shop and asked to see some pearl necklaces and diamond rings. He selected goods worth £2,550 and a ring for £450. He then offered to pay by cheque, saying that he was Sir George Bullough and giving his address. P verified from the telephone directory that Sir George did live at that address and accepted the cheque. N asked if he could take the ring before the cheque was cleared as it was for his wife's birthday. N pawned the ring with B and the cheque was dishonoured (not paid by the bank). P sought to recover the ring from B. The question for the court again was one of contract: 'Did P intend to contract with N (in which case there would be a contract) or with the man N said he was, i e Sir George, (in which case there would be no contract)?' Or put in another way, 'Was the false representation as to identity material to P's decision to contract with the physical person standing before him?' The court found that the false statement affected P's decision whether to part with the ring before the cheque was cleared (paid) and did *not* influence his decision to sell to the person standing before him. The contract between N and P was, therefore, voidable for misrepresentation, i e valid until avoided by P. Before P knew of the fraud upon him N had pawned the ring with B, who had acted in good faith and who thus became the true owner. In the words of Horridge J,

> 'The minds of the parties met and agreed upon all the terms of the sale, the thing sold, the price and the time of payment, the person selling and the person buying. The fact that the seller was induced to sell by the fraud of the buyer made the sale voidable not void'.

On the facts the presumption that P intended to sell to the person before him had not been rebutted. It is always a question of fact depending on the circumstances whether the question of identity is important and in this connection a distinction may be drawn between a rogue who borrows the name of a real person and a rogue who employs a fictitious name. In the first case the identity may be material and thus produce operative mistake, whereas in the second it is less likely to have this effect.

The operation of this principle can be seen in the case of a man who in buying a motor car represented himself to be Richard Greene, a well-known television star. The seller (L) asked for proof of identity and was shown a special admission pass to Pinewood Film Studios bearing the name R. A. Green and showing a photograph of the rogue. The seller then accepted a cheque for the car from the buyer who later could not be traced. The rogue sold the car to A. The cheque proved worthless. The court held that for L to upset the presumption that he was selling to the person physically present in front of him L would need to show that he intended to contract with some other person. This he failed to do on the facts. The contract between L and the rogue was, on the facts, voidable for misrepresentation and the ownership of the car passed from the rogue buyer to A *before* L took steps to avoid the contract. L could not recover the car (*Lewis v Averay* (1971)).

In the decided cases just discussed it is well to note that one of the parties knew that the other was mistaken and so the parties were not *ad idem*.

4 *Mistake of which the other party is aware.*   Where, though outwardly the offer and acceptance correspond, one party has made a mistake as to the subject-matter and the other party is aware of this the contract will be void. Thus, if in *Smith v Hughes* (p 275, above) the seller of the oats had known of the buyer's mistake there would have been no contract. In *Hartog v Colin and Shields* (1939) a seller of hare skins offered them at a price 'per pound' in mistake for 'per piece'. The buyer, knowing that this was a mistake, accepted the offer. The seller refused to deliver the skins and was sued by the buyer for breach of contract. The court held that there was no contract between the parties. One party *knew* that the other did not intend to contract on the terms expressed.

By way of contrast in *Centrovincial Estates plc v Merchant Investors Assurance Co Ltd* (1983) a landlord offered to renew the lease of his tenant at a rent of £65,000 pa in mistake for £126,000 pa. The tenant *did not know* of this error and accepted the offer. The Court of Appeal held that the mistake had no effect upon the contract, which was binding.

Equitable remedies for mistake

From the above discussion of mistake it can be seen that the common law recognises mistake as invalidating consent in a few situations only. Equity will, within very narrow limits, relieve a party from the effects of his mistake where the common law would hold him to his contract. The possible equitable remedies are:

1 *Rescission on terms.*   A court order which sets the transaction aside and restores the parties to their original position is known as rescission. This may be granted whether or not the mistake is fundamental provided that the party seeking to set the contract aside was not at fault. In *Solle v Butcher* (1950) the parties entered into a lease in the belief that the rent chargeable under the Rent Restriction Acts was £250. In reality it was only £140. However, in an action involving a claim by the lessee to excess of rent and a counterclaim by the lessor for the possession of the flat on the grounds that the lease was void for mistake, the Court of Appeal held that there was not such a mistake as to render the contract void at common law. Nevertheless in the exercise of its equitable jurisdiction the court allowed the lessor rescission of the lease provided that he offered the

tenant a new lease on the same terms and conditions as before and at a rent not exceeding £250 after giving the proper statutory notice of such an increase of rent. This case was followed in *Grist v Bailey* (1967) where both parties thought that, because a house could only be let at a controlled rent under the Rent Restriction Acts of not more than a certain amount, it was not worth more than £850. In fact the house was not subject to rent control and so was worth £2,250. An agreement for the sale of the house for £850 was therefore set aside in equity for common mistake on the terms that the vendor should offer the house to the purchaser at an 'open market' price.

2 *Rectification.*   Equity will in certain circumstances rectify (correct) a written document so that it coincides with the true agreement of the parties:

(a)   There must have been agreement between the parties on a particular aspect or provision of the agreement, *and*

(b)   the agreement must have continued unchanged up to the time it was put into writing, *and*

(c)   the writing fails to express the *agreement* (not the intention) of the parties.

Where all three requirements are satisfied equity will rectify the writing and give specific performance (see p 350, below) of the rectified document. In *Craddock Bros Ltd v Hunt* (1923) there was an oral agreement for the sale of a house *exclusive* of an adjoining yard. The written agreement and later conveyance *included* the yard. Equity granted rectification of both documents. *Frederick E. Rose (London) Ltd v William H. Pim Jnr & Co Ltd* (1953, CA) is an example of a mistake which is recognised neither by the common law nor by equity. A buyer made an enquiry about 'feveroles' and the seller answered by saying that they were 'horsebeans'. The subsequent negotiations and agreement referred to 'horsebeans'. 'Feveroles' are *not* the same as horsebeans. Equity would not grant rectification of the written agreement because it correctly represented the *agreement* (but not the *intention* of the parties). Denning LJ said, 'when the parties to a contract are to all outward appearances in full and certain agreement, neither of them can set up his own mistake, or the mistake of both of them, so as to make the contract a nullity from the beginning'.

3 *Specific performance* (see p 350, below).   The equitable decree of specific performance might be withheld where to grant it would be highly unreasonable in view of the hardship it would cause. In *Malins v Freeman* (1837) F bought an estate at an auction in a 'hasty and inconsiderate manner'. Later F realised he had bought the wrong property and refused to pay for it. The application of M for a decree of specific performance was refused leaving M to his remedies at common law. (As the mistake

was not operative at common law his only possible remedy would be damages for breach of contract.)

A case which well illustrates the difficulties which arise in considering problems of mistake is *Magee v Pennine Insurance Co Ltd* (1969). A proposal for car insurance was incorrectly filled out by a friend of M, without M knowing of the inaccuracy. Later M's car became a complete wreck when it crashed through a shop window. The company then offered to pay £385 under the policy and M accepted this sum. Soon after this agreement the insurance company discovered the material inaccuracy and refused to pay M. M sued the company on their offer to pay the £385. The Court of Appeal held, by a majority, that the claim failed, each member of the court having a different reason for his decision. Denning MR held that the contract of insurance was valid at common law but the agreement to pay £385 was liable to be set aside in equity as there had been a fundamental misapprehension and the party seeking to set the contract aside in equity was not himself at fault. Fenton Atkinson LJ also found in favour of the insurance company but on a different ground: he held that the contract of insurance was invalid at common law. Winn LJ dissented on the ground that the law did not recognise a mistake such as this. In entering into a contract to pay £385 by way of compromise of a claim (if any) under the policy the insurance company and M were acting on a common mistake of fact similar to the mistake made in *Bell v Lever Bros Ltd*.

Non est factum

Before leaving the topic of mistake it is convenient to deal with another situation where an apparent contract might be regarded as void. Normally a person is absolutely bound by the terms of a document he signs (see p 359, below) but a person who is induced by fraud to sign a document which contains a contract fundamentally different in nature or character from that which he contemplated is not bound by his signature. When sued on the contract he may claim that his mind did not accompany his act with the result that the signature was not written with the intention of giving the signer's authority to that kind of document. This defence is known as a plea of *non est factum* (it is not my act). There is an element of mistake here in that the person signing contemplated a different type of document from the one signed but the signature is not invalid because of this mistake but because the signature was fraudulently induced. Three points must be noted in this connection:

1 *Signature induced by fraud.* The signature must have been induced by a trick or fraud. A comparatively old case on this point is *Foster v Mackinnon* (1869), though the plea of *non est factum* goes back to the early days of the forms of action. A asked B to sign a contract of guarantee. B signed the document put before him, which later turned out to be a bill of exchange

on which his signature made him liable. The court held that B was not bound by his signature. Similarly, in *Lewis v Clay* (1897), the court held the signature of C to be invalid. C had signed a document as a witness, the rest of the document, apart from the space for the signature, being covered by blotting paper. In fact the document was a promissory note for over £11,000 with C as the promisor.

2 *Document different in nature.*   The document signed must be different in nature or character from that thought to be signed; mistake as to the contents will not suffice unless the document then becomes different in substance. Where A executed a mortgage in the belief, fraudulently induced by B, that it was a conveyance he was bound by his signature because both the mortgage and the conveyance involved the *transfer* of the *legal estate* in land. The two documents were similar in nature (*Howartson v Webb* (1907)). In *Saunders v Anglia Building Society* (1970, HL) a widow aged 78 was induced to sign an assignment of her house by way of security when she believed she was signing a deed of gift. At the time she signed the document she did not read it as her glasses were broken. She relied on the explanation given to her. A building society advanced money against the deeds as security and retained the deeds on default in repayment. When she learned the true facts the old lady sought to recover the deeds, raising the plea of *non est factum*. The court held that on the above facts the plea was not made out. The document signed was not substantially different in character or nature from that which she thought she was signing.

3 *The burden of proof lies on the party seeking to avoid liability on the document and he must show he acted with reasonable care.*   In *Saunders v Anglia Building Society* Lord Reid said:

> 'The plea cannot be available to anyone who was content to sign without taking the trouble to try to find out at least the general effect of the document. Many people do frequently sign documents put before them for signature by their solicitor or other trusted advisers without making any enquiry as to their purpose or effect. But the essence of the plea *non est factum* is that the person signing believed that the document he signed had one character or one effect whereas in fact its character or effect was quite different. He could not have such a belief unless he had taken steps or been given information which gave him some grounds for his belief. The amount of information he must have and the sufficiency of the particularity of his belief must depend on the circumstances of each case.
>
> Further, the plea cannot be available to a person whose mistake was really a mistake as to the legal effect of the document, whether that was his own mistake or that of his adviser.'

N.B. The origin of the plea of *non est factum* lies in it being the only defence available to a person sued on his covenant and was only available to blind and illiterate persons signing after explanation. Later this defence was extended to other documents. It may now be regarded as covering the situation of a person signing who is permanently or temporarily unable through no fault of his own to have any real understanding of the purport of a particular document, whether this be the result of defective education, illness or innate incapacity, (per Lord Reid, *Saunders v Anglia Building Society*).

2 Misrepresentation

Sometimes a person may enter into a contract as a result of a statement made to him which is false. If that statement is a term of the contract he will have a remedy for breach of contract (see p 355, below). If that statement is *not a term of the contract* it is called a mere misrepresentation and no remedy for breach of contract will lie. The contract will be voidable (not void) and as a consequence will be valid unless and until it is set aside by the person to whom the false statement has been made (p 279, above). In this section we will concern ourselves with the questions of what amounts to a mere misrepresentation not a term of a contract and what are its consequences.

What is a misrepresentation?

A misrepresentation is an untrue statement of fact which is one of the causes which induces the contract

'*Untrue*'. Clearly, if the statement made is true, the complaining party has no ground of complaint.

'*Statement*'. This can be in any form – spoken, written or by conduct as where a person by his dress 'states' that he belongs to a particular organisation. As a general rule mere silence cannot amount to a misstatement. The buyer should ask questions to safeguard himself (this is an example of caveat emptor) but there are exceptions to this rule:

(a) Where there is a fiduciary relationship between the parties (p 290, below).
(b) Where the contract is one of the utmost good faith (p 292, below).
(c) Where a half-truth is offered. A half-truth occurs where a person states true facts which, by virtue of what is not expressed, convey a false impression. A company in a prospectus advertised that even during the years of depression it had paid a regular dividend, thereby implying that it was on a sound financial footing. It had in fact paid the dividend but the company failed to disclose the fact

that this was paid out of profits accumulated before the years of depression. The court held that in these circumstances there had been an untrue statement of fact (*R v Kylsant* (1931)).

(d)   Where a statement which was true when made later becomes false the maker must disclose the alteration or the statement will be taken as false. This rule is based on the principle that a statement once made continues right up to the time of the contract. In *With v O'Flanagan* (1936) a doctor stated to a potential buyer that his practice was worth £2,000 pa. The contract was finally agreed four months later during which time the doctor had been seriously ill and most of his patients had gone elsewhere. The Court of Appeal held that the failure to disclose the changed circumstances amounted to a misrepresentation.

'*Fact*'.   Fact must be distinguished from law. This presents no problem where the statement is purely one of law (e g 'A bill of exchange must be in writing') or where the statement is purely one of fact (e g 'X has red hair'). Where the statement involves law *and* fact the question is difficult. It is suggested that where the point of law is a conclusion drawn from the facts the statement is one of law; otherwise not (e g 'As this contract is not evidenced by writing it is unenforceable', is a statement of law).

Fact must also be distinguished from future intention. A person who states that he intends to do something in the future is not stating as a fact that something will be done but he is stating a fact as to his *present* intention that it will be done. If therefore he has no such intention at the time of making the statement, the statement is false. In *Edgington v Fitzmaurice* (1885) a company had invited a loan from the public stating that the aim of asking for the loan was to finance future expansions. The true intent was to pay off certain debts. Bowen LJ, discussing the question of fact and intention, said,

> '. . . the state of a man's mind is as much a fact as the state of his digestion. It is true that it is very difficult to prove what the state of a man's mind at a particular time is, but if it can be ascertained it is as much a fact as anything else. A misrepresentation as to the state of a man's mind is, therefore, a misstatement of fact'.

Also, fact must be distinguished from opinion. Opinion is a conclusion based on grounds some of which are incapable of proof. A statement of fact may be inherent in an expression of opinion, especially where the person giving the opinion is an expert or has special knowledge. In one case the vendor of certain land gave it as his opinion that the land would carry 2,000 sheep. The vendor had no special knowledge. The Privy Council held that this was a statement of opinion (*Bisset v Wilkinson* (1927)).

In another case the landlord described the tenant of a flat he was selling as 'most desirable'. The vendor knew that it was difficult to persuade the tenant to pay his rent. The Court of Appeal said this was a statement of fact. (*Smith v Land and House Property Corpn* (1884)).

'*Induces*'. The representee will have a remedy only if the untrue statement influenced him in his decision to contract. A representation will not be regarded as having this effect where a person did not know of the misrepresentation. In *Horsfall v Thomas* (1862) the buyer of a gun did not examine it before the purchase. Therefore, the concealing of a defect in the gun did not affect his decision to purchase it. Under other circumstances the representee might know of the representation but act on some other information, such as his own judgment or advice of his own agents, thus not allowing the misrepresentation to induce him to enter the contract at all. Also the misrepresentation will not induce the contract when the representee knew that it was untrue. This knowledge of the untruth must be actual knowledge not a mere suspicion or the possession of information which, if checked, would have revealed the falsehood. Thus, in *Redgrave v Hurd* (1881), the vendor of a law practice stated its annual income at the same time flipping over various papers said to be bills. In fact the bills never amounted to the sum claimed and not all were paid, but as the purchaser did not examine the papers he was held not to know of the untruth of the vendor's statement.

Innocent and fraudulent misrepresentation

A fraudulent statement is one which the maker knows to be false, or does not believe to be true or where the person making it is recklessly careless whether it be true or false. In all other cases statements are innocent. The leading case on the meaning of 'fraudulent' is *Derry v Peek* (1889, HL). A company procured the passing of an Act of Parliament empowering it to run horse-drawn tramcars in Plymouth and, subject to the consent of the Board of Trade, tramcars by steam power. It submitted plans to the Board of Trade for the operation of steam driven tramcars and the company's directors thought that this consent would be given as a matter of course. The prospectus stated that the company had authority to run steam-driven tramcars. Shares were bought in the company in reliance on the prospectus. The Board of Trade refused its consent to the use of steam and the company was wound up with many investors losing money. The directors were sued in the tort of deceit. The House of Lords held that as the directors believed that the consent of the Board of Trade was practically concluded by the passing of the Act they were *not* dishonest but were inaccurate. Inaccuracy does not amount to fraud. 'Fraudulent' was then defined as above stated. Gross carelessness or deliberate abstaining from investigation prior to making a statement may amount to a fraudulent statement if it can be regarded as a complete disregard for the truth.

Consequences of misrepresentation

Remedies for misrepresentation.   The victim of the misrepresentation has several courses which he may possibly follow:

(a)   If the contract is nonetheless for his benefit he may enforce it. Misrepresentation does not render the contract void (except in the rare case where it induces operative mistake).

(b)   If the contract is entirely executory and the misrepresentee does not wish to proceed with performance, he may remain passive and use the misrepresentation as a defence to any action for specific performance of the contract.

(c)   Damages. (i) *Statutory damages* may be available to the victim of an innocent misrepresentation under the Misrepresentation Act 1967. The Act enables a person to sue another for damages where that other has induced him to enter into a contract with that other person by means of a misrepresentation innocently made. But the maker of the misrepresentation may have the statutory defence that he had reasonable ground to believe and did believe up to the time the contract was made that the facts stated were true. In effect where neither party is at fault the loss will lie where it falls. However, the court will award damages only where it is equitable to do so: in other cases of innocent misrepresentation it may issue a decree of rescission.

In the first case to be reported under the Act the plaintiff recovered damages for a misrepresentation which was not fraudulent. Gosling negotiated for the purchase of one of three flats in a house owned by Anderson. Agents for Anderson told Gosling that planning permission had been given for a garage to be erected on the house site. Anderson knew that this was not true. The contract between Gosling and Anderson, and the conveyance, showed a parking area but did not refer to planning permission. In fact planning permission was later refused. Gosling sought damages for the misrepresentation about the garage which induced her to purchase the flat. The Court of Appeal awarded Gosling damages under s 2 (1) of the Misrespresentation Act 1967 (*Gosling v Anderson* (1972)).

(ii) *Damages at common law.*   Damages for deceit may be obtained where a fraudulent statement as defined in *Derry v Peek* has been made (p 285, above). Up till 1963 it was said that no damages were obtainable at common law for an *innocent* misrepresentation. However, the case of *Hedley Byrne & Co Ltd v Heller & Partners Ltd* (p 161, above) has dispelled this view. it would now appear that liability in damages for an innocent misrepresentation can arise in tort under the head of negligence where a duty of care, in the sense enunciated in *Donoghue v Stevenson* (1932), has arisen. This is termed negligent misrepresentation or negligent misstatement. The principle stated by the House of Lords in the *Hedley Byrne Case* may be summarised thus: Wherever in the course of business or professional affairs and in response to a request a person gives advice or information, in circumstances in which a reasonable man would know that his words would be relied on and without clearly denying responsibility for his words, a duty of care arises to exercise such care as is reasonable in the circumstances. If this care is not exercised and damage results an action for damages will lie at common law in accordance with the usual principles of negligence. The principle of the *Hedley Byrne Case* has been applied by the Court of Appeal to the case where a petrol company, Esso, acting through its dealer representative of 40 years' experience, represented that a garage would have an annual throughput of 200,000 gallons. This was based on an estimate made *before* the local authority insisted on changes being made to the plans of the site, resulting in a lesser sales potential. Relying on the representation, Mardon entered a three year tenancy agreement and lost a considerable sum of money. Esso sued Mardon for petrol money due and possession of the garage. Mardon counter-claimed for rescission of the tenancy and damages to cover his loss of capital investment and loss of earnings. The Court applied the *Hedley Byrne* principle and Mardon recovered on his counter-claim. (*Esso Petroleum Co Ltd v Mardon* (1975).)

Also, since the Companies Act 1948, persons responsible for the issue of a prospectus advertising for sale shares in a company have been liable to compensate any shareholder who purchased shares in reliance on a misleading prospectus.

(d) The misrepresentee may ask for a court declaration that the contract is rescinded. This is possible where restitution (restoration of the property passing under the contract) is effected without the aid of the court or where the contract is wholly executory.

(e) The misrepresentee can apply to the court for an order rescinding the contract and in this case the court will give directions as to restitution.

Rescission. Rescission by court order is subject to several limitations. Rescission, as with all equitable remedies, is at the discretion of the court. Its aim is to restore the parties to a contract to their pre-contract position (in contrast to damage: see p 279, below) and where this cannot be done then equity will not grant its decree. Restitution of property handed over (known as *restitutio in integrum*) involves each party returning to the other benefits received, such as money, shares and paintings, while burdens assumed by one party under the contract must again be taken over by the other party, e g liability for future calls on shares. Also, and this is the difficult point, the party seeking the rescission must be *compensated* for the money which he has *necessarily* expended under *obligations* imposed on him *by the contract.* Equity will not give a complete indemnity for all the consequences of the untrue statement for this would be to award common law damages. The distinction between liability under the contract, which will be the subject of compensation, and consequential damage, which will not, is well drawn in the case of *Whittington v Seale-Hayne* (1900). W took a lease of land after negotiations with the agent of S-H who had said that the premises were in a sanitary condition and good state of repair. The lease did not contain these statements but it did provide that the tenant (W) should pay rent, rates, do repairs or any work required by the local authority. W started a poultry farm, employing a manager and buying stock. As a result of the poor state of the drains the stock died, the manager became ill and the local authority required the drains to be put in order. In the action W claimed compensation, inter alia, for (1) value of stock lost, (2) loss of profits, (3) medical expenses, (4) rates, (5) rent, and (6) cost of repairs as ordered by the local authority. The court held that (1), (2) and (3), although a result of the contract, were not necessarily incurred under it. If W had not bought stock or incurred expenses he would not have broken the terms of his lease. Items (4), (5) and (6) were necessarily incurred. If W had not expended money on these he would have been in breach of the covenants in the lease.

Normally, rescission by a party will involve words or acts revoking the contract being communicated to the party in default. However, where communication is impossible owing to the conduct of the defaulting party, as where he commits fraud and then absconds, some overt act of rescission will suffice. In *Car and Universal Finance Co Ltd v Caldwell* (1965, CA) the court held that where a defrauded party informed the police that he had been induced to part with possession of his car on accepting payment by cheque which turned out to be worthless, and asked them to recover it for him, there had been a sufficient overt act of rescission.

Cases where rescission will not be granted.   The court will *not* order rescission of a contract in the following circumstances:

1 Misrepresentation renders the contract *voidable* at the option of the representee but where he affirms the contract he loses his option to avoid. Moreover, though lapse of time is not of itself a bar to rescission it may indicate a waiver of the right to rescind and in all cases of delay equitable remedies may be withheld because they are discretionary. In *Leaf v International Galleries* (1950) L bought a picture which he was told was by Constable. In fact it was not by Constable. L discovered this five years later when he tried to sell the painting. No remedy lay in contract because the statement was not a term of the contract. No remedy lay for the mistake because it was as to quality not identity. Therefore, the remedy sought by L was rescission. This was denied to him on account of the delay which runs from the time the plaintiff *should* have discovered the misrepresentation even if in fact he did not actually discover it until some time later.

2 *Restitutio in integrum* must be possible. If the parties cannot be restored to their pre-contract position then rescission is clearly impossible. Generally, equity will grant rescission where it can do 'what is practically just' even though it cannot restore the parties precisely to their pre-contract position. In *Hulton v Hulton* (1916) W (a wife) brought an action against H (her husband) for rescission of a deed of separation on the ground of fraud. The deed had been operative for five years and under it H paid W an annuity of £500 a year. H claimed the return of the annuity as a condition of rescission. The court ordered rescission of the deed but did not order the return of the money. H had got during those years exactly what he bargained for under the deed.

The principle of restitution is applied less strictly in the case of fraud than in the case of innocent misrepresentation.

3 Where third parties have in good faith and for value acquired rights in property they become the owner at law and in equity. Thus, if B buys what is believed to be a genuine painting from A and sells it to C, who discovers that it is a fake, B cannot rescind as against A because he cannot return to A the painting, which belongs to C. (The situation would be different where any misrepresentation by A induces operative mistake. Here the contract between A and B would be void; so also the contract between B and C.)

Innocent misrepresentation and negligent misstatement compared

To suceed in an action based on an innocent misrepresentation the plaintiff must show that he has entered into a contract in reliance thereon. The defendant may then raise the statutory defence that he had reasonable grounds to believe and did believe up to the time the contract was formed that the facts stated were true. There is no need for a plaintiff to establish a duty of care.

In an action based on common law negligent misstatement the plaintiff need not show that a contract has been entered into but must show that a duty of care has arisen because of a special relationship between the plaintiff and the defendant and that the duty has been breached resulting in damage to the plaintiff (including financial loss). By way of defence the defendant may show reasonable grounds for his belief that the statement he made was true. (See *Howard Marine and Dredging Co Ltd v A. Ogden & Sons (Excavations) Ltd* (1978) CA.)

3 Duress and undue influence

At common law duress is actual or threatened violence to, or restraint of, the person of a contracting party and has no relation to his goods. The threat must be an illegal one so that a threat of lawful imprisonment does not constitute duress. Whether the effect of duress is to render the contract *void* or *voidable* is in doubt. The Privy Council in *Barton v Armstrong* (1976) has held that the effect of duress is to render the contract void. Thus, where a former Chairman of a company made threats against the life of its Managing Director with a view to forcing the Managing Director into signing an agreement to buy the former Chairman's shares the threats constituted duress and the contract eventually signed was void (*Barton v Armstrong* (1976) Privy Council). In modern times cases of duress are rare.

As the common law concept of duress was narrow in scope equity developed an application of its own doctrine of constructive fraud known as undue influence, which was much wider. Consent could be affected by many more influences than crude physical violence and equity took notice of these in granting rescission in appropriate cases. In equity the cases of undue influence fall into two classes: those cases where the party alleging the undue influence has to prove it and those cases where the relationship between the parties gives one an ascendancy over the other so that equity presumes that there has been undue influence exercised. The effect of the presumption is to shift the burden of proof so that the party against whom undue influence is alleged is under the obligation to prove there was no such influence.

Undue influence has never been clearly defined but equity generally grants relief wherever in the opinion of a court of equity free will and deliberate judgment have been excessively influenced. The exact position of the dividing line between undue influence and permissible persuasion is always one for the court. The attitude of equity is clearly seen in *Williams v Bayley* ((1866) HL). A son forged his father's signature on several promissory notes which were passed to the son's bank. At a meeting called to discuss the matter, the banker hinted at 'transportation' as a convict in consequence of some satisfactory solution not being found, whereupon the father gave the bank certain security in consideration for the return of the promissory notes. This agreement was held to be invalid as the banker had *exploited* the anxiety of the father for the son.

Examples of the relationships which give rise to the presumption of undue influence are: trustee and beneficiary, guardian and ward, solicitor and client, religious and medical advisers and those they advise, parent and child but *not* husband and wife. Undue influence is presumed in the parent and child relationship so long as the parent exercises parental influence over the child, even though the child may be an adult and married (*Lancashire Loans Ltd v Black* (1934)). The person against whom the undue influence is alleged may rebut it by showing that the person making the promise to him was in a position to form a free and unfettered judgment. It is desirable to show independent legal advice or advice of an expert. It has been suggested that where the relationship is of solicitor and client, the solicitor must show that the transaction was advantageous to the other party and that he disclosed all known relevant facts (Scrutton LJ in *Moody v Cox and Hatt* (1917)).

The principles on which the concept of undue influence are based have been in existence for some time. The present day question is whether the law will take the bolder and wider step of setting a transaction aside merely because one of the parties is poor, ignorant or weak. Moves in this direction can be seen in the cases and they may well develop into a wider doctrine of economic duress. In *D and C Builders v Rees* (p 231, above), where the debtor's wife held the creditor to ransom, the consent of the creditor to accept less than the full sum which was due was held by Lord Denning MR to be 'no true accord. . . . The creditor was in need of money to meet his own commitments and she knew it'. Mrs Rees had taken advantage of the builders' economic weakness.

Another situation where there was inequality of bargaining power is to be found in *Lloyd's Bank Ltd v Bundy* (1974). A father who owned family properties banked at the same branch of Lloyd's Bank as did his son who ran a plant-hire company. The son's company developed serious financial problems. The bank was willing to continue the company's overdraft facilities only if the father extended his guarantee and charge on his property. The bank did not fully explain to the father the weak state of the son's company. The father did as the bank asked him to do. In agreeing to this course the father was not only benefiting his son's company was also benefiting the bank because its loan to the son's company was secured by the father's guarantee and charge. The bank owed a duty to *both* customers. Later, on a receiving order being made, the bank stopped the son's overdraft facilities and proceeded against the father on the guarantee and charge.

The Court of Appeal held that the bank was under a duty to the father to see that he received *independent* advice when entering a transaction which also benefited the bank. The guarantee and charge were set aside as the father was likely to be influenced by the plight of his son in his dealing with the bank. In the course of his judgment, Lord Denning MR, obiter, reviewed the cases on this area of the law and suggested that

'through all these instances there runs a single thread. They rest on "inequality of bargaining power". By virtue of it, the English law gives relief to one who, without independent advice, enters into a contract on terms which are very unfair or transfers property for a consideration which is grossly inadequate, when his bargaining power is grievously impaired by reason of his own needs or desires, or by his own ignorance or infirmity, coupled with undue influences or pressures brought to bear on him by or for the benefit of the other. When I use the word "undue" I do not mean to suggest that the principle depends on proof of any wrongdoing. The one who stipulates for an unfair advantage may be moved solely by his own self-interest, unconscious of the distress he is bringing to the other. I have also avoided any reference to the will of the one being "dominated" or "overcome" by the other. One who is in extreme need may knowingly consent to a most improvident bargain, solely to relieve the straits in which he finds himself. Again, I do not mean to suggest that every transaction is saved by independent advice. But the absence of it may be fatal'.

Subsequently, Lord Scarman in the Privy Council case of *Pao On v Lau Yiu* (1979) has said that 'there is nothing contrary to principle in recognising economic duress as a factor which may render a contract voidable, provided always that the basis of such recognition is that it must amount to a coercion of will, which vitiates consent. It must be shown that the payment made or the contract entered into was not a voluntary act.' However, as the law now stands there has been no case decided in which the advantage taken by one party of the economic weakness of the other has been given as the ground for avoiding a contract. The distinction between a hard bargain and improper advantage will, in any event, prove a difficult one to draw. (Consider *Alec Lobb (Garages) Ltd v Total Oil GB Ltd* (1983).)

4 Contracts *uberrimae fidei*

In the case of certain contracts the law imposes a duty to disclose certain information. These are known as contracts *uberrimae fidei* (of the utmost good faith). In these cases the absence of misrepresentation or fraud by the party under the duty to disclose will not suffice as a defence. Where such duty arises failure to disclose relevant information may give rise to rescission.

The most important of the contracts within this class are contracts of insurance. A party seeking insurance of any kind must disclose all material facts within his knowledge. 'Material' was defined in relation to contracts of marine insurance in the Marine Insurance Act 1906 as every fact 'which would influence the judgment of a prudent insurer in *fixing the premium* or *determining whether he will take the risk*'. It has since been extended to all forms of insurance. A case which illustrates the point is *London Assurance v Mansel* (1879). M failed to disclose the fact that other insurance companies had refused to insure, and the London Assurance sought to use this failure to disclose as a ground for rescission. The court held that this was a material fact which should have been disclosed and rescission was granted. More recently, in 1975, a lady, who renewed an existing policy on her jewellery, failed to disclose her husband's recent criminal conviction. The Court of Appeal, although critical of the existing law, held that the lady had failed to disclose a material fact and the policy of insurance was avoided (*Lambert v Co-operative Insurance Society Ltd* (1975)).

The duty to disclose material facts is confined to facts known to the insured person. In life insurance applications, it is common for insurance companies to ask questions such as, 'Do you suffer from any heart disease?' The applicant may honestly answer 'No', when unknown to him he has an adverse heart condition and, in so doing, he will not break his obligation of good faith. To protect themselves it is usual for insurance companies to insert a clause providing that the accuracy of the answers to the questions is the basis on which the contract is made. The policy of insurance is thus avoided by an honest but inaccurate answer.

Other circumstances where the duty to disclose arises are: (1) promoters who issue a prospectus advertising shares in a company, (2) vendors of land are under a duty to disclose matters affecting title to the land but not physical defects, (3) partners are under a duty to disclose to each other all information concerning the partnership once the partnership is afoot, but an existing partner is under no duty of disclosure to an incoming partner who must take the necessary steps to protect his own interest, (4) a wide range of family arrangements fall within this category.

5 Illegality

The expression 'illegal' has different meanings in different contexts. It may be used, for example, to refer to a so-called contract that is ineffective to do anything at all, or to a contract that is unenforceable by action in the courts, or to a contract that is enforceable in court at the instance of only one of the parties to it.

Any contract in which the promise, the consideration or the object is unlawful will be void and, from the point of view of one or both of the parties, will be unenforceable. This situation may arise because the contract is (a) illegal at common law, or (b) illegal by statute, or (c) void by statute.

Contracts that are illegal and contracts that are void are similar in that neither can be enforced in court, but different in that an illegal contract, unlike a void one, will make unenforceable any collateral contract that depends on it.

Contracts illegal at common law

These contracts are of three types: (a) contracts where the object is the commission of a crime or a civil wrong; (b) contracts depending for their performance on sexually immoral acts; (c) contracts in contravention of public policy.

(a) Contracts where the object is the commission of a crime or a civil wrong

A contract to commit a burglary or to libel somebody will be illegal. If a contract is drawn up in such a way as to deceive a local or national taxation authority it too will be illegal and, therefore, unenforceable. Thus in *Napier v National Business Agency Ltd* (1951) a company agreed to pay an employee a salary of £13 a week and expenses of £6 a week. As the figure of £6 was much in excess of genuine expenses it was held that the contract had been drawn up to deceive the taxation authority and therefore was illegal.

(b) Contracts depending for their performance on sexually immoral acts

A contract for *future* illicit cohabitation is illegal whether it is a simple contract or under seal. If a contract is made in consideration of *past* illicit cohabitation it will be unenforceable if it is a simple contract because past consideration will not support a subsequent promise; if the contract is under seal, it will be valid. The cases in support of this analysis of the law are mainly Victorian. Today, in the light of current thinking, cohabitation contracts are likely to be legal.

(c) Contracts in contravention of public policy

Public policy is a vague expression which has never been precisely delimited. Pollock defined public policy as 'a principle of judicial legislation or interpretation founded on the current needs of the community'. This could be taken to mean a policy derived from political expediency but in fact legal decisions based on this ground have not been prompted by political considerations. The courts have used as a guide, when considering whether or not to enforce contracts, the most abstract conception of the general public good. There are a number of well recognised categories of contract that contravene public policy. Although in modern times the courts have refrained from declaring new categories of contracts to be contrary to public policy, they have, where necessary, altered the rule to keep pace with changing conditions. In *Fender v St. John Mildmay* (1938) the House of Lords showed itself to be emphatically against the extension of public policy if this could be avoided but did not go so far as to say that there cannot be any new categories.

The following are contracts which have been held to contravene public policy:

(i) *Marriage-brokage contracts.* These are agreements to bring about a marriage or to introduce two persons with a view to marriage in return for a reward. Contracts made by marriage bureaux are within this category.

(ii) *Contracts in total restraint of marriage.* These are contracts whereby a person promises not to marry at all. The category has been held to extend to a contract not to marry anybody except a certain person. A contract restraining a person from marrying one individual or one of a limited class, e g a protestant, or restraining somebody from remarrying is not contrary to public policy.

(iii) *Contracts interfering with marital duties.* A contract for a possible future separation of a husband and wife will be illegal. This does not apply to a contract providing for an immediate separation which actually follows, however, because in this case the separation will actually have become inevitable, nor does it apply to reconciliation arrangements.

(iv) *Contracts to the administration of justice.* A contract not to prosecute, or to interfere with criminal proceedings is illegal if the prosecution is for an offence that concerns the public, but not if the offence is of a private character. In *Fisher & Co v Apollinaris Co* (1875) a company whose trademark had been infringed had the option of prosecuting or suing the offender because the infringement was both a criminal and a civil wrong. They instituted a prosecution but abandoned it under the terms of a contract which gave them the right to publish an apology. The contract was held to be enforceable.

(v) *Contracts tending to promote corruption in public affairs.* This includes contracts for the sale of public offices. In *Parkinson v College of Ambulance Ltd* (1925) it was held that a contract to secure a knighthood for a man who gave money to a charity was illegal. (Such conduct is now criminal.)

(vi) *Contracts made with an alien enemy in wartime.* If a British subject lived voluntarily in an enemy or enemy-occupied country in wartime he would, for this purpose, be considered an alien enemy. Conversely, a national of an enemy country who received permission to reside in England while his country was at war with ours would not be treated as an alien enemy. A contract in this category will be valid if Crown permission to make it is obtained.

(vii) *Contracts directed against the welfare of a friendly foreign country.* In *Foster v* Driscoll (1929) a contract to enable whisky to be smuggled into the USA at a time when the sale of liquor was forbidden there was held to be illegal.

(viii) *Contracts to oust the jurisdiction of the courts.* It was held in *Bennett v Bennett* (1952) that an agreement by a wife, who was petitioning for divorce, not to apply to the court for a maintenance order was contrary to public policy. It is common for an arbitration agreement to contain a clause providing that the parties must await an award by an arbitrator before taking a dispute to court; this is not regarded as an attempt to oust the jurisdiction of the courts and such a clause will be valid. This type of stipulation is known as a '*Scott v Avery* clause' after the case in which it was first held to be valid in 1856.

(ix) *Contracts in restraint of trade.*   A contract imposing an unreasonable restriction on a person's right to carry on his trade or profession will be void and unenforceable.

A complete prohibition against trading is called a general restraint while a prohibition limited in time or place is known as a partial restraint. Until 1894 general restraints were regarded as always being void and partial restraints as being prima facie valid. In that year the House of Lords held in *Maxim-Nordenfelt Guns and Ammunition Co v Nordenfelt* that a general restraint was, in the particular circumstances, valid. In that case an inventor of guns, who had sold his world-wide business, had agreed not to compete with his successors for twenty-five years. In *Mason v Provident Clothing Co Ltd* (1913) the House of Lords held that partial restraints were prima facie illegal.

The present law is as follows:

1   All restraints, whether general or partial, are prima facie contrary to public policy and therefore illegal.
2   A restraint will be held valid if it is shown to be reasonable as regards the public interest as well as the interests of both parties.
3   In considering the question of reasonableness the court must be satisfied that the agreement as a whole is reasonable in the sense that the factors of area covered, period of time, and the scope of the restraint are all properly balanced against one another. The court is likely to allow a wider area where, for instance, the time factor is shorter.
4   The court must be satisfied that some interest of the promisee requires protection.
5   Sometimes a person who has promised not to compete in business fails to keep his promise. This may give rise to an action in which the promisor will contend that the contract binding him not to compete was illegal, while the promisee will say that it was legal. The burden of proving that, as between the parties, the restraint is *reasonable* lies on the promisee; but the burden of proving that, as far as the public is concerned, the restraint is *unreasonable* lies on the promisor.

There are four types of contracts in restraint of trade; these are as follows:

(a) Contracts for the sale of the goodwill of a business containing an agreement by the vendor not to compete with the purchaser.

> The restraint will be effective only where it is no more than reasonably necessary to protect the particular business bought by the purchaser. In *British Reinforced Concrete Engineering Co Ltd v Schelff* (1921) S sold his business in 'Loop' road reinforcements to British Concrete who carried on a large scale business in 'B.R.C' road reinforcement. S covenanted not to compete with British Concrete

in the business of road reinforcements and not to act as a servant of any person concerned in the sale of road reinforcements in any part of the United Kingdom. The court held that this restriction was wider than necessary to protect the interest sold.

The aim of the restraint must not be to protect the purchaser against all competition by the vendor. If, for example, the owner of several shops situated in different towns sold one of them, he could not, by imposing a restraint in the contract of sale of that shop, prevent the purchaser from competing with his other shops. Unless the restraint is accompanied by a genuine sale of a business the purchaser will acquire nothing capable of being protected and the restraint will be illegal. Thus in *Vancouver Malt and Sake Brewing Co Ltd v Vancouver Breweries Ltd* (1934) a company that had a licence to brew beer but did not in fact brew any, agreed to sell its goodwill and to refrain from manufacturing beer for 15 years. As no goodwill really passed to the purchasers the restraint amounted only to an agreement not to compete and was illegal. Also, the brewery had no interest to protect.

(b) Contracts between traders or business men by which prices, output, or methods are regulated.

The Restrictive Trade Practices Act 1956 (see now 1976 Act below) greatly reduced the importance of the common law rules applying to this subject. Before 1956 it was lawful for a number of traders to band together to force others to sell goods at a certain price by threatening collective action; this collective action often took the form of cutting off supplies. The 1956 Act made collective enforcement of prices unlawful. As the parties are business men they will be likely to have equal bargaining power and so in cases of this category it is often difficult to show that a restraint is unreasonable.

(c) Contracts in which an employee undertakes not to compete with his employer when he leaves him, by working on his own or for another employer.

If an employer seeks to restrain a former servant only to prevent competition from the servant, the restraint will be illegal. A restraint is legal only if it protects the former master against disclosure of trade secrets or against loss of customers to the former servant. If the restraint does protect one of these two interest, the fact that incidentally it reduces the competitive power of the former servant will not invalidate it. Argument as to the reasonableness of contracts of this type centres round two factors, the area of the restraint and the length of time for which the former employer seeks to impose it. In order to decide whether the area and duration are reasonable it will often be necessary to take into account the importance of the servant, whether he had access to secrets, and whether he came into contact with customers. The following cases illustrate the principles involved. In *Mason v Provident Clothing and Supply Co Ltd* (1913) a clothing company's canvasser was restrained from working in a similar position within 25 miles of London for three years. The House of Lords held the restraint to be illegal as being wider in area than necessary to protect the employers. In *Fitch v Dewes* (1921) a restraint on a solicitor's managing clerk, preventing him from ever engaging as a solicitor within seven miles of Tamworth, was upheld by the House of Lords because the area was not too wide in view of the fact that the clerk had gained a knowledge of the private affairs of the clients and they were likely to establish a connection with him if he practised in the neighbourhood. In *Littlewoods Organisation Ltd v Harris* (1978) the Court of Appeal enforced a restraint against an executive director of a mail-order business because in the course of his work for his employer he had gained a knowledge of confidential information about the business. The restriction was limited in point of time to 12 months from leaving his employment. The restraint operated against Harris working for Great Universal Stores or any of its subsidiaries. Great Universal Stores was a strong rival of the Littlewood Organisation but carried on a very wide range of business throughout the world. Although the job aspect of the restraint was very wide the Court of Appeal said it could be construed more narrowly to apply only to the Great Universal Stores mail-order businesses in the United Kingdom. On this narrower interpretation of the meaning of the clause, the true construction, it was reasonable and enforceable as being no wider than necessary to protect the confidential information about the mail-order side of the employer's mail-order business.

(d) Contracts in which a person agrees to limit his mode of trade by accepting orders from one person only or by agreeing to make only one type of machine.

A solus agreement is one in which a trader agrees to restrict his orders to one supplier. Such an agreement can be part of a mortgage or a lease whereunder, in return for a loan or a lease, a trader promises to buy only the goods of the mortgagee or lessor. A solus agreement *in gross* is one which is not connected with a lease or mortgage. In *Petrofina (Gt. Britain) Ltd v Martin* (1966) the court held that the doctrine of restraint of trade (i e that contracts in restraint of trade must be reasonable as between the parties and not injurious to the public interest) applied to a solus agreement. M, in return for a rebate on petrol sold, agreed with Petrofina to sell only their petrol. The agreement was to remain in force for 12 years. Also, M was to get any purchaser from him to enter into a similar solus agreement with Petrofina. M broke the agreement by selling other petrols and Petrofina sought to enforce it by injunction. The Court of Appeal held that the agreement was unenforceable as it was in unreasonable restraint of trade because (i) the obligation to sell only to a purchaser willing to enter into a similar solus agreement might make the garage unsaleable, and (ii) the period of 12 years was too long. In a later case, *Esso Petroleum Co Ltd v Harper's Garage (Stourport) Ltd* (1967) Lord Reid gave his opinion that a tying covenant in a mortgage was subject to the doctrine of restraint of trade. The House of Lords held that a 21-year's agreement was too long but enforced an agreement for four years and five months because in all the circumstances the time was not too long – the restraint was not unreasonable. However, in the *Petrofina Case* Denning MR clearly stated, obiter, that the doctrine had no application to a tied house in the brewery trade. A licensee who took a lease of premises from a brewer or who bought the premises on mortgage from a brewer and who was bound to take only the brewer's beer is bound by the terms of the lease or mortgage and cannot argue that the restraint is unreasonable and buy his beer elsewhere.

N.B. The House of Lords in the *Esso* Case took into account the recommendations of the Monopolies Commission Report, 1965, which called for a five-year limit on all 'tied garage' agreements.

Contracts illegal by statute

A statute may be designed to raise revenue, to protect the public or to achieve some other object and the court will have to construe the statute to decide upon its exact meaning. In some cases neglect to observe the provisions of a statute will render the offending contract illegal; in other cases it may not.

In *Smith v Mawhood* (1845) a tobacconist was able to sue on a contract for the sale of tobacco although he did not have a licence prescribed by the statute. This was so because the sole object of the statute was to raise revenue. It was not intended to vitiate contracts for the sale of tobacco without a licence.

The Life Assurance Act 1774 makes contracts on the life of a person in whom the proposer has no 'insurable interest' (explained below) illegal.

Under the Consumer Credit Act 1974 any unlicensed trader who enters a contract for which a licence is required commits a criminal offence.

The Truck Acts 1831–1940 lay down that most classes of manual workers must be paid in current coin of the realm and provide that any contract requiring a worker to spend his wages in a specified shop is illegal. The Payment of Wages Act 1960, which came into force in 1963, amended the Truck Acts and now, provided that the worker consents, it is lawful to pay him by cheque, postal order, money order or by crediting his bank account directly.

Before 1956 it was common for trade associations to make contracts with their members by which it was agreed that if one member of the association sold goods below a stated price, the others would join together to cut off his supplies. This collective enforcement of price-fixing was made illegal by the Restrictive Trade Practices Act 1956. As will be seen below, certain provisions of the same Act made some other contracts merely void.

Contracts void by statute

Restrictive trade practices

Under the Restrictive Trade Practices Act 1976, as amended by the Restrictive Trade Practices Act 1977 and the Competition Act 1980, collective agreements between two or more persons under which restrictions are accepted in respect of prices, quantities or descriptions of goods to be produced must be registered with the Director-General of Fair Trading, as also must be such agreements which restrict the supply of services. It is the duty of the Director-General to lay registered agreements before the Restrictive Practices Court. The function of the court is to decide whether or not any restrictions in the agreement are contrary to the public interest. The Act lays down that the court must begin with the assumption that the restrictions are contrary to the public interest and that it is for the parties to the agreement to justify them. If the parties can show that their agreement is beneficial, by proving that it comes within one of the eight sets of circumstances detailed in the Act, and can show in addition that the benefit proved is not outweighed by some disadvantage to the public, it will be held valid. The eight sets of circumstances mentioned above include such situations as the following: that the restriction is necessary to protect the public against injury, that the removal of the restriction would cause unemployment, or that the removal of the restriction would reduce the export trade. If the court decides that the restriction is against the public interest it becomes void by virtue of the statute.

In conclusion it should be noted that although the Resale Prices Act 1976 makes contracts for the collective enforcement of resale price maintenance unlawful, it puts a weapon into the hands of suppliers who wish to keep up the prices of their products. Section 26 permits a supplier to fix a minimum price at which goods may be sold to the public even though he sells to wholesalers who resell to retailers. The supplier must insert in his contract with the wholesaler, a *lawful* condition regulating resale prices and he can enforce this condition against any retailer who sells at a lower price provided that the retailer acquires the goods with notice of the condition, and despite the fact that there is no privity of contract (see p 262, below) between the supplier and the retailer. The effectiveness of this provision was for a while reduced by the practice of issuing trading stamps which amount to a form of price cutting.

Furthermore, the increasing dissatisfaction with the law has led to the present position now in the Resale Prices Act 1976. This Act provides that any condition in a contract between a supplier and a dealer for the sale of goods, which provides for the establishment of a minimum resale price of the goods, is void unless it is specifically exempted by the Restrictive Practices Court on any one of five grounds listed in the Act, all of which place emphasis on the public interest e g in the absence of a minimum resale price the number of retail outlets would drop substantially. Only where an exemption order has been made would the resale price condition be *lawful*. The sanction for failure to comply with a prohibition against a minimum resale price provision is an action for damages for breach of statutory duty at the suit of a person affected by such non-compliance.

Wagering and gaming contracts

Both wagering and gaming contracts are void. A wagering contract is defined in *Carlill v Carbolic Smoke Ball Co* (1892) as

> 'one by which two persons, professing to hold opposite views touching the issue of a future uncertain event, mutually agree that, dependent upon the determination of that event, one shall win from the other, and that other shall pay or hand over to him, a sum of money or other stake; neither of the contracting parties having any other interest in that contract than the sum or stake he will so win or lose, there being no other real consideration for the making of such contract by either of the parties'.

By way of contrast the essence of an insurance contract is that the person paying the premiums has an 'insurable interest', i e if the event insured against happens, he will lose something whether or not he has an insurance contract, and the object of the contract of insurance is to restore him to his former position.

In a wagering contract as defined above, *either* party may win or lose; such is not the case with football pools where the promoters take a percentage of the stake money and are financially unaffected by the accuracy or otherwise of the forecasts made by those taking part. It follows from this that a football pool coupon is not a wagering contract, and is therefore unaffected by statutes directed against gaming and wagering. This means that an agreement between a member of the public and a football pool company would ordinarily be a valid and enforceable contract. To avoid this football pool companies expressly negative the intention to enter legal relations, by providing on the coupon that the agreement shall be 'binding in honour' only. It was held in *Jones v Vernon's Pools Ltd* (1938) that the use of an expression such as that mentioned did in fact prevent the formation of a contract (see further p 238, above).

Gaming is defined by the Betting, Gaming and Lotteries Act 1963, a consolidating statute, as 'the *playing* of a game of chance for winnings in money or money's worth'; a game of chance is defined so as to include a game of chance and skill combined. Athletic games and sports are expressly excluded from the definition of games of chance. It follows from the definition that only the players of the game can make a gaming contract. If persons who are not playing the game stake money on the outcome, their contract will be a wagering contract on the game, which is not the same thing. The Act makes gaming lawful but only if it is conducted in accordance with rules laid down by the Act; these rules include a condition that the chances in the game must be equally favourable to all the players.

The Gaming Act 1845, s 18 makes all contracts of gaming or wagering void, and unenforceable in the courts, although it does not make them illegal.

The Gaming Act 1892 prevents a betting agent from suing his principal either for money paid out in bets on the principal's instructions or for the agent's commission or fee. Thus in *Tatam v Reeve* (1893) a plaintiff who had settled four debts for the defendant without realising that they were incurred by wagering was held unable to recover the amount paid because his action was held to have been brought 'in respect of' a wagering contract, within the meaning of s 1 of the Act which renders null and void 'Any promise, express or implied, to pay any person any sum of money paid by him under or in respect of any contract or agreement rendered null and void by the Gaming Act 1845 . . .' A principal cannot sue an agent who does not carry out his betting instructions, but if an agent wins money as the result of placing a bet for his principal, the principal may sue him for the winnings, as money had and received to the use of the principal.

The Gaming Act 1835 renders irrecoverable money lent under a contract which stipulates that it is to be used for betting. Money lent on the understanding that it is to be used only to pay betting debts is likewise irrecoverable by virtue of the Gaming Act 1892. If, however, the borrower is not obliged to pay betting debts with the loan even though he is likely to do this, then, as was decided in *Re O'Shea* (1911), the loan is recoverable by action.

The consequences of illegality

It is customary, in considering the consequences of illegality, to draw a distinction between contracts that are illegal from the outset, and contracts that, although innocent at the outset, become illegal because one party intends to use the contract to achieve an illegal purpose.

Contract illegal from the outset

Contracts that are illegal from the outset fall into two categories: (i) contracts that are, from their very nature, quite incapable of lawful performance such as a contract to commit a crime. In contracts of this type both parties are always treated as equally at fault; (ii) contracts that would be capable of lawful performance but which are intended to be performed unlawfully, such as a contract for the hire of a brougham (a horse-drawn carriage) where, as in *Pearce v Brooks* (1866), the brougham was to be used by a prostitute to further her activities. In contracts of this type the parties are treated as equally at fault if both knew of the unlawful purpose, but if only one of them knew of it, he will be treated as guilty and the other will be treated as innocent. This is true also where a contract when formed is intended to be performed lawfully but to the knowledge of one or both parties is performed unlawfully. The party tainted with knowledge of the illegality cannot sue on the contract. In *Ashmore, Benson, Pease & Co Ltd v Dawson Ltd* ((1973) CA) the plaintiff failed to recover compensation for the damage done to his 'tube tank' when it fell off the defendant's lorry. The load was over the legal weight limit to the knowledge of the plaintiff so he had no rights on the contract for the carriage of the 'tube tank'.

The legal maxim, *ex turpi causa non oritur actio* (from a bad cause no action arises) applies to the contract. The maxim means that neither party has any rights under the contract, but the courts do not always rigidly follow this rule because to do so would cause unfair hardship to innocent parties. The following rules are adopted by the courts:

(i) As a general rule the contract is void and unenforceable and no property rights pass under it.

(ii) Collateral transactions are void. This means that any other contract founded on the illegal one will be void, and any bond (promise under seal) given for money owed on the illegal contract will be unenforceable. Thus in *Fisher v Bridges* (1854) a bond was given in respect of money owed on land that the purchaser was buying for an illegal purpose. It was held that no action lay on the bond because it was collateral to the illegal contract for sale.

(iii) Generally money or property handed over under an illegal contract cannot be recovered. This situation is described in the maxim *in pari delicto potior est conditio defendentis* (where the parties are equally at fault the position of the defendant is the stronger one). An illustration is provided by *Parkinson v College of Ambulance* (1925) where the plaintiff was misled by the secretary of the defendant charity into believing that if he contributed to the funds of the charity he would get a knighthood. Although the plaintiff paid, he was not knighted, and when he sued for the return of his donation he was unsuccessful because the contract was illegal as contravening public policy.

There are the following exceptions:

(a) If the party that handed over the property can prove some right to it without having to rely on the illegal contract he may assert that right and recover his property, as in *Bowmakers Ltd v Barnet Instruments Ltd* (1945). In this case the plaintiff hired some tools to the defendants under an illegal contract. The defendants wrongfully sold the tools and thereupon the right to the tools reverted automatically to the plaintiffs because the defendants had committed a tort against them. The plaintiffs sued for, and were awarded, damages on the basis of their right of ownership to the tools. Their claim did not depend on the illegal contract.

Another example of property being recovered despite an illegal contract, because it was possible to make out a claim independent of the illegal contract, is afforded by *Mistry Amar Singh v Kulubya* (1964). This was an appeal from Uganda to the Judicial Committe of the Privy Council. For the protection of Africans there was in force a law making it illegal for an African to lease certain land to a non-African without permission from the government. The plaintiff, who was the registered owner of some of the land in question, was an African and he purported to lease a plot of it to the defendant, an Indian, without permission. The defendant did not pay the rent and the plaintiff sued for rent, damages, mesne profits, and recovery of possession. When the defendant pleaded that the contract was illegal the plaintiff dropped his claim for everything except possession. In this claim he was successful because it was not necessary for him to rely on the illegal contract. He was awarded possession on the ground that he was the registered owner of the land.

A further point of interest in the case is that the parties were held not to be equally at fault because the plaintiff was a member of a class (African landowners) that was intended to be protected.

(b) If a party to an illegal contract genuinely repents before the illegal purpose has been substantially performed he may recover his money or property. It is, however, essential that the party seeking to recover what he has handed over should be able to convince the court that his repentance was real. In *Bigos v Bousted* (1951) an attempted recovery of property handed over failed because there was no real repentance. In this case the defendant sent his wife and daughter to Italy but, owing to currency restrictions, was unable to provide them with as much Italian money as he would have wished. To overcome the difficulty he entered into an illegal contract with the plaintiff under which the plaintiff was to supply Italian lire in Italy in return for the payment of £150 in England. The defendant handed over a share certificate as security. The plaintiff did not pay any Italian money over but nevertheless sued for the £150. The defendant had to plead the facts which constituted the illegal contract in his defence, and he added a counterclaim for the return of the share certificate. Although the defendant was able to point to the fact that he had not carried out the illegal contract, he was unsuccessful in his attempt to get his share certificate back because the court took the view that his so-called repentance was really the result of inability to sin and therefore not genuine.

(c) If the parties are not equally to blame or, in more legal phraseology, not in pari delicto (equally at fault), the less guilty one may recover what he has handed over. There are various circumstances in which the parties are regarded as not in pari delicto. Some of these are as follows:

(i)   If the one who handed over the property has suffered oppression at the hands of the other. Forcing somebody into a contract would be oppression.

(ii)   If the party handing over the property was induced to do so by fraud. This might take the form of a deliberate misrepresentation.

(iii)   If one of the parties belongs to a group of persons who are protected by a statute from another group, he may recover his money or goods even though he has transferred them under a contract prohibited by that statute. This was the situation in *Mistry Amar Singh v Kulubya* (above).

It should be noted that if both parties made an illegal contract while acting under the same mistake of law, being equally innocent, they would be regarded as in pari delicto.

Contract where one party intends to use it for an illegal purpose

The consequences will not be the same for both parties. The party responsible for the illegal performance will be in a much weaker position than the innocent party. No remedy will be available to the guilty party, so that he will neither be able to sue on the contract nor to succeed in an action against the innocent party should the latter repudiate the contract before the intended illegal performance is carried out. Thus in *Cowan v Milbourn* (1867) the defendant agreed to let rooms to the plaintiff, but refused to carry out the contract when he discovered later that the rooms were to be used for giving blasphemous lectures, which was an unlawful purpose. It was held that the plaintiff, who was the guilty party, had no remedy.

The innocent party, if he is to retain his status as innocent, must, as soon as he is aware of the illegality, repudiate the contract or refuse to proceed further with it. He has the following rights:

(i) He may sue on a quantum meruit for anything he has done under the contract before becoming aware of the illegality. In *Clay v Yates* (1856) a printer who had agreed to print a book for the defendant discovered in the course of the work that part of the book was libellous and omitted this part. The defendant did not pay for the printing because of the omission. In an action by the printer it was held that he was entitled to recover for the work he had carried out.

(ii) The parties may have made a collateral contract placing a duty on the guilty party to do something (such as getting a licence) to prevent the main contract from becoming illegal. If the main contract becomes illegal because the collateral contract has not been carried out, both parties will be tainted by the illegality and neither will be able to sue on the main contract. The innocent party will, however, be able to obtain damages for the breach of the collateral contract. This situation is illustrated by *Strongman Ltd v Sincock* (1955) where the plaintiff builders had carried out work under a contract with an architect. By a collateral contract the architect had agreed to get the proper licences that were necessary to make the construction work lawful, but he failed to do this. As a result the plaintiffs were unable to sue on the main contract which was an illegal one since it was carried out without the necessary licences. Despite this the plaintiff builders were awarded damages against the architect under the collateral contract because of his failure to get the licences.

Severance

There may be a number of promises in a contract and, if some of these are unlawful, the question may arise as to whether the whole contract is unlawful. If it is possible to separate, or 'sever', the lawful promises from the others, the contract will remain valid but will be enforceable only in respect of the lawful promises. The law is not entirely clear as to the circumstances in which severance is to be allowed.

It has been suggested that if the unlawful promise is only an unimportant part of the contract, the rest of the contract can be severed from it and enforced but that if the unlawful promise was the most important one, severance will not be possible.

Another suggestion that has been put forward is that severance is permissible only if it will leave the nature of the contract unaltered. In *Goldsoll v Goldman* (1915) the plaintiff bought the business of the defendant who traded in *imitation* jewellery in the United Kingdom; one of the terms of the contract was that the defendant would not trade in *imitation or real* jewellery in the *United Kingdom or* in a number of specified *foreign countries*. In an action on the contract it was held that the references to real jewellery and foreign countries could be severed and that the contract could be enforced in respect of the sale of *imitation* jewellery in the *United Kingdom* only. In the *Nordenfelt Case* (p 296, above) a promise not to engage in 'any business competing or liable to compete with' the company was held to be too wide and was severed from the valid promises.

Although it is not possible to be dogmatic about the effect of the cases it is suggested that promises can be severed if (i) the promise is a relatively unimportant part of the contract, (ii) the severance leaves the nature of the contract unaltered, and (iii) the severance does not entail re-wording the contract. It should be remembered that if a contract contains an unlawful promise that cannot be severed, the *whole contract* will be unlawful.

Supervening illegality

If a legal contract becomes illegal before it is due to be performed, through a change in the law, such as a declaration of war, it is at once abrogated and there need be no performance.

Common Market rules

Under Art 84 of the EEC Treaty and Regulations made thereunder, persons (including, e g, English companies) making contracts which may affect *trade between member countries* and which may prevent, restrict or distort competition within the Common Market, may be fined by the European Commission, subject to an appeal to the European Court of Justice.

Chapter 18
Discharge of contracts

Where all the essentials of a contract are present the parties thereto will have rights and obligations. These rights and obligations come to an end (are discharged) in various ways which are the subject for study in the present chapter.

1 Performance

The general rule

As a general rule parties must perform *precisely all* the terms of the contract in order to discharge their obligations. This is the mode of discharge contemplated by parties when entering into a contract. In relation to contracts for the sale of goods statute has provided in the Sale of Goods Act 1979, s 30 that where a seller delivers less or even more goods than he contracted to sell, or mixed goods, the buyer may reject whatever is delivered. There are many illustrations of this strict rule. Thus where S agrees to sell to B so many tins of fruit in 30-tin cases and in fact delivers the correct number of tins but some are in 30-tin cases and others are in 24-tin cases B may reject the lot (*Re Moore & Co and Landauer & Co* (1921)). Where M agrees to supply and install machinery in a factory but before all the machinery is installed everything is destroyed by fire the buyer is not obliged to pay for the part of the machinery which was supplied and installed at the time of the fire (*Appleby v Myers* (1867)). This situation is now governed by the Law Reform (Frustrated Contracts) Act 1943, p 329, below).

The party in default cannot recover the work he has done because:

(a) The contract is based on an implied condition precedent. From the agreement between the parties it is presumed that complete performance of one part is a condition which must be satisfied before the obligation of the other arise.

(b) A *quantum meruit* action is not available because there cannot be an implied promise to pay a reasonable sum when there is an express contract in being. A quantum meruit action is one brought to recover as much as is merited by the circumstances of the case, as opposed to the contract price, if any. A quantum meruit action may be contractual or quasi-contractual (see also p 245, above). It will be contractual where there is a contract in being but no price has been fixed in return for the plaintiff's consideration. Here the plaintiff will recover the value of the work done. Where goods are sold without provision as to price and there is no previous course of dealing between the parties the buyer must pay a reasonable price. What is a reasonable price is a question of fact dependent on the circumstances of each particular case (Sale of Goods Act 1979). The action will be quasi-contractual where the plaintiff does not base his claim on a contract but merely claims the value of a benefit he has conferred on another who was in a position to accept or reject the benefit but who nevertheless accepted it. An illustrative case is *Forman & Co Proprietary Ltd v The Liddesdale* (1900). P contracted with S to effect repairs to his ship for a certain sum. P did repairs in a workmanlike manner but he did not do precisely what he had contracted to do – in fact some of the materials he used were more suitable for the job and more expensive than those required by the contract. S refused to pay for the work and the Privy Council held that P could recover nothing for the work he had done. P could not recover under the contract because he had not performed it in accordance with its terms nor could he recover on a quantum meruit for the work actually done, because S had not been in a position to accept or reject the work done. The ship belonged to S and the fact that he retook the ship did not amount to an acquiescence in the work of P. A more recent illustration of the principle is to be found in *Gilbert & Partners v Knight* (1968, CA). K agreed with a firm of surveyors to supervise building work for a fee of £30. The surveyors undertook additional supervision and submitted an account for £30 plus £105 for the additional work. K paid only the £30. The court held that the surveyors were not entitled to the extra £105 on a quantum meruit basis as the original contract still subsisted. A new contract could not be implied while the old one was still afoot.

Exceptions to the rule

The above rules, though clearly stated and in the above cases rigidly applied, obviously can in practice work in an unreasonable way. If A builds a house for B and fails to use the correct quality rain spout then under the strict rule B will have to pay nothing for his house. Not surprisingly there are several important exceptions.

(i) Divisible contracts

Where it is possible to regard part of the consideration of one party as being due on performance of part of the consideration of the other then, when that part is performed, a right of action to enforce the appropriate part of the consideration of the other arises. It is a question of construction whether a contract is entire or divisible. An entire contract is one where the agreement provides that complete performance is a condition precedent to contractual liability or one where the consideration is a lump sum without provision for the setting off of part of the performance against part of the consideration. An example of an entire contract is *Appleby v Myers* (above). Divisible contracts are frequently to be found in the building trade, eg where a builder agrees to build a house for £2,500. £1,000 is to be paid on completion of the foundations, £1,000 on erection of the superstructure and £500 six months after completion of the house in accordance with the specification. If after the foundations have been laid the builder fails to do any further work, he can, nonetheless, recover £1,000. Compare this case with *Sumpter v Hedges*, below.

(ii) Acceptance of partial performance

Where the person to whom the promise of performance was made (the promisee) receives the benefit of partial performance of the promise under such circumstances that he is able to accept or reject the work, and he accepts the work, then the promisee is obliged to pay a reasonable price for the benefit received. The case of *Sumpter v Hedges* (1898, CA) is an example of circumstances where the promisee had no choice but to accept the work done. In this case S contracted with H to erect two houses and a stable on H's land for £565. S did work to the value of £333 and then abandoned the contract, whereupon H himself completed the buildings. S brought an action to recover for the work done and materials provided. The Court held that S could not recover the value of the work done as H had no option but to accept it. H was not obliged to leave the buildings in an unfinished state as in that state they would be a nuisance and, in the absence of other circumstances from which a new contract could be inferred, the plaintiff would fail in his action.

(iii) Where the performance is prevented by the promisee

Where a party to an entire contract is prevented by the promisee from performing all his obligations, then he can recover a reasonable price for what he has in fact done on a quantum meruit. In one case P agreed to write a book on 'Costume and Ancient Armour' for a Juvenile Library series and was to receive £100 on completion of the book. After he had done the necessary research but before the book had been written the publishers abandoned the idea. Here no claim would lie on the contract for £100 because P had not performed *all* the terms precedent to recovery but he was successful in an action based on a quantum meruit (*Planchè v Colburn* (1831)).

(iv) The doctrine of substantial performance

This doctrine is an example of the courts, in their desire to do justice between the parties, mitigating the harshness of the law by the

original contract altogether (rescission) and create a new one, or intend merely to vary the original contract (variation), is a question of fact to be determined in the light of all the circumstances of each particular case.

That the distinction between variation and rescission can be vital can be seen from a consideration of *Goss v Nugent* (above). The plaintiff, who was the *vendor*, failed in his action because the oral agreement which he sought to enforce was an ineffective variation. The result would have been the same if the oral agreement had been construed as a rescission. There would then have been no original contract to enforce and any new agreement would have lacked written evidence. *But* if the *purchaser* had sued on the contract and if the oral agreement were construed as a variation the purchaser could have enforced the original contract (subject to the possible effect of waiver: see below). If the words were construed as a rescission there would be nothing for the purchaser to enforce. Thus from the point of view of the vendor, whether the oral agreement is a variation or a rescission he will fail but, from the point of view of the purchaser, the distinction is crucial. If the oral agreement is a variation he may succeed on the original contract; if the oral agreement amounts to a rescission he is in no better position than the vendor.

Waiver. The word 'waiver' is used in different senses. Sometimes it is the equivalent of rescission, other times it means the same as variation, and it can mean e g forbearance. In the present context the word is used with the last meaning. Under the ordinary pressures of commerce and industry, such as postal delays and labour troubles, it frequently arises that it is not possible for one of the parties to keep strictly to the terms of his contract. Thus the buyer of goods may ask the seller to deliver less than the agreed number of articles one month and make up the number on later monthly deliveries or the seller may not be able to deliver all the goods contracted for by the delivery date. In the first case the seller will waive (i e forbear from insisting on the exact performance of the contract) his strict rights under the contract for the benefit of the buyer and in the second case waiver is by the buyer in the interest of the seller. There is a substituted time or mode of performance.

At *common law* there are cases which suggest that a waiver is binding on a party at whose request it is granted (i e would be binding on the vendor in *Goss v Nugent*) and that the party who grants indulgence cannot go back on his promise (i e the purchaser in *Goss v Nugent* cannot withdraw his consent to accept a defective title). This common law position is far from satisfactory. In effect it makes enforceable a promise (the promise to forbear) which is unsupported by consideration. The truth would appear to be that the judges strive to give effect to the intentions of the parties and, where the rules relating to waiver allow them to do this but the rules relating to variation do not, the judges incline to interpret the later words of the parties as a waiver which is enforceable rather than a variation which is not.

In *equity* the doctrine of quasi or equitable estoppel is of possible application. The effect in equity of waiver is seen in the *High Trees Case* (p 232, above). The promise to forbear, or the concession or indulgence as it is sometimes called, creates no new rights and is effective only until withdrawn on reasonable notice. The facts of the case of *Charles Rickards Ltd v Oppenheim* (1950, CA) illustrate the circumstances in which and the way in which the promise to forbear may be withdrawn and how time may be made the essence of the contract. Early in 1947 the defendant instructed the plaintiffs to build a body on a Rolls Royce chassis which he had bought. Sub-contractors to the plaintiff said that they could do the work 'within six or at the most, seven months'. On this basis the defendant gave the plaintiffs a firm order on 11 July 1947. The specification for the bodywork was not finally agreed until 20 August 1947, so, running time from this date, the car should have been ready for delivery at the latest on 20 March 1948. The work was not completed on that date. Instead of cancelling the contract the defendant pressed for delivery of the finished car and so waived the stipulation that the car would be finished within 'at the most, seven months'. As delivery was not forthcoming by June 1948, the defendant wrote to the plaintiffs informing them that the car must be delivered within four weeks or the order would be regarded as cancelled. The car was delivered on 18 October 1948, but the defendant refused to accept delivery. In an action by the plaintiffs for breach of contract by the defendant in not accepting delivery of the car, the Court of Appeal held, agreeing with the trial judge, that there was an initial stipulation as to time, making time of the essence, that this had been waived by the defendant but that he had subsequently made time of the essence again by the giving of reasonable notice. As this notice had not been complied with the plaintiffs themselves were in breach of contract in not delivering the car by 25 July and their action against the defendant failed. However, in the course of his judgment, Denning LJ, considered what the position would have been if the facts had been slightly different. (His words are, therefore, obiter dicta: see p 43, above.) He considered the position of the defendant if he had waived the stipulation for delivery by March 1948 and had later refused to accept a delivery made before the date given in his letter of June which made time of the essence.

> 'If the defendant, as he did, led the plaintiffs to believe that he would not insist on the stipulation as to time, and that, if they carried out the work he would accept it, and they did it, he could not afterwards set up the stipulation in regard to time against them. Whether it be called waiver or forbearance on his part, or an agreed variation or substituted performance, does not matter. it is a kind of estoppel. By his conduct he evinced an intention to affect their legal relations. He made in effect, a promise not to insist on his strict legal rights.

That promise was intended to be acted on, and was, in fact, acted on. He cannot afterwards go back on it. . . . It is a particular application of the principle I endeavoured to state in *Central London Property Trust Ltd v High Trees House Ltd*' (see p 232, above).

In equity there is no distinction drawn between variation and waiver and in this respect the approach of equity is more realistic.

(b) Unilateral discharge

A unilateral discharge takes place where one party only has rights to surrender. Thus where one party has entirely performed his part of the agreement he is no longer under obligations but has rights to compel performance of the agreement by the other party. Thus, A agrees to sell a hundredweight of coal to B for £5 and A delivers the coal only to find that B has suddenly incurred a tremendous expense. A, out of sympathy, agrees that B shall not pay for the coal. But where is the consideration moving from B (the promisee) in support of A's promise to forego his right to the £5? There is none. There is merely a bare agreement. The agreement is one-sided. Only A makes a promise. For this type of discharge, unless the agreement is under seal, consideration must be furnished in order to make the agreement enforceable. In this particular context the agreement is termed the accord and the consideration which makes it binding is known as the satisfaction. It must be remembered that in the case of a bilateral discharge, since both parties have rights to surrender, the agreement generates its own consideration. The judicially-accepted definition of accord and satisfaction is taken from an established textbook, Salmond and Winfield on *Contracts*:

'Accord and satisfaction is the purchase of a release from an obligation, whether arising under contract or tort, by means of any valuable consideration, not being the actual performance of the obligation itself. The accord is the agreement by which the obligation is discharged. The satisfaction is the consideration which make the agreement operative.'

In the above example of unilateral discharge which was not enforceable because of lack of consideration, B should give A something of value with which he would buy A's promise to forego the £5. For instance, B could give A a pencil in return for his promise, or could give him a quarter of a pound of sweets or help to load the coal lorry.

A well-known case, which illustrates this branch of the law and which is authority for the proposition that in appropriate circumstances even a promise to do an act is sufficient consideration even though the act is not in fact performed, is the case of *British Russian Gazette Ltd v Associated Newspapers Ltd* (1933, CA). In this case T brought an action against the defendant newspapers claiming damages for libel. The defendants offered to pay T a sum which he accepted in satisfaction of his claim. His letter of acceptance ran, 'I accept the sum of one thousand guineas on account of costs and expenses in full discharge and settlement of my claims . . . and I will forthwith instruct my solicitors . . . to end the proceedings now pending.' But before the payment was in fact made T disregarded the agreement (accord) and proceeded with the action. In the action the defendants pleaded the accord and satisfaction as a defence. T argued that although there was an accord there was no satisfaction until the payment was actually made and he had commenced his action before any payment was made so the accord was no defence. The Court of Appeal said that it was a question of construction whether the parties intended the promise to pay the thousand guineas to be consideration for the promise to forbear or whether they intended that only actual payment should be sufficient. On the facts of this case the Court of Appeal held that the parties intended the promise to pay a thousand guineas to support the promise to discontinue the proceedings. The defence of accord and satisfaction, therefore, succeeded.

The Bills of Exchange Act 1882 provides an exception to the general rule that a unilateral discharge requires consideration. Where the holder of a bill or promissory note unconditionally renounces his rights against the acceptor the bill is discharged. The renunciation must be in writing or the bill must be delivered up to the acceptor.

(c) Novation

Novation is the name given to a particular type of discharge by agreement. It occurs where there are two contracts, each with a creditor and debtor, and the same person is a debtor under one contract and a creditor under the other. The creditor of one agrees to accept the debtor of the other in return for the release of his own debtor, and the debtor of the other agrees to pay the first creditor in return for his creditor's promise to release him from his obligation. For example, A owes B £100. C owes A £100. C agrees to pay B £100 if he will release A from his debt to B. Thus the first two contracts are discharged and a new one created. (This topic is discussed further on p 274, below.)

(d) Condition subsequent

The parties to a contract may at its formation agree that in a certain event the contract shall come to an end. The contract thus makes provision for its own discharge. An example would be where a manufacturer sells his products as 'guaranteed free from defect and if any defect appears within six months of purchase the manufacturer guarantees to refund the purchase price' on the return of his product. X buys one of the products and a defect appears. The conditions under which the product was sold result in the contract of sale automatically coming to an end and X being entitled to the return of his purchase price. The condition as to the refund of the purchase price is known as a condition subsequent because it can take effect only *after* the contract of sale has been concluded and *after* the defect has appeared. (A condition precedent, on the other hand, is a provision which makes the arising of a right depend upon the prior occurrence of a certain event where at the time of making the contract the parties do not know whether the event has occurred. Examples are *Corpe v Overton* (1833) and *Couturier v Hastie* (1852) (pp 246 and 276, above)).

3 Frustration

Under the doctrine of frustration a contract may be discharged if, after its formation, something happens to make its performance impossible.

A contract may be impossible of performance for various reasons, not all of which amount to a frustration in law. First, it might be legally or physically impossible on the face of the contract. In either of these cases there will, in law, be no contract because the agreement lacks one of the elements essential to a valid simple contract, i e legality of object and possibility of performance. An interesting case on the latter point is the case where a contract for a trip to the moon was declared impossible of performance. Perhaps today it would be better to give the example of a contract for a trip to the sun. Second, unknown to either party at the time of contracting, it might be impossible to perform the contract, as where the goods contracted for have already been destroyed (see *Couturier v Hastie* (1852) p 276, above). Third, the contract might be perfect at its formation but before the time for performance has arrived some event may occur which makes the contract incapable of performance. An example of this would be where a music hall, hired for the performance of a concert, is destroyed by fire after the agreement was reached but before the concert was held. In the first two types of impossibility the contract, at its formation, cannot be legally performed. There is no frustration here. In the third type of impossibility the contract is capable of performance but becomes impossible of performance by some event coming between the agreement and the performance of the agreement. This is termed a supervening or subsequent impossibility. The valid contract is said to be frustrated.

The doctrine of frustration is best understood historically. It is an exception to the rule which was early established in our law. *The rule as to absolute contract says that where there is a positive contract to do a thing not in itself unlawful the promisor must perform the contract or pay damages.* The rule is clearly stated in the case of *Paradine v Jane* (1647). A tenant was sued for arrears of rent and in his defence pleaded that for the last three years he had been dispossessed by the King's enemies. The court rejected the plea and the tenant was held liable for the rent.

'When the party by his own contract creates a duty or charge upon himself, he is bound to make it good, if he may, notwithstanding any accident by inevitable necessity, because he might have provided against it by his contract. . . . Now the rent is a duty created by the parties upon the reservation, and had there been a covenant to pay it, there had been no question but the lessee must have made it good, notwithstanding the interruption by enemies, for the law would not protect him beyond his own agreement.'

In *Paradine v Jane* the tenant could not take the benefit of his lease but was nonetheless obliged to pay the rent because he had promised to pay it.

The doctrine of frustration is an exception to the rule as to absolute contracts enunciated in *Paradine v Jane*. Under the doctrine, at common law, the parties are discharged from liability for further performance by the occurrence of the frustrating event. Early in the nineteenth century the rule as to absolute contracts was modified in a case of supervening illegality. A contract to load a ship at a foreign port was frustrated (discharged) by the outbreak of war between this country and the foreign country where the port was situated. The element of public policy is obvious here. Other modifications were recognised and in 1903 there appeared what is known as the 'frustration of the common venture' in the case of *Krell v Henry*. It was said in this case that the frustration was not limited to complete physical impossibility but also covered cases where, although the contract could be performed, because of the occurrence of some event, the performance of the contract is rendered radically different from what the parties agreed to perform. This last type of frustration is clearly difficult to assess and equally clearly is most flexible. We will now consider the various heads of frustration which the law recognises and the 'frustration of the common venture' head in particular as this is where most difficulty will arise.

Illustrations of the application of the doctrine of frustration

So far we have considered what is meant by frustration and how the doctrine of frustration arose as an exception to the general rule about absolute contracts in *Paradine v Jane*. Now we will consider a range of particular instances where a frustration has been recognised by the courts or where one of the parties thought that, in law, frustration had occurred. The cases will be studied under three heads.

1 *Supervening illegality*

The first type of case is where the contract is frustrated on account of a supervening illegality. An obvious type of case is where after a contract is made legislation is enacted which renders such contracts unlawful. An illustration of this would be a situation where the parties had entered into a contract to build a house within five months and before the house was completed Parliament passed legislation prohibiting all building for two years. Other illustrations would be where there is a contract for personal services and the promisor is interned or conscripted for military service.

Where the illegality affects the whole contract there is no problem. But where it does not affect the contract in toto (ie the whole contract) problems do arise. If the illegality affects some major object of the contract there is frustration in law. A very good illustration of this is the case of *Denny, Mott and Dickson Ltd v James B. Fraser & Co Ltd* (1944, HL). There was an agreement to come into effect in 1929 between the parties for the sale of timber over a period of years. The agreement expressly provided that to enable the agreement to be carried out the respondents should let a certain timber yard to the appellants and it also gave the appellants option to take a long lease or to purchase. Various Control of Timber Orders from 1939 onwards had the effect of halting the import of timber and thus making the performance of the agreement legally impossible. The appellants, however, sought to enforce the option to purchase the timber yard. The House of Lords held that the *whole* contract had been discharged because performance of its main purpose, trading in timber, had become illegal.

Where, however, the main purpose is not frustrated the illegality will not discharge the contract and the rights of the parties are regulated by the general rule that they must perform what they promise or pay damages. In *Eyre v Johnson* (1946) a tenant, who was under a covenant to do repairs, was held liable in damages for breach of the covenant to do the repairs even though war-time regulations had the effect of making such repairs illegal. Anomalous as it might seem, the tenant was held liable in damages for failing to do an illegal act.

2 *Physical impossibility*

There are many illustrations of situations where a contract becomes physically impossible of performance.

(a) *Destruction of subject matter.*   Here the subject matter, or a major part of the subject matter, is destroyed so as to defeat the main purpose of the contract. The leading case on this topic is the case of *Taylor v Caldwell* (1863). The defendant agreed to hire to the plaintiff 'The Surrey Gardens and Music Hall' on certain days in the summer of 1861 for the purpose of giving a series of four grand concerts. Before any of the concerts had been held the hall was destroyed by fire and the courts held that the parties were discharged from their obligations under the contract. In *Turner v Goldsmith* (1891) the court held, on balance, that the main purpose of the contract was not defeated. The plaintiff was employed as agent for a period of years to sell goods 'manufactured *or* sold' by the defendant. The defendant's factory was burned down,. The court held that this did not frustrate the contract because the plaintiff could still continue as agent for sale in relation to goods 'sold', but not necessarily manufactured, by the defendants.

(b) *Non-availability of subject matter.* Non-availability discharges a contract where a person or thing ceases to be available for the purposes of the contract. It may be that there is no question of the destruction of the subject matter but, simply, the subject matter is no longer available. Where the non-availability is merely temporary a question of construction arises. The court has to consider the relationship between the contract as a whole and the effect of the temporary non-availability on that contract. There will be a frustration if the delay makes the performance of the contract substantially different from that originally undertaken. The following cases illustrate the principle.

(i) J chartered a ship to carry cargo from Newport to San Francisco in the spring of 1872. The ship ran aground and was not available until repaired in the autumn of 1872. It was held that the contract was discharged. The voyage was as different as if it had been described as intended to be a spring voyage, while the one after repair would be an autumn voyage (*Jackson v Union Marine Insurance Co Ltd* (1874)).

(ii) A charter-party was arranged for a period of 12 months without any stipulation as to when the 12 months should begin to run. Part of the agreement ran, 'That the steamer shall be delivered under the charter not before 1 April 1915, and should the steamer not have been delivered latest on 30 April 1915, charterers to have the option of cancelling this charter.' Before delivery the ship was requisitioned and not released until September 1915. It was held that, though not expressed, it was understood between the parties that it should be an April to April charter-party. The requisitioning of the vessel frustrated this purpose. It

> 'destroyed the identity of the chartered service and made the charter as a matter of business a totally different thing. It hung up the performance for a time, which was wholly indefinite and probably long. The return of the ship depended on considerations beyond the control and ken of either party.'

(*Bank Line Ltd v Arthur Capel & Co* (1919, HL)).

(iii) A British tank steamship was chartered for five years from 4 December 1912. Under the terms of the charter the vessel was to be used for carrying crude oil or other suitable cargo and the charterers agreed to pay the freight charge. In February 1915 she was requisitioned by the government and converted into a troopship. The sum paid by the government for the requisitioned vessel exceeded the freight. If the charter continued to be valid this sum would be payable to the charterers. If the requisition and conversion of the tanker to a troopship frustrated the contract it was at an end and the sums would be payable to the owners. The House of Lords held that the charterparty was not frustrated. The parties never contemplated that the charterers should do anything other than pay the agreed freight and this they were prepared to do. However, that the question of frustration is sometimes difficult to decide is evident from the fact that the decision of the House was by a bare majority and the minority Lords thought that the very foundation of the contract had disappeared ((*F. A. Tamplin Steamship Co Ltd v Anglo-Mexican Petroleum Products Co Ltd* (1916)).

(c) *Non-availability of party.* In some cases the subject matter may be available where a person essential to performance is not. Here again the court has to consider the effect of the delay on the contract as a whole and where the contract involves a performance on a particular day or for a particular period of time the time factor is most important. The best example of non-availability of the person is, of course, death. Death of either party will frustrate the contract. In cases of contracts for personal services, illness, internment or conscription for military service will frustrate the contract if the non-availability caused by these happenings substantially affects the performance. The following cases illustrate the point. A piano player was engaged to perform at a concert but was ill on the day. The Court of Exchequer in an action against the piano player for breach of contract held that the contract had been frustrated (*Robinson v Davison* (1871)). The defendant music hall artist employed the plaintiff as his manager for ten years from 1938. In 1938 the plaintiff was called-up for service in the army for the duration of the war, an uncertain, and probably long, time. The plaintiff sought damages for breach of contract in that on certain occasions the defendant accepted engagements without his consent. The King's Bench Division held that the contract had been frustrated (*Morgan v Manser* (1947)).

However, where the contract is in the nature of general employment ordinary illness will not put an end to the contract in the business sense and so no frustration will arise. The effect of the illness is merely to excuse the employee's non-attendance. But here again *all* the facts are considered. If the illness is likely to be permanent and to prevent the employee from fulfilling his contract ever, or for a long time, then the parties will be discharged.

(d) *Method of performance impossible.* The particular method of performance contemplated by the parties might become impossible. Where this is so and the parties *stipulated* for the particular mode of performance the contract will be frustrated. If the parties merely anticipated that a certain method of performance would be used the impossibility of that method would not end the contract. The position is well illustrated by the events which followed the closure of the Suez Canal in 1956.

In one case there was a contract for the sale of Sudanese ground-nuts, shipment to be made in November/December, 1956. No express provision was made for the route the ship was to take but the only suitable port was Port Sudan and at the time of the contract the customary route was through the Suez Canal. At the time of shipment the canal was closed as a result of the events following the invasion of Egypt so the seller did not ship the groundnuts. The arbitrator, to whom the case was referred, found that there was no implied term that shipment should be via Suez and that the journey round the Cape was not commercially a fundamentally different one from that through the canal. The House of Lords upheld the finding of the arbitrator (*Tsakiroglou & Co Ltd v Noblee and Thorl, GmbH* (1961)).

3 *Foundation of contract destroyed*

The contract may also be frustrated where performance is not illegal or physically impossible but where later events have destroyed the foundation on which the contract rests. Where this occurs it is said that the common venture, i e the performance provided by the parties, is no longer possible. This would appear to be a very flexible principle but the courts have been most reluctant to invoke it. In particular the common venture is not frustrated where the contract merely becomes more burdensome to one or both of the parties.

This particular type of frustration was first recognised in the case of *Krell v Henry* ((1903) CA). The facts are that in 1902 the defendant hired from the plaintiff for two days a flat in Pall Mall from which the forthcoming coronation processions could be seen. The defendant paid £25 down and agreed to pay a further £50 two days before the hiring was to take place. The coronation processions did not take place because of the serious illness of the King. The plaintiff sued for the £50 balance and the defendant counterclaimed for the return of his £25. The court took the view that this was not a case of mere letting of a room but was a 'licence to use rooms for a particular purpose and none other'. The fact that the processions were intended to pass by the flat 'was regarded by both contracting parties as the foundation of the contract', and since what both of them regarded as essential did not take place the contract was frustrated. The plaintiff could not recover the £50. (For the position of the £25 already paid see p 329, below.)

In the course of his judgment in *Krell v Henry*, Vaughan Williams LJ considered the situation where A asks a cabman to take him to Epsom on Derby Day and even agrees to pay £10 over the normal fare. If the Derby is cancelled the contract is not frustrated. The cab has no special qualities which led to the selection of this particular cab and so long as A instructs the cabman to drive to Epsom and he agrees the cabman has no right to enquire of the purpose of the journey. If he refused to take A to Epsom he would be liable for breach of contract.

A case to contrast with *Krell v Henry* is the case of *Herne Bay Steam Boat Co v Hutton*, also decided in the Court of Appeal in 1903. This concerned the charter of a steam boat to see the naval review at the time of the coronation *and* for a day's cruise round the fleet. The naval review was cancelled, the cruise never took place and the plaintiff owner sued the charterers for the balance of the cost of hire. However, the fleet remained in position and the court held that there had not been sufficient change of circumstances to amount to a frustration. The charter was interpreted as a single hire of a boat. The plaintiff recovered the balance due.

The case of *Davis Contractors Ltd v Fareham Urban District Council* ((1956) HL) is a most important case on this branch of the law. In 1946 the parties entered into a contract whereunder the plaintiff was to build 70 houses for the defendants within eight months. The price was fixed at £92,425. Owing to bad weather and labour troubles it took 22 months to build the houses. The defendant was willing to pay the contract price but as events turned out this was less than the cost to the plaintiff. Therefore, the plaintiff sought to have the contract discharged on the ground of frustration – both parties had agreed that the work should be done in eight months – and to seek payment on a quantum meruit basis when at least they would recover their costs. However, the House of Lords took the view that basically the contract was for the building of houses and the changed circumstances as to materials and labour had not rendered the contract *radically different*. Houses were in fact built. The effect of the altered circumstances was largely to make the contract unexpectedly *more burdensome to one* of the parties. This was not a frustration.

Limitations to the application of the doctrine

There are limitations to the doctrine of frustration. Where the limitations are found by the court the contract will not be discharged and the party promising performance will be liable in contract for any non-performance by him.

1 *Self-induced frustration.* A party alleging that the contract is discharged cannot rely on a frustration if he is himself responsible for it. In other words he cannot rely on a self-induced frustration. The leading case on this topic is *Maritime National Fish Ltd v Ocean Trawlers Ltd* ((1935) Privy Council) where Lord Wright said, 'The essence of "frustration" is that it should not be due to the act or election of the party.' A chartered from B a steam trawler for fishing. This vessel was useless for this purpose unless fitted with an otter trawl which to the knowledge of both parties could lawfully be used only under licence from the Canadian Minister of Fisheries. A already had four other ships so he applied for five licences. He was in fact granted only three licences which he appropriated to his own vessels and sought to return the chartered ship alleging that the known basis of the hire had been frustrated. The Privy Council refused to find a

frustration where the party alleging it had been in part himself responsible for the impossibility. The burden of proving that the frustration was self-induced lies on the party raising the allegation. Thus, where on the day before a chartered ship was due to unload her cargo, an explosion in the boiler-room blew up the ship, thereby preventing performance, the defence of frustration succeeded in an action by the charterers against the defendant owners as the charterers were unable to show that the defendants had been negligent (*Joseph Constantine Steamship Line Ltd v Imperial Smelting Corpn Ltd* (1941) HL).

Another interesting case on the limits to the doctrine of frustration is *Ocean Tramp Tankers Corpn v V/O Sovfracht* ((1964) CA). Here the charterers of a ship under a time charter dated 8 September 1956, allowed the ship to continue into the Suez Canal (a known danger zone) in breach of terms of the charter which prohibited sailing into a danger zone. The ship became trapped for over two months when the canal was blocked. The trip contemplated was from Genoa 'to India via Black Sea', a journey which would take 108 days via the Suez Canal and 138 days round the Cape. The cargo was of iron and steel. The charterers sought to have the contract declared frustrated. The court held that even if there were a frustration here the charterers could not rely on it as it had been brought about by their own breach of contract in entering the danger zone. And even on the hypothetical basis of the ship never having entered the canal there would have been no frustration because in all the circumstances of the case (particularly the journey times and the type of cargo) a situation had not arisen which rendered performance of the contract 'a thing *radically different* from that which was undertaken by the contract' (see p 325, above).

2 *Effects of event greater than foreseen.* Where the parties make express provision for an event which in fact occurs but which is far more extreme in its effects than they imagined would be the case, a difficult question of construction arises. The aim of the doctrine of frustration is to decide who has to bear the loss occasioned by unforeseen events. If the parties anticipate certain difficulties by express provision in the contract then in general the doctrine has no relevance because the contract can be performed either in the original manner contemplated or in accordance with that part of the contract which comes into play only when the unforeseen events have in fact occurred. But one of the parties may raise the argument that, although provision is made to cover the type of event which had occurred, the parties did not have in mind such an extensive and far-reaching catastrophe as has in fact occurred. In such a case, it may be argued, there are, in effect, no words covering the catastrophe and the contract is discharged by frustration. Here the court has to decide what interpretation is to be put upon the words used and to consider, in the light of this interpretation, whether they cover the events which

happened. Thus, in one case where the contract provided for the charter of certain ships between 1914 and 1918 and provided that if war broke out the charters might be *suspended* at the option of either party, the court held that the outbreak of such a catastrophic war was not contemplated and the contract was discharged. Without doubt the contract provided for suspension of the charter on the outbreak of war but the court's interpretation of this clause said that it did not cover such a large-scale war with its far-reaching effects on business ventures.

However, there are cases, such as *Bank Line Ltd v Arthur Capel & Co* (p 322, above), where the parties made adequate provision to cover the events which have occurred but nevertheless the court held the contract to have been frustrated by those very events. When the courts act in this way the difficult question as to the underlying theory of frustration arises. Clearly in this type of case the theory applied is the one which says that the court intervenes to impose a just solution where events unforeseen by the parties have occurred and prevented performance.

NB. For many years argument took place on the question whether the doctrine of frustration applied to leases. The view of many writers, including the present authors, was that it did not. However, in *National Carriers Ltd v Panalpina* (1981) the House of Lords held that the doctrine of frustration can in law apply to a lease but in practice is 'hardly ever' likely to do so.

Effect of a frustrating event

At common law the consequences of frustration did not always work the justice that one might hope for and, as the common law itself did little to mitigate the harshness of its rules, legislation was introduced in 1943 to alleviate the common law position. This legislation does not apply in certain cases and may be excluded by the parties, so we must first study the effects of frustration at common law and then by statute, noticing particularly the circumstances in which the statute will not apply.

The common law rule. Simply the common law rule was that frustration fixes the rights and liabilities of the parties as at the time of the frustrating event. All rights which have occurred before the event can be enforced. All rights which arise after the event are not enforceable. The contract is not destitute of effect. Property passing before the moment of frustration cannot be recovered. A frustrated contract is not void ab initio. It merely ceases to have legal effect from the time of the frustrating event. A leading illustrative case is *Chandler v Webster* (1904). The defendant agreed to let the plaintiff a room in Pall Mall for the purpose of viewing the coronation processions. The processions were never held. The payment of £141 15s was to be made immediately. The plaintiff paid £100 on account before the illness of the King was known and sued to recover this £100. The defendant counter-claimed for the payment of the balance due. The

Court of Appeal held that as the full sum was due before the occurrence of the frustrating event anything due which had been paid could not be recovered and anything due and unpaid could be sued for. The plaintiff failed to recover his £100 and the defendant succeeded on his counter-claim for £41 15s. The injustice of the rigid application of this rule of thumb can be seen by comparing *Chandler v Webster* with the similar case of *Krell v Henry* (p 324, above). In the latter case there was a hiring of similar rooms for a similar purpose, but it happened that the parties had agreed for a down payment with the balance of the hire paid later. Between the date of the down payment and the date for payment of the balance the processions were cancelled. In this case the owner of the rooms sued for the balance of £50 and failed to recover on the ground that the frustrating event discharged the contract as from the time of frustration. The counter-claim of the defendant for the return of the £25 down payment also failed. The reason here is that the money was due before the frustrating event occurred and therefore was paid under a valid contract.

Thus whether money could be recovered or was to be paid depended whether the payment was to be made on a day before the unforeseen illness occurred – not a very just solution.

The common law was to make one modification to these rigid rules but even this lacked the element of discretion to enable the court to do full justice. The rule was that where the consideration had *wholly* failed a party could recover any payment he has made before the frustrating event. This was decided in the *Fibrosa Case* ((1942) HL). In July 1939 the respondents (the defendants at first instance) agreed to sell to the appellants (plaintiffs at first instance) machinery for £4,800 of which £1,600 was to be paid when the order was placed. Delivery was to be at Gdynia in Poland. In fact £1,000 was paid with the order. In September war broke out and Poland was occupied by Germany. The appellants sued for the return of the £1,000. If *Chandler v Webster* had been applied the appellants would have recovered nothing and indeed this was so held at first instance and in the Court of Appeal. However, the House of Lords held that money paid could be recovered where the consideration had totally failed. Thus the appellants recovered their £1,000. The rule is not a just one as presumably the appellants would have failed to recover their £1,000 and would have been liable for the further £600 due with the order if the respondents had delivered some small part of the machinery to the value, say, of £1.

The *Fibrosa Case* enables the maker of payment to recover it if the consideration totally failed but does not assist him if it fails only in part. To this extent it alleviates the position of the payer, but it does nothing for the payee. The payee may be compelled to repay the money he has recovered where the consideration totally fails even though he has incurred expenses in endeavouring to carry out the contract before the frustration occurs.

Apportionment of loss by statute. It is abundantly clear that, where A promises to do something for B in return for payment on completion of the task and the performance is frustrated without the fault of either party but after A has incurred considerable expense, justice demands that some attempt should be made to apportion the loss between them. The law as stated in *Chandler v Webster* and the *Fibrosa Case* would simply mean that A would not be liable to B for breach of contract but would not enable him to recover any sum for the work he had done.

In an attempt to remove hardship the Law Reform (Frustrated Contracts) Act 1943 was passed. Generally the Act gives the court discretion as to what sum shall be payable or recoverable and allows a sum to be recovered where there has been no total failure of consideration, and allows a party who has done something in performance of contract before the frustrating event to claim compensation for any valuable benefit he has bestowed on the other. The Act provides as follows. Section 1 (1) states that the Act applies only where the contract is governed by English law and has been discharged by frustration. Section 1 (2) provides:

> 'All sums paid or payable to any party in pursuance of the contract before the time when the parties were so discharged (in this Act referred to as "the time of discharge") shall, in the case of sums so paid, be recoverable from him as money received by him for the use of the party by whom the sums were paid, and, in the case of sums so payable, cease to be so payable'.

Thus the claim of the flat owner in *Chandler v Webster* for the balance of the sum due would now fail, and the sum paid by the hirer would be recoverable, subject to the proviso in this subsection. The right to recover money paid is available whether the failure of consideration is total or partial. Section 1 (2) goes on:

> 'Provided that, if the party to whom the sums were so paid or payable incurred expenses before the time of discharge in, or for the purpose of, the performance of the contract, the court may, if it considers it just to do so having regard to all the circumstances of the case, allow him to retain or, as the case may be, recover the whole or any part of the sums so paid or payable, not being an amount in excess of the expenses so incurred.'

Thus, if the payment by the hirer were recoverable under the first part of the subsection and the owner had incurred expenses in preparing the flat for the better viewing of the processions, then the owner may be allowed to retain such part of the money paid in advance as the court sees fit – but not exceeding the expenses so incurred. In similar circumstances the owner would be able to recover a part of the money payable. Subsection (3) of s 1 lays down:

'Where any party to the contract has, by reason of anything done by any other party thereto in, or for the purpose of, the performance of the contract, obtained a valuable benefit (other than a payment of money to which the last foregoing subsection applies) before the time of discharge, there shall be recoverable from him by the said other party such sum (if any), not exceeding the value of the said benefit to the party obtaining it, as the court considers just, having regard to all the circumstances of the case and, in particular, (a) the amount of any expenses incurred before the time of discharge by the benefited party in, or for the purpose of performance of the contract including any sums paid or payable by him to any other party in performance of the contract and retained or recoverable by that party under the last foregoing section, and (b) the effect, in relation to the said benefit, of the circumstances giving rise to the frustration of the contract.'

This subsection alleviates the hardship of the party to whom the sums were paid or payable and who ceases to have a right to them under the Act. He is enabled to claim his expenses from the sums paid or payable. It follows that if the contract made no provision for payment before performance no claim for expenses can be made.

The working of s 1 (3) can be seen in *BP Exploration v Hunt* (1979). Hunt, who owned an oil concession in Libya, entered an agreement for its development with BP Exploration. Under the agreement, BP were to provide the capital and expertise and when, and if, the oil were developed and sold BP would be paid back out of Hunt's share of the oil. After BP had done considerable work and incurred great expense in developing the oil field successfully, the Libyan government withdrew the concession. The agreement between BP and Hunt was thus frustrated. BP submitted a claim under s 1 (3). The court held that BP had incurred expense under the contract and, as a result, a benefit had been conferred on Hunt in the form of an increased value in his share of the concession. The court took into account the value of the oil already received by Hunt and the value of a possible claim for compensation against the Libyan government. This was the 'valuable benefit'. In calculating the sum to be recovered by BP the court took into account the sums it had already received from Hunt.

The remaining provisions of the Act may be summarised as follows:

Section 1 (4) makes provision for taking into account overhead expenses and work done personally in estimating the expenses incurred by any party for the purpose of the above subsections.

Section 1 (5) says that the court is not to take into account any insurance moneys which have become payable by reason of the frustrating event unless the insurance was called for by the contract or by statute.

Section 2 (2) states that the Act is to bind the Crown.

Section 2 (3) provides that if the contract on its true construction makes provision covering the frustrating event, the court shall give effect to the Act so far as is consistent with the provision of the contract.

Section 2 (4) provides that where the contract is severable and part is performed and part is frustrated, the frustration of the remainder alone is subject to the Act.

Section 2 (5) states that the Act does not apply: (a) To most charterparties or to a contract for the carriage of goods by sea. (b) To a contract for the sale, or sale and delivery, of specific goods where the contract is frustrated because the goods have perished. Therefore, the Act will apply to goods, where the source of the goods is identifiable but not the particular goods (e g the sale of two bottles of wine from the wine merchant's cellar) and where the contract is for the sale of unascertained goods (e g a sale of 'two bottles of wine') because genus numquam perit (a class never perishes), e g where A promises to supply wine and all his wine is destroyed he still has to supply wine. All the wine in the world is not destroyed and his promise was not to supply some of *his* wine, although this may have been his intention. (c) To a contract of insurance, save as provided in s 1 (5).

Because the Act does not apply in all cases it is necessary today to be familiar with the common law as it was before the Act and indeed still is.

The question is often asked how *Appleby v Myers* (1867) would be decided today. In that case, it will be recalled, the plaintiff agreed to erect machinery on the defendant's premises and keep it in order for two years for a payment of £459. When the machinery was almost complete the premises were destroyed by fire. The plaintiff sued for £419 for work done and materials supplied but failed. At first glance it would appear that the supplier of the machinery which was destroyed would now be able to recover something under the 1943 Act but the problem arises as to the meaning of 'valuable benefit' in s 1 (3). Some writers take the view that the defendant received nothing of value to him so nothing would be payable; others argue that 'valuable benefit' means anything done in pursuance of the contract. The present writers suggest that the latter view is preferable as it gives the court a discretion to do justice and this, in general, is the aim of the Act.

Underlying theory of the doctrine of frustration

There are several views of the juristic (legal theoretical) basis of the doctrine of frustration but only two seem to have gathered considerable support.

(a) *The implied term theory.* In accordance with this theory the court regards a contract as discharged only where it can imply a term in the contract that in the events which happened the contract is to be regarded as at an end. This theory rests on the presumed intention of the parties and is really a manifestation of the 'officious bystander test' explained below (p 360) when discussing the doctrine of *The Moorcock* (1889). A well-known expression of this theory is the statement of Lord Loreburn in the *Tamplin Case* (p 323, above):

> 'No court has an absolving power, but it can infer from the nature of the contract and the surrounding circumstances that a condition which was not expressed was the foundation upon which the parties contracted.'

(b) *The just solution theory.* This theory maintains that the presumed intention of the parties is not the criterion but that the court interferes with the contractual arrangement in order to do justice in circumstances which have prevented performance and which occurred without the fault of either party. It is essential that the law should assist the parties otherwise the altered circumstances would result in the parties being bound by a contract they did not make. Under this theory, the contract is discharged by operation of law as soon as the frustrating event occurs. A leading statement of this theory is to be found in the judgment of Lord Wright in the case of *Denny, Mott and Dickson Ltd v Fraser* (p 321, above).

> 'Where, as generally happens, and actually happened in the present case, one party claims that there has been frustration and the other party contests it, the court decides the issue and decides it ex post facto on the actual circumstances of the case. The data for decision are, on the one hand the terms and construction of the contract, read in the light of the then existing circumstances, and on the other hand the events which have occurred. It is the court which has to decide what is the true position between the parties.'

Weighty support is lent to the just solution theory by the speech of Lord Radcliffe in the case *Davis Contractors Ltd v Fareham UDC* (p 325, above). In the course of his speech Lord Radcliffe disapproved of the implied term theory, pointing out that there is 'a logical difficulty in seeing how the parties could even impliedly have provided for something which ex hypothesi they neither expected nor foresaw'. He continued,

> ' . . . so perhaps it would be simpler to say at the outset that frustration occurs whenever the law recognises that without default of either party a contractual obligation has become incapable of being performed because the circumstances in which performance is called for would render it a thing *radically different* from that which was undertaken by the contract. *Non haec in foedera veni.* It was not this that I promised to do.'

This theory has received further support from Lord Denning MR in the *Ocean Tramp Tankers Case* (p 326, above) where he stated that the doctrine of frustration would apply even in cases where the parties had foreseen the possibility of the frustrating events occurring but had failed to make provision for such eventualities in the contract.

A review of the several theoretical bases for the doctrine of frustration is to be found in the judgment of Lord Hailsham LC in *National Carriers Ltd v Panalpina* (1981) (p 327, above).

4 Discharge by breach

Meaning of breach

Breach means failure to comply with the terms of a contract. To say that a party is in breach is a wide statement. He may be in breach of some comparatively unimportant point, as where goods are delivered late under a contract where time is not of the essence. On the other hand the term of the contract which is broken may be of great significance as where a party fails to deliver at all, or where a watch repairer negligently repairs a watch so that even after repair it does not work.

The topic of discharge by breach is a misnomer and is placed in the present chapter as a matter of convenience. A breach does not automatically discharge a contract as frustration does. As discussed below (p 357) most breaches of the terms of a contract fall into two categories according to the different consequences which flow from the breach. First, those breaches which result in the innocent party having a right to sue for *damages only*, and, second, those breaches which give the innocent party an *option* to treat the contract as repudiated by the contract breaker *and sue for damages* for failure to comply with the terms of the contract. In the first case the term is frequently described as a warranty and is a comparatively minor term of the contract. In the second case, it is referred to as a condition and is a more important term of the contract. Whether the facts of a particular case fall within one category or the other is a question of construction for the court. Breach does not discharge the contract but merely in some cases (cases of repudiation and substantial failure of consideration) gives the innocent party the right to treat the contract as repudiated. It is this point which is behind the decision of the House of Lords in *White and Carter (Councils) Ltd v McGregor* (1962) (p 346, below). The plaintiff was under no obligation to mitigate his loss when the defendant told him that he had no intention of carrying out his obligations because this breach gave the plaintiff the *option* of treating the contract as discharged and did not discharge the contract automatically.

How and when breach may occur

A breach which is sufficiently serious to discharge a contract may occur in either of two ways. One party may show by express words or implications from conduct that he no longer intends to observe his obligations under the contract, or he may in fact break a major term under circumstances which amount to a substantial failure of consideration. An option to treat the contract as discharged arises where there is an express repudiation or where a repudiation can be read into the facts of the case. The innocent party may elect no longer to be bound by the contract and may immediately sue for damages. Examples of this type of contract are where T, who has engaged H to act as courier in the summer, writes to him in the spring saying that he has changed his mind. H is entitled to sue in the spring when he receives the letter (*Hochster v De La Tour* (1853)).

Repudiation in either of the above ways may occur before or during performance. Where the breach occurs *during performance* a very difficult question of construction arises. The court has to decide whether an act alleged to be a breach sufficient to give one party an option to treat the contract as repudiated is to have this effect in law. A leading case on this branch of the law is the case of *Mersey Steel and Iron Co v Naylor* (1884). The facts are as follows. N sold to MS 5,000 tons of steel which were to be delivered at the rate of 1,000 tons a month. Payment was to be made within three days of the receipt by the buyer of the shipping documents relating to the steel. With his first delivery N delivered only half the correct quantity, then made a second delivery but shortly before payment was due proceedings were taken to wind up the N Co (the sellers). MS (the buyers) received legal advice to the effect that pending the proceedings they could not make the payments without leave of the court. Therefore, MS refused to make payment until this leave was obtained. The legal advice was incorrect and MS could safely have paid the money to N. N regarded the non-payment by MS as a repudiation entitling them to hold themselves discharged from further performance. The court held that in the circumstances it was impossible to ascribe to the buyers an intention to repudiate the contract. The buyers thought there was a difficulty in the way of performance and merely thought that they were following the correct way round the difficulty. They acted on a wrong interpretation of the law and this amounted to a breach of contract but did not amount to *an intention not to be bound by* the contract. Therefore, the option to treat the contract as discharged did not arise. Guidance on this difficult question has been given by the Court of Appeal in *Maple Flock Co Ltd v Universal Furniture Products (Wembley) Ltd* (1934) where it was said that the question of whether, in an instalment contract, breach discharges the contract is to be determined by the objective test of the relation in fact of the default to the whole purpose of the contract. The factors for consideration are: 'first, the ratio quantitatively which the breach bears to the contract as a whole, and, secondly, the degree of probability or improbability that the breach will be repeated.' The *Mersey Steel and Iron Case* is illustrative of this. The refusal of the buyers to make payment for the deliveries received did not, in all the circumstances of the case, evidence an intention not to proceed with the contract. In the earlier case of *Freeth v Burr* (1874), which was approved in the *Mersey Steel and Iron Case*, the same approach was adopted. F agreed to buy iron from B. The iron was delivered in two instalments and payment was to be by cash within fourteen days of delivery. When the first payment was due F claimed to be entitled to a reduction in price for late delivery and refused to pay. Whereupon B refused all further performance. It was held that F's conduct did not show an intention not to be bound by the contract and B was not entitled to treat the contract as discharged. B's remedy for the refusal of payment by F was a remedy in contract for damages. Lord Coleridge said,

> 'The real matter for consideration is whether the acts or conduct of the one do or do not amount to an intimation of an intention to abandon and altogether refuse performance of the contract'.

Where the breach occurs *before the time fixed for performance*, known as anticipatory breach, the innocent party is not under any obligation to wait until the date fixed for performance before commencing his action (for example, *Hochster v De La Tour*). It may be thought that if, in February, S contracts to deliver coal to B in June but in April informs B of his change of mind, S is not in breach until the June when he fails to perform. In April he is under no obligation to perform. However, the law says that in April S breaks his promise to deliver, a promise which is supposed to continue until June when it is fulfilled by performance. Thus B can, if he so wishes, sue for damages in April. If, however, he does not accept the repudiation, the contract is not discharged and S remains under the obligation to deliver in June. The contract is said to open for the benefit of and at the risk of both parties. If S fails to deliver, as he has indicated will be the case, then B will recover as his damages his loss at the time of the breach in June. Therefore, if the price of coal rose between April and June, B would recover as damages the difference between the contract price and the market price on the day of the breach in June.

That the contract remains at the risk of both parties is illustrated by the well-known case of *Avery v Bowden* (1855). B chartered A's ship and agreed to load her with cargo at Odessa within 45 days. After a while B told A that he had no cargo and advised him to go away. A waited at Odessa hoping that B would fulfil his promise. Before the end of the 45-day period the Crimean War broke out between England and Russia and the performance of the contract then became illegal. The refusal by B to provide a cargo was an anticipatory breach which would have entitled A to sue immediately for breach of contract. But A did not sue. Therefore, the contract remained on foot until performed. However, within the time allowed for performance it was frustrated by the outbreak of war and the parties were discharged. Consequently B was not liable to A for breach of contract.

Warning has been given by the House of Lords that anyone seeking to rely on an anticipatory breach will be allowed to do so only where the other party has *clearly* indicated, by words or conduct, his intention not to be bound by the contract. In a case where the defendant, who had contracted to buy land, but then found that it was subject to compulsory acquisition proceedings, *attempted to rescind* the contract *under a clause providing for rescission* in certain circumstances, the House of Lords held that there was *no* rescission. The purchaser was, albeit erroneously on the facts, attempting to exercise his rights under the contract and could hardly be said to be repudiating his contractual obligations. Repudiation is a drastic conclusion which should be held to arise only in clear cases of a refusal to perform contractual obligations going to the root of the contract (*Woodar Investment Development Ltd v Wimpey Construction UK Ltd* (1980)).

Chapter 19
Remedies for breach of contract and the limitation of actions

A. Remedies

(i) Damages

The common law remedy for breach of contract is damages. Equitable remedies, which are possibilities depending on the circumstances of the case, are specific performance, injunction, rectification (p 280, above) and rescission (p 279, above).

Where the breach is so serious that the aggrieved party has an option of treating the contract as repudiated by the other party and does so elect, he may, in addition to refusing all further performance, sue for damages; or, instead of a claim for damages for breach of contract, he may sue on a quantum meruit for the value of any work he may have done (see *Planché v Colburn* (1831) p 310, above).

Where the breach does not give rise to an option to treat the contract as discharged, the general common law remedy is an action for damages. In considering an award for damages the court has to consider two problems. *First* of all, it has to ask itself whether the damage suffered can properly be made the subject of compensation or whether the damage is too remote. This question of remoteness of damage arises because the law says that it is unreasonable to make a man liable for all the events which follow from his breach of contract. Some events are so far removed from a breach that the law regards the damage suffered as not being caused by that breach. Thus such damage cannot be the subject of compensation even though it is a direct result of the breach. An example would be where A breaks his contract with B. B consults his solicitor about the legal position instead of returning home early to drive his wife to her doctor's surgery. His wife makes her own way to the doctor's surgery and is killed while walking across a zebra crossing. The sequence of events is clear but A will not be liable to B for the death of his wife even though the death is a consequence of A's breach of contract. This is, of course, an extreme example, but it suffices here to show what is meant by saying that damage is too remote so that, as a result, no compensation will be awarded by the court. The *second* question for the court, once it has concluded that in particular cases the injury is not too remote, is to assess the damages (compensation) to be awarded. The court has to use some principle as a guide in fixing the amount (quantum) of its award. The general principle here is that the aim of damages is to put the parties, as far as money can enable the court to do this, in the position they, or at least the innocent party, would have enjoyed if the contract had been performed. Thus, quite simply, if A agrees to sell B a car 'next Monday' for £100 and defaults so that B has to pay £120 for a similar car the quantum of damages would be the difference between the contract price and the price B had to pay elsewhere for a similar article, i e £20. When B receives the £20 he has in effect got a car for £100, as was intended to be the case under the contract. Note that if B had bought a similar car for £90 he would not have lost by the breach and A would have had to pay him nominal damages only (say £1).

Remoteness of damage

Now let us consider these two factors in more detail. An early case on remoteness of damage, and the best-known, is *Hadley v Baxendale* (1854). The facts were as follows: The crankshaft of a mill had broken and it was necessary to send it to the manufacturers as a pattern for a new one. Carriers, whose duty it was to proceed without delay, agreed to carry the crankshaft to the manufacturers. However, the carriers delayed and the millers were without their crankshaft, and suffered loss of profit, greater than would have been the case if there had been no delay by the carriers. The millers sued to recover their loss of profit. The defendants argued that the damage was too remote. The Court of Exchequer found as a fact that at the time the contract was made the only circumstances indicated by the millers to the carriers were that 'the article to be carried was the broken shaft of a mill'. In the course of his judgment Baron Alderson stated that the question of remoteness of damage turned on the knowledge of the parties. Where the damage could be foreseen the contract-breaker would be liable for that damage:

> 'Where two parties have made a contract which one of them has broken, the damages which the other party ought to receive in respect of such breach of contract should be such as may fairly and reasonably be considered either as arising naturally, i e according to the usual course of things, from such breach of contract itself, or such as may reasonably be supposed to have been in the contemplation of both, at the time they made the contract, as the probable result of the breach of it. Now, if the special circumstances under which the contract was actually made were communicated by the plaintiffs to the defendants, and thus known to both parties, the damages resulting from the breach of such a contract, which they would reasonably contemplate, would be the amount of injury which would ordinarily follow from a breach of contract under the special circumstances so known and communicated.'

Baron Alderson then applied this principle to the facts of the case. As the carriers did not know that the millers had only one crankshaft and relied on it for their livelihood they could not be held liable in damages for the loss of profit caused by the delay. It was reasonable to suppose that the millers had a spare crankshaft. On the state of knowledge of the carriers, they did not know that they were responsible for carrying the *only* crankshaft the millers had. The loss of profit was, therefore, too remote as a head (i e an item) of damage.

In subsequent cases this passage from the judgment of Baron Alderson has been analysed into two parts. A contract-breaker is always liable for the loss which flows naturally and in the normal course of events from the breach. As a reasonable man he is taken to know what this *normal loss* will be. He is fixed with *imputed knowledge* of the loss, i e he is taken to know the consequence of his breach, whether he in fact knows of them or not, and will be liable in damages to the innocent party. If there are special circumstance which give rise to *special loss* then the guilty party will be liable for only such loss as he can foresee is likely to result from his breach. If he does not know of the special circumstances he will not be liable for the loss occasioned in those special circumstances. This was the ground of the decision in *Hadley v Baxendale*. However, cases subsequent to *Hadley v Baxendale* have said that mere knowledge of the special circumstances will not give rise to liability for the special loss. Before a contract-breaker can be held liable for a special loss he must *know of the special circumstances and contract on the basis of them.*

In the example given above of A selling a car to B and failing to deliver it at the agreed time A must be taken as a reasonable man to realise that B would then have to buy in the open market and pay whatever was then the market price. That B would have to pay more is a possibility which A should have foreseen. If, however, B had sub-contracted to sell the car at a greater profit and, because of A's default in delivery, B had lost the profit on this sub-contract, A would not be liable to compensate B for this loss. A does not know of this sub-contract and is not fixed with knowledge of anything which does not flow automatically from the breach of the contract as he understands it to be. However, if A knew of the sub-contract and promised to deliver the car without fail so that B would gain advantage of his favourable bargain with the second purchaser, then A would be liable for the loss of the profit on the resale as he knew of the special circumstances and contracted on the basis of them. Where the buyer fails to accept and pay for goods he will be liable for his breach of contract if he reasonably ought to foresee loss to the seller. If the seller has a ready market for his goods then his loss will be nominal only but if he has no ready market and, as a result of the breach, sells one article less, the buyer will have to compensate the seller by the payment of damages equal to the loss of profit.

The case of *Simpson v London and North Western Rly Co* (1876) is an example of the application of the second part of the rule in *Hadley v Baxendale* to a contract for the carriage of goods. The plaintiff, who exhibited his products at agricultural shows, consigned his samples to a show ground at Newcastle under such circumstances that the court found as a fact that the defendants knew that they were to be exhibited at the Newcastle show. The goods were marked 'must be at Newcastle on Monday certain'. The samples failed to arrive on time and the plaintiff sought to recover the prospective profits lost by virtue of his inability to exhibit at Newcastle. The court held that the defendants, knowing of the special circumstances and agreeing to accept the goods on the basis of them, were liable to compensate the plaintiff for his prospective loss of profit. However, in ordinary circumstances the court is less likely to hold a carrier of goods liable for loss of profits than a seller. A carrier less frequently knows the purpose for which the goods are being carried whereas the seller of a particular article is more likely to know the use to which the article will be put.

Another case which illustrates the working of the rule in *Hadley v Baxendale* is *Victoria Laundry (Windsor) Ltd v Newman Industries Ltd* (1949). In this case the plaintiffs, who were launderers and dyers, wanted another boiler to enable them to expand their business and in particular to take on certain other lucrative dyeing contracts. The defendants agreed to sell the plaintiffs a second-hand boiler and to deliver on 5 June 1946. The boiler was damaged while being dismantled and was not delivered until 8 November 1946. The plaintiffs claimed damages as follows: (i) £16 per week for loss of new custom which they would have taken on; and (ii) £262 per week for loss of the lucrative dyeing contracts they would have had with the Ministry of Supply. The defendants knew that they were supplying a boiler to launderers and that the launderers wanted to put it into use as soon as possible. The Court of Appeal referred the fixing of damages to the Official Referee with the direction that he should award as damages such sum as the defendants might reasonably be expected to know would result from their breach. The plaintiffs would, therefore, recover the ordinary loss of business but not the loss of the specially lucrative contracts.

Hadley v Baxendale has been the subject of an exhausting analysis before the House of Lords where much of their Lordships arguments is merely about words and the judgment of the court remains substantially unaltered. A seller of sugar chartered a ship, *The Heron II*, for the carriage of sugar to Basrah, a journey which would take 20 days. The shipowner deviated from the normal route and the cargo of sugar arrived nine days later than it would otherwise have done. In those nine days the price of sugar on the market at Basrah fell considerably. The delay constituted a breach of contract and the House of Lords had to decide whether the fact that the owner of the sugar intended to sell his sugar in Basrah could be foreseen and whether the shipowner could be held liable for the loss as arising in the normal course of things. The House of Lords held that on the knowledge available to the shipowner when the contract was made, the sale of the sugar on the market at Basrah on the ship's arrival was so probable that it should be regarded as arising in the normal course of events and, therefore, as being within the contemplation of the parties at the time of the contract.

Also, although not necessary to the decision, four of the Law Lords including Lord Reid, said that the *measure* of damages in contract and in tort is not the same. In contract, the injured party may protect himself by directing the other party's attention to a particular risk before the contract is made. In tort there is no opportunity to do this, so the wrongdoer cannot justifiably complain if he has to pay for unusual but foreseeable damage resulting from his wrongdoing (*The Heron II* (1967)).

Quantification of damages

With regard to the assessment of the sum awarded as damages the words of Baron Parke in *Robinson v Harman* (1848) are instructive.

> 'The rule of the common law is, that where a party sustains a loss by reason of a breach of contract, he is, so far as money can do it, to be placed in the same situation, with respect to damages as if the contract had been performed.'

This principle can be seen at work in *C & P Haulage (a firm) v Middleton* (1983) where an engineer, who had been unlawfully ejected from his business premises by the owner of the premises, sued to recover the cost of installing equipment in the premises for his business use. Under the terms of his licence to use the premises the engineer was not entitled to remove fixtures put in by him at the end of the licence period. The licence period was for six months renewable. The engineer was about to move some of his equipment to his home from where he worked for the next 12 months. The Court of Appeal held that 'it is not the function of the courts where there is a breach of contract knowingly, as this would be the case, to put the plaintiff in a better financial position than if the contract had been properly performed. In this case, [the engineer], if he was right in his claim, would indeed be in a better position because . . . had the contract been lawfully determined, as it could have been . . . there would have been no question of his recovering these expenses'. If the contract had been properly performed and not renewed the engineer would not have been compensated for the loss he claimed because to return him financially to his *pre*-contract position would be to compensate him for his own bad bargain. During the remaining part of the six-month period from his unlawful ejection the engineer worked rent-free from his home. He was awarded £10 nominal damages only.

In some circumstances, as a result of the breach of contract, the innocent party may lose some *chance* of a benefit. Where possible loss is not too speculative the courts may award damages as a matter of good sense. Examples are the loss of possible tips or the loss of a chance of entering a beauty contest. The question of the assessment of damages may be a matter of pure conjecture as where a theatrical manager contracted with an actress that if she would attend for interview with 49 other actresses he would select 12 for remunerative work. The notice he gave calling the plaintiff actress to the interview was unreasonably short, thereby causing her to lose her opportunity to be selected for the work. The Court of Appeal found a breach of contract here and upheld an award of £100 as damages. This figure had been arrived at with difficulty as it was by no means certain that the plaintiff would have been selected for the work. In the circumstances it was a matter of pure guesswork (*Chaplin v Hicks* (1911)).

In relation to contracts for the sale of goods the Sale of Goods Act 1979 has made provision for measuring the compensation to be paid in certain types of breach of contract. The provisions are only prima facie rules and, therefore, do not constitute a rigid yardstick in cases where injustice would result from their application. In an action for damages for non-delivery s 51 provides that the measure of damages is the estimated loss directly and naturally resulting, in the ordinary course of events, from the seller's breach of contract. Where there is an available market for the goods the measure of damages is the difference between the contract price and the market or current price at the time when the goods should have been delivered, or if no time for delivery was fixed, at the time of the refusal to deliver. If there is no available market the market value must be otherwise ascertained, for instance, by reference to a resale price, if any. The Act makes a similar provision in relation to the assessment of damages for non-acceptance of, and failure to pay for, goods delivered. Section 50 provides that where there is an available market the sum awarded as damages is the difference between the contract price and the current market price at the time when the goods should have been accepted or at the time of the refusal to accept them. An example of a situation where the prima facie rule will not apply is *Thompson (W.L.) Ltd v Robinson (Gunmakers) Ltd* (1955). In this case the defendant refused delivery of a car sold to him by the plaintiffs who were car dealers. The plaintiffs could possibly have sold the car to another person at the same price, which was fixed by the manufacturers, but in fact returned the car to their suppliers. The defendants admitted that they were in breach of contract but argued that they were not liable for the profit lost by the plaintiffs but only for nominal damages for breach as the plaintiffs had returned the car to the supplier. It was held that, as in this case the provisions of s 50 expressed with reference to the current market price would not indemnify the plaintiff for his loss of profit on the sale, the section was inapplicable. The damages awarded were the loss of profit to the seller on that particular sale.

In assessing the amount of damages to be awarded the court may take into account the inconvenience, sense of frustration and annoyance to the innocent party. Although possible, this measure of damages is not frequently employed. In *Jarvis v Swans Tours Ltd* (1973, CA) the plaintiff paid £63.45 for two weeks' winter sports holiday, which fell substantially short of what was advertised. At the hotel there was little in the way of holiday atmosphere and in the second week he was the only holidaymaker in the hotel and was unable to speak the language of the staff there. Although he received accommodation and food the plaintiff recovered £125 by way of damages taking into account his upset and annoyance at losing the opportunity of enjoying his two weeks' holiday from his employment. An employee who was demoted in breach of contract and as a consequence suffered depression and illness recovered damages by way of compensation for the breach (*Cox v Philips Industries Ltd* (1976)). In another case a surgeon, who was suspended from duty in breach of contract by a Regional Health Authority for refusing to undergo a psychiatric examination, was entitled to damages in respect of his 'distress, frustration and vexation' as well as to damages for loss of income from his private practice (*Bliss v South East Thames Regional Health Authority* (1983)).

A factor which may affect the assessment of damages is the incidence of taxation. In cases where damages are awarded for breach of contract by the wrongful dismissal of an employee, as where a person working under a contract of service for five years which has two years to run is given three months' notice, the tax payable on the salary which would have been given to the employee over a period of time if he had not been dismissed is to be taken into account. At first glance one would think that the damages payable would be the sum of wages which the dismissed employee lost as a result of the breach (subject to the duty to mitigate the loss: see p 345, below). However, the aim of damages is to put the innocent party in the position he would have enjoyed if the contract had been performed. If it had been performed he would have received his wages less tax; therefore, this is the the the sum which the contract-breaking employer must pay him. Thus if there is no work for the employee it is probably cheaper for the employer to dismiss him in breach of contract and pay damages than to perform the contract by paying him while does no work. This principle is known as the principle in *Gourley's Case* and was decided by the House of Lords in 1956. *Gourley's Case* concerned a plaintiff, who, as a result of *negligence* by the defendants, was seriously injured and lost earnings of £37,000. If there had been no injury, the plaintiff's £37,000 earnings would have been taxed and he would have received £6,000. The House of Lords held that the aim of damages is to compensate for loss sustained and the loss to the plaintiff was not £37,000 but £6,000 and this latter sum was awarded as damages. In the assessment of damages for loss of earnings the incidence of taxation is to be taken into account. *Gourley's Case* involved an action in tort but the same principle applies to contract. In *Parsons v B.N.M. Laboratories Ltd* (1963), a case where damages for wrongful dismissal were claimed, the Court of Appeal, by a majority decision, held that at common law the principle in *Gourley's Case* applied to the assessment of damages for breach of a contract of service and income tax liability was deducted from the nominal earnings lost. (However, it should be noted that by virtue of the Finance Act 1981 sums of more than £25,000 are taxable in the hands of the person dismissed, so in such a case the *Gourley* principle will not apply.)

Inflation can be a factor which influences the assessment of damages. In a road accident case a widow's tort damages were increased to take into account the likely increased earnings of her husband had he lived to receive the higher wages paid in an inflationary spiral (*Miller v B.R.S.* (1967)).

The effect of devaluation of the pound sterling can be seen in a case in contract. An English company contracted with a Swiss company, the law governing the contract being Swiss and the money sums being expressed in Swiss francs. The English company failed to pay for the goods delivered. At the time of the court action the pound had fallen in value. The House of Lords ordered payment in Swiss francs. This resulted in the English company having to pay a much larger sum for the francs than it would otherwise have had to pay (*Miliangos v George Frank (Textiles) Ltd* (1975)).

Summary of rules on remoteness and measure of damages

By way of summary of the topics of remoteness of damage and the measure of damages the following extract from the judgment of Asquith LJ in the Court of Appeal in the *Victoria Laundry Case* (above) may be studied:

'(1) It is well settled that the governing purpose of damages is to put the party whose rights have been violated in the same position, so far as money can do so, as if his rights had been observed.... This purpose, if relentlessly pursued, would provide him with a complete indemnity for all loss de facto resulting from a particular breach, however improbable, however unpredictable. Hence,

(2) In cases of breach of contract the aggrieved party is only entitled to recover such part of the loss actually resulting as should at the time of the contract have been in reasonable contemplation as liable to result from the breach.

(3) What was at that time reasonably foreseeable depends on the

knowledge then possessed by the parties, or, at all events, by the party who later commits the breach.

(4) For this purpose, knowledge "possessed" is of two kinds – one imputed, the other actual. Everyone, as a reasonable person, is taken to know the "ordinary course of things" and consequently what loss is liable to result from a breach of that ordinary course. This is the subject-matter of that "first rule" in *Hadley v Baxendale*, but to this knowledge, which a contract-breaker is assumed to possess whether he actually possesses it or not, there may have to be added in a particular case knowledge which he actually possesses, of special circumstances outside the "ordinary course of things" of such a kind that a breach in those special circumstances would be liable to cause more loss. Such a case attracts the operation of the "second rule" so as to make additional loss also recoverable.

(5) In order to make the contract-breaker liable under either rule it is not necessary that he should actually have asked himself what loss is liable to result from a breach. As has often been pointed out, parties at the time of contracting contemplate, not the breach of the contract, but its performance. It suffices that, if he had considered the question, he would as a reasonable man have concluded that the loss in question was liable to result. . . .

(6) Nor, finally, to make a particular loss recoverable, need it be proved that on a given state of knowledge the defendant could, as a reasonable man, foresee that a breach must necessarily result in that loss. It is enough if he could foresee that it was likely so to result. . . .'

Limitations on the rules concerning remoteness and measure of damages

1 *Duty to mitigate the loss.* Generally the law imposes on all persons the duty to mitigate the loss which flows from the breach. In assessing the damages to be awarded the court will take into account whatever the innocent party has done, or has had the means of doing and ought as a reasonable man to have done, to minimise his loss. This rule is well illustrated by the case of *Brace v Calder* (1895) where the plaintiff had been employed as a manager in a business carried on by four people in partnership. Two of the partners died and this amounted to a termination of the contract of employment with the plaintiff without due notice being given. The surviving partners wished to carry on the business so they gave the plaintiff notice terminating his employment by the four and offering him immediate re-employment on the same terms by the two. The plaintiff resented this technical dismissal, refused the offer of re-employment and sought damages from the original firm for

wrongful dismissal. The Court of Appeal held that the plaintiff was under the obligation to mitigate the loss. He, therefore, recovered nominal damages for the breach but did not recover the total loss of wages until his re-employment elsewhere:

> 'The plaintiff as a prudent, reasonable man should have accepted the offer of the two remaining partners to retain him in their service.'

However, in certain cases of personal service, care must be taken in applying *Brace v Calder*. If the circumstances of the dismissal are grossly insulting it may be that the 'prudent, reasonable man' would not be expected to accept an offer of re-employment.

Another illustration of the duty to mitigate loss is provided by the case of *Darbishire v Warren* (1963). D owned and maintained in excellent condition a 1951 Lea Francis shooting brake, which was badly damaged in an accident caused by the admitted negligence of W. The plaintiff was advised that, as the value of the car was about £85 and the costs of repair £192, repair would be uneconomic. Nevertheless, the plaintiff had the car repaired and claimed as his damages from the defendant the £192 less the sum received from his insurance company (£80), plus the costs of hiring another vehicle until his damaged one was repaired (£25). The defendant argued that on the market there were similar shooting brakes at about £85 purchase price (though not a 1951 Lea Francis) and that the plaintiff should not have taken the uneconomic step of having his car repaired but should have mitigated his loss by buying a replacement vehicle on the open market. The Court of Appeal held that as the car was not an irreplaceable article the cost of repairs was not justified. The plaintiff had not taken all reasonable steps necessary to reduce his loss and its replacement as a total loss should be the measure of damage. The plaintiff thus recovered the replacement value (£85) plus the cost of hiring a substitute vehicle (£25) less the sum received from his insurance company (£80).

However, in the case of the so-called 'anticipatory breach' the innocent party has the right to elect to keep the contract open *or* to accept the breach and sue for damages immediately. His election to keep the contract open may work to his disadvantage as in *Avery v Bowden* (p 335, above) or to his advantage as in *White and Carter (Councils) Ltd v McGregor* (1961), a case which came before the House of Lord on appeal from the Scottish Court of Session. The facts are as follows: Advertising contractors agreed to display advertisements for a garage business for a period of three years. On the very day that agreement was reached between the contractors and an agent for the garage business, the owner of the business, McGregor, wrote to the contractors asking to cancel the contract. The contractors refused this request and at the appropriate time five months later they displayed the advertisement. The contract provided that payments should be paid annually in advance with the first instalment due seven days after the first advertisement was displayed and further provided that where an instalment fell due and was four weeks in arrear then the whole sum for the three years immediately became payable. McGregor refused to pay any sums at all and in the resulting action the contractors claimed the full three-year sum. The House of Lords held in favour of the contractors. The House held that the act of McGregor in seeking to cancel the contract was a repudiation which it was open to the contractors to accept or reject. The contractors decided to reject and so the contract remained open for the benefit and at the risk of both parties. The contractors were merely suing to recover what was due under the contract. The duty to mitigate the loss did not arise until the date of the breach, which was on the failure by the garage business to pay all sums due for the three-year period.

It has been suggested that the principle of *White and Carter (Councils) Ltd v McGregor* will not apply where the innocent party needs the co-operation of the person repudiating or where the innocent party ought in all reason, to accept the repudiation and sue for damages. An example of the former would be where there is a contract to paint a house and the house-owner repudiates the contract. Here the painter cannot gain access to the property to start or complete the contract. His remedy is in damages.

An example of the latter is where an expert is engaged to carry out an expensive survey and report. Before the work is started the contract is repudiated. It is argued that the expert ought not to be allowed to incur useless expense. His remedy is to sue for damages as at the time of cancellation, rather than do the work and sue for the contractual payment, thereby saddling the repudiator with the full contract price. If he were to recover the contract cost, having incurred expenditure, he would not be significantly better off financially than if he had sued for damages on cancellation (see Cheshire and Fifoot's *Law of Contract* (10th edn, p 554).

2 *Provisions in contract as genuine pre-estimate of loss.* When entering into contractual relations the parties may anticipate a breach in certain circumstances and make provisions as to the sum of money to be paid by way of compensation should this breach occur. If the provision is a *genuine pre-estimate of the loss* the courts will allow the plaintiff to recover this sum without proving that in fact he has suffered any loss at all. The sum provided for in this way is called *liquidated damages*. However, where the sum payable on breach is not a genuine pre-estimate of the loss which would probably flow, it is said to be held over the heads of one party 'to terrorise' him into performing. The sum provided for in these circumstances is said to be a *penalty*. Equity has always given relief against this form of agreed damages and the courts will not allow such a sum to be recovered.

Whenever a contract contains words fixing in advance the damages to be paid in a certain event or events, *it is a question of construction for the court to determine whether the words used amount to liquidated damages or a penalty.* If the sum is found to be liquidated damages and no more it is recoverable on a breach of contract and the usual rules as to damages are excluded. In *Cellulose Acetate Silk Co Ltd v Widnes Foundry (1925) Ltd* (1933) a *penalty* of £20 for each week's delay was inserted in a contract. The actual delay was 30 weeks and the plaintiff's loss was far greater than £600. The plaintiff sued for the full loss but the House of Lords held that as the sum stipulated was for less than the possible loss it was not *in terrorem* and therefore not a penalty. The so-called penalty clause merely fixed in advance the agreed damages and the plaintiff was limited to their sum.

If the sum is held to be a penalty the clause is ignored and the plaintiff may recover his actual loss in accordance with the normal rules explained above. An instance where a clause was construed as a penalty is to be found in the case of *Landom Trust Ltd v Hurrell* (1955). The defendant bought a car from the plaintiffs on hire-purchase terms. The hire-purchase price was £558. The defendant paid off £302 and then defaulted. The plaintiffs retook possession of the car and resold it for £270. Thus the plaintiffs had by this time received £302 plus £270 for the car priced at £558. The hire-purchase agreement provided that if the agreement was terminated by the plaintiffs on the breach of the defendant the latter should pay as agreed compensation for depreciation the difference between the sums paid and £425. (£425 is roughly 75% of the purchase price of £558.) The plaintiffs, therefore, claimed £123 which would have given them a total of £695 for the car. The court held that as at the time of the formation of the contract it was possible that the defendant might default and the plaintiff retake possession of the car *after* payment of the first instalment, with the consequence that roughly £425 would be payable as agreed compensation, the sum would be treated as a penalty and would be irrecoverable. The sum of £425 was clearly not a genuine pre-estimate of the loss in those circumstances.

The legal principles relating to this question of damages fixed in anticipation of a breach were reviewed by Lord Dunedin in the leading case of *Dunlop Pneumatic Tyre Co Ltd v New Garage and Motor Co Ltd* (1915) as follows:

1   Whether or not the parties use the words 'liquidated damages' or 'penalty' to describe the payment agreed on, it is for the court to determine whether in all the circumstances the case judged at the time of the formation of the contract the payment amounts to liquidated damages or a penalty.

2   The essence of *liquidated damages* is a *genuine pre-estimate* of the loss and the essence of a *penalty* is that it is a money payment held *in terrorem* of the contract-breaking party.

3   The following tests were suggested as helping to decide the issue:

(a)   If the sum stipulated for is extravagant and unconscionable in comparison with the greatest loss which could conceivably be proved to have followed from the breach it is a penalty. A corollary of this is that where the breach consists of the non-payment of a sum of money and the sum to be paid on this breach is greater than the sum which ought to have been paid the sum to be paid on the breach is a penalty.

(b)   There is a presumption that where a single lump sum is to be paid on the occurrence of one or all of several events, some of which may be serious, others not, the lump sum is a penalty.

(c)   On the other hand the courts may regard a single lump sum as a genuine pre-estimate where precise estimation of the consequences of breach is almost an impossibility.

Illustrative examples of the application of the above principles are as follows:

In the *Dunlop Pneumatic Tyre Case* manufacturers supplied goods to dealers under an agreement which fixed damages in anticipation of certain breaches. In consideration of receiving a trade discount the dealers promised not to sell below list prices, not to supply certain named persons, not to exhibit any of the goods and to pay £5 'by way of liquidated damages and not as a penalty' for each item in breach of the agreement. The House of Lords held that this was enforceable as a genuine pre-estimate of the loss. Damage to the manufacturers from the general breach of the agreement would be certain but damage from any one sale in breach would be impossible to forecast. In the words of Lord Dunedin:

'It is just, therefore, one of those cases where it seems quite reasonable for parties to contract that they should estimate that damage at a certain figure, and provided that the figure is not extravagant there would seem no reason to suspect that it is not truly a bargain to assess damages, but rather a penalty to held in terrorem'.

In *Ford Motor Co v Armstrong* (1915) a retailer, in consideration of receiving supplies from Fords, agreed not to sell any car or parts below listed price, not to resell cars bought under the agreement to other dealers and not to exhibit such cars without the permission of Fords. It was provided that the retailer would, in the event of each and every breach, pay £250 as 'agreed damages which the manufacturer will sustain'. The Court of Appeal held that this sum was a penalty. It was a substantial payment, payable on every breach and designed to be held in terrorem over the head of the retailer to compel him to perform.

In *Kemble v Farren* (1829) an actor contracted to appear at a theatre for four seasons, to conform to the regulations and to receive in return £3 6s 8d a day. The agreement provided that in the event of a breach by either party the party in default should pay £1,000 to the other as liquidated damages. The court held that the sum of £1,000 was a penalty. If the manager of this theatre failed to make one payment of £3 6s 8d he would be obliged to pay £1,000 as agreed damages. The payment of a large sum on default in paying a small sum must in its nature be a penalty.

(ii) Specific performance and injunction

The decree of specific performance is an equitable remedy which orders a person to perform his obligations. It is an early example of acting in personam. Equity did not award damages but ordered the contract-breaker to fulfil his obligations and in default would put him in prison. Thus the Court of Appeal decreed specific performance of the contract for the sale of land, although it was outside the jurisdiction of the English courts, because the *defendant* was within the jurisdiction and the decree could be made effectively against him (*Richard West Ltd v Dick* (1969)). The origin of specific performance lies in the fact that in certain types of situation the common law remedy of damages is inadequate. Like all equitable remedies it is discretionary and will be granted only where it is just and equitable to do so taking into account all the circumstances of the case. In particular it will not be granted to one party if it could not be granted to the other. For example, the decree of specific performance will not be granted to a minor to enable him to secure performance of a contract which could not be enforced against him on account of his minority (*Flight v Bolland* (1828)). Also, there is the maxim that delay defeats equity and a tardy application for the decree may be refused on the basis of the delay alone.

In modern times the decree will, in most cases, be appropriate only in contracts for the sale of land. If A agrees to sell goods to B and then refuses to sell to B so that B is forced to buy at a higher price elsewhere, B will recover damages from A under the principles described above. This will put B in the same financial position he would have enjoyed if the contract had been performed. In this case the remedy of damages is adequate. But if A agreed to sell well-situated building land to B and then refused, damages would not be an adequate remedy for B, because in most cases he would not be able to buy other suitable land. Therefore, the court of equity may give its decree ordering A to perform his promise to B by conveying the land to him. However, although the decree will not normally be given where chattels form the subject-matter of the contract, the decree will be given for the transfer of specific chattels of great antique or unique value or which are not ordinary articles of commerce.

In *very rare* circumstances damages may be given *in substitution for* specific performance. For example, where the vendor of a house and land needed the proceeds of the sale of the properties to repay the mortgages thereon, he contracted to sell to a purchaser who failed to complete the sale. The vendor obtained an order for specific performance. Before he took steps to enforce the order (and thereby obtain the agreed purchase price) his mortgagees (lenders) enforced their rights in default of mortgage payments by the vendor and sold the properties. The vendor was thus, on the principle of mutuality, unable to enforce his order for specific performance against the purchaser. The Court of Appeal, on these facts, awarded damages to the vendor in lieu of specific performance and directed enquiry to settle the damages suffered by the vendor as a result of the purchaser's failure to complete (*Johnson v Agnew* (1978)). It is likely that damages will be given in substitution for specific performance, once the vendor has elected for specific performance rather than damages, only in circumstances where not to award damages instead of specific performance would cause prejudice to the vendor, as on the above facts.

Two types of case where specific performance is not granted are contracts requiring supervision and contracts for personal service. On the principle that equity does nothing in vain, equity will not order something to be done which needs continuous supervision. The transfer of land or a chattel is one act which can be compelled but provision of service as part of an agreement for the lease of a flat cannot satisfactorily be compelled for the duration of the lease. Equity, therefore, leaves the parties to their common law remedy of damages (*Ryan v Mutual Tontine Westminster Chambers Association* (1893)).

On the same principle contracts for personal services cannot be made the subject of a decree. If the contract is with an actor or singer the court cannot compel him to give the quality of performance that was contracted for, so no decree will be awarded. However, in certain circumstances the equitable remedy of an injunction may be awarded to *encourage* performance of a contract for personal services and thus achieve the same object as the decree of specific performance itself. Every contract to work for someone implies a promise *not* to work for someone else but the injunction restraining a breach of contract will be granted only to restrain the breach of an *express negative stipulation*. Thus, if A promises to sing at a concert organised by B on 16 October, B will not be able to obtain a decree of specific performance if A should indicate that he has changed his mind. However, if A promises to sing and 'not to sing elsewhere on that date' then the court may grant an injunction restraining A from breaking the contract by singing elsewhere on that date. This will *not compel* A to sing but it will certainly *encourage* him to do so. The action prevented in the negative part of the contract must relate to the positive part. For example, a person engaged to act can be restrained from acting elsewhere but not from working at all elsewhere on the day in question. A well-known case is *Warner Bros Pictures Inc v Nelson* (1936). The defendant film actress agreed with the plaintiffs that she would give them her exclusive services as a film actress and that, during the period of the contract, she would *not* act for anyone else. The defendant contracted to act for a third party and the plaintiffs applied to the court for an injunction. The court granted an injunction restraining the breach of the negative stipulation. To order the defendant not to break the negative part of her contract with the plaintiff was not the same as ordering specific performance of a contract of service because the injunction did not order compliance with the positive part of the contract. If she still refused to work for the plaintiff she could find work other than as a film actress, e g as a waitress. Moreover, damages were not an adequate remedy as no other suitable actress could be found.

B. Limitation of actions

Discharge of right of action

A right of action can be discharged in three ways:

1 *Consent of the parties.* This may be by accord and satisfaction or by release under seal (see p 313, above).

2 *Judgment of a court of competent jurisdiction.* The right of action on the contract is discharged by the judgment or is merged in the solemn form of contract of record.

3 *Lapse of time.* Actions for breach of contract must be commenced within a certain time or else *the right to sue* will be taken away. The Limitation Act 1980 now makes specific provision for this.

Limitation Act 1980

It is said to be in the interest of society that there should be an end to litigation. Certainly it is in the interest of the plaintiff that he should sue while documents and witnesses are still available. Also, it is in the interest of a defendant that a possible action should not be left hanging over his head indefinitely. With these factors in mind Parliament has from time to time passed Limitation Acts which have fixed a limit of time within which an action must be commenced. The latest Act is the Limitation Act 1980, a consolidatory measure.

An action which cannot be brought because of the provisions of the Limitation Act 1980 is known as 'statute-barred'. The Act provides that actions for breach of a simple contract are barred six years, and actions based on a specialty (a deed) are barred twelve years, after the date on which the right of action (or cause of action) first occurs (i e date on which the breach of contract occurs).

Failure to discover breach. Where the plaintiff fails to discover the breach within the six-year period the running of time will generally not be affected. Section 32 of the Act makes special provision for cases of fraud, mistake or concealment as follows:

In any action to which the Act applies and

(a) the action is based on the fraud of the defendant; or
(b) any fact relevant to the plaintiff's right of action has been deliberately concealed from him by the defendant; or
(c) the action is for relief from the consequence of mistake;

the period of limitation shall not begin to run until the plaintiff has discovered the fraud, concealment or mistake or could with reasonable diligence have discovered it.

Section 32 applies to the situation where a builder contracted to build a house on a particular type of foundation. The work on the foundation was done badly and in parts not at all with the result that several years later, outside the six-year period, the house became dangerous and unsafe for habitation. The Court held that there had been concealment of the defective foundations and allowed the action to proceed outside the fixed period of six years from the breach of contract by the builder (*Applegate v Moss* (1971)).

Disability. If on the date on which the right of action accrues the person aggrieved is suffering from a disability, the action may be brought within six years (or 12) from the date when disability ceases or the person dies, whichever event first occurs. The disabilities now recognised by law are *unsoundness of mind* and *minority*. Where one disability ceases and another at the same instant, or earlier, arises, the second disability also prevents time from running, e g where a minor becomes of unsound mind. Once time has begun to run it is not stopped by the later occurrence of a disability.

Acknowledgement. Where the right of action to recover a debt or other liquidated sum has accrued and the person liable (a) acknowledges indebtedness in the form of a written, signed acknowledgement, or (b) makes any payment in respect thereof, time shall begin to run again from the date of such acknowledgement or part payment. This rule applies only where the acknowledgement or part payment is made during the limitation period. It has the effect of starting the period anew. Thus if A failed to pay B £100 due on 2 January 1984, B's right to sue would be barred after six years, i e in January 1990. If in 1989 A makes a payment to B of £5 as part payment of the debt the time limit of six years begins to run again and B's right to sue for the remaining £95 will not be barred until 1995. The sum of money owed need not be stated in the acknowledgement so long as it may be discovered by reference to extraneous evidence (e g tax returns of interest – *Dungate v Dungate* (1965, CA)) but there must be a clear acknowledgement of the debt and not merely an acknowledgement that a dispute exists (*Good v Parry* (1963, CA)).

Equitable claims.　Section 36 (1) of the Limitation Act 1980 expressly states that it is not to apply to claims for specific performance, injunction or other equitable relief except so far as the periods may be applied by analogy. The common law periods were, before the 1939 Act, applied by analogy to cases where the common law had a remedy which was subject to limitation and equity had a corresponding or similar remedy. The 1980 Act intends that this practice should be preserved. Thus, where at common law the remedy of account is barred after six years from the time the right to the account arose, so, by analogy, the equitable remedy of account was barred after six years. In other cases the equitable doctrine of 'laches' (delay) is applied. If, on considering all the circumstances of the case, the court is of the opinion that the plaintiff has been dilatory in bringing his action, then the court will refuse its equitable relief In the case of *Pollard v Clayton* (1855) the defendant agreed to sell to the plaintiff all the coal raised from a particular mine. When he sold elsewhere in breach of the agreement the plaintiffs objected and were referred to the defendant's solicitors. After a delay of 11 months the plaintiff filed a bill in Chancery for specific performance of the contract and the court refused the decree on the principle that equity will not lend its aid to stale claims ('delay defeats equity').

Chapter 20
Terms of the contract

Incorporation of express terms in the contract

When considering what are the terms of a contract the first problem is to discover what was said, done or written and then to enquire how far these express actions constitute a part of the contract. Whether a statement is a term of the contract or not is always a question of the intention of the parties objectively considered. If the statement is written the question of its meaning is one of law and the appropriate remedy for its breach is usually damages. If statements are not written there is a preliminary question of what was in fact stated, then arises the question of the meaning to be attributed in law to these words. Where a statement is not a term of the contract the appropriate remedy for any inaccuracy will possibly be damages for deceit or damages under the *Hedley Byrne Case* (p 286, above) or under the Misrepresentation Act 1967. In each case rescission is a possibility also.

A contract may be expressed entirely in writing, or part in writing and part by word of mouth, or possibly in writing accompanied by oral words of explanation. Under an approach to questions involving the incorporation of terms in a contract known as the parol (oral) evidence rule, no evidence may be given in court to add to, vary or contradict the terms of a written contract. As part of their objective approach to questions of formation of contract the courts are concerned with the outward intentions of the parties rather than an examination of their actual or subjective intentions. Under this rule, evidence of the parties' preliminary negotiations and post-contract conduct may *not* be introduced to show what the parties intended by what they had written. An application of the parol evidence rule can be found in *Henderson v Arthur* (1907) where a lease contained a covenant (promise under seal) for the payment of rent quarterly in advance. Prior to the drawing up of the lease the parties had agreed that the rent could in effect be paid in arrear. When the tenant was sued on the lease for non-payment in advance he pleaded this prior oral agreement. The Court of Appeal held that it was not permissible to substitute the terms of a prior oral agreement for the terms of a subsequent formal contract dealing with the same matter. The subsequent writing had the effect of destroying the previous agreement on the rent issue.

Although the parol evidence rule is a basic rule of evidence used by the courts from time to time to discover the intention of the parties, the courts have not always found that it leads to satisfactory results. As a consequence, several ways of side-stepping the rule have evolved.

Evidence of custom or trade usage may be admitted to show the background against which the parties contracted and, in so doing, to give to the written words used by the parties the meaning which they probably intended the words to have (see p 40, above).

Oral evidence may be admitted to show that (a) the written contract was intended to become operative only on the happening of an event and was not intended to become immediately operative, and (b) that such an event has not yet occurred. In *Pym v Campbell* (1856) by a *written* agreement a person bought a share in an invention but the parties orally agreed that the agreement was not to become operative until the invention had been approved by an independent expert. The court viewed the two agreements together. Such written agreement is said to be subject to a *condition precedent*.

In equity evidence may be admitted to show that a common mistake gave rise to the signing of a document, in which event the decree of rectification may be issued (for rectification see p 280, above).

In some situations the parties to a contract express their contract partly in writing and partly by word of mouth. For the courts to apply the parol evidence rule in such circumstances would be for them to ignore the reality of the agreement between the parties. This, indeed, was the position in *Couchman v Hill* (1947), where the Court of Appeal linked the auctioneer's written conditions and catalogue with the oral statement that the heifer up for auction had not been served (in calf). In another case growers of oranges orally agreed to ship their produce from Spain straight to England. The parties signed the standard bill of lading which allowed the shipowners to proceed by any route, direct or indirect, to England. In fact the ship called first at Antwerp and the oranges missed a favourable market. The growers alleged a breach of contract. The court held that the written bill of lading was *evidence* of an agreement between the parties. The court enforced the oral agreement as to the direct route to England as being in all the circumstances what the court thought the parties had intended (*SS Ardennes (Cargo Owners) v SS Ardennes Owners*) (1950)).

Sometimes a *collateral contract* may come to the aid of one of the parties. In discussions prior to the drawing up of a written contract one party might give an assurance to the other as to the meaning or effect of a proposed term in order to persuade him that there is no difficulty in connection with that point in the proposed agreement. Where the written agreement is then signed in reliance on the statement made, the courts may well find two contracts. One is clearly the written contract. On listening to the oral evidence the courts may also find a contract, subsidiary to and dependent upon the main written one, in which a particular provision of the main contract is to be interpreted in a certain way. One party says in effect, 'I will sign this document if you will assure me that it means . . .'. Such a document will then be read in the light of the oral agreement which is itself called a collateral contract. In one case a tenant signed a shop lease, which contained a clause limiting the use of the premises to 'showrooms, workrooms and offices only'. The tenant overcame his reluctance to agree to this clause when he was assured orally that, if he signed the lease, he would be allowed to sleep on the premises as he had done in the past. When he in fact slept on the premises the landlord sought to forfeit the lease. The court held that the tenant was in breach of the lease but that oral evidence of the collateral contract would be admitted by way of defence (*City and Westminster Properties (1934) Ltd v Mudd* (1958)).

Once a statement is adjudged to be a term of the contract the exact weight to be given to it is for the court to decide. Terms of a contract are of two main classes – minor terms of the contract called warranties and major terms of the contract called conditions. Whether a term is a warranty or condition is a question of construction for the courts to determine. It is not decided conclusively by the use of the word 'condition' in the contract (*Schuler A G v Wickman Machine Tools Sales Ltd* (1973) HL). A breach of warranty is remediable by damages only. However, a breach of condition gives the innocent party to the contract an option. He has the right to treat the contract as repudiated by the other party and sue for damages for non-performance of the contract. In this case he must return property received under the contract. In the alternative, the innocent party may opt to enforce the contract if it is for his benefit and treat the breach of condition as a breach of warranty entitling him to damages. In this case he may keep the property passed to him under the contract. When the innocent party elects to do this he is said to treat the condition as a warranty ex post facto (after the breach is known). Where a contract excludes liability for breach of warranty and a condition is broken the innocent party may elect to sue for damages for breach of warranty ex post facto. His right to elect to treat the contract as repudiated *or* to affirm it and sue for damages is not affected in these circumstances. For the purpose of the exclusion clause the condition is still a condition – once a condition, always a condition. The above principles can be seen at work in the following cases:

In *Hopkins v Tanqueray* (1854) a statement made the day *before* an auction as to the soundness of a horse to be auctioned was held not to be a contractual term as the statement was not made with a view to contracting. This case may be contrasted with *Couchman v Hill* (1947) where, at an auction but before bidding had commenced, the plaintiff asked both the defendant owner and the auctioneer if the heifer to be auctioned was served. Both answered in the negative. Relying on this the plaintiff bought the heifer which died on account of bearing calf too young. The sale was subject to the 'usual conditions' which provided that lots were sold with all faults. The court held that the plaintiff could recover damages here because the oral statement was intended to be part of the contract. Moreover, the statement as to the heifer being unserved was clearly a condition but, as it was dead, the plaintiff could not return it so he elected to sue for damages as for breach of warranty.

Where one party seeks to enforce the terms of an unsigned document he has to show that the other party knew of the terms and accepted them as part of the contract. This is done by either drawing the other party's attention to the terms or in some other way giving him reasonable notice of their existence. This must be done before the contract is concluded. Again a consideration of the cases will help towards an understanding of principle.

In *Olley v Marlborough Court Ltd* (1949) a man and wife booked in to a hotel for the first time. In the foyer the man agreed to take a room in the hotel. On entering the bedroom his eye caught a notice telling him, for the first time, that no responsibility was accepted for valuables not deposited for safe-keeping. His wife's furs were stolen from the wardrobe. The court held that the notice, drawn to the husband's attention after the contract was concluded, formed no part of it and did not debar the husband from suing to obtain compensation for loss of the furs. A more modern application of this principle can be found in the case of *Thornton v Shoe Lane Parking Ltd* (1971) which involved an automatic car park. T approached the barrier at the entrance to the park where a notice was prominently displayed saying, 'cars parked at the owner's risk'. T placed his money in the automatic machine and received his ticket. On parking his car T saw further conditions written at length in small print on the wall of the car park. These conditions also excluded liability for injury to customers. T was injured and sued the defendant company who relied on the exclusion clause. The court held that the contract was concluded when T put his money into the machine, and conditions drawn to T's attention *thereafter* could not be part of the contract. The exclusion clause in the car park was therefore of no benefit to the defendant.

A previous course of dealing between the parties on certain terms may be sufficient notice to justify the application of the previous terms to a present contract. Whether the previous course of dealing has this effect is a matter for the court to determine. In *Hollier v Rambler Motors (A.M.C.) Ltd* (1972) H had taken his car to R Ltd's garage for repair on only three or four occasions over the past five years. On each occasion he signed an invoice for the work. The invoice contained these words, 'The company is not responsible for damage caused by fire to customers' cars on the premises'. On the occasion in question H was not in fact presented with an invoice and the car was destroyed by fire owing to R Ltd's negligence. When sued by H, R Ltd sought to rely on the exclusion clause. The Court of Appeal held that the company could not do so as there was insufficient course of previous dealing between the parties to justify the inclusion of the clause in the arrangement between them.

Where the contracting parties are in the same trade a knowledge of the usual trade terms will readily be implied and become part of an oral contract between the parties. I Ltd hired a crane from B Ltd, the negotiations being carried out by telephone. Both parties were in the plant-hire business. During the negotiation no reference was made to the position should the crane become stuck in marshy ground and become expensive to return to its owner. In the trade the usual written conditions placing the burden of cost on the hirer covered this event. In this case the written conditions sent by the owner (B Ltd) did not reach the hirer until *after the crane had become bogged* down. The court held that the hirer (I Ltd) should meet the costs as both parties knew of the usual terms and their oral agreement was made against this background. Such a term would be implied (*British Crane Hire Corpn Ltd v Ipswich Plant Hire Ltd* (1975)).

Subject to the above the law requires that notice of the terms should be on the face of any contractual document handed over or in a reasonably prominent position in a public place. If one contracting party is subject to a disability such as blindness, it is a misfortune and not a privilege. If notice is reasonable, judged by the standard of the reasonable person, then the law is satisfied (*Thompson v LMS Rly Co* (1930)). In *Chapelton v Barry UDC* (1940) C hired a deck chair from the council By the stack of chairs was a notice which read, 'Hire of chairs 2d per session of 3 hours'. C paid his 2d and received a ticket which he put in his pocket unread. On the back of the ticket were printed words excluding liability for damage arising from the hire of deck chairs. C sat on the chair which broke and he was injured. The court held that insufficient steps had been taken to draw C's attention to the conditions and his right to sue was not affected by the exclusionary words. In *Sugar v LMS Rly Co* (1941) the ticket handed to a passenger did have the words 'For conditions see back' on the face of the document but these were obliterated by the date stamp put on the ticket by the issuing clerk. Here again, the court held that insufficient notice had been given.

However, where a party signs a written document he is absolutely bound by the terms of the document he has signed whether he has read them or not – except where he is induced to sign by innocent misrepresentation or fraud. In *L'Estrange v Graucob* (1934) a lady signed a hire-purchase agreement for a slot-machine. She never read the agreement which contained, in very small print, these words, 'Any express or implied condition, statement or warranty, statutory or otherwise, is hereby excluded'. The machine proved defective and the lady was without remedy. If there is any misrepresentation as to the nature of the document signed, the signor will not be bound (see *Foster v*

Mackinnon, p 281, above). Where a lady signed a document, limiting liability for damage to a dress being laundered, as a result of a misrepresentation made in all honesty, it was held, in the event of damage to the dress, that the document signed could not be raised against her (*Curtis v Chemical Cleaning and Dyeing Co* (1951)).

Implied terms

Not every contract contains expressly all the terms by which the parties intend to be bound. They may contract with reference to a particular trade or terms may be implied by law. In this way much time and effort is saved. However, it should be noted that a term cannot be implied contrary to an express term (*expressum facit cessare tacitum*) if the parties expressly agree on certain terms they cannot be taken to have contracted on the basis of *contrary* terms which would otherwise be implied by law. A term was not implied to extend the time for the completion of Stage III of a building contract in *Trollope and Colls Ltd v North West Metropolitan Regional Hospital Board* (1973, CA). The contract provided for the completion of Stage III by 30 April 1972 and for the work to be started within six months of the completion of Stage I. Had the completion of Stage I not been delayed 30 months would have been allowed for Stage III. As it was, only 16 months were available. The court refused to imply a term extending the completion date by 14 months as the terms agreed by the parties were express and unambiguous. Another term might have been more appropriate but the court would not imply a term contrary to an express term.

In the following circumstances terms not expressed may be incorporated into a contract.

1 *Trade usage.* For a discussion of terms which will be implied by conventional trade usage, see p 40, above.

2 *Custom.* See p 37, above.

3 *Precedent.* Where a usage or custom has been judicially approved it will be binding in future cases in accordance with the scheme of judicial precedent outlined at p 41, above.

4 *Statute.* Statute may imply certain terms. Thus under the Sale of Goods Act 1979 conditions may be implied in contracts for the sale of goods that the goods are fit for the purpose for which they are required, that they are of merchantable quality and that, where goods are sold by sample, the bulk corresponds with the sample.

5 *Doctrine of the Moorcock.* Under the doctrine of *The Moorcock* (1889) the common law may imply a term to give 'business efficacy' to a contract. This principle must be carefully considered as the courts will not rewrite a contract for the parties and the judges are reluctant to invoke the

doctrine. The test used to determine whether a term should be implied is the 'officious bystander' test. If, at the time of the negotiations, an officious bystander had said to the parties, 'Is so and so a term of the contract?', and they would have replied, 'Of course it is!', then such a term will be implied. In the words of Bowen LJ

> 'the law is raising an implication from the presumed intention of the parties, with the object of giving to the transaction such efficacy as both parties must have intended that at all events it should have'.

In the case of *The Moorcock* D contracted to allow P to unload cargo from his ship at D's jetty and it was understood that at low tide the ship should be twelve feet from the jetty. The ship sank on to hard ground at low tide and was damaged. The contract contained no stipulation as to the safety of the mooring. The Court of Appeal implied a term in order to give efficacy to the contract to the effect that the bed of the river would be suitable for mooring and allowed P to recover damages for its breach.

In *Charnock v Liverpool Corpn* (1968, CA) in order to give 'business efficacy' to a contract the court implied a term, in a contract for the repair of a car left in a garage, to the effect that the repairs would be carried out in a reasonable time.

The House of Lords in *Liverpool City Council v Irwin* (1976) implied a term in a tenancy agreement between a local authority and its tenants in order to give efficacy to the agreement. The tenants had withheld payment of rent in respect of flats in a tower block because the stairs were unlit, lifts did not work and rubbish chutes were often blocked. There was a list of tenants' obligations prepared by the landlord but there were no express landlord's undertakings. The House implied a term to the effect that the landlord was obliged to take reasonable care to maintain the common parts of the tower block in a reasonable state of repair.

In another case, where a principal and an agent agreed that, on a sale by the principal to a third party under a contract negotiated for the principal by the agent, a commission would be payable to the agent, the Court of Appeal held that there would be an *implied term* that the principal would not withdraw from the contract so as to avoid the sale with the result that the agent would not become entitled to his commission. This term was implied to give business efficacy to the contract and the plaintiff recovered damages for breach of the implied term. The facts of the case were that the agent introduced a buyer for his principal's cement. The agent was to receive a commission based on tonnage sold. The principal contracted with the buyer, then withdrew from the contract. No sale took place. The agent recovered damages for breach of the implied term that the principal would not break the contract so as to deprive the agent of his commission (*Alpha Trading Ltd v Dunnshaw-Patten Ltd* (1981)).

Part three

Statutory encroachments on the freedom of contract

Summary

Chapter 21

Introduction

The law of contract developed during a period of freedom in economic development. Any interference by the law was usually on the basis of the parties being able to agree otherwise. Members of the public buying goods or services often had their rights taken away by their own agreement. The alternative was to do without the goods or services they required. Freedom of choice has been endangered by the practice of company mergers creating a situation where one or two companies gained a dominant position in a particular market area. While the common law has tried to protect the underdog (which has long been its traditional role) as is evidenced by many of the cases involving exclusion clauses (see p 367, below), Parliament has also over recent years made attempts to reverse this trend whereby, under the guise of freedom of contract, freedom of the consumer has been severely restricted. The Misrepresentation Act 1967 restricts the right of the parties by agreement to exclude liability for a misrepresentation. The Unfair Contract Terms Act 1977 (see p 371, below) removes the consumer's freedom to agree away his rights in respect of compensation for death or personal injury. Restrictions are also placed on manufacturers' guarantees which often took away more rights than they gave. The Monopolies and Mergers Acts 1948 and 1965 placed restriction, in the public interest, on the freedom of one company to merge with another, where this would lead to a monopoly in the supply goods and services and the application of processes to goods. The Board of Trade is empowered to refer a merger to the Monopolies and Mergers Commission, which is a body set up to investigate monopoly situations, and to produce a report thereon to be laid before Parliament. The Board of Trade is given wide powers to control a mischief caused by a monopoly situation revealed in any report by the Monopolies and Mergers Commission. Where a merger would result in one company controlling one-third of the goods or services in question the Board of Trade may refer the merger to the Commission for investigation and report. In 1984 the Secretary of State for Trade and Industry accepted the advice of the Commission and refused to sanction a proposed takeover in the motor vehicle component industry on the ground that the takeover would reduce competition in that part of industry and would be against the public interest. The Acts have particular application to newspaper mergers in the interest of freedom of speech. If all newspapers were under the same control, freedom of speech (including the freedom to give written expression to your views) would be in danger of suppression. The freedom to merge newspapers is restricted in the public interest.

Statute has also made important inroads into 'freedom of contract' by protecting the consumer in the sale of goods, the supply of goods and services and the giving of credit to the consumer. These topics form the subject-matter of the ensuing chapters.

Chapter 22
Exclusion and limitation clauses

In many contracts today one party insists on the insertion of a clause excluding, or limiting, his liability for breach of contractual terms (as, for example, in *Scrutton's Case*, p 262, above). This most frequently occurs where a large-scale business enterprise or a member of a federation of business organisations is dealing with an individual or small organisation. As there is often considerable disparity between the bargaining powers of both sides, the idea that a contract is a bargain struck by two or more people of equal bargaining power cannot be maintained. In such cases the terms of the contract cannot be said to be freely negotiated but rather are imposed by the more powerful party. There is therefore a danger that such terms may operate harshly on the weaker party. This is particularly true of exclusion clauses. It is not surprising, therefore, that the courts have attempted to mitigate the harshness of such clauses wherever possible. In *Olley v Marlborough Court Ltd* (1949) and in the two ticket cases explained above (p 359) the court held the clause had not even become a contractual term, and in several cases where one aspect of possible liability has been excluded (e g for breach of warranty) the court has held that the breach was in fact of a different nature (e g a breach of condition). Although interpreting the clause so that it does not cover the breach is a help in many cases, legal draftsmen also learn from the cases and now may exclude liability in the widest possible terms, e g 'liability is excluded for breach of condition or warranty, express or implied by common law, statute or otherwise, and for negligence'. Such a clause would have left a buyer of goods with but little hope of redress if the goods he bought were unsatisfactory in some respects. Even the worst cases of injustice can be prevented only by judicial interpretation of the words used so that they do not cover the breach which has occurred.

A typical illustration is *Karsales (Harrow) Ltd v Wallis* (1956). W agreed to buy a Buick car under a hire-purchase agreement which included this clause, 'No condition or warranty that the vehicle is roadworthy or as to its age, condition or fitness for any purpose is given by the owner or implied herein'. One night the car was towed to W's house and W found it outside next morning. Parts of the car were missing, others broken and the car was incapable of self-propulsion. W was sued for the hire-purchase instalments which he refused to pay, Karsales relying on the exclusion clause to support their claim. The Court of Appeal held the exclusion clause was <u>not intended to cover so wide a breach as this</u>.

Also illustrative of the approach of the courts to the question of the effect or scope of an exclusion clause is the case of *Mendelssohn v Normand Ltd* (1969). M left his car in a garage on written terms which <u>excluded liability for the theft of luggage</u>. The terms also stated that no variation <u>could be made unless expressed in writing and signed by the manager</u>. M <u>did not read the terms. On the occasion in question M wanted to leave valuables in the car and to lock it but the attendant insisted that it remained unlocked according to garage rules</u>. However, the attendant <u>assured M that he would lock the car later</u>. The valuables were stolen from the unlocked car. In an action by M to recover damages for the loss of his property the Court of Appeal held that the garage could not rely on the exception clause because (i) th<u>e oral promise</u> of the defendant to lock the car <u>overrode the written exclusion</u> term, and (ii) the garage carried out the contract in a way other than that envisaged by the parties. In *Hollier v Rambler Motors (A.M.C.) Ltd* (p 368, above) the Court of Appeal also discussed the interpretation of the exclusion clause and stated that R Ltd's liability would be primarily for negligence as bailees. The exclusion clause could be interpreted as a warning that the company did not accept liability for fire damage caused without negligence. However, where the words of exclusion are not clear the clause will be interpreted against the interest of the party responsible for the clause (<u>contra proferentem</u>). The words were not sufficiently clear to exclude liability for damage by fire started by the negligence of R Ltd.

In a number of cases, particularly in the Court of Appeal, the view had been expressed that as a rule of law no exclusion or limitation clause could operate to exclude or limit the liability of one of the parties for the breach of a <u>fundamental term.</u> By way of obiter dicta in the House of Lords it was clearly stated that the contra proferentem rule of construction (the words of a wide exclusion clause should be interpreted against the person seeking to enforce it) may operate to avoid the harsh effect which such a clause may otherwise have. This view of the House of Lords may now be regarded as firmly established as a result of a number of cases beginning with *Photo Production Ltd v Securicor Transport Ltd* (1980) where the law relating to the interpretation of exclusion and limitation clauses was reconsidered. The facts are as follows: The plaintiffs owned a factory. The defendants contracted to provide <u>security services</u> including night patrols. An employee of the defendants on night duty deliberately started a <u>small fire which got out of control</u> and caused damage to the value of £615,000. When sued for breach of contract the defendants pleaded an exemption clause to the effect that '<u>under no circumstances</u>' would the <u>defendants be 'responsible for any injurious act or default by any employee . . . unless such act or default could have been foreseen and avoided by due diligence on the part of the defendants</u> as his employer: nor, in any event' were the defendants to be liable for any loss suffered by the plaintiffs as a result of 'fire or any other clause except in so far as such loss' was 'solely attributable to the negligence of the' defendants' employees acting in the course of their employment. It was not alleged that the defendants were negligent in employing the particular employee who started the fire. The House of Lords unanimously held in favour of the defendants. On the facts the defendants were in breach of their implied obligation to operate their service with due regard for the safety of the plaintiff's premises. However, the words of the clause in a contract between two businessmen were clear and unambiguous and operated to protect the defendants. *Where there is a fundamental breach or breach of a fundamental term, the effect of words of exclusion still depends on the construction of the words used in relation to the contract as a whole.* In commercial cases, where the parties are not of unequal bargaining power, the parties should normally be left to apportion the risks as they think fit. Each party may effect his own insurance. If a substantial element of the risk were undertaken by one party this would affect the fee which he charged for his service. In this case if defendants had accepted liability for fire risk their fee charged for the security service would have been much higher. The parties had struck a balance which they, and the House of Lords, considered reasonable.

In 1981 the House of Lords heard a case on appeal from Scotland dealing with limitation clauses (*Ailsa Craig Fishing Co Ltd v Malvern Fishing Co Ltd* (1983)). The House reaffirmed the view, expressed in the *Photo Production* case, that the contra proferentem approach was the correct one and went on to say that clauses merely limiting liability were not to be construed as rigidly as clauses totally excluding liability because a limitation clause was more likely to reflect the true intention of the parties, having regard to the possible loss on the one hand and the price charged for the service on the other. Lord Wilberforce said:

> 'Whether a condition limiting liability is effective or not is a question of construction of that condition in the context of the contract as a whole. If it is to exclude liability for negligence, it must be most clearly and unambiguously expressed, and, such a contract as this, must be construed contra proferentem . . . one must not strive to create ambiguities by strained construction. . . . The relevant words must be given, if possible, their natural, plain meaning. Clauses of limitation are not regarded by the courts with the same hostility as clauses of exclusion; this is because they must be related to other contractual terms, in particular to the risks to which the defending party may be exposed, the remuneration which he receives and possibly also the opportunity of the other party to insure.'

These decisions of the House of Lords were applied by the House in the case of *George Mitchell (Chesterhall) Ltd v Finney Lock Seeds Ltd* (1983). A seed merchant supplied Dutch winter cabbage seed to a farmer at a cost of

£201. The seed in fact was an inferior variety which grew badly over the
winter and had to be ploughed back into the ground. The farmer
complained about his time, labour, the use of 63 acres of land and profit
on sales which were all lost to him. As damages for breach of contract he
claimed £61,000. When delivered the seed was accompanied by an
invoice which had been used throughout the seed trade for many years.
The invoice set out the words of a limitation clause. In the event of
defective seeds being delivered the seed merchant limited his liability to
either the replacement of the seeds or the refund of the price paid for
them. Expressly excluded was liability for any loss or damage arising
from the use of the seeds and for any consequential loss. The House held
that the words limiting liability were clear and unambiguous when given
their ordinary meaning and that at common law the words did cover the
breach of contract by the seed merchant. However, at the present time, the
Sale of Goods Act 1979, s 55 and Sch 1, para 11 permits such clauses to be
enforceable only where they are fair and reasonable. When considering whether
it is 'fair and reasonable' to allow reliance on a term the courts will look at
the circumstances *at the time of the breach* rather than at the time the
contract was formed. The clause was *not enforceable* because (a) in the past
where a defect in seed had appeared the seed merchants had negotiated a
settlement with the farmer concerned, (b) the defective seed was supplied
as a result of the negligence of an associated company and, (c) the seed
merchant could have insured against the risk. Applying the common law
rules relating to (a) incorporation of terms, and (b) the scope and
meaning of the clause incorporated, and then (c) looking at the result in
the light of legislative modifications to the common law, the House of
Lords concluded that the limitation clause could not be enforced.

While the common law has been changing slowly over the years to
protect parties from the harsh effects of exclusion and limitation clauses,
Parliament has only relatively recently directed itself to the questions
raised by such clauses. Attacks on exclusion and limitation clauses were
made in the Misrepresentation Act 1967 and in the Supply of Goods
(Implied Terms) Act 1973. The relevant provisions are now to be found
in the Unfair Contract Terms Act 1977.

It is well to note that under the Unfair Contract Terms Act 1977 any
provision excluding or restricting any liability or remedy for a
misrepresentation (i e an untrue statement inducing a contract) is of *no
effect in law except to the extent that it is fair and reasonable* bearing in mind the
circumstances which were known or ought reasonably to have been
known to the parties at the formation of the contract. It is for a party
claiming the term is reasonable to prove it.

Under the Sale of Goods Act 1893 certain conditions and warranties
were normally implied in a contract, but the practice of vendors in
protecting themselves by insisting on an exemption clause that took away
the purchaser's statutory protection has been the subject of a great deal of

criticism. However, the Law Commission investigated and reported on the problems involved in 1969 and 1975. Under the Unfair Contract Terms Act 1977 the seller's implied statutory undertaking as to title cannot be excluded or restricted at all. Nor can the other implied terms (conformity with description or sample, fitness or quality) be excluded or restricted where one party is a consumer. In cases of non consumer sales, liability can be restricted or excluded but only so far as is reasonable. A *consumer sale* generally involves three elements: a sale *by a seller* in the ordinary course of business *of goods* ordinarily bought for private consumption *to a buyer who is not buying them in the course of business*. Sales of apples, books, clothes and motor cars by retailers to customers for their own use would be consumer sales. A sale of apples to a restaurateur for use in his restaurant would not be.

The Unfair Contract Terms Act 1977 also covers the situation where a business contract attempts to exclude liability for negligence. The Act says that liability for negligence, including breach of the common duty of care under the Occupiers' Liability Act 1957, causing death or personal injury cannot be excluded or restricted. Liability for other loss or damage can be excluded or restricted, but only to the extent that it is reasonable to do so. See also the Occupiers' Liability Act 1984, p 174, above.

Where one of the parties deals as a consumer, on the other's written standard terms, he cannot have enforced against him by the party at fault an exclusion or restriction clause except to the extent that the clause is reasonable. Nor can such person claim under a clause to be entitled to make a performance substantially different from what was reasonably expected of him or to render no performance at all.

As a result of the Act all previous cases must be looked at anew. Cases where an exclusion clause has been upheld may today fail as *not* being *reasonable*. Cases which have failed in the past on the ground that insufficient notice of the clause was given, so that it did not become a contractual term, will continue to fail in the future for the same reason, no matter how reasonable the clause may be.

It should be noted that the effect of the Act may be to allow the courts to ignore an exclusion or limitation clause, thus letting the plaintiff succeed in his action. His action must have been based on a breach of an express term of a contract, or a breach of an implied term or in tort. His action is *not* based on the Act which can never provide in itself a cause of action.

N.B. Schedule I to the Unfair Contract Terms Act 1977 contains a number of types of contract to which the Act does *not* apply. This means that the case law applicable before the Act will be operative in such cases. For instance, the old rules will continue to apply to any contract of insurance, to contracts for the creation or transfer of an interest in land, to company formations and to the rights and obligations of the corporators.

Chapter 23

The contract of employment

A major area of the law where freedom to contract on the terms agreed by the parties has been curtailed is the area of employment law which will be discussed in this section.

At common law there is no satisfactory definition of a contract of employment. It is easier to recognise one when seen than it is to describe. Occasionally a statute defines 'employee'. The Employment Protection (Consolidation) Act 1978 defines an employee as 'an individual who has entered into or works under (or, where the employment has ceased, worked under) a contract of employment'. No definition of 'contract of employment' is given. In practice this is left to the courts and tribunals.

Looking at the facts of any problem situation a court or tribunal would look for *significant* facts, or *indicia*. Where a person is *selected* for work by another, is liable to be *dismissed* by him and is *controlled* in the work he does and how he does it he is likely to be an employee. The *payment* of wages, *ownership* of tools, equipment (by the employers), chance of *profit* and risk of *loss* are also indications in favour of a contract of employment. In *Ready Mixed Concrete (South East) Ltd v Minister of Pensions and National Insurance* (1968) McKenna J said that a contract of employment (also known as a contract of service) exists where three tests are satisfied:

(i)   The employee agrees that in return for a *wage* or other consideration he will provide his *own work* and skill in performing a service for his employer.

(ii)   The employee agrees, expressly or impliedly, that in performance of the service he will be subject to the other's *contract in a sufficient degree* to make the other an employer.

(iii)   The other provisions of the contract are consistent with its being a contract of service. In the course of his judgment McKenna J considered five examples:

> (i) A contract obliges one party to build for the other, providing at his own expense the necessary plant and materials. This is not a contract of service, even though the builder may be obliged to use his own labour only and to accept a high degree of control: it is a building contract. It is not a contract to serve another for a wage, but a contract to produce a thing (or a result) for a price.

(ii) A contract obliges one party to carry another's goods, providing at his own expense everything needed for performance. This is not a contract of service, even though the carrier may be obliged to drive the vehicle himself and to accept the other's control over his performance: it is a contract of carriage.

(iii) A contract obliges a labourer to work for a builder, providing some simple tools, and to accept the builder's control. Notwithstanding the obligation to provide the tools, the contract is one of service. That obligation is not inconsistent with the nature of a contract of service. It is not a sufficiently important matter to affect the substance of the contract.

(iv) A contract obliges one party to work for the other, accepting his control, and to provide his own transport. This is still a contract of service. The obligation to provide his own transport does not affect the substance. Transport in this example is incidental to the main purpose of the contract. Transport in the second example was the essential part of the performance.

(v) The same instrument provides that one party shall work for the other subject to the other's control, and also that he shall sell him his land. The first part of the instrument is no less a contract of service because the second part imposes obligations of a different kind. . . .

I can put the point which I am making in other words. An obligation to do work subject to the other party's control is a necessary, though not always a sufficient, condition of a contract of service.'

The contracts in (i) and (ii) above are often referred to as contracts *for services*.

The facts of the *Ready Mixed Concrete Case* were that a company which manufactured and delivered concrete wished to separate the manufacturing side of its business from the delivery side. It introduced a system of delivery by owner-drivers. A worker entered into a contract with the company for the delivery of concrete under which he was to be paid at fixed rates per cubic yard of concrete for each radial mile. The lorry was to be bought on hire-purchase terms from an associated company and was to be painted in the company's colours and carry its name. The worker was to make the lorry available at *all* times to the Company and not to allow it to be used for any other purpose. He was to drive the lorry for the hours permitted by law, wear the Company's uniform and obey all instructions 'as if he were an employee of the company'. He was to pay the running costs but the company insured the vehicle. He could engage a substitute driver who would be subject to the Company's approval. The Company did not instruct the worker in the driving of the vehicle, or the routes he should take. The contract declared that he was an independent contractor (not under a contract of service). The question the court had to decide was whether the worker was an 'employed person' under a contract of employment (a contract of service) for the purposes of s 1 (2) (a) of the National Insurance Act 1965.

In his judgment McKenna J considered the various indicia in the above facts. Was it a contract of service which would make the worker an employee or was it one of carriage which would make him an independent contractor? The contract left the worker to buy, maintain and drive his own lorry, while free to choose the routes he followed and where he obtained his petrol and services in connection with the vehicle. He was paid at a rate per mile. All these factors indicated a contract of service. Against these factors must be balanced the fact that he was not free to use the lorry as he pleased, to engage anyone he wished to drive it and he accepted the superintendence of the company as an aid to the efficient running of his operations. On balance McKenna J held that the contract was for the carriage of goods and was not a contract of service.

The importance of the employment relationship

Whether a person is an employee working under a contract of employment is often a very important question. Examples of situations where the law applies to employees engaged under a contract of employment are as follows:

1   An employee is entitled to a written statement of his terms and conditions of employment within 13 weeks of the commencement of his employment (Employment Protection (Consolidation) Act 1978).

2   An employee is protected by the rules against unfair dismissal (the 1978 Act above).

3   An employee who loses his job on the grounds of redundancy may receive a payment as a form of compensation (see the 1978 Act).

4   Rules making discrimination on ground of race or sex unlawful apply in the area of employment (Sex Discrimination Act 1975 and the Race Relations Act 1976).

5   The equal pay laws apply to people working under contracts of employment (Equal Pay Act 1970, Art 119 of the Treaty of Rome and European Directives).

6   A woman who is employed has maternity rights in respect of her employment. She is entitled to certain payments and has the right to return to her old job after having been absent from work for her confinement (Employment Protection (Consolidation) Act 1978).

7 Unemployment benefit is available only to people who have been employed under a contract of employment (Social Security Act 1975).

8 Sickness benefit payments under the national insurance scheme are payable to employees only (Social Security Act 1975).

9 Industrial injury benefit is payable to employees injured at work in the course of their employment (Social Security Act 1975).

10 Occupational pension schemes operate for the benefit of employees.

11 In contracts of employment a clause limiting the liability of an employer is void but one limiting the liability of an employee is not. In contracting with an independent contractor the employer may limit his liability (Unfair Contract Terms Act 1977).

12 Under the rules relating to vicarious liability an employer is liable for the torts committed by his employee in the course of the employment as explained at p 157, above.

The above list illustrates situations where it is important to know whether a person is engaged under a contract of employment because only an employee has the appropriate legal right. The list covers a wide range of situations in which ordinary working people are likely to find themselves at sometime in their life. It should be noted that complete rules are not given above and relevant statute and case law should be consulted before any conclusion is drawn in a practical situation.

Terms of the contract

The terms of a contract of employment may arise because they have been expressly agreed between the parties. In addition terms may be implied to give 'efficacy' to the contract (see p 360, above). In addition to terms implied under the doctrine of the *Moorcock* (1889), terms may also be applied more readily by the courts simply because the relationship of employer and employee exists. 'I think that an implied term is something which, in the circumstances of a particular case, the law may read into the contract if the parties are silent and it would be reasonable to do so; . . . the phrase "implied term" can be used to denote a term inherent in the nature of the contract which the law will imply in every case unless the parties agree to vary or exclude it'. (Lord Reid in *Sterling Engineering Co Ltd v Patchett* (1955).) In employment law terms may be implied from *collective bargains*, between employers and unions, which are the background against which a contract of employment is formed. A term may also be implied from the *works' rules* which commonly exist in large organisations to set out the practice in the running of the company, As has already been noticed (p 40, above), trade custom may imply a term.

Implied duties

The common law implies certain duties in a contract of employment.

Employer's duties

1   To pay the agreed wages.
2   Generally there is *no* common law duty to provide *work*. However, in certain situations the remuneration of the employee might in part depend on the work he does; for example, work paid on piece rates or on commission on sales. In such cases the employer is under an implied duty to provide work.
3   Generally the employer must exercise reasonable care in relation to the employee. In practice this leads to four implied duties:
   (a)   To provide competent fellow employees. This is to safeguard an employee from the activities of dangerous workers, both the unskilful and the practical joker.
   (b)   To provide a safe system of work. For example, in mining operations there must be an efficient warning system before blasting takes place.
   (c)   To provide safe premises, tools and equipment. Poor quality drills which chip in use and are a danger to eyes etc. must not be provided.
   (d)   To indemnify the employee against expenses incurred in the course of his employment, as where a lorry driver pays for the repair of a burst tyre.
4   To treat the employee with respect. The employer must not use abusive behaviour to or swear at an employee especially where the employee is in charge of others who are close enough to see or hear what is going on.

Employee's duties

1   The employee must *co-operate* with the employer in carrying out orders and instructions which are lawful and reasonably within the scope of his contract of employment. This is often referred to as the duty of obedience.
2   The employee owes a duty of care to his employer in carrying out his duties not to damage equipment, waste materials or injure a fellow-employee.
3   The employee must act in good faith (the duty of fidelity).

This duty could be broken by the employee working for a competitor in his spare time, by selling confidential information, developing in his spare time ideas picked up at work and impeding the work of his employer.

Statutory interference with the contract of employment

From the above implied terms and duties it can be seen that common law placed terms, which had not been agreed by the parties, in a contract of employment. But at common law those terms could, and still can, be excluded by express agreement of the parties.

From 1963 onwards there have been many statutory impositions in employment law. Almost all of them *cannot be excluded* by agreement between the parties and they have the effect of reducing the freedom of contract. The relationship between an employer and his employee used to be one of contract, one of their own making and on their own terms. Today, it is largely one of *status*. Once the contract is formed by the parties and the employment relationship is born the legislation automatically applies because of employee status. A number of examples of this interference will be studied below.

It is well to note that frequently legislation refers to 'a contract *of service*' when referring to what is more popularly known as 'a contract of employment' and to 'a contract *for services*' when referring to a contract with an independent contractor.

1 *Written statements.* The requirement that an employee is to be given a *written statement* (not a contract) containing the main terms of his contract of employment was introduced in 1963 by the Contracts of Employment Act of that year.

The *contract* comes into existence when the parties reach agreement. The written statement is evidence of it. The Act also provided for minimum notice periods.

The rules relating to written statements were altered in 1972 and are now to be found in the Employment Protection (Consolidation) Act 1978. Now an employee who works under a contract for 16 hours or more per week is entitled to a statutory period of notice. Where he has worked for less than two years he is entitled to one week's notice. Where he has worked for two years or more he is entitled to one week's notice for each completed year of service up to a maximum of 12. The parties may agree a longer period but not a shorter one. Thus, a contract terminable by one month's notice gives an employee a right to one month's notice as a minimum. Where he has worked for five years he is entitled to five week's notice. To qualify the service must be continuous.

2 *Redundancy payments.* The redundancy payments scheme was introduced in 1965 to cover the situation where a man was dismissed, through no fault of his own, on the ground of redundancy. The Redundancy Payments Act 1965 has now been consolidated with other legislation in the Employment Protection (Consolidation) Act 1978. Redundancy

arises where there is a cessation or reduction of work, actual or intended, at a particular place, or in the need for a particular skill. An employee who has worked continuously for at least two years since the age of 18 under a contract of service requiring him to work for 16 hours a week or more is entitled to a redundancy payment. The payment is based on a week's pay for each year worked. Years between the ages of

> 18 to 21 count for one half week
> 22 to 40 count for one week
> 41 to 65 count for one and a half week.

There is a maximum weekly pay which is allowed (reviewed annually in February 1984 was £145). The multiplier is a maximum of 30 years. A man aged 46 years who has worked continuously for his employer during the 12 years up to his dismissal on the grounds of redundancy will receive 15 times his weekly pay as a redundancy payment (six years over 40 count as $1\frac{1}{2}$ each. $6 \times 1\frac{1}{2} = 9$ plus six years age 40 and under). At common law there is no right to a redundancy payment, sometimes referred to as a severance payment. Strictly a severance payment may include not only any redundancy payment which is made but also other payments, such as a payment *in lieu* of notice, which become payable by agreement or otherwise on the termination of employment.

3 *Equal pay.* The Equal Pay Act 1970 came into operation in 1975 on the same day as the Sex Discrimination Act 1975, with which it forms one code. The Equal Pay Act applies equally to men or women claiming equal pay with a member of the opposite sex. The Act provides that where a woman is engaged on 'like work' with a man in the 'same employment' any term in the woman's contract which is 'less favourable' than the man's is to be modified so as to be not less favourable and any term in the man's contract which is not in the woman's contract is to be included in such contract. All employment contracts are deemed to include an equality clause. Men and women are employed on like work where the work they do is the same or broadly similar. Where a woman is *in charge* of a work section and is paid less than the men she supervises, the Act will not help her as she is not engaged in like work.

Where a job evaluation scheme is in operation a woman must be paid according to the valuation put upon her job. In this way men's jobs and women's jobs can be evaluated by comparison of demands made on them such as training, skill, working conditions etc and a payment made accordingly without reference to sex. Under the 1970 Act an employer could not be compelled to introduce a job evaluation scheme. Under new rules introduced in 1984 job evaluation can be called for by an Industrial Tribunal. These rules and others have been introduced to a great extent as a result of pressure from the European Community in the form of directives and European Court decisions. There is a statutory defence open to an employer where he can show that the variation between the woman's contract and the man's was genuinely due to a material difference other than the difference of sex. Other exceptions also exist.

Article 119 of the Treaty of Rome, which became part of English law on 1 January 1973, provides for equal pay for 'work of equal value'. The wording of the Sex Discrimination Act suggests a comparison between the work or tasks actually performed by a man and a woman. The Article in the Treaty suggests equality of pay where there is equality of value to the employer in the work done. The Treaty of Rome is part of English law and where the two conflict the Treaty rules prevail.

At common law an employer is not obliged to consider the sex of his employee when fixing a wage. If he wishes to pay his female staff (or male) less than he pays his male staff (or female) he may do so.

4 *Unfair dismissal.* At common law an employee could be given his contractual notice terminating his employment at any time and without reason given. To mitigate this injustice the concept of unfair dismissal was introduced by the Industrial Relations Act 1971 and the statute law is now to be found in the Employment Protection (Consolidation) Act 1978. The Act gives an employee who has the necessary qualifying service (52 weeks' continuous service under a contract involving 16 hours' work or more per week) the right not to be unfairly dismissed. If he is so dismissed he has a right to claim re-instatement, re-engagement in another capacity or compensation.

To succeed, the dismissed employee must show that he has the necessary qualifying service and that he has been dismissed as defined in the Act. The employer, to avoid a finding against him, must show what was the principal reason for the dismissal and that this was one of the reasons set out in the statute, eg lack of qualification, or poor performance. It is then for the Industrial Tribunal to consider all the circumstances and decide whether 'the employer acted reasonably in treating the reason he gave as sufficient reason for dismissing the employee'. Where the employee succeeds it is rare for the Tribunal to order his former employer to re-employ him. He will usually be awarded compensation made up of a basic award, calculated as for a redundancy payment, and a compensatory award, the limit for which is raised annually in February. The maximum compensatory award for 1984 is £7,540.

5 *Discrimination.* At common law a woman could be lawfully discriminated against on account of her sex. Statute has now intervened. The Sex Discrimination Act 1975 says that a woman is discriminated against where, on the ground of sex, she is treated 'less favourably' than a man (the direct form). Also, she is discriminated against where a condition is required of her that is also applied to a man but is such that less women than men are able to comply with it, which cannot be justified

'irrespective of sex' and which is to her detriment because she cannot comply with it (the indirect form). The Act also applies the above definition to discrimination against men and the Race Relations Act 1976 extends a parallel definition to discrimination on the grounds of race. The 1975 Act also defines discrimination as covering discrimination against *married* persons. Discrimination by victimisation is defined as treating a person 'less favourably' than another would be treated because the person victimised has brought proceedings, or intends to bring proceedings, or is even suspected of intending to bring proceedings under the 1975 Act or the 1970 Equal Pay Act.

The above definition of discrimination is found in part I of the Act. Part II makes discrimination in several areas of employment *unlawful*. For example, it is unlawful to discriminate in arrangements made for interviewing applicants for a job, the terms on which any offer is made, access to promotion, transfer, training, dismissal or other detriment. To offer home-loan facilities to male employees only is direct discrimination on the grounds of sex, as is a requirement that only the men do particularly dirty work. To have a height requirement of 6ft 2in. for a shop assistant would amount to indirect discrimination because fewer women than men can comply with it.

Discrimination in advertising is unlawful. The willingness to consider either a man or a woman for a job must be clearly shown. The words 'waiter', 'salesgirl', 'postman' and 'stewardess' must not be used unless other words are also used to show there is no discriminatory intention, e g 'Postman wanted, male or female may apply' is acceptable.

At common law an employer may employ whichever sex or race he prefers for whatever reason and on any terms to which he and his employee agree. The freedom of the employer to negotiate terms of an employment contract are very considerably reduced by these legislative provisions.

6 *Maternity rights.* Under the Employment Protection (Consolidation) Act 1978, as amended, a woman who is pregnant, depending on various other conditions, has a number of maternity rights. She has the right to time off to attend a clinic in connection with her pregnancy, and for her confinement, the right to payment from her employer during part of her maternity leave and the right to return to her employment at any time within 29 weeks of the birth of her baby. A woman may be unfairly dismissed if the reason for her dismissal is that she is pregnant or is a reason connected with her pregnancy.

Similar rights to the above do *not* exist at common law where the parties are free to contract on the terms they agree. The Act now severely restricts that freedom.

Chapter 24
Sale of goods

The many cases which had been decided over centuries were codified with little change in the Sale of Goods Act 1893. This Act applied only to sales of goods. The Sale of Goods Act 1893 has now been repealed and replaced by the Sale of Goods Act 1979 with most of the old law remaining unchanged. Sales of services and the supply of goods and/or services were not included in the Sale of Goods Acts and were subject to the common law until the Supply of Goods and Services Act 1982.

A sale is defined as the transfer, or the agreement to transfer, of the ownership of goods from the seller to the buyer for a price (a consideration in money). Ownership passes from the seller to the buyer when the parties intend it to pass. Failing their agreement on this matter, and consumers seldom consider it, the ownership passes in accordance with rules laid down in the Act. The precise moment when ownership passes becomes important when deciding questions of risk, e g who bears the loss in the event of theft or destruction by fire?

The word 'goods' is not defined in the Act. A contract for the sale of a service, such as a haircut or window cleaning, was not covered by the Act. Difficulties arose where the sale combined goods and services, as where the repair of a television set involved the fitting of a new tube. There are many cases on this area of the law and decisions on the facts of each case are not always clear. A contract to paint a portrait has been held to be a contract for services (*Robinson v Graves* (1935)). A contract to build ships' propellers was a contract for sale (*Cammell Laird and Co Ltd v Manganese Bronze and Brass Co Ltd*) whereas a contract for a meal in a restaurant was a contract of sale (*Lockett v A and M Charles Ltd* (1938)). Each case depends on its own facts and the principle appears to be based on the balance of goods used as opposed to the skill and labour in achieving the end product. Where the substance of the contract was of skill and labour the use of ancillary materials would be a minor consideration and the contract would not be one of sale (*Robinson v Graves*).

Implied terms – Sale of Goods Act 1979

The Sale of Goods Act 1979 protects consumers who are buyers by implying terms into contracts for the sale of goods. Since 1973 the law has curtailed the extent to which these implied terms can be excluded. The implied terms appear below. References to sections are to sections in the Sale of Goods Act 1979.

(a) *Title.*   Section 12 (1) implies a condition to the effect that the seller has the right to sell the goods and will pass a good title to the buyer. If the seller fails to comply with this term, the buyer is entitled to recover the price of the goods as there has been a total failure of consideration even where he has used the goods for some time (*Rowland v Divall* (1923)). Section 12 (2) covers the situation where the seller's title may be uncertain and the buyer agrees to take whatever title the seller has. Several warranties are implied to protect the buyer against claims made against him by the seller or a person claiming through him. Liability for any of the obligations under this section cannot be excluded or limited by contract (Unfair Contract Terms Act 1977, s 6).

(b) *Description.*   Section 13 provides that, 'where there is a contract for the sale of goods by description, there is an implied condition that the goods will correspond with the description'. Goods sold by reference to a sample as well as a description must comply with both the sample and the description (s 13 (2)). Goods may be sold by description where the seller uses a lengthy description; a descriptive phrase, such as hot-water bottle, bottle of wine; one word, such as bicycle; or merely displays articles for sale. Where goods are displayed for sale, as in a supermarket, and the customer selects them himself, there will be a sale by description (s 13 (3)). In *Grant v Australian Knitting Mills Ltd* (1936) Grant asked for underwear and was shown some woollen underpants, which he bought. This was a sale by description and when he developed dermatitis as a result of an excess of sulphites in the wool the implied condition in s 13 was shown to have been broken. As is explained below, the implied conditions of fitness for purpose and of merchantable quality were also broken. Additionally, the manufacturer was held liable to the buyer in negligence. In *Godley v Perry* (1960) a retailer was shown a sample catapult by a wholesaler. He ordered the goods which proved defective in use. Although they were in fact catapults, the goods delivered had a flaw not possessed by the sample. This constituted a breach of s 13.

In most instances where goods are sold and there is a breach of the implied condition as to description there will often also be a breach of an express term, or of the implied condition of fitness for purpose, or another implied condition. For example, where a person buys a 'gold watch', which is gold-coloured but not made of gold, there has been a breach of s 13 and there has been a breach of the express term 'gold'. In *Arcos Ltd v Ronaasen* (1933) the sale was of half-inch-thick wooden staves. A large number of the staves were slightly over this thickness. The House of Lords held that, although the staves were fit for the purpose required and were of merchantable quality, they did not comply with the implied condition that they would comply with the description. The buyer was entitled to reject them. Lord Atkin said, 'If the . . . contract specifies conditions of weight, measurement and the like, those conditions must be complied with. A ton does not mean about a ton, or a yard about a yard'.

As s 13 is not limited to sales 'in the course of business' it can apply to private sales, whereas terms which are implied only in the case of a business sale cannot apply to a private sale (see s 14).

As against a person dealing as a consumer (see p 371, above), liability for breach of the obligations under s 13 cannot be excluded or limited by contract. As against a person dealing other than as a consumer, liability for breach of any obligation under s 13 can be excluded or limited only in so far as the term satisfies the test of reasonableness as laid down in s 6 of the Unfair Contract Terms Act 1977.

(c) *Merchantable quality*.   By s 14 (2) the Act may imply a condition of merchantable quality in the sale of goods. Section 14 (2) states:

> 'Where the seller sells goods in the course of a business, there is an implied condition that the goods supplied under the contract are of merchantable quality, except that there is no such condition –
> (a)   as regards defects specifically drawn to the buyer's attention before the contract is made; or
> (b)   if the buyer examines the goods before the contract is made, as regards defects which that examination ought to reveal.'

Breach of this implied condition gives the buyer the right to rescind the contract and recover damages.

A simple application of the implied condition of merchantable quality can be seen in *Godley v Perry* (1960) where the hidden defect in the catapult made it not of merchantable quality.

This subsection does not apply to private sales but will apply to the usual consumer sale in a retail shop or other retail outlet.

The word 'supplied' under the contract, rather than 'sold', indicates that the whole package must be considered, e g the box or dividing paper as in a box of chocolates. In one case a buyer ordered 'Coalite'. When used in an ordinary domestic grate the Coalite exploded as a result of gelignite in the fuel. The supplier argued that there was nothing wrong with the 'Coalite'; it was merely accompanied by gelignite which was not part of the sale. The Court of Appeal rejected this argument and held that the Coalite containing the gelignite was not of merchantable quality (*Wilson v Rickett, Cockerell and Co Ltd* (1954).)

The two exceptions to s 14 (2) must be met *before* the contract is entered into. A seller of goods as 'shop-soiled' must specifically draw the attention of the buyer to the defect before the sale is agreed. The provision relating to examination by the buyer puts the buyer under no obligation to examine the goods. If he does *not* examine the goods the condition will be implied. If he does examine the goods the condition will not be implied in respect of any defect which his examination ought to have revealed. Thus a cursory examination of the outside of a packet would not be expected to reveal a defect in the contents and the conditions of merchantable quality would be implied. A cursory examination of the contents of a packet might not reveal a defect which a more thorough examination would have revealed. In this situation the exception may apply and the condition would not be implied.

What amounts to merchantable quality has been a difficult question for the courts on many occasions. The concept was not defined in the Sale of Goods Act 1893. However s 14 (6) of the 1979 Act, adopting the Supply of Goods (Implied Terms) Act 1973, describes goods as being of merchantable quality where they are 'as fit for the purpose or purposes for which goods of that kind are commonly bought as it is reasonable to expect having regard to any description applied to them, the price (if relevant) and all other relevant circumstances'. The application of this definition to a real-life problem is frequently difficult.

Goods sold for a particular use, such as underpants in *Grant v Australian Knitting Mills Ltd* (above), must be capable of that use or there will be a breach of the implied condition of merchantable quality, as there will also be where a Bath bun contains a stone (*Chapronière v Mason* (1905)).

Goods which are used in the mechanical sense, such as a car, a watch or a food mixer, may well be bought as much for their appearance as their mechanical accuracy. Where such goods are chipped or scratched the court will take into account all the circumstances of the case in order to determine whether there has been a breach of the implied condition of merchantable quality. A buyer might reasonably expect second-hand goods to show signs of wear and the price might also be an indication of the condition of an article sold. The life expectancy of second-hand goods would similarly be determined by reference to price and any statement made by the seller. A car which is stated to have done 80,000 miles will have a lesser life expectancy than a new car or one which has done only 20,000. A second-hand sewing machine which is stated to be five years old but seldom used would be expected to last longer than a cheaper model which was 15 years old, all other considerations being equal.

Price may be an indicator of the quality to be expected but goods sold at a 'discount price' or 'sale goods' are impliedly of a quality meriting a higher price. A quality corresponding to the discounted price could be interpreted as a breach of the implied condition of merchantable quality. However, an extremely low or throw-away price might indicate a low quality of goods being offered for sale. (See the judgments in *B. S. Brown and Son Ltd v Craiks Ltd* (1970) HL.)

In a case decided under the Fair Trading Act 1973 (*Cavendish-Woodhouse Ltd v Manley* (1984)) the Court of Appeal considered the meaning of the words 'bought as seen' when attached to furniture in a showroom. The buyer inspected the goods before buying them. The

Court held that there was no sale by description but the phrase did not exclude the implied terms of merchantable quality and fitness for purpose in respect of defects which could *not* be seen. In the event of a dispute between the parties about the condition of the goods at the time of the sale, the words indicated that it was not a sale by description but that it was a sale of the goods only after the buyer had seen them and had purchased them as a result of what he saw.

As against a person dealing as a consumer, liability for breach of the implied condition of fitness for purpose cannot be excluded or limited. As against a person dealing other than as a consumer, liability can be excluded or limited only to the extent that it is reasonable to do so (s 6 of the Unfair Contract Terms Act 1977).

(d) *Fitness for purpose.* A frequently relied upon provision of the Sale of Goods Act is to be found in s 14 (3):

> 'Where the seller sells goods in the course of a business and the buyer, expressly or by implication, makes known –
> (a) to the seller, or
> (b) ... any particular purpose for which the goods are being bought, there is an implied condition that the goods supplied under the contract are reasonably fit for that purpose, whether or not that is a purpose for which such goods are commonly supplied, except where the circumstances show that the buyer does not rely, or that it is unreasonable for him to rely, on the skill or judgment of the seller. ...'

Breach of the implied condition of fitness for purpose gives rise to a right to rescind and recover damages.

As is the case with the implied condition of merchantable quality, the condition of fitness for purpose will be implied only where the goods are sold in the course of *a* business.

Section 14 (3) will not apply where the buyer does not rely on the skill and judgment of the seller, as where the buyer orders goods under a trade or brand name so that the seller must supply those goods and only those goods under the contract. The buyer is not relying on the seller in this situation.

As a result of experience and knowledge of his product the seller is likely to know more about the goods he sells than the buyer. Thus the inference that the buyer relied on the seller's skill and judgment readily arises. If the seller does not know the characteristics of his goods he should make this clear to the buyer who will not then be able reasonably to rely on him, neither will he be reasonable in relying on the seller where he makes his own careful examination of the goods to be bought and realises or should realise that they are not appropriate to his needs. The purpose for which goods are required may be made known by the buyer to the seller or it may be implied from the circumstances. It is obvious what a fountain pen, a Bath bun, underpants, a hot-water bottle or Coalite are wanted for. Where the buyer has a special purpose in mind this must be made known to the seller if s 14 (3) is to apply. A person who has an abnormal skin sensitivity must make this known to the seller when buying for his own use clothing which could irritate him. A lady who did not disclose that she had abnormally sensitive skin and who developed dermatitis as a result of wearing a Harris tweed coat she bought, failed in her action based on the implied condition of fitness for purpose (*Griffiths v Peter Conway Ltd* (1939)).

Goods bought need only be 'reasonably fit' for the purpose stated. This provision is intended to make allowance for such factors as price, age and the condition of the goods. Whether goods are reasonably fit for the purpose required is often a difficult question for the courts. In the case of a complete failure to work (e g a kettle which will not heat water) goods are clearly not fit for the purpose required. Where they work for a short time only or wear out quickly difficulties arise. Not only will a question of balance arise (how long should a jumper last before a hole is worn at the elbow?) but the seller will be in a position to argue that the goods were fit for the purpose required when sold but have since been misused or subjected to extraordinary wear.

It is not unusual for the provisions of both s 14 (2) and s 14 (3) to be implied in the same contract of sale. A hot-water bottle which bursts is not of merchantable quality nor is it reasonably fit for the purpose required (*Preist v Last* (1903)). (See also *Godley v Perry* (1960), below).

As against a person dealing as a consumer, liability for breach of the implied condition of fitness for purpose cannot be excluded or limited. As against a person dealing other than as a consumer, liability can be excluded or limited only to the extent that it is reasonable to do so (s 6 of the Unfair Contract Terms Act 1977).

(e) *Sale by sample*.   Goods may be bought by reference to a sample. An example would be where a buyer sees a dining suite in a furniture showroom and orders a similar suite to be delivered from the warehouse. The description of the suite is by reference to sample. A retailer will often look at a sample article shown to him by a commercial salesman and, relying on the sample, he will place a bulk order. In these cases s 15 will be relevant. It provides:

'(1)   A contract of sale is a contract for sale by sample where there is an express or implied term to that effect in the contract.

(2)   In the case of a contract for sale by sample there is an implied condition –

   (a)   that the bulk will correspond with the sample in quality;

   (b)   that the buyer will have a reasonable opportunity of comparing the bulk with the sample;

   (c)   that the goods will be free from any defect, rendering them unmerchantable, which would not be apparent on a reasonable examination of the sample.'

Again breach of the implied condition gives rise to a right to rescind and recover damages. Like s 13 the section is not confined to business sales (contrast s 14). 'Unmerchantable' is to be construed in the same way as the implied condition of merchantable quality.

In *Godley v Perry*, a retailer, Perry, examined a sample catapult shown to him by a wholesaler. The catapult looked sound and was tested by Perry who firmly drew back the elastic. Perry ordered several catapults. Later Perry sold one of the catapults to Godley. When being used normally a shaft broke, as a result of a hidden defect, and injured Godley's eye. Godley sued Perry for a breach of contract. The court held that the purpose for which the catapult was required was readily inferred from the facts and as it was not fit for that purpose there was a breach of the implied condition of fitness for purpose. The court also held that a catapult with a hidden defect was not of merchantable quality. Perry also recovered from the wholesaler as the particular catapult sold to Godley did not correspond with the sample in quality and the catapult was not free from a defect, rendering it unmerchantable, which was not apparent on the reasonable examination of the sample undertaken by Perry.

A buyer in a sale by sample is protected from the effects of a contract term excluding or limiting liability of the seller for a breach of s 15 by s 6 of the Unfair Contract Terms Act 1977.

Chapter 25
Liability of the manufacturer

Usually a consumer buys his goods from a retailer. He has rights under his contract both in respect of express terms and implied terms. He has no contractual right against the manufacturer of the goods bought, should they prove defective in some way, because he has no contract with the manufacturer – no privity of contract.

However, in a limited range of circumstances outside the contract of sale, the manufacturer may be made liable to the buyer/consumer.

(a) In negligence

A manufacturer owes a duty of care to anyone he foresees could be injured by his product. When he breaks that duty by failing to exercise reasonable care in all the circumstances with the result that damage is caused to a person within the area of reasonable foreseeability, he commits the tort of negligence (see p 158, above).

By way of defence the manufacturer need show only reasonable care and skill in his manufacturing process. The burden of proving that the manufacturer is negligent lies on the consumer and this is often difficult for him to discharge.

A thermos flask manufactured in Durham, could cause injury at Lands End where the consumer lives. Obtaining evidence about the manufacturing process in Durham would be difficult and expensive. In any event the availability of compensation for a purely economic loss or for a consequential loss is a developing area of law making proof of a claim more difficult and risky (see *Junior Books Ltd v Veitchi Co Ltd* (1982) above, p 164).

(b) Manufacturer's guarantee

Frequently manufacturers guarantee their products. The guarantee appears on the side of the packing or box in which the goods are marketed or on a slip of paper inside a box. A typical example is usually found on a chocolate bar wrapper. In most cases where a buyer contacts the manufacturer to make a claim, the claim will be met within the terms of the guarantee. The question which arises is whether the buyer can sue the manufacturer on the guarantee. (N.B. this is a different use of the word 'guarantee' from that used in the section on writing and the law of contract at p 253, above.)

The buyer has no contract with the manufacturer in the absence of offer, acceptance, consideration etc.

In a limited range of circumstances a collateral contract might arise (see p 356, above), under which the buyer claims that he bought the goods from the retailer in reliance on and in return for the promise (guarantee) by the manufacturer. In *Carlill v Carbolic Smoke Ball Co* (p 210, above), Mrs Carlill sued the manufacturer on his promise in spite of the fact that she bought the smoke ball from a retailer. The buyer must *know* of the manufacturer's promise before he buys the goods which later are the subject of complaint (see p 214, above).

Largely as a result of s 5 of the Unfair Contract Terms Act 1977 the practice of some manufacturers asking for a guarantee to be signed by the buyer has in the main disappeared. Where the buyer signed the guarantee he would often be signing away his common law or statutory rights. Under a guarantee where: (i) the goods are ordinarily supplied for private use, (ii) they are defective in use by a consumer, and (iii) the manufacturer did not sell the goods to the consumer, any excluding words are ineffective.

The result is that under such a guarantee the manufacturer cannot effectively take away common law and statutory rights in connection with defects in the goods or damage arising from negligence but he can provide additional rights in the terms of the guarantee. A manufacturer of an electric kettle, who provides a guarantee which states, 'the manufacturer undertakes to replace, free of charge, any parts proved to be defective in use and in return the purchaser surrenders all other rights given by common law or statute', cannot escape liability in negligence if the kettle explodes in normal use injuring the purchaser in the eye.

(c) Consumer Safety Act 1978

The Consumer Safety Act 1978 replaced Acts of 1961 and 1971 with a view to increasing control by the Secretary of State (at the passing of the Act this was for Prices and Consumer Protection) over the manufacture and labelling of goods in the interest of the 'safety of consumers'. The number of people killed and injured in the home each year is broadly the same as for people killed or injured on the roads. Powers now exist in respect of safety regulations, prohibition orders, prohibition notices and notices to warn. Interestingly the Act was introduced to Parliament as a Private Members' Bill.

The Secretary of State may make regulations covering the composition, design and labelling of goods. Failure to comply with the regulations is a criminal offence. A *prohibition order* can be issued to prevent the supply of a class of goods he considers to be unsafe and a *prohibition notice* can be served on an individual to prevent him supplying a particular product. Also, a *notice to warn* can be served on an individual trader requiring him to publish warnings about goods he has already supplied.

Failure to comply with the above provisions (except 'notice to warn') gives any injured person a right to civil remedy which cannot be excluded by agreement (s 6 of the Consumer Safety Act 1978). Any claim under s 6 is confined to classes of goods which have been made the subject of an order by the Secretary of State.

Chapter 26
Supply of goods and services

Throughout this chapter references to sections are in the Supply of Goods and Services Act 1982, unless otherwise stated.

The Sale of Goods Acts apply only to *goods* which are sold for cash. This protective legislation does not cover dealing in goods other than by way of sale (e g by way of hire, as of a suit or a car or a television) and does not cover the payment of cash or other consideration in return for services (e g a haircut, the repair of a burst tyre, transport). Many principles had been established by cases decided at common law. It was clearly unsatisfactory to have codifications of the law relating to misrepresentations, implied terms in contracts for the sale of goods and exclusion clauses (see the Misrepresentation Act 1967, the Sale of Goods Act 1979 and the Unfair Contract Terms Act 1977) while at the same time leaving the law relating to the supply of goods and services uncodified. As a result of the Law Commission's consideration of this area of law the Supply of Goods and Services Act 1982 was passed.

Transfer of goods

Section 1 of the Supply of Goods and Services Act 1982 excepts certain types of contract from its operation. Among these are contracts for the sale of goods and the hire-purchase of goods, both of which are governed by other legislation. Contracts analogous to sale under which ownership of goods passes, or is to pass, to a buyer are within the scope of this Act. Section 1 (3) makes it clear that the Act applies to contracts for the transfer of goods whether or not services are also provided (e g the supply and fitting of a sun roof to a car) and irrespective of the nature of the consideration furnished in return for the goods and services. Sections 2 to 5 of the Act imply conditions as to title, description, merchantable quality, fitness for purpose and correspondence with sample which closely follow those implied into contracts for sale of goods by the Sale of Goods Act 1979, ss 12 to 15 (see p 382, above).

The conditions implied by ss 2 to 5 would now apply in a number of cases previously decided by the courts as not being covered by the Sale of Goods Act 1893. By way of example should be considered, the repair of a car (*G. H. Myers and Co v Brent Cross Service Co* (1934)), painting a portrait (*Robinson v Graves*), application of a hair dye (*Watson v Buckley, Osborne, Garrett and Co Ltd* (1940)) and roofing a house (*Young and Marten Ltd v McManus Childs Ltd* (1968), where the House of Lords reviewed a number of the older cases).

Attempts by the parties at excluding the implication of any of the above terms are subjected to severe limitations by statute. Section 17 (2) amends s 7 (3) of the Unfair Contract Terms Act 1977 with the result that the implied terms about title cannot be excluded or limited. By s 7 of the Unfair Contract Terms Act 1977 the terms implied by ss 3 to 5 cannot be excluded or limited as against a consumer. As against a person dealing other than as a consumer, liability for a breach of the implied terms can be limited only insofar as the test of reasonableness is satisfied.

Hire of goods

Although hire-purchase agreements and contracts where goods are bailed on the redemption of trading stamps are expressly excluded, s 6 of the Act defines a contract for the hire of goods to which ss 7 to 10 apply as one under which 'one person bails or agrees to bail goods to another by way of hire'. The bailor gives possession of his goods to the bailee to be used for such purposes as are agreed in return for a consideration. By s 7 there is an implied *condition* that the bailor has a right to transfer possession of the goods by way of hire or will have such right at the time of the bailment. By ss 8, 9 and 10 there are implied *conditions* which closely follow the sale of goods provisions, i e implied conditions as to description, merchantable quality, fitness for purpose and correspondence with sample. At common law the courts had followed three different lines of thought in respect of the liability of the bailor of goods. The Act takes the view that the implied terms in a contract of hire should parallel as far as possible the implied term in contracts for the sale of goods.

The statutory implied conditions will apply to the following types of case involving hire: the hire of a horse which was unfit for the journey (*Chow v Jones* (1841)), a wheel which broke on a hired bus (*Jones v Page* (1867)), a hired sack which burst (*Vogan and Co v Oulton* (1848)) and a saddle which slipped on a hired bicycle (*White v John Warwick and Co Ltd* (1953)).

The implied terms relating to the right to transfer possession cannot be excluded or limited. The other implied terms in a contract of hire cannot be excluded or limited as against a consumer and in other cases can be excluded or limited only to the extent that they satisfy the 1977 Act's test of reasonableness (Unfair Contract Terms Act 1977).

Supply of services

In 1981 the National Consumer Council published the results of its survey into the provision of services under the title 'Service Please – services and the law: a consumer view'. Largely as a result of this work the provisions relating to the supply of services were inserted in the Act.

A contract for the supply of a service is one 'under which a person ("the supplier") agrees to carry out a service' (s 12). Contracts will fall within this definition even where goods are also included and where a consideration other than money is involved. The following *terms* are implied in contracts for the supply of a service.

(a) *Care and skill*

Section 13 provides:

'In a contract for the supply of a service where the supplier is acting in the course of a business, there is an implied term that the supplier will carry out the service with reasonable care and skill.'

The section implies a *term*, not a condition as in the case of most of the above. As a result the consequences of a breach of the implied statutory obligation will depend on its importance in the contract. If it is of little importance (a warranty) the innocent party will recover damages only. If it is of considerable importance (a condition) he will be able to rescind the contract and recover damages. It must be noted that the implication is confined to contracts where the supplier is acting in the course of *a* business.

The basic philosophy behind this implied term is to be found in *The Moorcock* (p 360, above) where it was established that in business contracts the common law will imply a term to give such 'business efficacy' to a contract as must have been intended by the parties. The term will now be implied in cases such as where a car has been repaired with a defective part (*G. H. Myers and Co v Brent Cross Service Co* (1934)), or skill is used in the choice and application of a hair dye (*Watson v Buckley, Osborne, Garrett and Co Ltd* (1940)), or dentures are repaired (*Samuels v Davis* (1943)), or a carpet is layed in an unworkmanlike manner (*Kimber v William Millett Ltd* (1947)) and where a carpet was stolen after it had been collected for cleaning (*Levison v Patent Steam Carpet Cleaning Co Ltd* (1977)).

Whether the care and skill which has been used will be reasonable depends on all the circumstances of the case and leaves the court with an element of discretion. Where the parties expressly agree a term involving care and skill in its achievement such a term must be strictly adhered to as a matter of contract. One party could be in breach of contract even though reasonable care and skill had been used. This position could arise where a lady asks a hairdresser to dye her hair and to ensure that the dye does not cause her hair to drop out. The hairdresser selected the dye using all known facts about the effect of dyes on hair and applied it to the lady's scalp. In spite of the care taken the dye caused the lady's hair to drop out. Section 13 has been complied with. There is no breach of the implied term of care and skill but there has been a breach of the *express* term that the hair will not drop out as a result of using the dye. The liability of the hairdresser is strict for the breach of this express contract term.

(b) *Time for performance*

Section 14 provides:

'(1) Where, under a contract for the supply of a service by a supplier acting in the course of a business, the time for the service to be carried out is not fixed by the contract, left to be fixed in a manner agreed by the contract or determined by the course of dealing between the parties, there is an implied term that the supplier will carry out the service within a reasonable time.

(2) What is a reasonable time is a question of fact.'

Again it must be noted that s 14 implies a *term*, which may be a condition or warranty depending on the facts. As with s 13 it is implied only in the case of contracts entered into in the course of *a* business.

Charnock v Liverpool Corpn (p 361, above) and *Charles Rickards Ltd v Oppenheim* (p 316, above) are cases containing facts where s 14 would be applied today.

(c) *The consideration*

Section 15 provides:

'(1) Where, under a contract for the supply of a service, the consideration for the service is not determined by the contract, left to be determined in a manner agreed by the contract or determined by the course of dealing between the parties, there is an implied term that the party contracting with the supplier will pay a reasonable charge.

(2) What is a reasonable charge is a question of fact.'

Section 15 implies a *term* in the case of a contract entered into in the course of a business. A painter who agrees to paint the outside of a house 'taking about one week depending on the weather, starting on Monday' makes *no* reference to the price for the job. When he has completed his work he is entitled to a reasonable price and *no more*. Where the price is *expressly* agreed it must, of course, be paid in full in the absence of any defect in the work done.

As 'reasonableness' is the basis of each of the three *terms* implied in contracts for the supply of services and as s 3 of the Unfair Contract Terms Act 1977 dealing with consumer sales permits the exclusion or limitation of terms only to the extent that such exclusion or limitation is reasonable, it follows that it cannot be reasonable by agreement to exclude or limit a reasonable term implied by statute. The conclusion is, therefore, that the three terms implied in contracts for the supply of services cannot be excluded or limited by contract.

Chapter 27
Unsolicited goods

A practice has developed rapidly since the 1960s of a supplier sending goods to a potential customer, without there being a prior request, in the hope that the 'customer' will decide to buy them or through inactivity keep them for so long that he feels obliged to pay for them. This practice has become known as 'inertia selling'. From *Felthouse v Bindley* (p 215, above) it can be seen that the sender cannot impose inactivity (silence) as an acceptance by the customer. The customer seldom knows the law and anxiety is frequently caused by this method of selling. The Unsolicited Goods and Services Act 1971 was passed to give further protection to the buyer in this type of situation.

A person who receives unsolicited goods other than in the course of a trade or business may either (i) treat the goods as an unconditional gift if the sender does not reclaim the goods within six months of their receipt, or (ii) give written notice to the sender stating that the goods were unsolicited and giving the address where the goods may be collected. In this case if the goods are not collected within 30 days they become the property of the recipient (s 1).

The recipient of unsolicited goods will not normally be liable for loss of or damage to them while in his possession before the end of the above statutory periods. The recipient is in the position of an involuntary bailee at common law.

In addition to the above civil law protection given to the recipient of unsolicited goods, criminal sanctions are imposed on the sender of unsolicited goods, who demands payment for them or threatens legal proceedings where he has no reasonable cause to believe he has a right to such payment (s 2).

Chapter 28

Credit – protection of the consumer

Credit is one of the features of a modern capitalist society. It enables consumers to buy goods or services which they could not otherwise afford. The credit explosion started with the arrival of consumer durables such as sewing machines, pianos and furniture and continued on its way with cars, televisions and video equipment. The recent expansion of the credit card system has made credit more readily available to a wider range of society. The providers of credit are often large companies, such as banks and finance houses, who deal on their own standard terms designed principally for their own benefit. The credit is offered to individuals as consumers of credit who may easily be tempted by the powers of advertising and persuasion to overreach their financial resources. As a result legislation was seen to be necessary to control many aspects of the giving of credit or the supply of goods on hire or hire-purchase (see the report of the Crowther Committee on Consumer Credit (1971) Cmnd 4596). The remaining part of this section deals with legal aspects of the subject of credit from the point of view of the individual consumer.

For the protection of the consumer major hire-purchase regulation was introduced in 1938 with further legislation in 1964 and 1965. The intention is that the latest Act, the Consumer Credit Act 1974, should replace all earlier legislation but the introduction of its provisions has been irregular and intermittent. By no means are all the provisions and regulations provided for by the Act operative at the present time. It is expected that by 1985 most, if not quite all, sections will be in operation. The length and complexity of the Act are considerable. For the sake of simplicity it is assumed that all provisions of the Act are currently operative. The purpose of the Consumer Credit Act 1974 is 'to establish for the protection of consumers a new system, administered by the Director-General of Fair Trading, of licensing and other control of traders concerned with the provision of credit, or the supply of goods on hire or hire-purchase and their transactions, . . .; and for related matters' (see the preamble to the Act).

The Director-General of Fair Trading is charged by statute with the duties, among others, of administering the licensing system set up by the Act as well as exercising judicial functions in connection with the issue, suspension and revocation of licences, and generally to superintend the working and enforcement of the Act (s 1). Unless otherwise stated references in this section are to the Consumer Credit Act 1974.

Definition of terms

The Act defines the terms it uses (see particularly Part II). Before considering any of the provisions of the Act it is desirable to clarify the meaning of the terms used in the areas of the Act to be examined.

Problems were first encountered in the law relating to hire-purchase agreements. In practice, where, eg furniture is bought on hire-purchase terms, the customer (also known as the buyer or consumer) asks the retailer (seller or, in the case of cars, the dealer) to make the necessary hire-purchase arrangements. The retailer then offers to sell the furniture to a finance company, while at the same time the customer offers to take the furniture from the finance company on hire-purchase terms. The finance company agrees to these arrangements. The dealer is in fact paid *not* by the customer standing in front of him *but* by the finance company. The customer's obligation to the finance company is to *hire* the furniture by the payment of regular instalments coupled with a *right* to buy the furniture with the payment of the last instalment. In the language of the Act the retailer is the *agent* of or *negotiator* for the finance company. The finance company is the *legal owner* of the goods until they are purchased by the payment of the last instalment. The finance company is also the *creditor*, to whom the payments are owed, and in law the *supplier* of the goods. The customer is the *hirer* of the goods as well as the *debtor* who is obliged to pay the hire-purchase instalments to the finance company. In the case of a hire-purchase agreement the hirer does not become the legal owner until the payment of the last instalment. Until the final payment it is possible for the finance company to repossess goods subject to the agreement (this is possible only by court order and subject to severe restraints – see below).

Under a credit-sale the ownership of the goods passes to the buyer at the time of the sale and *payment* is deferred on instalment terms. Under a credit-sale agreement the goods cannot be re-possessed by the seller whose remedy is to sue for the instalments still owed to him.

In the case of credit card sales also, the customer becomes the owner of the goods bought by the use of the credit card. By prior arrangement, the credit card company, such as Access, agrees to pay the retailer for the goods sold by him to his customer, who is the *debtor*. The credit card company later seeks payment from the customer.

A *personal credit agreement* is one where a creditor provides a debtor, who is an individual, with credit not exceeding £5,000. So long as it is not also an exempt agreement (defined by s 16 of the 1974 Act to include local authorities, building societies or a body specified as exempt by the Secretary of State), a personal credit agreement is a *regulated* agreement (ie subject to the protection of the Act (s 8)). The amount of credit extended (excluding any deposit or charge for the credit facility) determines whether the Act is applicable.

Formalities

The agreement must be written and the type of paper, print and other matters are controlled by regulation. The 1974 Act entitles the hirer or debtor to a copy of the document he signs both in the case where the document is to be signed by the creditor later and in the case where the document is executed by both parties at the same time. In the former case the hirer or debtor is entitled to a further copy of the agreement within seven days of its execution by the owner or creditor. Any failure to comply with the requirements as to formality make the executed contract *unenforceable by the owner or creditor* (ss 62 and 63). In practice a person buying furniture on hire-purchase would probably sign a hire-purchase agreement at the point of retail sale and would then be entitled to a copy for his retention. The signed document would then be sent by the retailer to the finance company who in turn would sign the document. The customer (debtor) is then entitled to a copy of the document actually signed by the finance company.

Cancellation

Under the general law of contract a hirer or buyer of goods on hire-purchase terms may withdraw his offer at any time before it has been accepted. The Act takes the rights of the hirer or buyer further than the common law. In certain circumstances he has the right to cancel the agreement i e to cancel after he has made his acceptance. In effect this provision gives a consumer the right to think again – a 'cooling-off' period (ss 67–73). Oral representation (persuasion) must have been made to the hirer or debtor and the agreement must have been other than at the business premises of the owner or creditor (or of a negotiator or of a party to a linked transaction such as a contract of insurance to guarantee payment). In practice this means that where an agreement is signed in the hirer's or debtor's home as a result of the visit of a doorstep salesman it will be a cancellable agreement. The hirer or debtor has five days from the receipt of his copy of the executed agreement (i e signed by the owner or creditor) within which to cancel the agreement by giving written notice to the owner or creditor or his agent. Cancellation is effective from the date of posting. Under s 56 the negotiator is treated as the agent of the owner or creditor. In the example given above in respect of furniture, the retailer is deemed to be the agent of the creditor. Notice of cancellation to the retailer would, therefore, be sufficient.

On the cancellation of an agreement the hirer or debtor is entitled to the return of money paid (s 70) and the owner or creditor is entitled to the return of the goods (s 72).

Termination

At any time before the last payment is due the debtor under a hire-purchase agreement may terminate the hiring (ss 99 and 100). The law attempts to hold the balance between this right of the debtor to terminate the hiring, and the interest of the creditor, who may have valuable goods returned to him after a few instalments only have been paid, leaving him with depreciated second-hand goods to dispose of. The Act requires the debtor to pay the creditor such sums as will bring the total repayments to one half of the total price. This is a maximum sum. The court has power to order the payment of a lesser sum equal to the loss sustained by the creditor as a result of the termination of the agreement.

The hirer of goods has a right to terminate the hiring after 18 months or such shorter period as is agreed by the parties (s 101).

Protection of the consumer against enforcement by owner or creditor

Where the hirer or debtor defaults in paying his instalments the owner or creditor will probably seek to terminate the agreement, repossess the goods and sue for compensation. Even where the consumer (hirer or debtor) is in default the Act operates to protect his interest:

(a) The person seeking to terminate the agreement must serve on the person failing to pay a default notice which sets out the nature of the breach of the agreement. The hirer or debtor may then make the outstanding payments or correct the breach and the breach will be treated as not having occurred (ss 87–89). The owner or creditor will then have no right to terminate the agreement.

(b) Where a hirer or debtor is behind with his payment or is in default in some other way (e g by failing to insure or to repair) the owner or creditor may take steps to enforce his rights. In these circumstances the hirer or debtor may apply to the court under s 129 for a 'time order'. If it appears to the court 'just' to do so, the court may make an order (i) for the payment by the hirer or debtor of any sum owed under the agreement as is reasonable having regard to the means of the hirer or debtor, and/or (ii) for the remedying of the breach within a specified period.

While a 'time order' is in force the owner or creditor is precluded from taking any action to terminate the agreement or repossess the goods until the time specified has elapsed.

(c) A retailer who seeks to repossess goods in default of hire-purchase instalments being paid must first serve a 'default notice' in prescribed form on the debtor giving him seven days in which to remedy the situation. Where there has been no payment within seven days of the 'default notice' the retailer will wish to recover his goods. He cannot enter premises to repossess them without a court order (s 92). Where the debtor has paid or tendered one-third or more of the total price the goods become 'protected goods' under s 90 and the creditor cannot then repossess them without a court order. A creditor who is unwise enough to flout the rule against possession without a court order will find that the agreement is automatically terminated, the debtor released from further liability and, worse, the defaulting debtor can recover all sums he has paid under the agreement (s 91).

Loans at exorbitant interest rates

Sections 137 to 140 apply to agreements which provide credit at exorbitant rates of interest. 'If the court finds the credit bargain extortionate it may re-open the credit agreement so as to do justice between the parties' (s 137). The credit bargain will be regarded as extortionate where it requires payments which are grossly exorbitant or where it grossly contravenes ordinary principles of fair dealing. Section 138 indicates the factors to be taken into account in deciding whether a credit bargain is extortionate. In respect of the debtor these include his age, health, business capacity and financial pressures. In respect of the creditor these include the risk, security, relationship to the debtor and whether a merely colourable cash price was quoted for goods or services. Also to be considered are the prevailing interests and any other relevant matter. In assessing whether the credit is extortionate the court will look at the interest rate which in itself may be too high and which might be expected to be below the prevailing rate where a sound security for repayment is given. An unsecured advance to a borrower who is in an unsound financial position may justify a high rate of interest, so long as the debtor fully understands the nature of his bargain and no advantage has been taken of his position. A bargain at an acceptable rate of interest may be re-opened as extortionate where it otherwise grossly contravenes ordinary principles of fair trading. The Act specifically lists a colourable cash price (probably a high cash price), which is quoted for goods or services, as a factor in deciding whether a bargain is extortionate.

When in the course of proceedings a debtor alleges that the credit bargain is extortionate the onus of proving to the contrary lies on the creditor (s 171).

The issue can be raised before the county court or the High Court. The court has power by order (i) to direct an account to be taken between the parties, (ii) to set aside the whole or any part of any obligation of the debtor or his surety imposed by the credit bargain, (iii) to require the creditor to repay sums received in whole or in part and to return a surety in whole or in part and (iv) to alter the terms of the credit agreement or surety.

Licensing

The Act provides licensing arrangements applicable to all persons involved in the consumer credit business including shops and department stores. The system is centrally administered and is designed to monitor and control effectively a contentious area of business activity. The Director-General of Fair Trading may grant or refuse a licence to provide credit facilities. A person granted a licence must be a 'fit' person in the opinion of the Director who may take into account any factors he thinks are relevant. It is a criminal offence to trade without a licence. (See Part III and ss 147 to 150.)

N.B. Small agreements fall outside the regulatory provisions of the Act. The Consumer Credit (Increase of Monetary Limits) Order 1983 limit now stands at £50.

Statutory protection of buyers/consumers

A historical summary

1893	Sale of Goods Act	terms were implied in contracts for the sale of goods but these could be excluded by agreement between the parties.
1938	Hire-Purchase Act	applied only to credit buyers and prohibited the exclusion of terms implied by the Act.
1967	Misrepresentation Act	rendered of no effect any clause excluding or restricting liability for a misrepresentation except to the extent that it was fair and reasonable.
1971	Unsolicited Goods and Services Act	the recipient of unsolicited goods was given ownership of them in certain circumstances.
1973	Supply of Goods (Implied Terms) Act 1973	in respect of the statutory implied terms buyers of goods for cash were placed on the same basis as buyers on credit.
1977	Unfair Contract Terms Act	applies to the sale and supply of goods, manufacturers' guarantees and misrepresentations and either outlaws certain exemption clauses or severely restricts them by reference to the test of reasonableness.

1979	Sale of Goods Act	repealed and substantially re-enacted the 1893 Act.
1982	Supply of Goods and Services Act	effectively prohibits the exclusion of the three terms implied by the Act on the basis of reasonableness.

Appendices

Appendix 1

Examination preparation and technique

We have often received letters from students asking for guidance in preparing for their exams. In an attempt to answer as yet unsent letters we hope that the following letter, offered from the perspective of over 20 years' combined experience of 'A' level law examining, will assist students in their preparation for their forthcoming exam.

Dear Student,

A most useful and much neglected starting-point is a study of the expanded syllabus notes, past exam papers (some of which are reproduced in Appendix 2) and examiners' reports, all of which are available from the relevant Examining Board. These indicate that the General Papers require more than the mere repetition of learnt facts. They require a critical appraisal and evaluation of such facts and this is all too often missing. In the Optional Papers the major weakness of candidates who attempt the problem type of question is their failure to spot the legal points raised by the question. Clearly, no matter how much law you have absorbed in long nights spent in the light of the guttering candle, it will all have been wasted from an exam point of view if you fail to realise that the story in front of you calls for a particular legal response. The best way to gain this kind of expertise is to practise on past papers of an equivalent difficulty. A final and equally important point, which has consistently appeared in the examiners' reports, is that you must ensure that you communicate your ideas to the examiner as clearly as possible. This requires that your command of English is adequate and that your writing is legible.

In addition to studying the material contained in this book it is essential that you consult other source material some of which is listed in Appendix 3. A particularly useful insight into the skills required of a student of law is provided by Glanville Williams' little gem of a book, *Learning the Law*. A most useful way of reading about the law in operation, criticisms of it and proposals for its reform is to read the weekly *New Law Journal* and to make a habit of reading a newspaper like *The Times*. The *Students' Law Reporter* is an invaluable aid to keeping up to date.

As you can see from the past exam papers reproduced in Appendix 2 the questions divide into two kinds, the essay or bookwork kind and the problem kind of question. Points to note and implement in the exam in relation to these two types of question are as follows:

1   Make the information you use relevant to the question asked. When you are writing you should constantly be asking yourself, 'Is this point I'm making advancing the argument?' If it is not, you are being irrelevant and wasting time which might be more usefully employed in attempting another question.

2   Always answer the question asked, not the one you would have liked to have been asked. Thus, for example, a good answer to question 1 on the 1983 Paper 1 (see p 411, below) must include a *critical* examination of the part laymen play in the administration of the law. Thus, your answer should include both the pros and cons of the system, e g their lack of expertise, the fact that they save a great deal of money. A mere recitation of their role will not suffice.

3   When answering problem questions make sure you do as you are requested. Advise the persons you are asked to advise and address yourself to the information you are asked to provide.

Experience tells us that students are at their weakest when it comes to tackling a problem. However, if you go about it systematically, a problem may be solved relatively easily. First, you must **IDENTIFY** the legal principles in issue. Second, you must **DEFINE** the legal terms involved, whether it is 'misrepresentation' in contract or 'deception' in criminal law. Third, you must **EXPLAIN** the law and this is done via the medium of relevant case law. Lastly, you must **APPLY** the law to the facts of the problem, always bearing in mind that it is unlikely that you will be given a full statement of the facts, in which case you must interpret the facts in a reasonable way. There may, of course, be more than one reasonable interpretation and you must follow each possibility to its legal conclusion. Application is the weakest aspect of students' exam technique. It is not a great deal of use merely to state the law and then say something like 'Applying the above A may sue for breach of contract'. This is not an application; it is a shamefaced admission of an inability to apply the law to the facts. You must *use* the facts and it may help to imagine that you are explaining the position to a client who has come to you with the story in the problem and showing him how the law applies to his particular situation. The mnemonic **IDEA** may help you to remember the above steps in problem-solving.

As an outline indication of how you might apply the above approach, we shall use question 1 on the 1982 Paper II, Option B, as an example:

I – the question involves the effect on a contract for the sale of goods of an exclusion clause, its extent and whether it has been incorporated into the contract. The notice relates to warranties, not conditions. Is the sale a consumer sale?

D – the legal terms used must be defined.

E – you must explain the law by using interpretative case law.

A – apply the law to the facts given, i e a half-price sale, kind of carpet bought, short period of wear, notice partially obscured. Finally, note that the question is split into two parts and answer accordingly.

On the exam day itself you are bound to be a little nervous but if you have prepared properly there should be no need to worry unduly. A degree of nervousness is a good thing. All that adrenalin coursing through your veins helps to put you on your mettle, to speed up your responses and your writing.

When you open your exam paper you must:

1 *Read the rubric* which gives you your exam instructions. It is absolutely vital that you answer the required number of questions, from the different sections if this is appropriate. Answer too many and you waste time. It is often practice for examiners to mark the number of questions required and to discount the last answer(s) over and above the required number. Answer too few and you forego possible marks which may make all the difference between a fail and a pass. If you are running short of time, an answer in note-form should be attempted, preferably those parts of a question which bear a greater proportion of the available marks as indicated on the paper, as this at least gives the examiner something for which he may be able to award some marks so as to make that all-important difference between failing and passing.

2 *Follow the instructions* about such matters as entering your name and correct exam number on your answer books and attaching any supplementary answer book(s) or paper to your original book.

3 *Read the questions carefully.* Do precisely as you are asked.

4 *Do not waste time.* Examiners are experts at spotting mere space-filling waffle and giving no marks for it! Don't waste time over trying to remember the name of a case or the date of an Act. The name of a case is not important; it is the legal principle which it established which matters. The date of a case is seldom worth remembering except where it is part of an argument. Provided you can identify the case and the Act you will be all right. It is also permissible to use abbreviations, e g S.O.G.A. (Sale of Goods Act), pl. (plaintiff), def. (defendant), provided that your meaning is clear.

We wish you the very best of luck in your exams and, whatever the outcome, we hope that you have enjoyed your study of law and that it may prove of some help to you in your daily life.

With all best wishes,

Appendix 2
Sample examination papers

The following papers are reproduced with the kind permission of the Joint Matriculation Board to whom the authors express their grateful appreciation.

June 1982

Answer four questions.
Each question carries 25 marks.
Sections of questions carry equal marks unless otherwise stated.

1 Describe and examine critically the part played by laymen in the administration of the law.

2 The common law has been described as 'the heart of the legal system'. To what extent is this a true statement of English law today?

3 'The Treaty [of Rome] does not touch any of the matters which concern solely England and the people in it. These are still governed by English law. They are not affected by the Treaty. But when we come to matters with a European element, the Treaty is like an incoming tide. It flows into the estuaries and up the rivers. It cannot be held back. Parliament has decreed that the Treaty is henceforward to be part of our law. It is equal in force to any statute. . . .' per Lord Denning MR in *Bulmer Ltd v Bollinger SA* [1974] CA.
Discuss.

4 (a) Discuss the ways in which a juvenile court differs from other courts of criminal jurisdiction.
(b) In what ways may a juvenile court deal with a juvenile offender?

5 Outline the provisions of the Bail Act 1976. To what extent has this Act been successful in improving the situation with regard to the granting of bail by magistrates and by the police?

6   'That degree is well settled. It need not reach certainty, but it must carry a high degree of probability. Proof beyond reasonable doubt does not mean proof beyond a shadow of doubt. . . . If the evidence is so strong against a man as to leave only a remote possibility in his favour which can be dismissed with the sentence "Of course it is possible but not in the least probable" the case is proved beyond reasonable doubt; but nothing short of that will suffice.' per Denning J in *Miller v Minister of Pensions* [1947].
Discuss this statement in relation to the required standard of proof in both civil and criminal cases in the English courts. Where does the burden of proof lie in each case?

7   It has been argued that the individual judge must be left with enough discretion to decide in the light of the circumstances everything that cannot be justly settled by general rule. Discuss this view of the function of the judge in relation to judicial precedent.

8   'The Rule of Law is a defence against arbitrary government.' Discuss.

June 1982

OPTION B   LAW OF CONTRACT
Answer four questions, including at least two from Part 1 and at least one from Part 2.
Each question carries 25 marks.
Sections of questions carry equal marks unless otherwise stated.

Part 1   Answer at least two questions from this part.

1   Roger buys a new carpet, which is to be fitted in his lounge, during a half-price January sale. On a wall in the store is a notice saying, 'No warranty is given with sale goods'. This notice is partly obscured by a roll of carpet lying against the wall.
After two months, the carpet becomes badly worn in front of the chair in which Roger sits while watching the television.
Consider Roger's rights, if any, against (a) the retailer, and (b) the manufacturer of the carpet.

2   Geoff, a plumber, advertises for the supply to him of copper piping and copper goods over a period of 12 months and not exceeding a total length of 10,000 metres. Stock submits a written tender on which he has written, 'if this tender is accepted, orders for piping must be notified in writing to the tenderer'. Stock's tender is accepted by Geoff.

One week later, Geoff posts a letter to Stock ordering 100 metres of copper piping but this letter never reaches Stock. Being dissatisfied at hearing nothing from Stock, Geoff telephones him, repeats the order and explains that a letter has already been sent. Stock then replies that the whole deal is off as he can sell his copper piping at a far higher figure elsewhere.

Advise Geoff.

3   John, a farmer, contracted with Sam, a demolition contractor, for the knocking down of an old farm building and the removal of the rubble from the site. The contract contained the following clause, 'The contractor undertakes the work on the express understanding that no liability is accepted by the contractor, his employees or agents for any damage or bodily injury no matter how caused'.

Unfortunately, the work is not done well. As one wall is collapsed it destroys an adjacent barn, injuring John at the same time. While bricks are being driven away in a lorry operated by Shift Company Limited, engaged by Sam to clear the site, the vehicle hits a farm gate which in turn destroys a beehive and breaks the leg of John's wife Mary, who is tending the beehive at the time.

Advise (a) John, and (b) Mary.

4   Socrates Tours Limited engaged Jane as a courier for a period of six months from 3 May 1982. Under the contract Jane is to attend regularly at a series of Greek lessons over the preceding winter. Jane has influenza for two weeks and is unable to attend classes for those two weeks but does attend for the remaining ten weeks of the course. In April 1982, the Company decides, as booking are low, that it will cancel its Greek tours and Jane is told that her services will not be required. Nonetheless, Jane travels to her workplace in Greece and stays there for six months.

Advise Jane who now wishes to recover the cost of travelling to Greece and the wages which she claims are due from Socrates Tours Limited while she is in Greece during the contract period.

5   Tony hired a hall with a seating capacity of 2,000 from the Seaside Corporation at a charge of £1,000 for one week. He also hired an internationally-known pop group to appear in concert at the hall for a fee of £3,000. All 14,000 concert tickets at £2 each were sold in advance of the concert week.

Two days before the first concert, Seaside Corporation informed Tony that his letting had been cancelled in favour of another client who was prepared to pay more for the hire of the hall.

(a) Advise Tony, who wishes to hold the Corporation to the agreement.

(b) What, if any, would be the difference to your answer if Tony could not persuade the Corporation to allow him the use of the hall and as a result he has been obliged to pay the group its fee for the week and return the £28,000 ticket money to the ticket holders.

Part 2   Answer at least one question from this part.

---

6 'A peppercorn does not cease to be . . . consideration if it is established that the promisee does not like pepper and will throw away the corn'. per Lord Somervell in *Chappel and Company Limited v Nestlé Company Limited* [1960].
Explain and comment.

7 'When two parties have come to a contract – or rather what appears, on the face of it, to be a contract – the fact that one party is mistaken as to the identity of another does not mean that there is no contract, or that the contract is a nullity and void from the beginning'. per Lord Denning MR in *Lewis v Averay* [1973].
How far is the above statement a true reflection of the law?

8 Explain and comment on the view that it it quite reasonable for the parties to a contract to estimate damage resulting from breach at a certain figure and, provided the figure is not extravagant, there seems to no reason to say that it is not truly a bargain to assess damages but rather a penalty to be held *in terrorem*.

June 1983

PAPER I

Answer four questions.
Each question carries 25 marks.
Sections of questions carry equal marks unless otherwise stated.

---

1 'They are a separate set of courts dealing with a separate set of rights and duties. Just as in the old days there were ecclesiastical courts dealing with matrimonial cases and the administration of estates and just as there was the Chancellor dealing with the enforcement and administration of trusts so

in our day there are the new tribunals dealing with the rights
and duties between man and the State.'

> Lord Denning in *Freedom Under The Law.*

Comment on this view of administrative tribunals.

2 Discuss the general charactistics of the English Common
Law system, making reference where appropriate to other
systems.

3 Discuss the importance of Equity in the development of
English Law.

4 How successful have the official law reform agencies been in
improving the law?

5 (a) By reference to the concept of judicial precedent explain
how case law is made.   15
(b) Give an account of any decided case which in your view
has made an important contribution to English Law and
explain how it has done so.   10 = 25

6 Give a critical account of the principal approaches applied
by the judges in ascertaining the meaning of statutes.

7 Discuss, and assess the success of, the arbitration system for
small claims in county courts.

8 'A court may use its powers of sentencing according to the
nature of the offence and the offender.' Discuss the various
ways in which the courts deal with convicted persons.

June 1983

OPTION B   LAW OF CONTRACT
**Answer four questions, including at least two from Part 1
and at least one from Part 2.**

Part 1   Answer at least two questions from this part.

---

1 Ormclocks Limited, an English company, manufactured
small alarm clocks. Mondule S.A., a French company
situated in Paris, imported clocks to France. By letter posted
in Paris on Tuesday 5 April, Mondule S.A. placed an order
with Ormclocks Limited for 1000 clocks and asked for
'immediate notification of acceptance' of the order. On
receipt of the order on Friday 8 April, Ormclocks Limited

straightaway posted an acceptance of the order to Mondule S.A. in France. On Thursday, 7 April, Mondule S.A. decided not to buy the clocks and posted a revocation of the order to Ormclocks Limited. This letter reached Ormclocks Limited on Monday 11 April.

Assume that English law applies.

(a)   Advise Ormclocks Limited.

(b)   What difference, if any, would it make to your advice if

(i)   Ormclocks Limited had accepted the order by telegram on Friday 8 April, and   **3**

(ii)   Ormclocks Limited had accepted the order by telex on Friday 8 April?   **3 = 25**

2   David wrote an account of the Spanish Civil War for a new publisher. His contract with the publisher provided that he would be paid £5000 cash on completion of the writing in return for the copyright in the work being assigned to the publisher. On completing the work, David sent the completed work to the publisher together with a form assigning the copyright to him. As David had received no reply after six weeks he visited the publisher demanding his money. The publisher said that he was short of funds to finance his various enterprises and David could have a cheque for £4000 payable after two weeks in full satisfaction or do without anything at all until after publication in twelve months' time. David accepted the cheque for £4000.

David, who has now cashed the cheque, wishes to sue for £1000 which he claims is the balance owed to him.

Advise David.

3   Larry booked a ticket for a cruise from Southampton round the Mediterranean islands. A condition of the booking was that 'neither the Company nor the Captain and crew are responsible for injuries caused to the passengers it carries by reason of negligence or otherwise of its Captain, crew members or any other person and in entering into this contract the Company is contracting on its own behalf and as agent for its Captain and crew'. The Captain supervised the lowering of the gangway for disembarkation at Southampton on the return journey. The gangway shook violently as Larry was coming down it carrying his hand luggage with the result that he fell over the side, landed on the quay, broke his back and lost his hand luggage in the sea.

Advise Larry who now wishes to sue

(a) the Company, and   **15**

(b) the Captain.   **10 = 25**

4 For several years Vera had carried on business as a restauranteur in various small towns in North West England and during this time she was very successful. In 1981 she decided to sell one of her businesses and advertised it in trade journals as 'most desirable premises and business to be sold as a going concern with an existing throughput of 200 diners each Saturday and prospects of further development'. Julia bought the business at the advertised price and at the end of the first year found that the business attracted only 200 diners per week with the prospect of a downfall in trade as a result of local authority roadworks causing a redirection of traffic. The contract between Vera and Julia made no reference to throughput of customers nor to annual turnover. Advise Julia of any rights she may have against Vera.

5 Alan bought a suit from Mensuit, a retail tailor. After six months' occasional use, the suit began to wear away at the knees and elbows. On examination of the suit by the manufacturer it was discovered that a chemical substance, used in the manufacture of the cloth, had impregnated the cloth and was the cause of the wear. Later it was realised that the cause of Alan's dermatitis was contact with this chemical in the suit.
Advise Alan.

Part 2   Answer at least one question from this part.

---

6 By reference to the aims of the Consumer Credit Act, 1974, explain the major ways in which the Act has attempted to protect the consumer in relation to the formation, enforcement and termination of regulated credit and hire agreements made in respect of goods.

7 Discuss the circumstances in which the law will allow a contracting party to recover 'damages' on a contract which he has not performed in full.

8 'In a little more than a decade the law relating to contract of employment has been radically altered by statute.' Discuss.

The authors gratefully acknowledge the kind permission of the Associated Examining Board permitting the reproduction of the following questions from the Board's special subject paper (Paper 2). The Board's paper 1 is broadly comparable to that of the Joint Matriculation Board.

June 1983
PAPER 2

OPTION 1 – NEGLIGENCE

Answer **all** *questions*

1   The passage is taken from *Hedley Byrne & Co Ltd v Heller & Partners Ltd* (1963).

> 'A reasonable man, knowing that he was being trusted or that his skill and judgment were being relied on, would, I think, have three courses open to him. He could keep silent or decline to give the information or advice sought: or he could give an answer with a clear qualification that he accepted no responsibility for it or that it was given without that reflection or inquiry which a careful answer would require: or he could simply answer without any such qualification. If he chooses to adopt the last course he must, I think, be held to have accepted some responsibility for his answer. . . .. (Lord Reid).

(a)   Which of the three courses' had the defendants in the case taken   (*2 marks*)

(b)   Which case of 1951 did this case regard as wrongly decided?   (*2 marks*)

(c)   How did *Hedley Byrne* explain or distinguish the statement in *Derry v Peek* (1889) that 'in the absence of contract, an action for negligence cannot be maintained when there is no fraud'?   (*4 marks*)

(d)   What other duty in respect of negligent statements, apart from a contractual one, had already been recognised by the House of Lords?   (*1 mark*)

(e)   State in your own words the situations where the Courts recognise a duty under *Hedley Byrne*.   (*4 marks*)

(f)   What gloss is placed upon *Hedley Byrne* by *Mutual Life and Citizens' Assurance Co Ltd v Evatt* (1971)?   (*3 marks*)

(g) What authority, according to the doctrine of stare decisis, is *Evatt*? Why? *(2 marks)*

(h) Why did the House of Lords in *Hedley Byrne* feel compelled to reconcile its decision with *Nocton v Lord Ashburton* (1914) and *Derry v Peek*? *(3 marks)*

(i) According to its 1966 Statement, when can the House of Lords depart from its own previous decisions? *(1 mark)*

(j) When will the House of Lords be unlikely to depart from its own previous decisions? *(3 marks)*

June 1983

OPTION 2 – THE CONSUMER

3 Gwen bought a 'reconditioned' television set from Harry, a dealer in new and second-hand radio and T.V. sets. At the time of sale Gwen told Harry that she was quite satisfied with her existing set, which was several years old and could not receive more than three channels, but that her husband was 'very keen to be able to have a choice of four channels.' Harry assured her that the reconditioned set would receive on four channels.

Gwen signed a receipt which stated: 'Reconditioned radio and T.V. sets are guaranteed for a period of 3 months from purchase against break-down due to mechanical or electrical fault. The dealer can accept no other liability whatsoever for the condition or quality of such sets, which are purchased on the clear understanding that they are of reconditioned standard only.'

Gwen and her husband continued to receive good quality pictures on the original three channels but poor quality pictures on the other. They complained to Harry, who advised them fit an amplifier to the aerial because reception in the area was weak. Gwen arranged for an aerial fitter to fit the amplifier but there was no improvement in picture reception. The fitter commented that the tube was worn out and that it needed replacement but that it was hardly worth it with such an old set. The fitter charged Gwen £30 for his services.

Advise Gwen as to her legal position. *(25 marks)*

Addresses of examining boards

Addresses of the examining boards offering papers at Advanced Level:

Associated Examining Board
Wellington House,
Station Road,
Aldershot,
Hampshire,
GU11 1BQ

Joint Matriculation Board,
Oxford Road,
Manchester,
M15 6EU

London Examining Board,
School Examination Department (GCE),
University of London,
Senate House,
Mallet Street,
London,
WC1

Oxford Examining Board,
Ewart Place,
Summertown,
Oxford

Welsh Joint Education Committee,
University of Wales,
245 Western Avenue,
Cardiff,
CF5 2YX

Appendix 4
Booklist

The following suggested booklist is compiled in the order in which, in whole or in part, the books appearing in it could be read to advantage while studying this textbook. Latest editions should be used. Reference should also be made to the guidance given on page 407.

O. Hood Phillips *A First Book of English Law* (Sweet & Maxwell)

O. Hood Phillips *Constitutional and Administrative Law* (Sweet & Maxwell)

J. A. G. Griffith *The Politics of the Judiciary* (Fontana)

J. H. Baker *An Introduction to English Legal History* (Butterworths)

M. Zander *The Law-Making Process* (Weidenfeld and Nicolson)

Walker and Walker *The English Legal System* (Butterworths)

The Law Society *Legal Aid Guide*

H. Street *The Law of Torts* (Butterworths)

J. Tillotson *Contract Law in Perspective* (Butterworths)

M. P. Furmston *Cheshire and Fifoot's Law of Contract* (Butterworths)

J. C. Smith and J. A. C. Thomas *A Casebook on Contract* (Sweet & Maxwell)

A. P. Dobson *Sales of Goods and Consumer Credit* (Sweet & Maxwell)

Ross Cranston *Consumers and the Law* (Weidenfeld and Nicolson)

Osborn *A Concise Law Dictionary* (Sweet & Maxwell)

Index